Presented by
ASAYA MIYANAGA

Nicola
Traveling
Around
The Demon's
World

contents

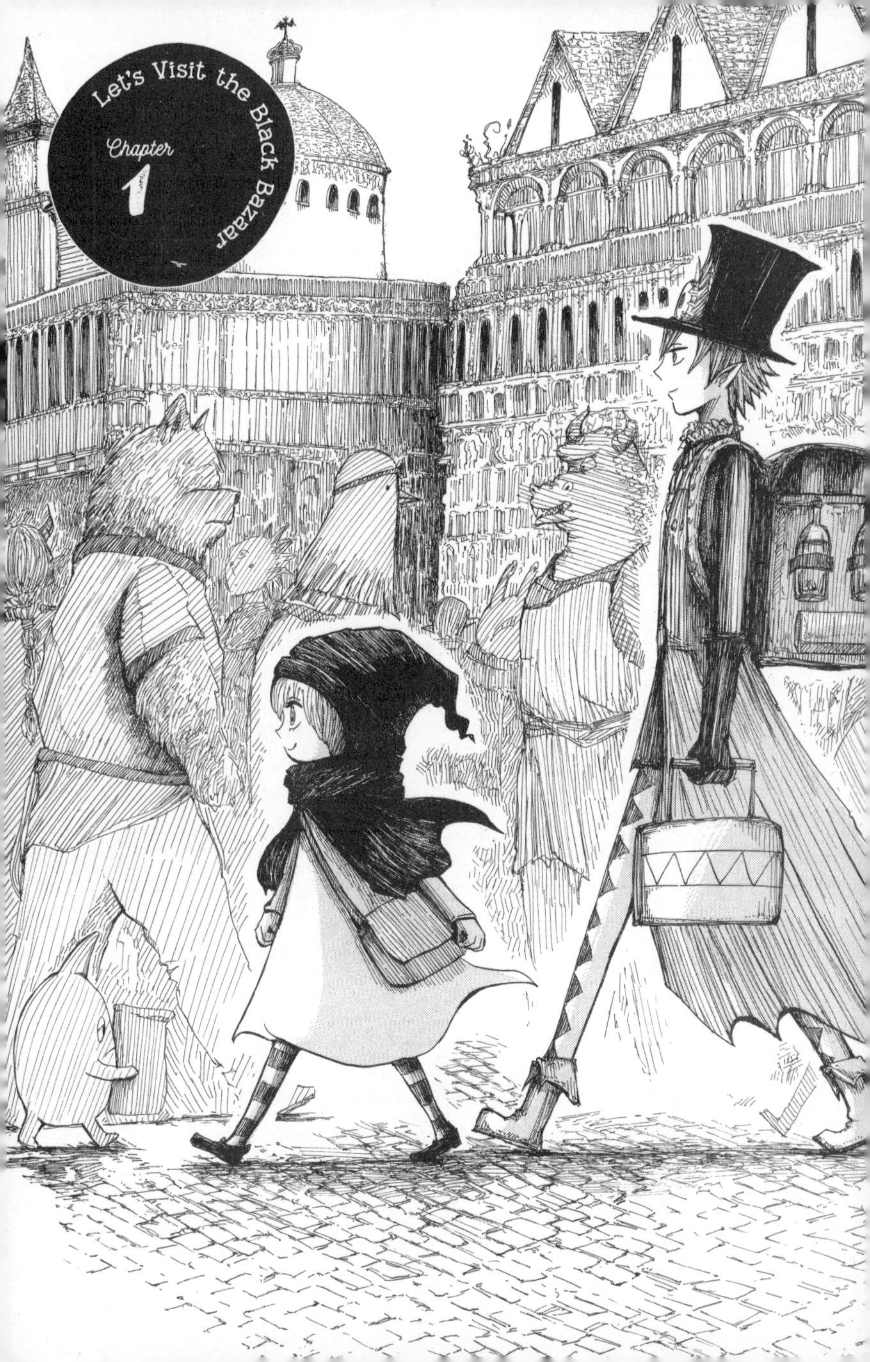
Let's Visit the Black Bazaar
Chapter
1

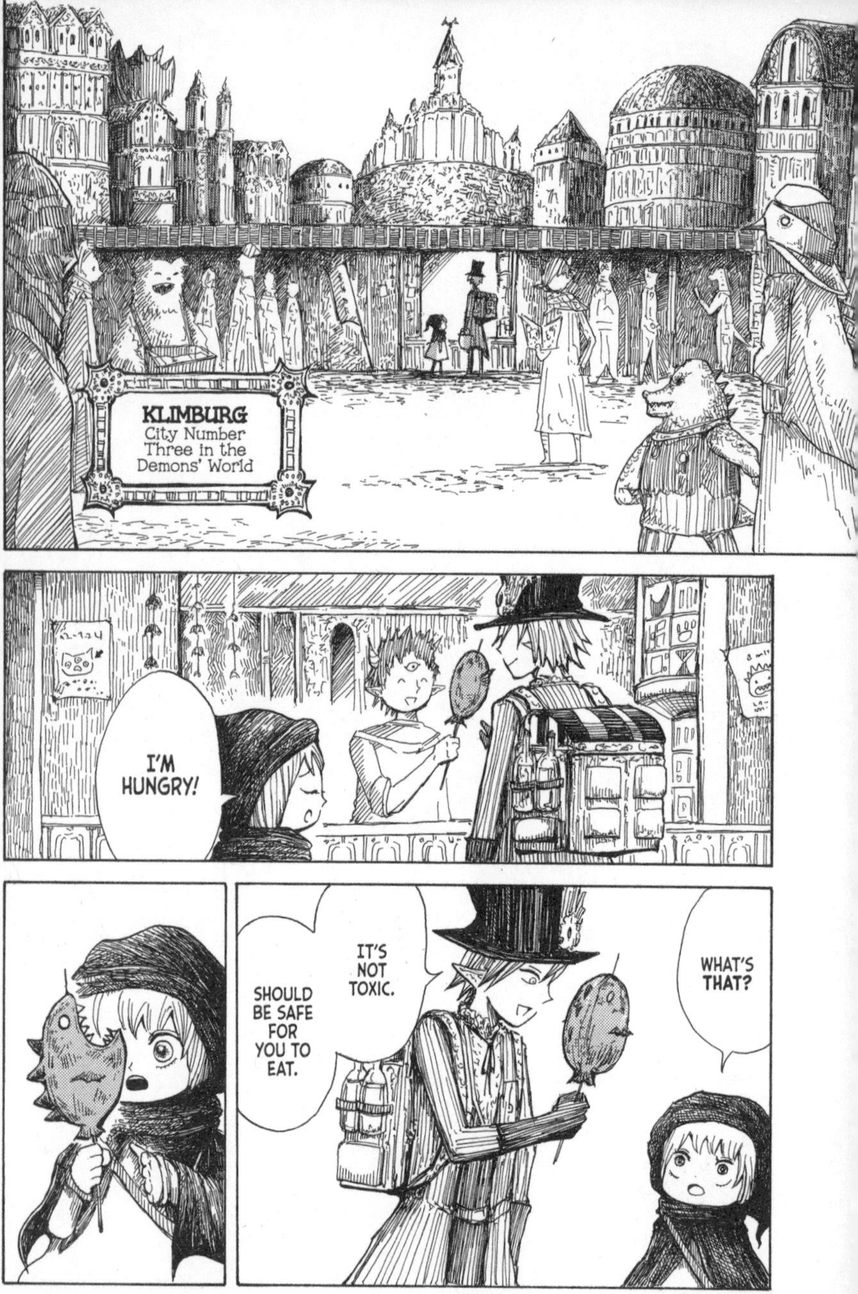
KLIMBURG
City Number Three in the Demons' World
I'M HUNGRY!
WHAT'S THAT?
IT'S NOT TOXIC.
SHOULD BE SAFE FOR YOU TO EAT.

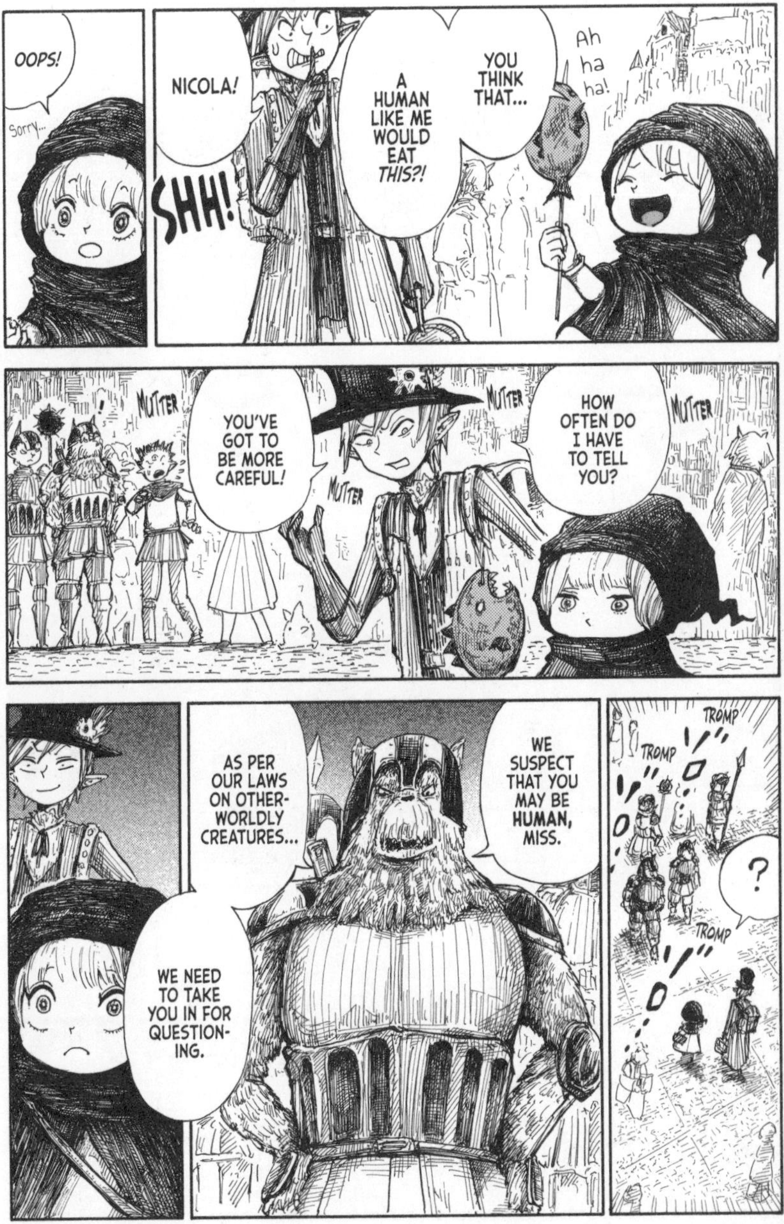
Ah ha ha!
YOU THINK THAT...
A HUMAN LIKE ME WOULD EAT THIS?!
NICOLA!
SHH!
OOPS!
Sorry...
MUTTER
HOW OFTEN DO I HAVE TO TELL YOU?
MUTTER
MUTTER
YOU'VE GOT TO BE MORE CAREFUL!
MUTTER
TROMP
TROMP
?
TROMP
WE SUSPECT THAT YOU MAY BE HUMAN, MISS.
AS PER OUR LAWS ON OTHER-WORLDLY CREATURES...
WE NEED TO TAKE YOU IN FOR QUESTION-ING.

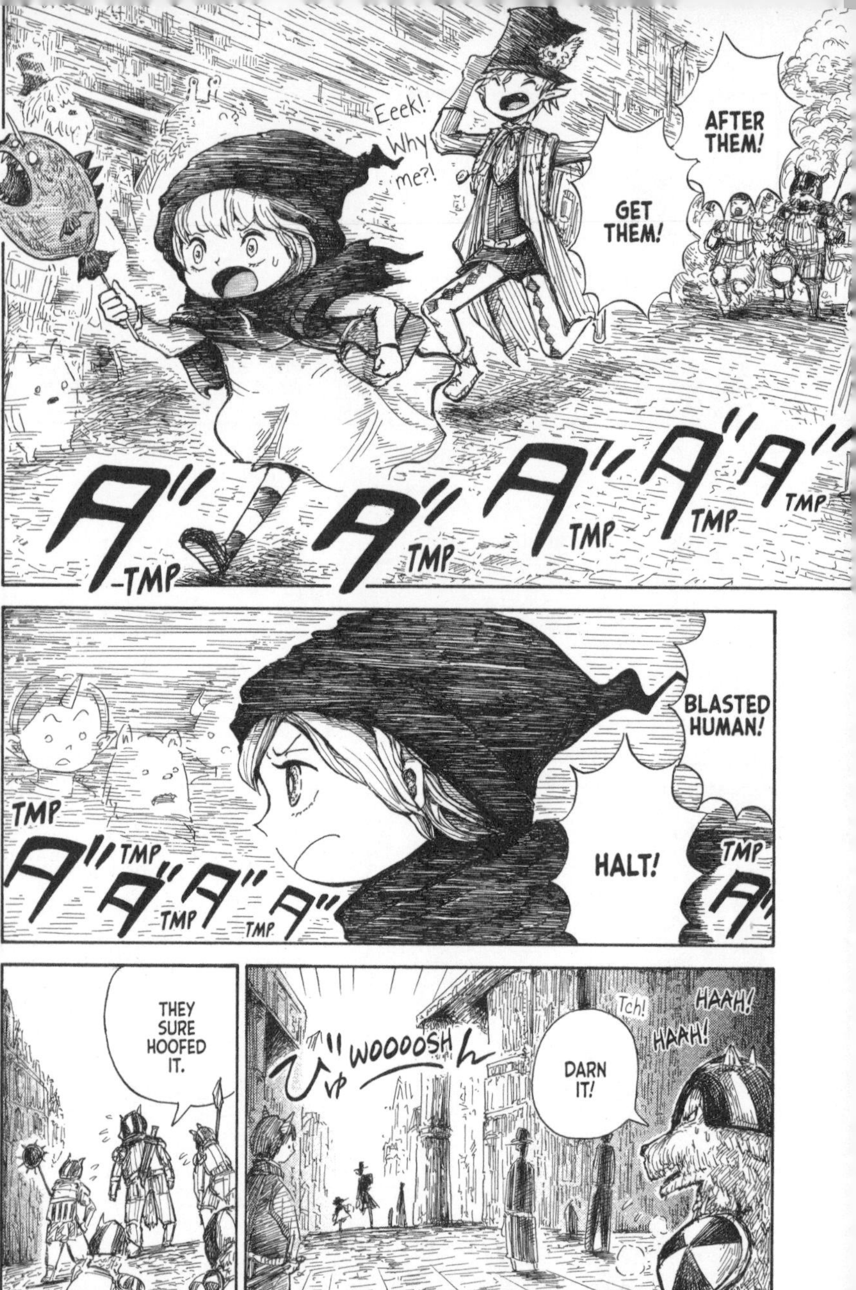
AFTER THEM!
GET THEM!
Eeek! Why me?!
TMP TMP TMP TMP TMP
BLASTED HUMAN!
HALT!
TMP
TMP TMP TMP TMP
HAAH! HAAH!
Tch!
DARN IT!
WOOOOSH
THEY SURE HOOFED IT.

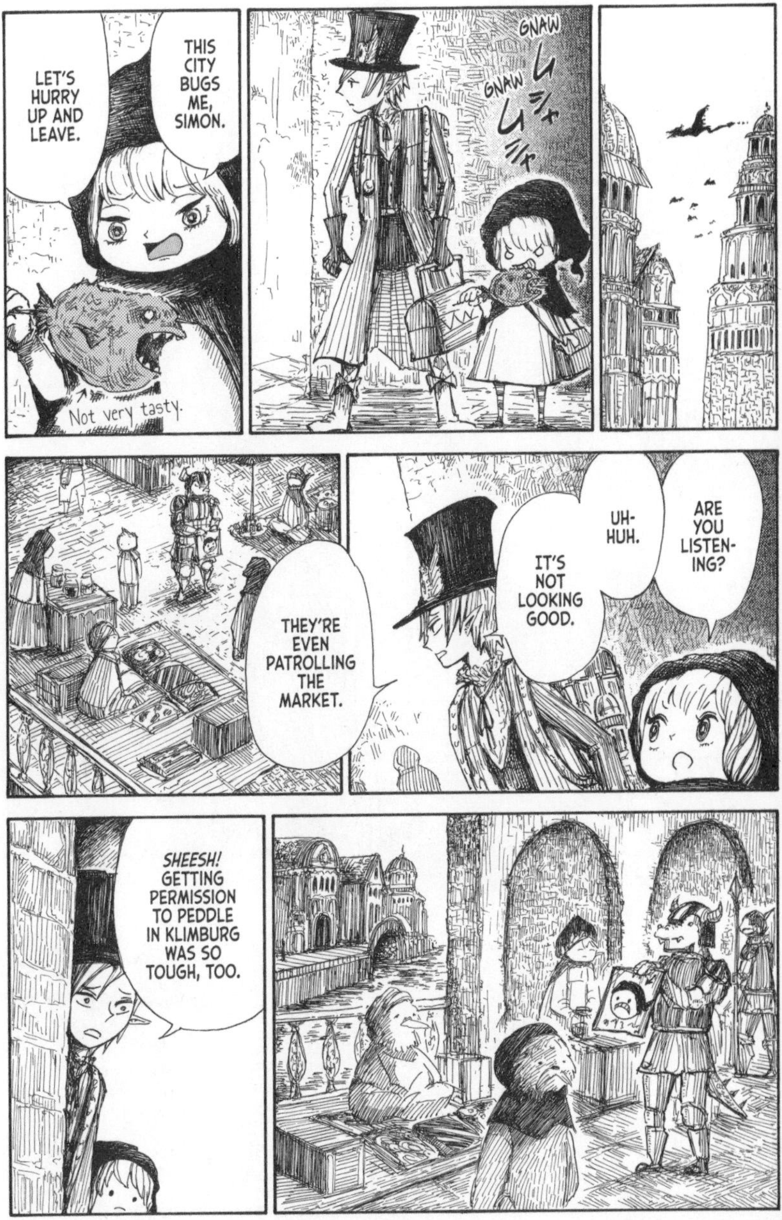

GNAW
GNAW
ムシャ
ムシャ
THIS CITY BUGS ME, SIMON.
LET'S HURRY UP AND LEAVE.
Not very tasty.
ARE YOU LISTENING?
UH-HUH.
IT'S NOT LOOKING GOOD.
THEY'RE EVEN PATROLLING THE MARKET.
SHEESH! GETTING PERMISSION TO PEDDLE IN KLIMBURG WAS SO TOUGH, TOO.

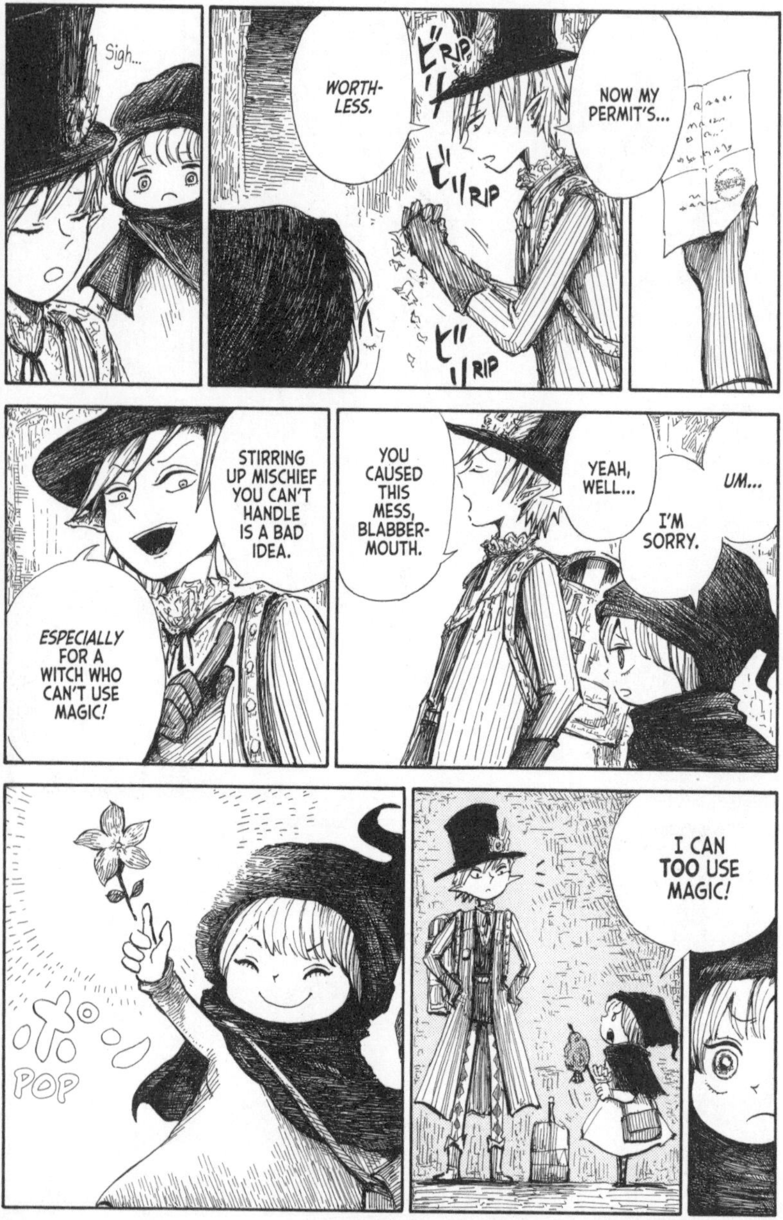
NOW MY PERMIT'S...
RIP
WORTH-LESS.
RIP
RIP
Sigh...
UM...
YEAH, WELL...
I'M SORRY.
YOU CAUSED THIS MESS, BLABBER-MOUTH.
STIRRING UP MISCHIEF YOU CAN'T HANDLE IS A BAD IDEA.
ESPECIALLY FOR A WITCH WHO CAN'T USE MAGIC!
I CAN TOO USE MAGIC!
POP

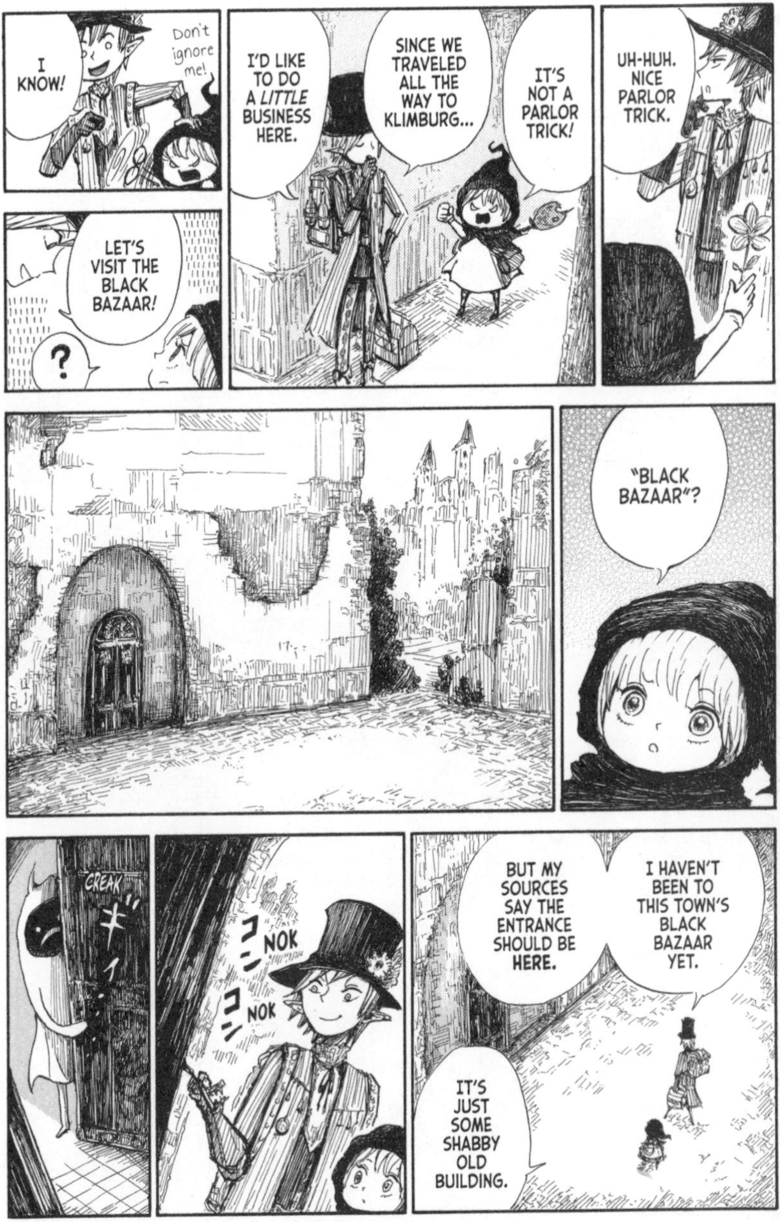
UH-HUH. NICE PARLOR TRICK.
IT'S NOT A PARLOR TRICK!
SINCE WE TRAVELED ALL THE WAY TO KLIMBURG...
I'D LIKE TO DO A *LITTLE* BUSINESS HERE.
I KNOW!
Don't ignore me!
LET'S VISIT THE BLACK BAZAAR!
?
"BLACK BAZAAR"?
I HAVEN'T BEEN TO THIS TOWN'S BLACK BAZAAR YET.
BUT MY SOURCES SAY THE ENTRANCE SHOULD BE HERE.
IT'S JUST SOME SHABBY OLD BUILDING.
コン NOK
コン NOK
CREAK ギイ

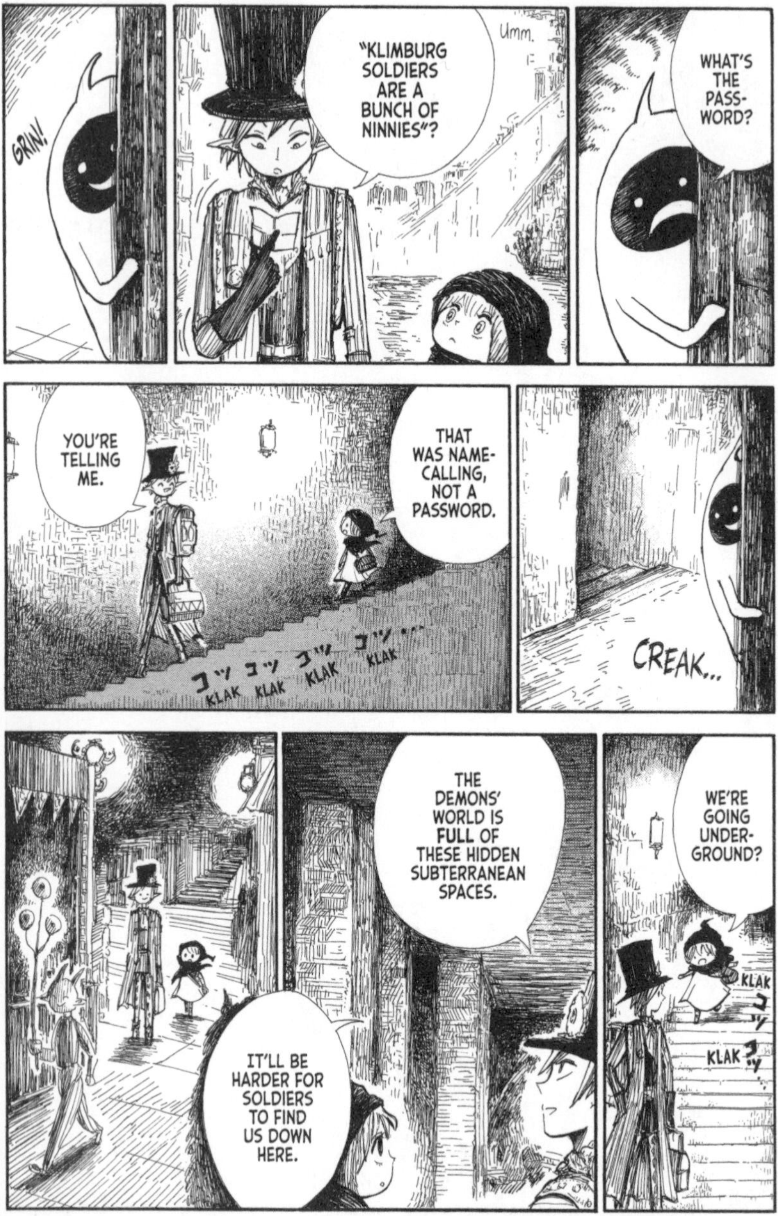
WHAT'S THE PASSWORD?
Umm.
"KLIMBURG SOLDIERS ARE A BUNCH OF NINNIES"?
GRIN!
CREAK...
THAT WAS NAME-CALLING, NOT A PASSWORD.
YOU'RE TELLING ME.
コツ KLAK コツ KLAK コツ KLAK コツ KLAK...
WE'RE GOING UNDERGROUND?
KLAK コツ
KLAK コツ
THE DEMONS' WORLD IS **FULL** OF THESE HIDDEN SUBTERRANEAN SPACES.
IT'LL BE HARDER FOR SOLDIERS TO FIND US DOWN HERE.

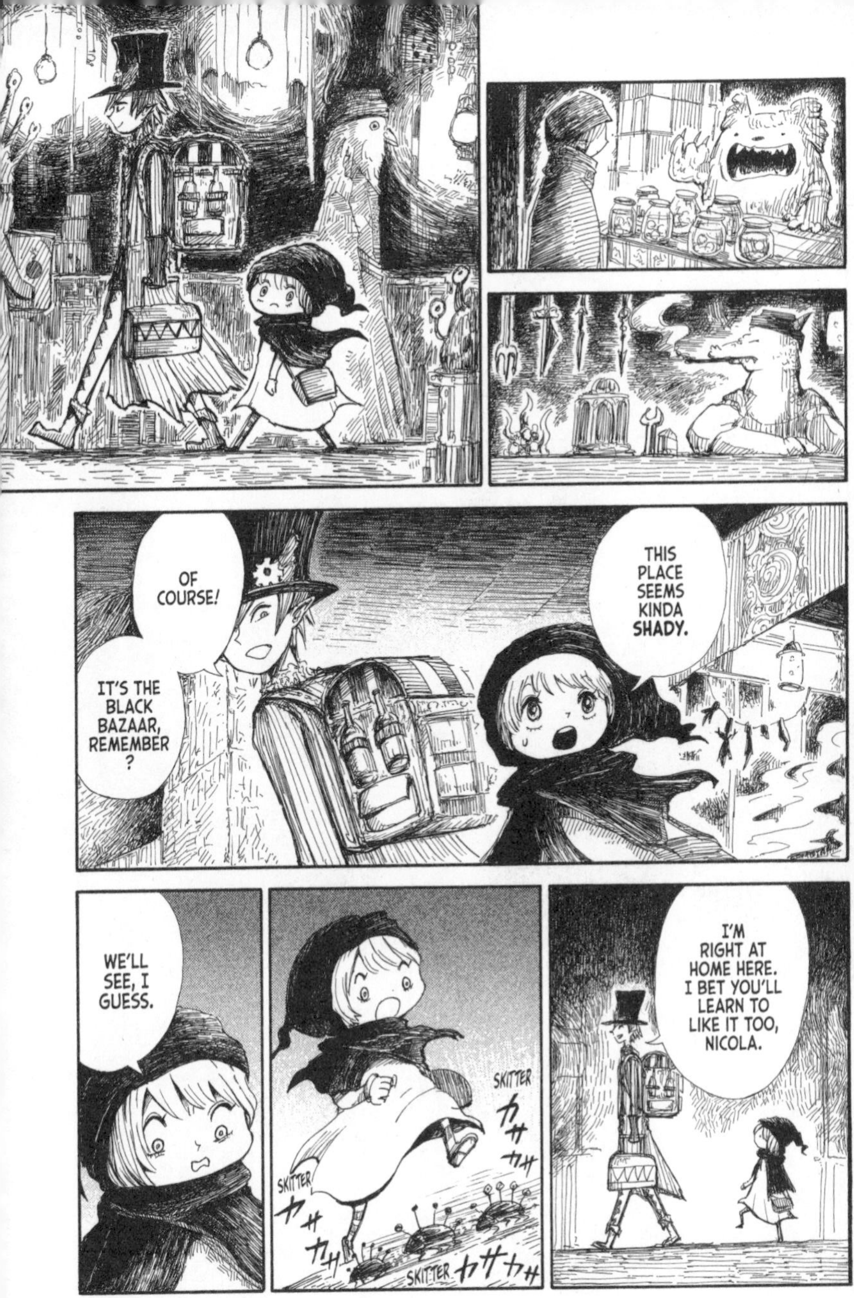
THIS PLACE SEEMS KINDA SHADY.
OF COURSE!
IT'S THE BLACK BAZAAR, REMEMBER?
I'M RIGHT AT HOME HERE. I BET YOU'LL LEARN TO LIKE IT TOO, NICOLA.
SKITTER
SKITTER
SKITTER
WE'LL SEE, I GUESS.

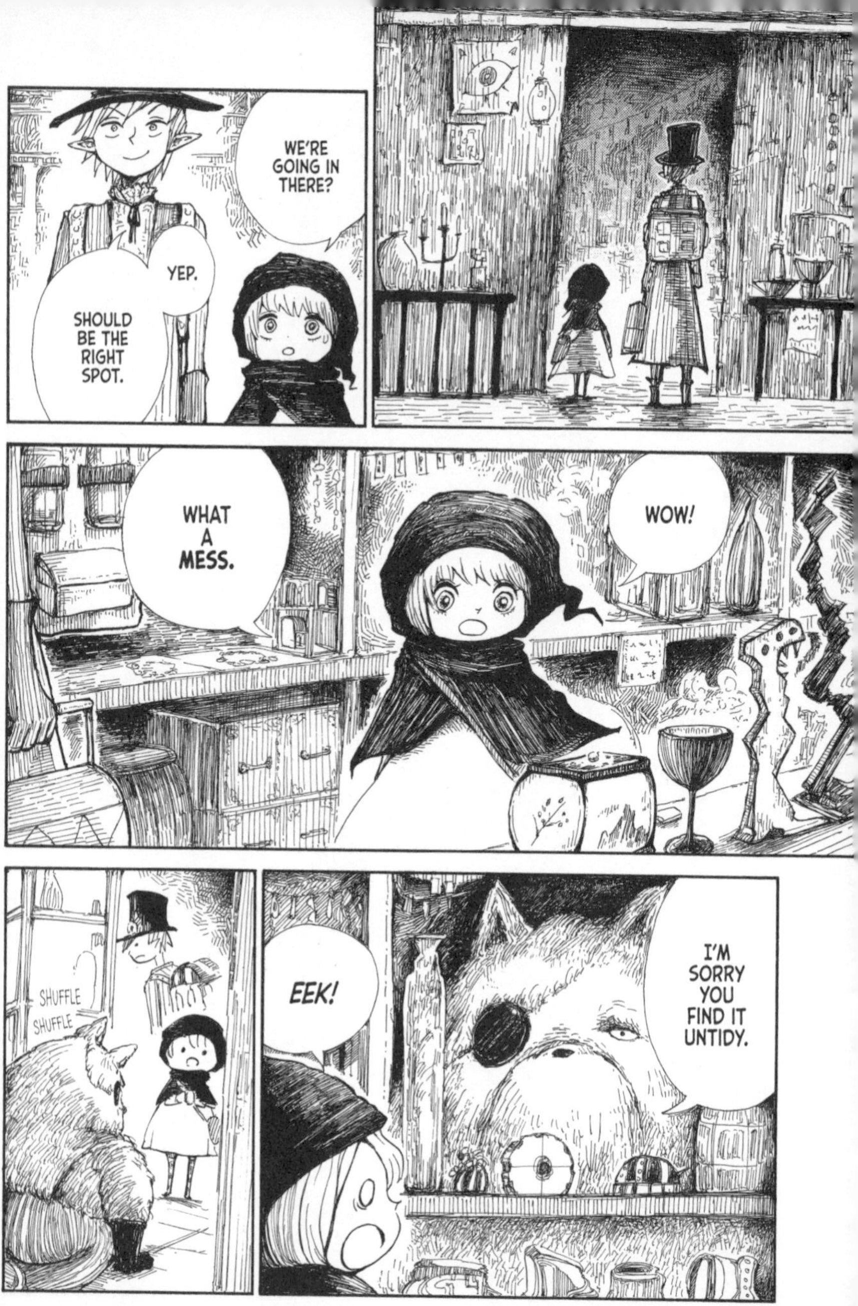
WE'RE GOING IN THERE?
YEP.
SHOULD BE THE RIGHT SPOT.
WOW!
WHAT A MESS.
I'M SORRY YOU FIND IT UNTIDY.
EEK!
SHUFFLE
SHUFFLE

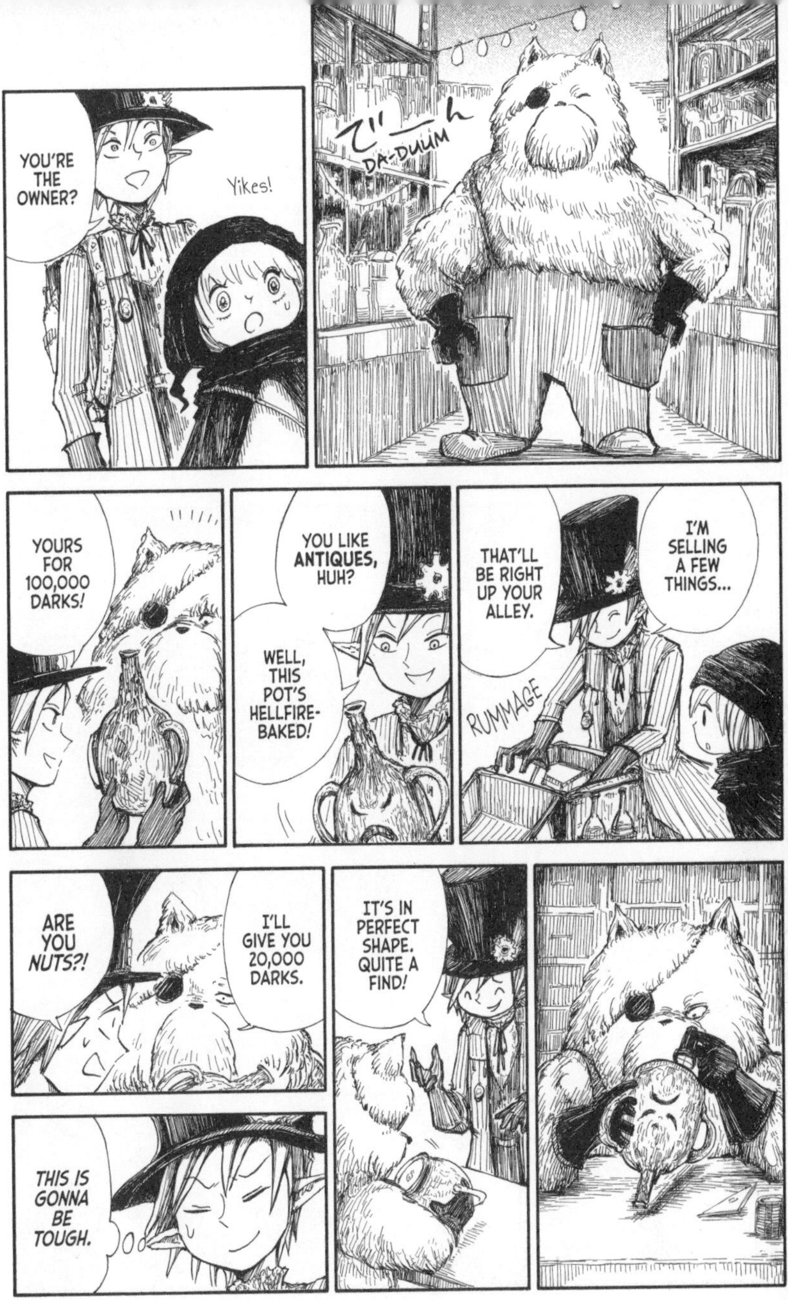
でーん
DA-DUUM
YOU'RE THE OWNER?
Yikes!
I'M SELLING A FEW THINGS...
THAT'LL BE RIGHT UP YOUR ALLEY.
RUMMAGE
YOU LIKE **ANTIQUES,** HUH?
WELL, THIS POT'S HELLFIRE-BAKED!
YOURS FOR 100,000 DARKS!
IT'S IN PERFECT SHAPE. QUITE A FIND!
I'LL GIVE YOU 20,000 DARKS.
ARE YOU *NUTS?!*
THIS IS GONNA BE TOUGH.

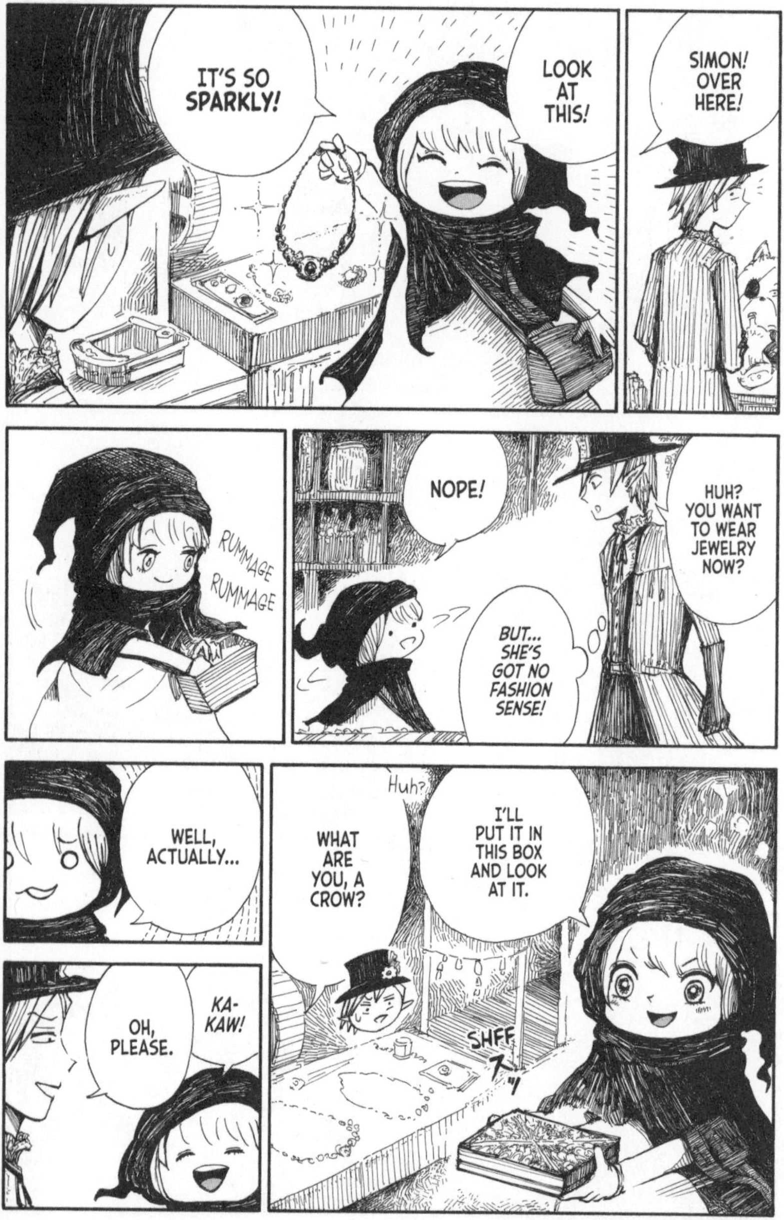
SIMON! OVER HERE!
LOOK AT THIS!
IT'S SO SPARKLY!
HUH? YOU WANT TO WEAR JEWELRY NOW?
NOPE!
BUT... SHE'S GOT NO FASHION SENSE!
RUMMAGE RUMMAGE
I'LL PUT IT IN THIS BOX AND LOOK AT IT.
Huh?
WHAT ARE YOU, A CROW?
SHFF
WELL, ACTUALLY...
KA-KAW!
OH, PLEASE.

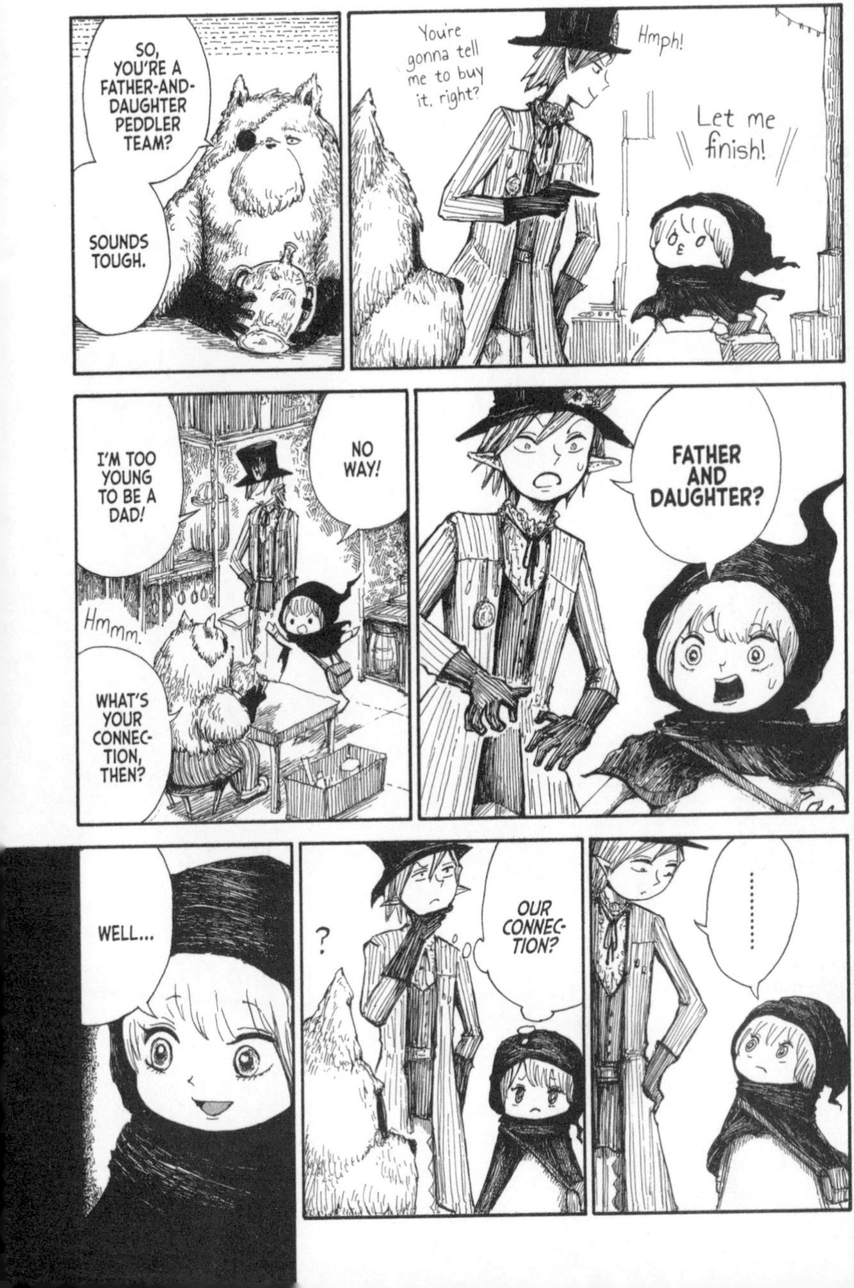
Hmph!
You're gonna tell me to buy it, right?
Let me finish!
SO, YOU'RE A FATHER-AND-DAUGHTER PEDDLER TEAM?
SOUNDS TOUGH.
FATHER AND DAUGHTER?
NO WAY!
I'M TOO YOUNG TO BE A DAD!
Hmmm.
WHAT'S YOUR CONNECTION, THEN?
....
OUR CONNECTION?
?
WELL...

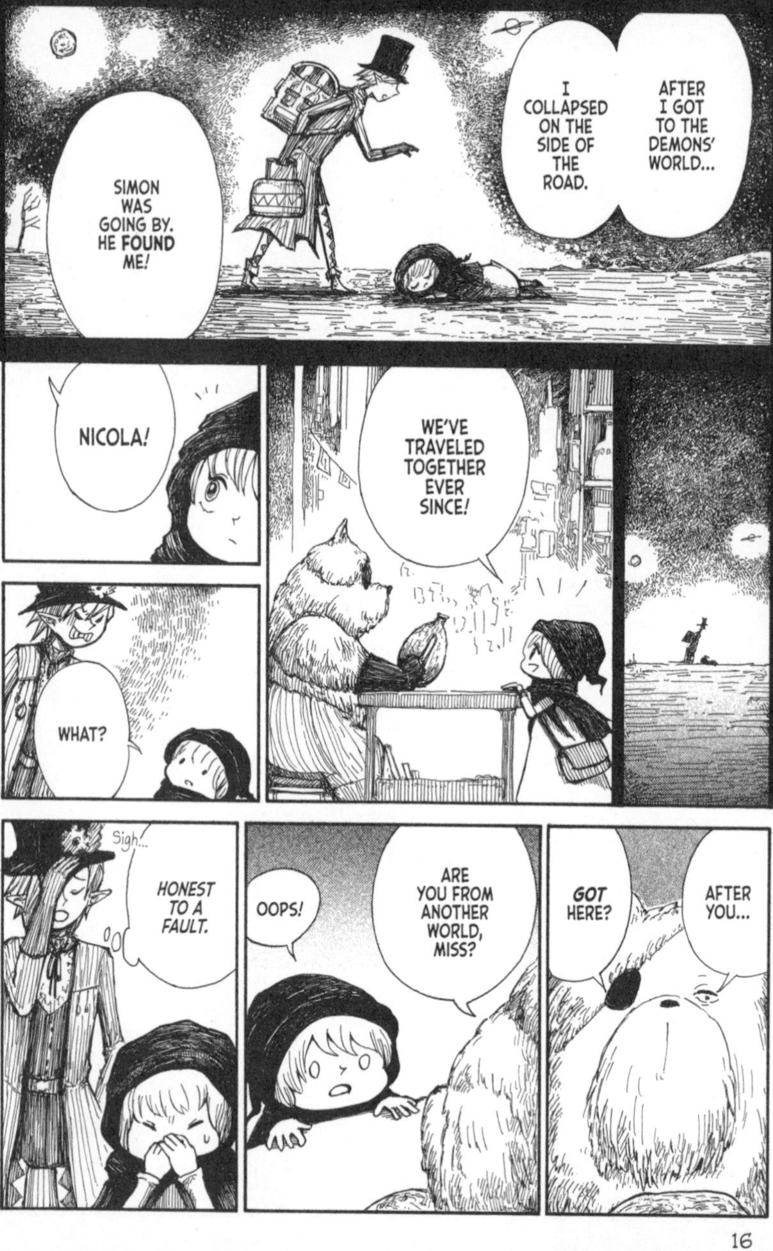
AFTER I GOT TO THE DEMONS' WORLD...
I COLLAPSED ON THE SIDE OF THE ROAD.
SIMON WAS GOING BY. HE FOUND ME!
WE'VE TRAVELED TOGETHER EVER SINCE!
NICOLA!
WHAT?
AFTER YOU...
GOT HERE?
ARE YOU FROM ANOTHER WORLD, MISS?
OOPS!
Sigh...
HONEST TO A FAULT.

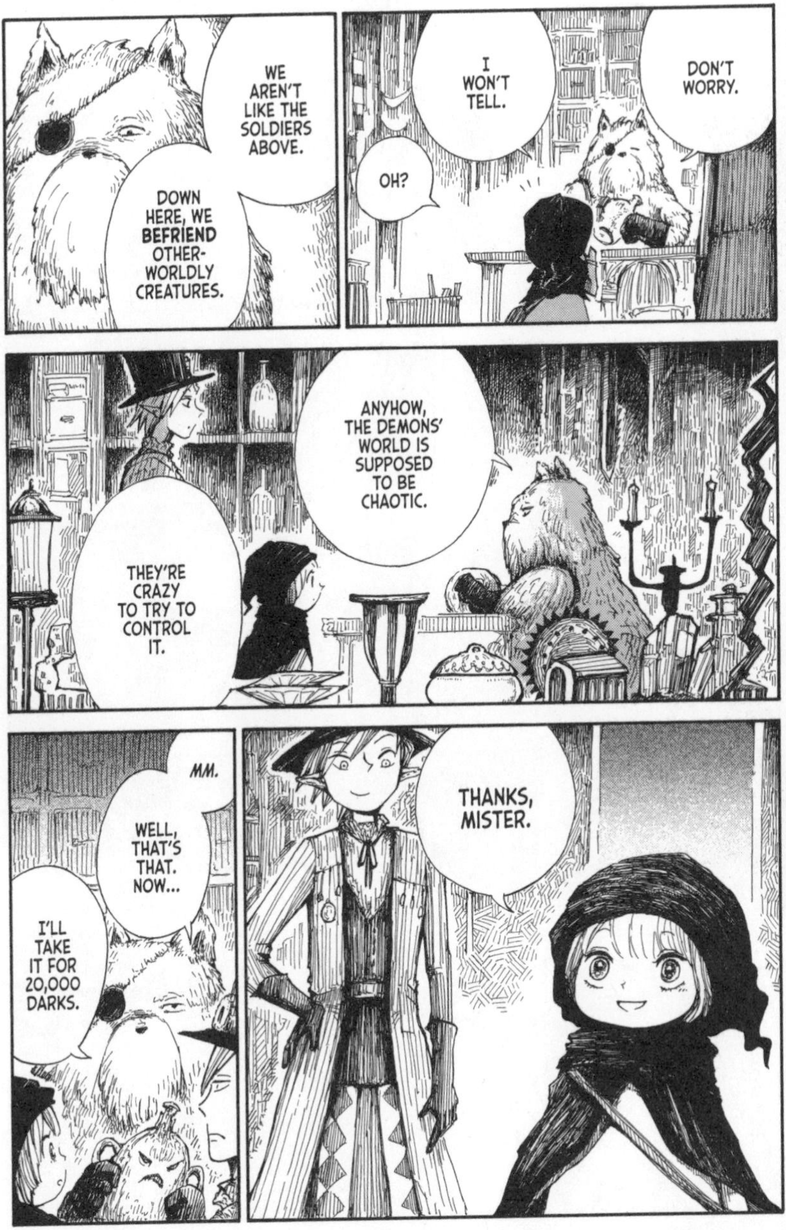
DON'T WORRY.
I WON'T TELL.
OH?
WE AREN'T LIKE THE SOLDIERS ABOVE.
DOWN HERE, WE **BEFRIEND** OTHER-WORLDLY CREATURES.
ANYHOW, THE DEMONS' WORLD IS SUPPOSED TO BE CHAOTIC.
THEY'RE CRAZY TO TRY TO CONTROL IT.
THANKS, MISTER.
MM.
WELL, THAT'S THAT. NOW...
I'LL TAKE IT FOR 20,000 DARKS.

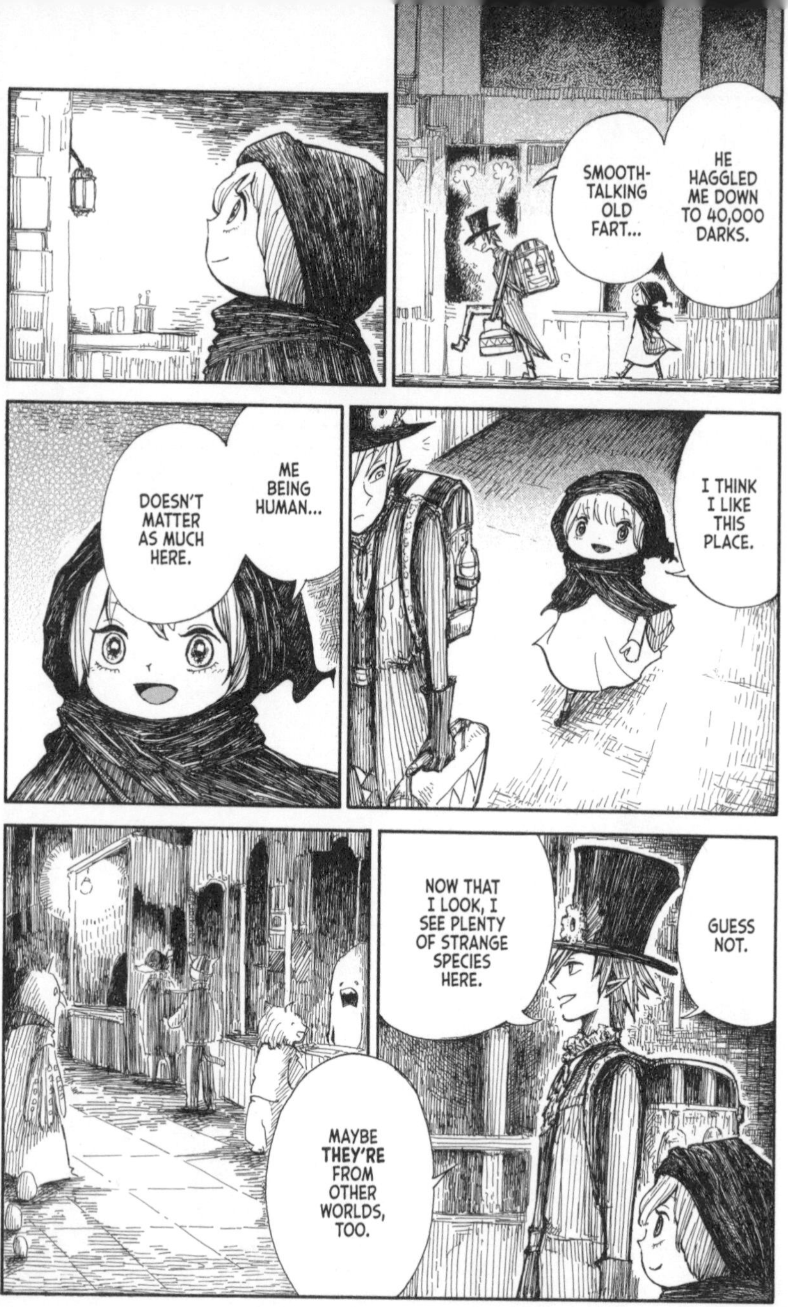
HE HAGGLED ME DOWN TO 40,000 DARKS.
SMOOTH-TALKING OLD FART...
I THINK I LIKE THIS PLACE.
ME BEING HUMAN...
DOESN'T MATTER AS MUCH HERE.
GUESS NOT.
NOW THAT I LOOK, I SEE PLENTY OF STRANGE SPECIES HERE.
MAYBE **THEY'RE** FROM OTHER WORLDS, TOO.

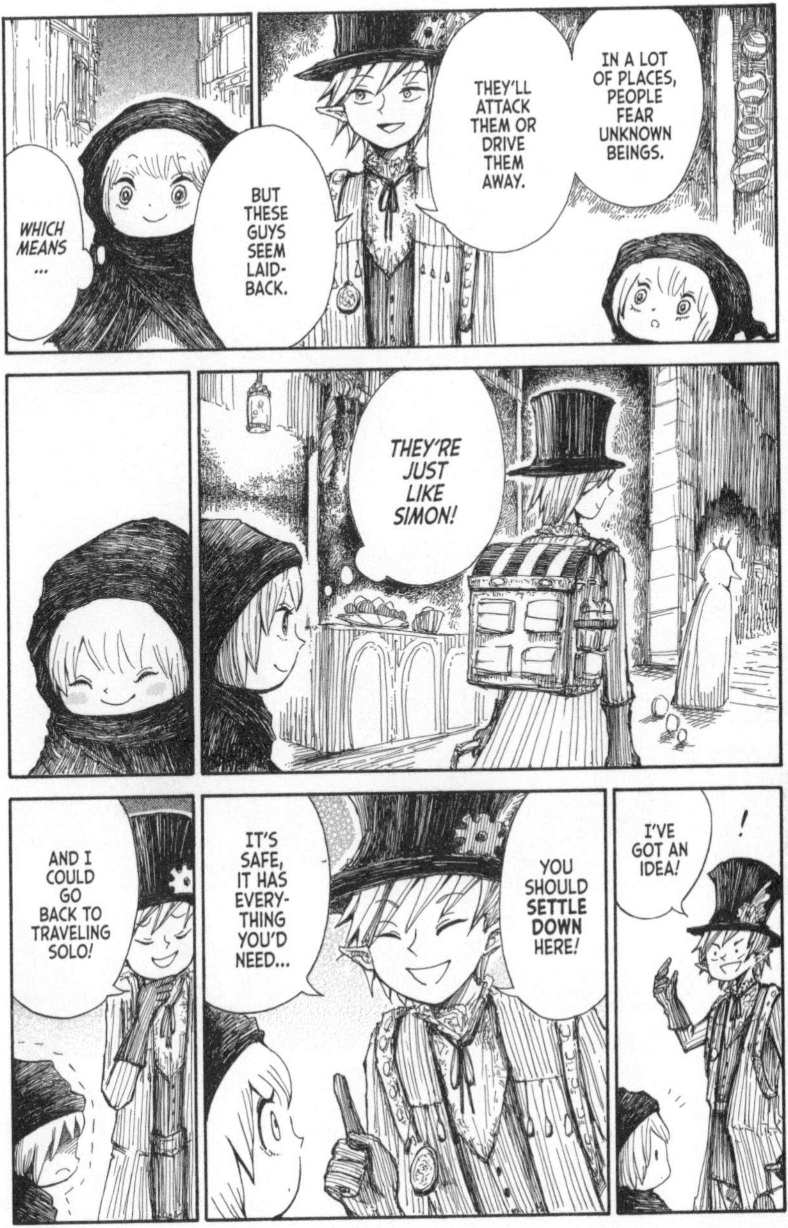
IN A LOT OF PLACES, PEOPLE FEAR UNKNOWN BEINGS.
THEY'LL ATTACK THEM OR DRIVE THEM AWAY.
BUT THESE GUYS SEEM LAID-BACK.
WHICH MEANS ...
THEY'RE JUST LIKE SIMON!
!
I'VE GOT AN IDEA!
YOU SHOULD **SETTLE DOWN** HERE!
IT'S SAFE, IT HAS EVERYTHING YOU'D NEED...
AND I COULD GO BACK TO TRAVELING SOLO!

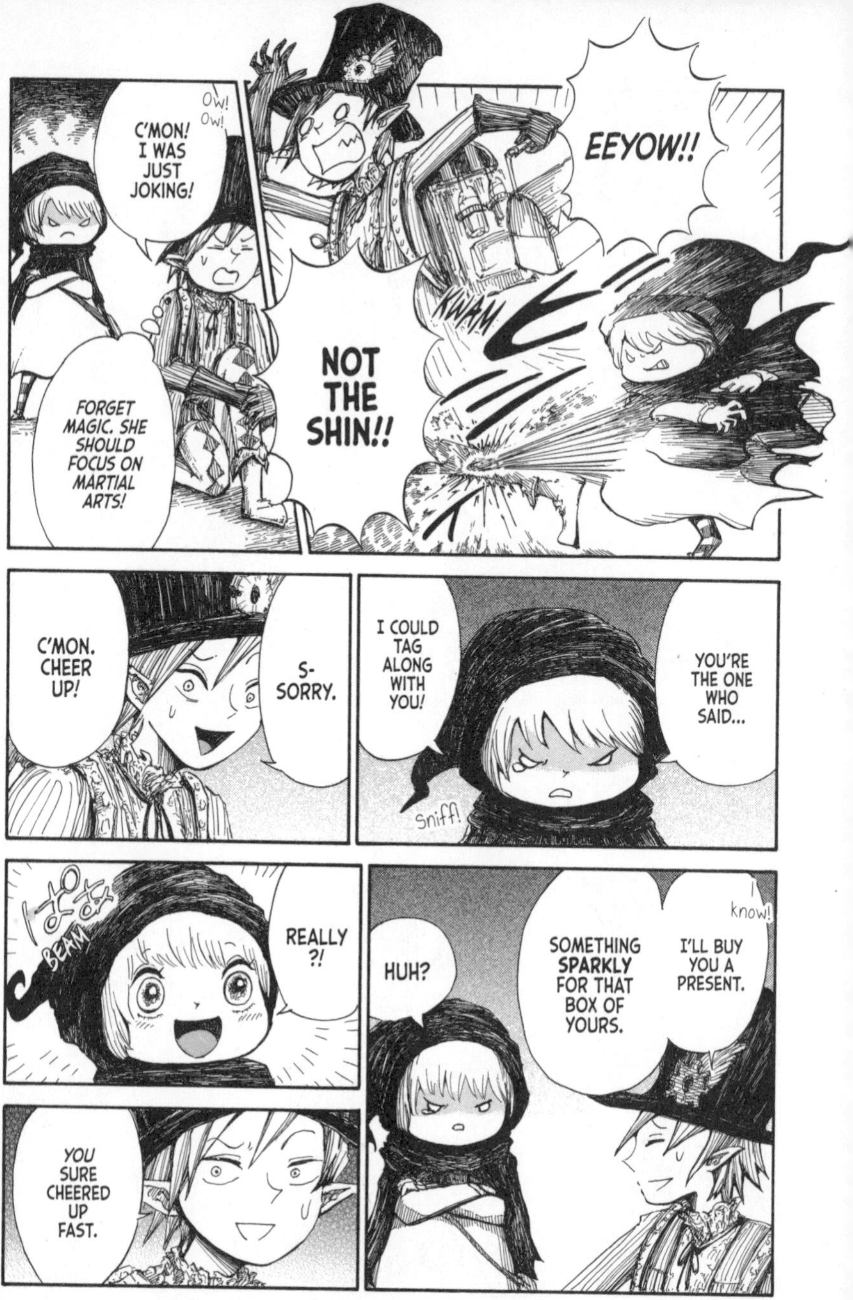
EEYOW!!
KWAM
NOT THE SHIN!!
Ow! Ow!
C'MON! I WAS JUST JOKING!
FORGET MAGIC. SHE SHOULD FOCUS ON MARTIAL ARTS!
YOU'RE THE ONE WHO SAID...
I COULD TAG ALONG WITH YOU!
Sniff!
S-SORRY.
C'MON. CHEER UP!
I know!
I'LL BUY YOU A PRESENT.
SOMETHING **SPARKLY** FOR THAT BOX OF YOURS.
HUH?
REALLY?!
BEAM
YOU SURE CHEERED UP FAST.

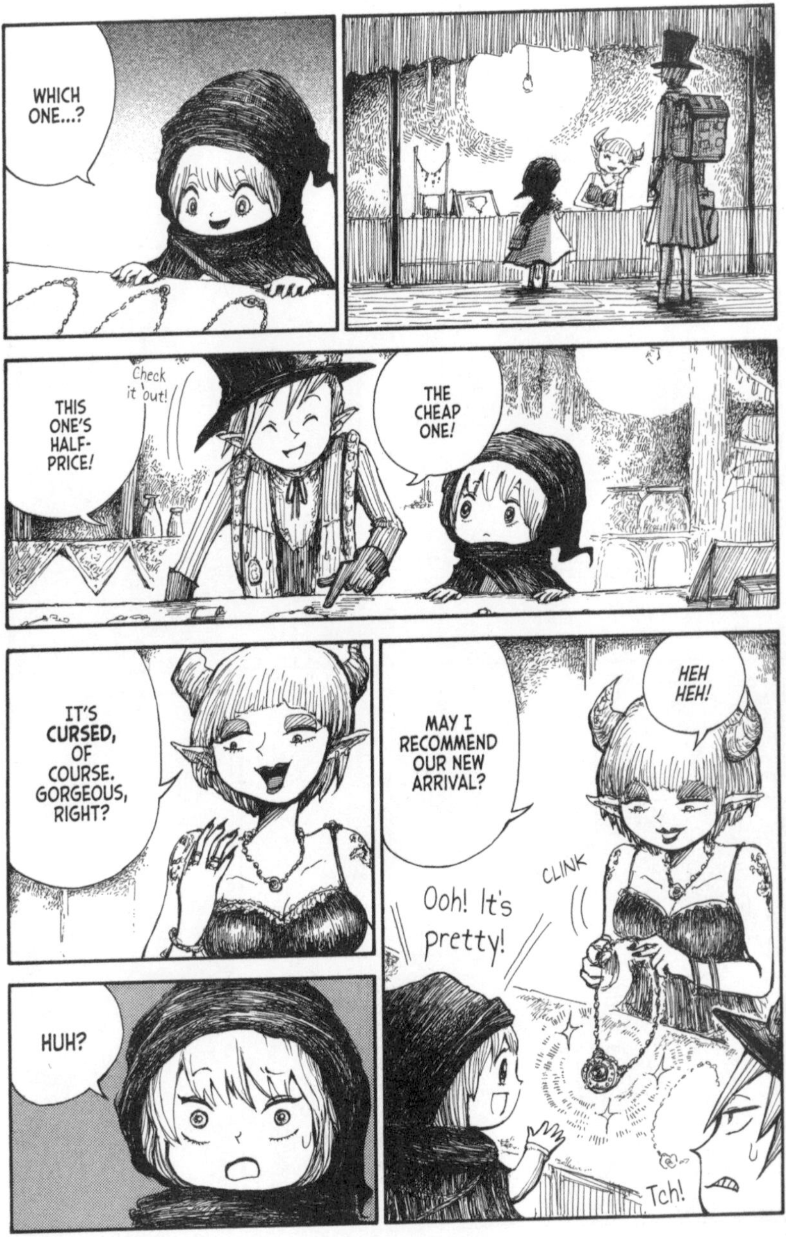
WHICH ONE...?
THE CHEAP ONE!
Check it out!
THIS ONE'S HALF-PRICE!
HEH HEH!
MAY I RECOMMEND OUR NEW ARRIVAL?
CLINK
Ooh! It's pretty!
Tch!
IT'S CURSED, OF COURSE. GORGEOUS, RIGHT?
HUH?

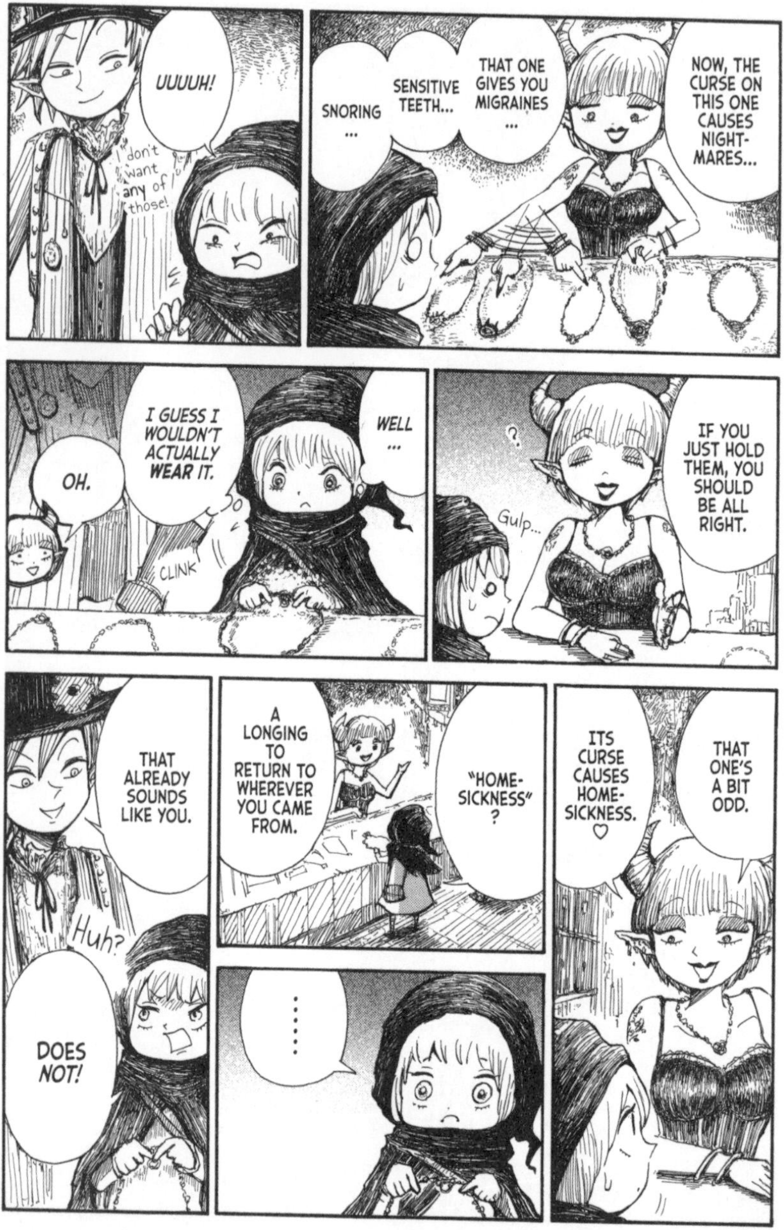
NOW, THE CURSE ON THIS ONE CAUSES NIGHT-MARES...
THAT ONE GIVES YOU MIGRAINES ...
SENSITIVE TEETH...
SNORING ...
UUUUH!
I don't want any of those!
IF YOU JUST HOLD THEM, YOU SHOULD BE ALL RIGHT.
?
Gulp...
WELL ...
I GUESS I WOULDN'T ACTUALLY WEAR IT.
OH.
CLINK
THAT ONE'S A BIT ODD.
ITS CURSE CAUSES HOME-SICKNESS. ♡
"HOME-SICKNESS" ?
A LONGING TO RETURN TO WHEREVER YOU CAME FROM.
......
THAT ALREADY SOUNDS LIKE YOU.
Huh?
DOES NOT!

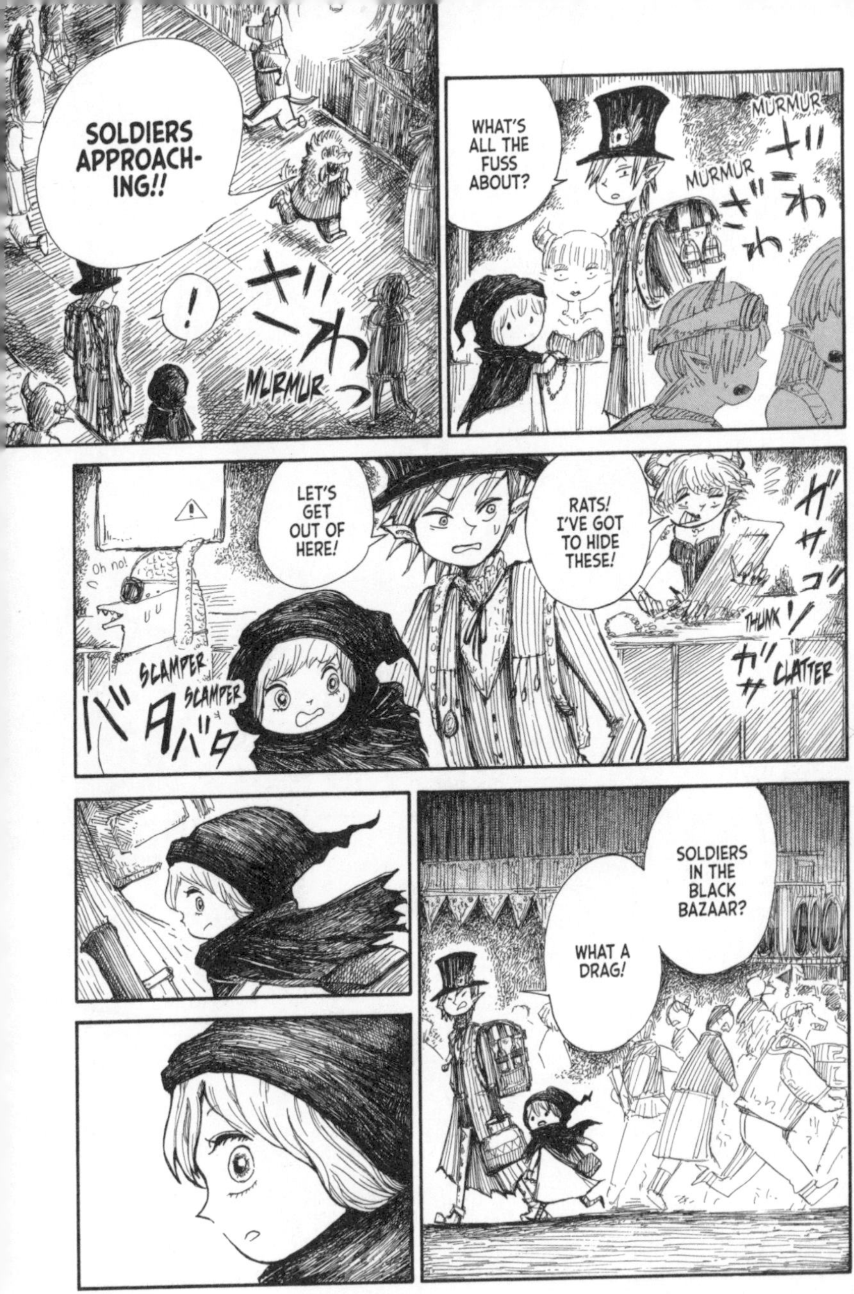
WHAT'S ALL THE FUSS ABOUT?
MURMUR
MURMUR
SOLDIERS APPROACHING!!
!
MURMUR
RATS! I'VE GOT TO HIDE THESE!
THUNK
CLATTER
LET'S GET OUT OF HERE!
Oh no!
SCAMPER
SCAMPER
SOLDIERS IN THE BLACK BAZAAR?
WHAT A DRAG!

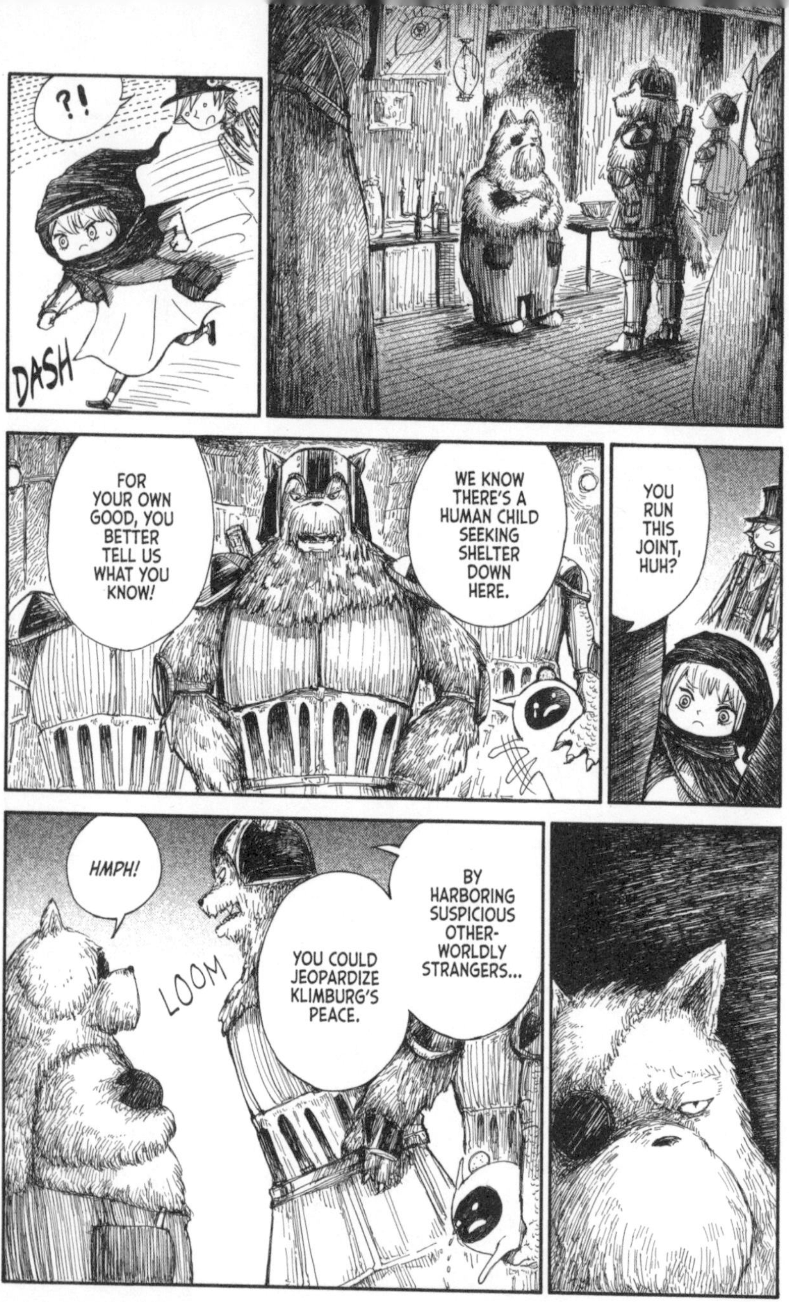
?!
DASH
YOU RUN THIS JOINT, HUH?
WE KNOW THERE'S A HUMAN CHILD SEEKING SHELTER DOWN HERE.
FOR YOUR OWN GOOD, YOU BETTER TELL US WHAT YOU KNOW!
BY HARBORING SUSPICIOUS OTHER-WORLDLY STRANGERS...
YOU COULD JEOPARDIZE KLIMBURG'S PEACE.
LOOM
HMPH!

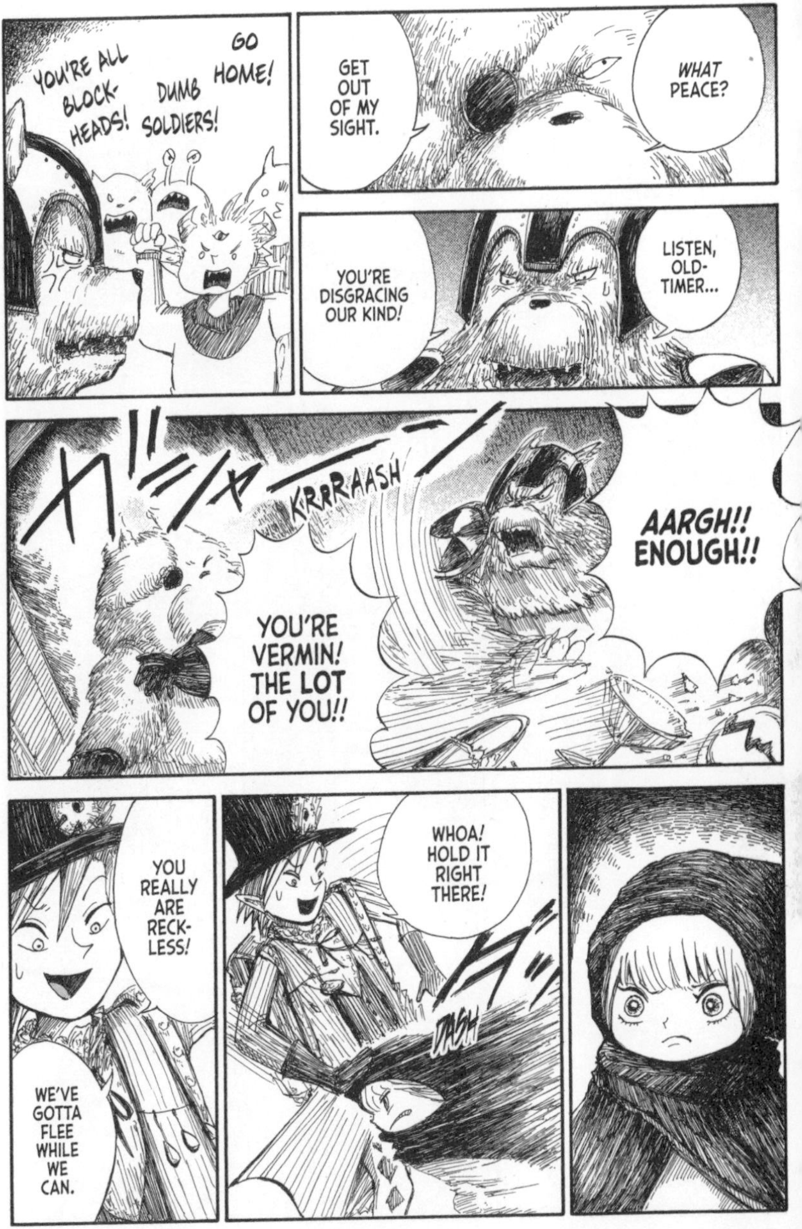
WHAT PEACE?
GET OUT OF MY SIGHT.
LISTEN, OLD-TIMER...
YOU'RE DISGRACING OUR KIND!
GO HOME!
DUMB SOLDIERS!
YOU'RE ALL BLOCK-HEADS!
AARGH!! ENOUGH!!
KRRRAASH
YOU'RE VERMIN! THE LOT OF YOU!!
WHOA! HOLD IT RIGHT THERE!
DASH
YOU REALLY ARE RECK-LESS!
WE'VE GOTTA FLEE WHILE WE CAN.

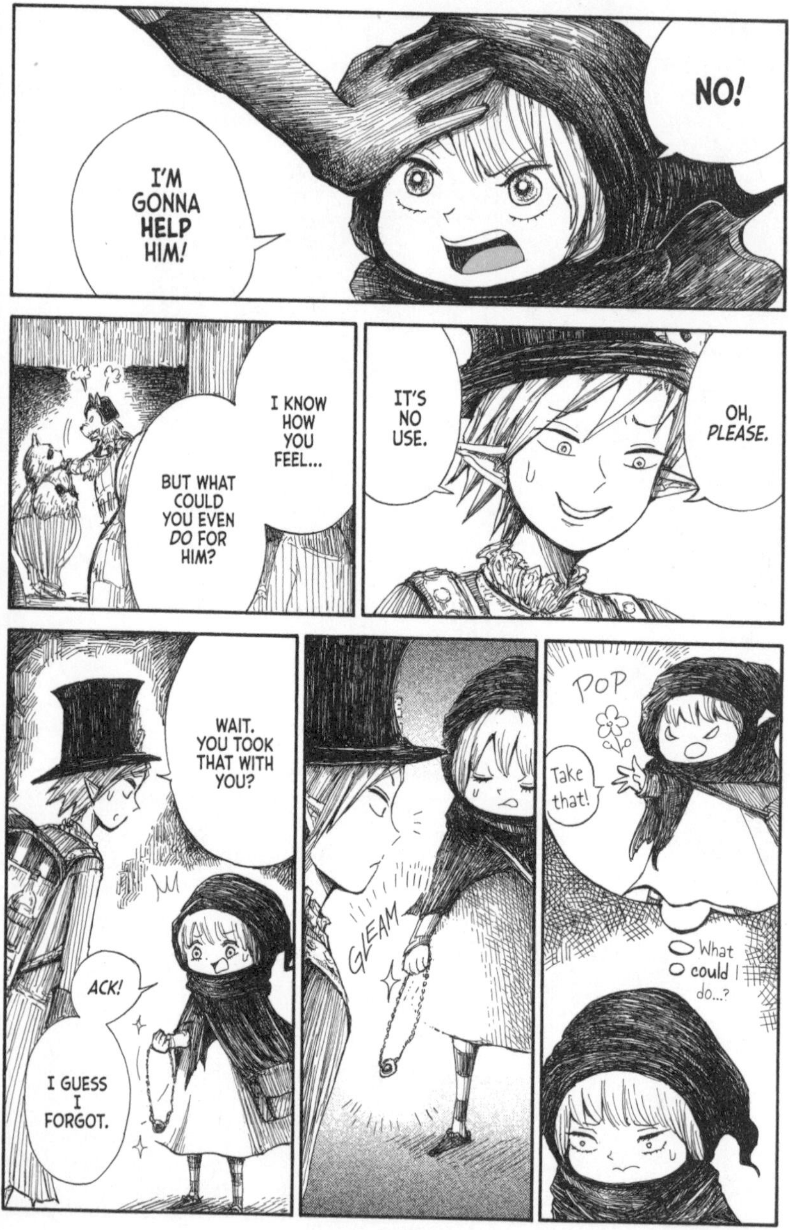
NO!
I'M GONNA HELP HIM!
OH, PLEASE.
IT'S NO USE.
I KNOW HOW YOU FEEL...
BUT WHAT COULD YOU EVEN DO FOR HIM?
POP
Take that!
What could I do...?
GLEAM
WAIT. YOU TOOK THAT WITH YOU?
ACK!
I GUESS I FORGOT.

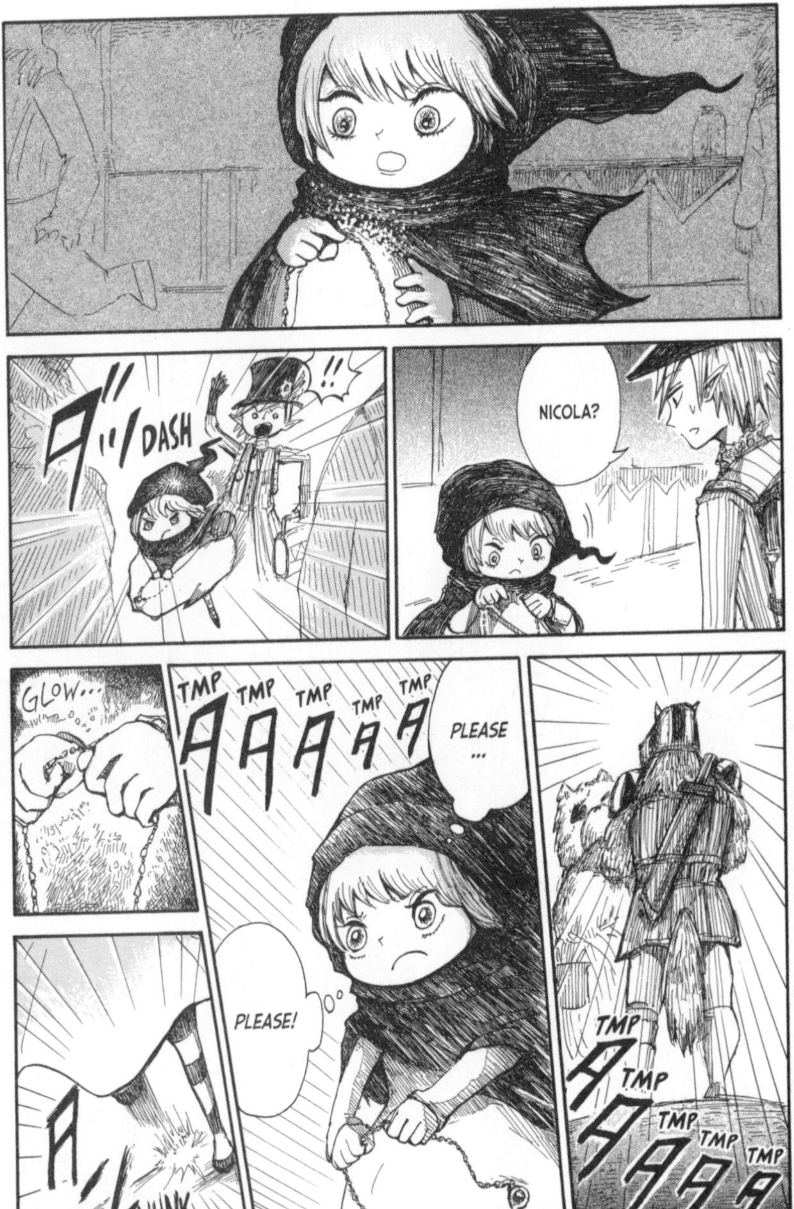
NICOLA?
!!
DASH
TMP
TMP
TMP
TMP
TMP
TMP
TMP
TMP
TMP
TMP
TMP
PLEASE ...
PLEASE!
GLOW...
THUNK

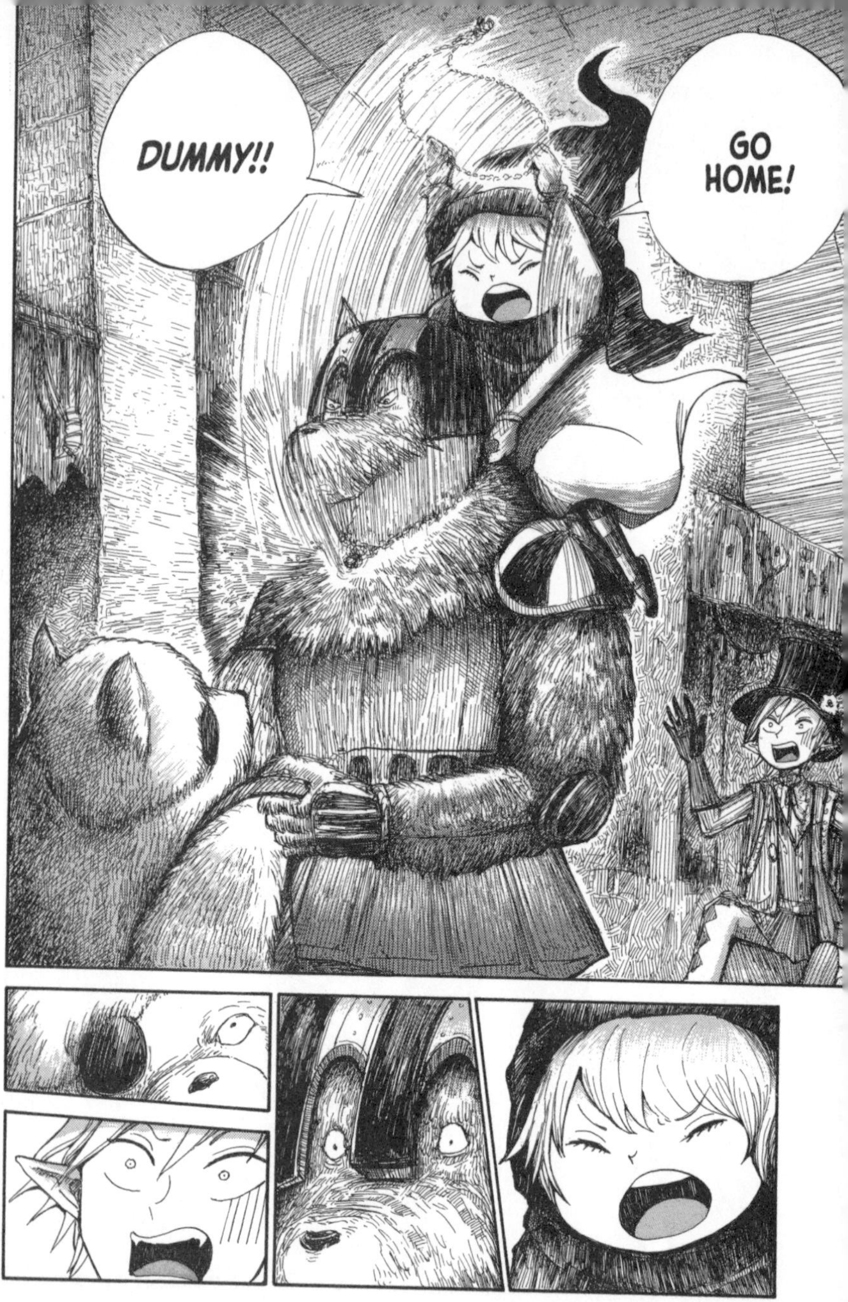
GO HOME!
DUMMY!!

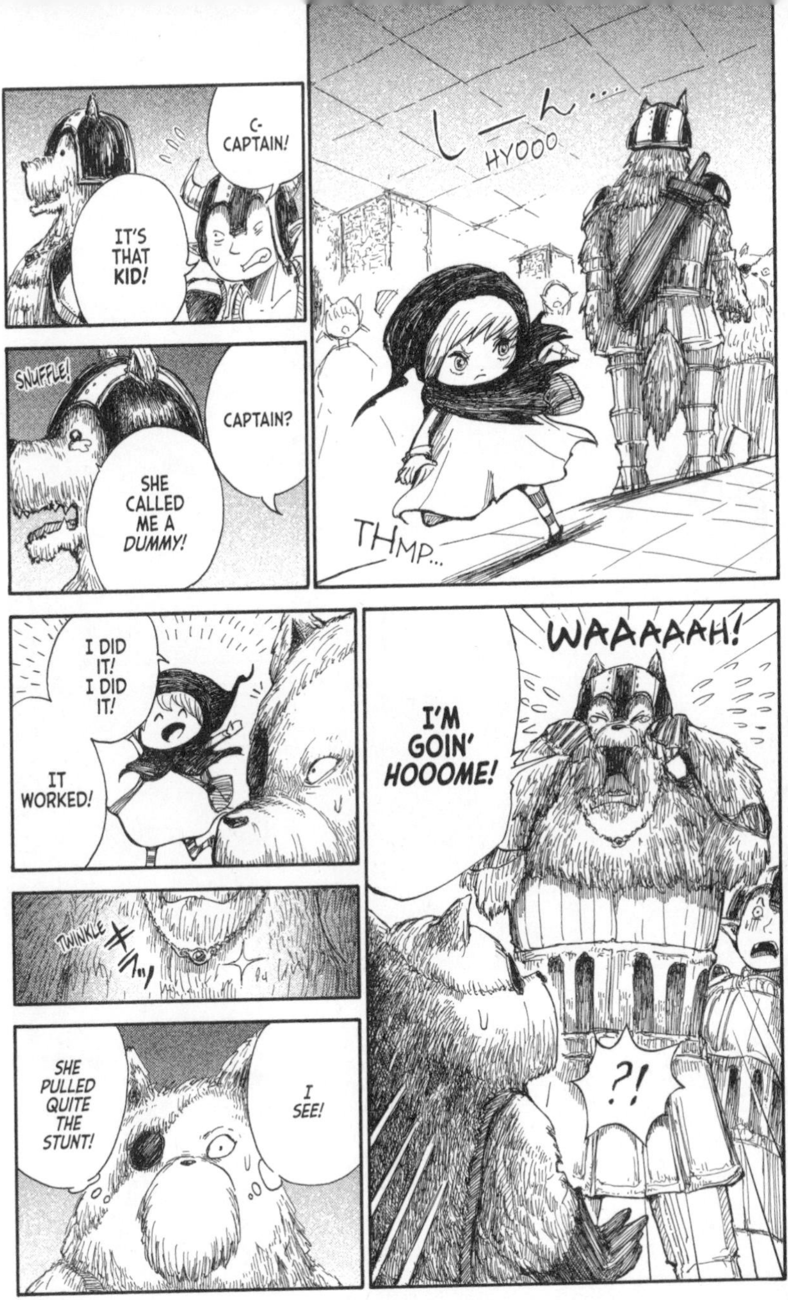

しーん…
HYOOO
THMP...
C-CAPTAIN!
IT'S THAT KID!
CAPTAIN?
SNUFFLE!
SHE CALLED ME A *DUMMY!*
WAAAAAH!
I'M GOIN' *HOOOME!*
?!
I DID IT! I DID IT!
IT WORKED!
TWINKLE
I SEE!
SHE PULLED QUITE THE STUNT!

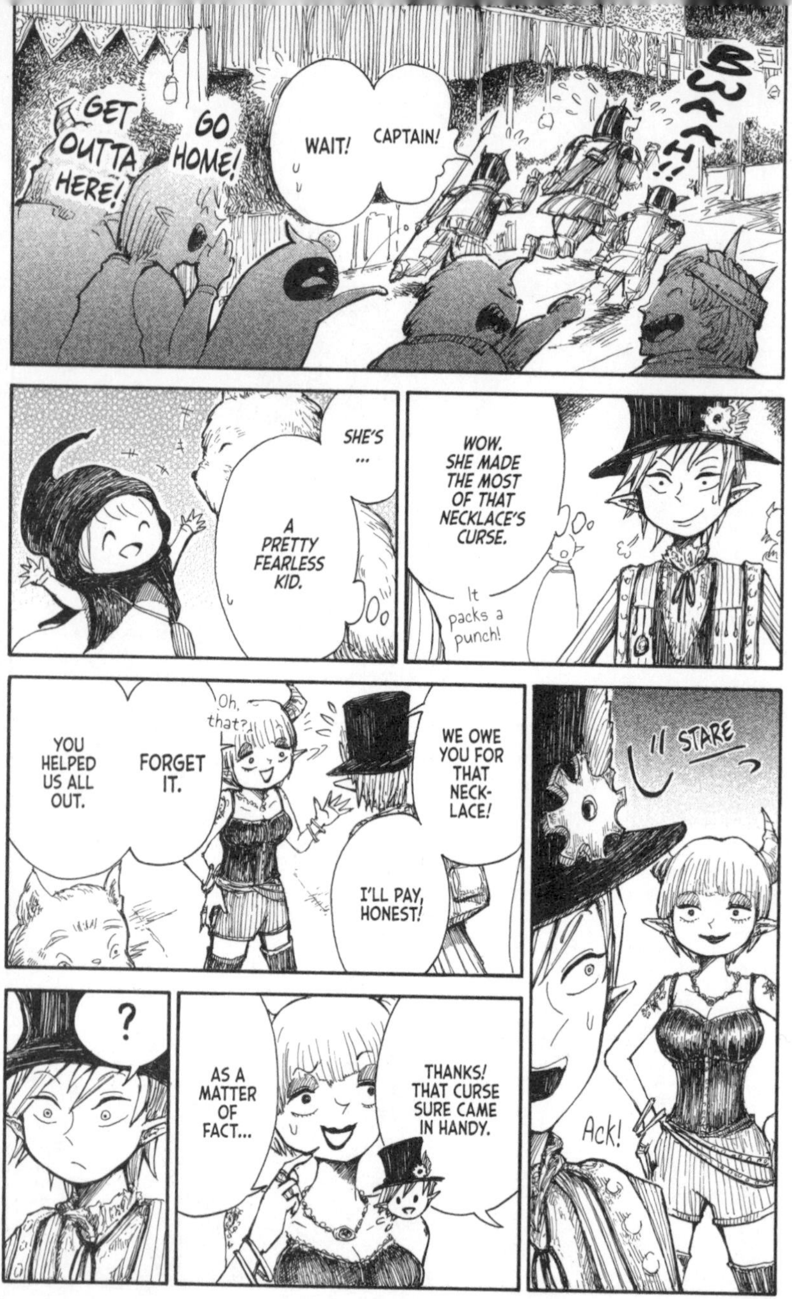
BWAAH!!
CAPTAIN!
WAIT!
GO HOME!
GET OUTTA HERE!
WOW. SHE MADE THE MOST OF THAT NECKLACE'S CURSE.
It packs a punch!
SHE'S ...
A PRETTY FEARLESS KID.
STARE
Ack!
WE OWE YOU FOR THAT NECK-LACE!
I'LL PAY, HONEST!
Oh, that?
FORGET IT.
YOU HELPED US ALL OUT.
THANKS! THAT CURSE SURE CAME IN HANDY.
AS A MATTER OF FACT...
?

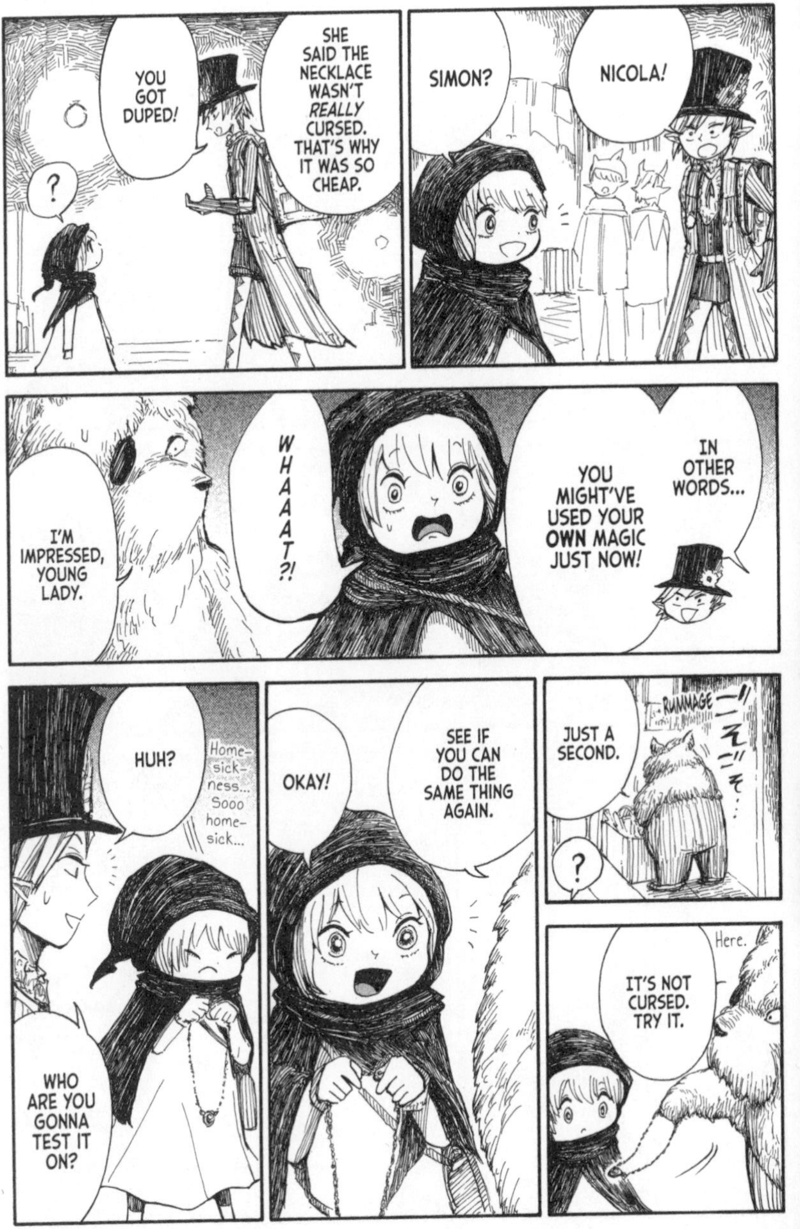
NICOLA!
SIMON?
SHE SAID THE NECKLACE WASN'T *REALLY* CURSED. THAT'S WHY IT WAS SO CHEAP.
YOU GOT DUPED!
?
IN OTHER WORDS...
YOU MIGHT'VE USED YOUR **OWN** MAGIC JUST NOW!
WHAAAAT?!
I'M IMPRESSED, YOUNG LADY.
RUMMAGE
JUST A SECOND.
?
Here.
IT'S NOT CURSED. TRY IT.
SEE IF YOU CAN DO THE SAME THING AGAIN.
OKAY!
Home-sick-ness... Sooo home-sick...
HUH?
WHO ARE YOU GONNA TEST IT ON?

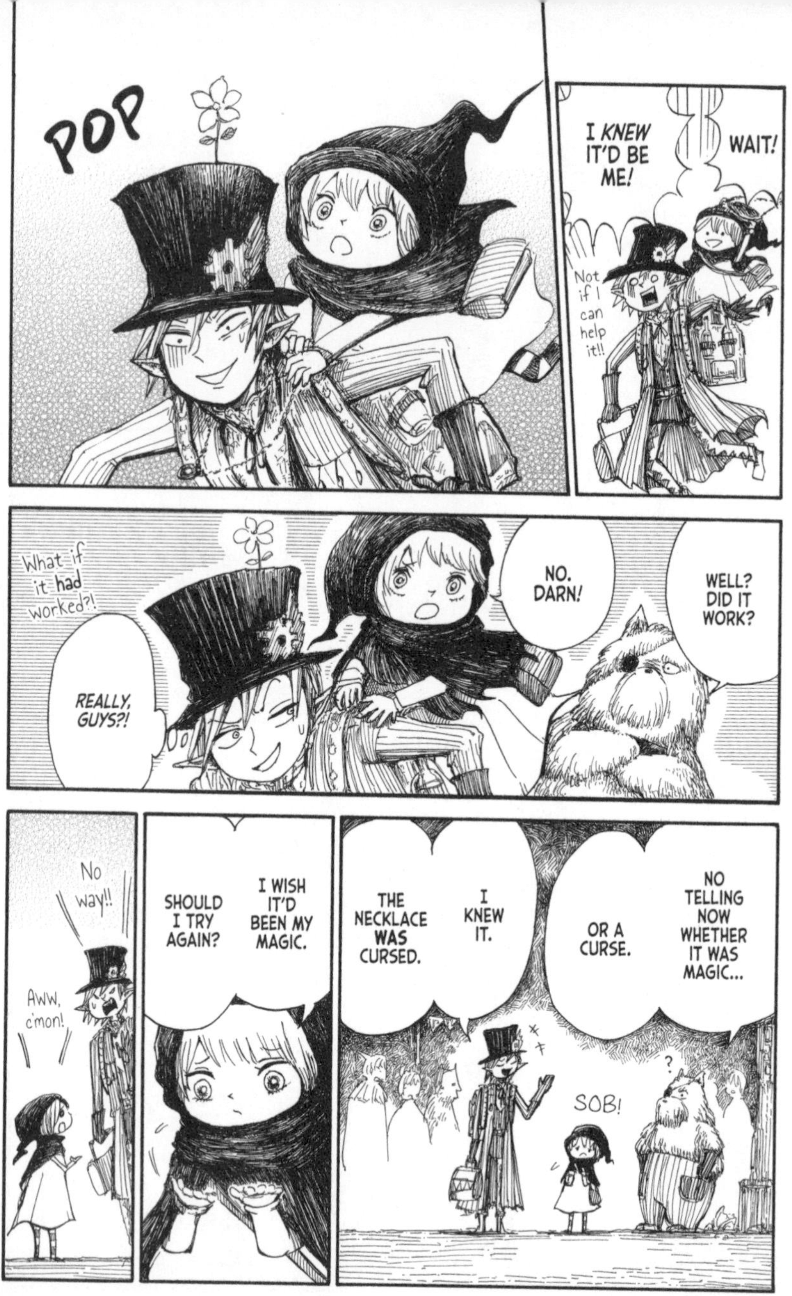
WAIT!
I KNEW IT'D BE ME!
Not if I can help it!!
POP
WELL? DID IT WORK?
NO. DARN!
What if it had worked?!
REALLY, GUYS?!
NO TELLING NOW WHETHER IT WAS MAGIC...
OR A CURSE.
I KNEW IT.
THE NECKLACE WAS CURSED.
?
SOB!
I WISH IT'D BEEN MY MAGIC.
SHOULD I TRY AGAIN?
No way!!
Aww, c'mon!

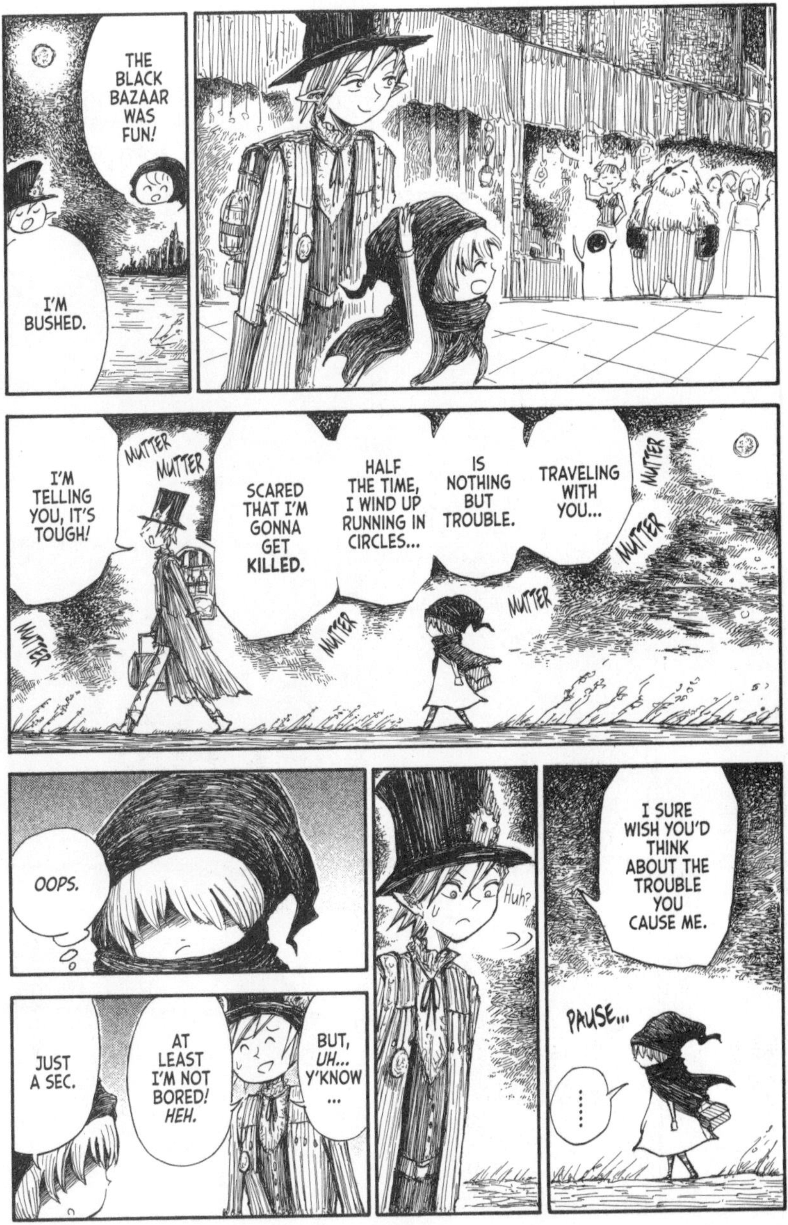
THE BLACK BAZAAR WAS FUN!
I'M BUSHED.
MUTTER MUTTER
TRAVELING WITH YOU...
IS NOTHING BUT TROUBLE.
HALF THE TIME, I WIND UP RUNNING IN CIRCLES...
SCARED THAT I'M GONNA GET **KILLED.**
I'M TELLING YOU, IT'S TOUGH!
MUTTER
MUTTER
MUTTER
MUTTER
I SURE WISH YOU'D THINK ABOUT THE TROUBLE YOU CAUSE ME.
PAUSE...
......
Huh?
OOPS.
BUT, *UH...* Y'KNOW...
AT LEAST I'M NOT BORED! *HEH.*
JUST A SEC.

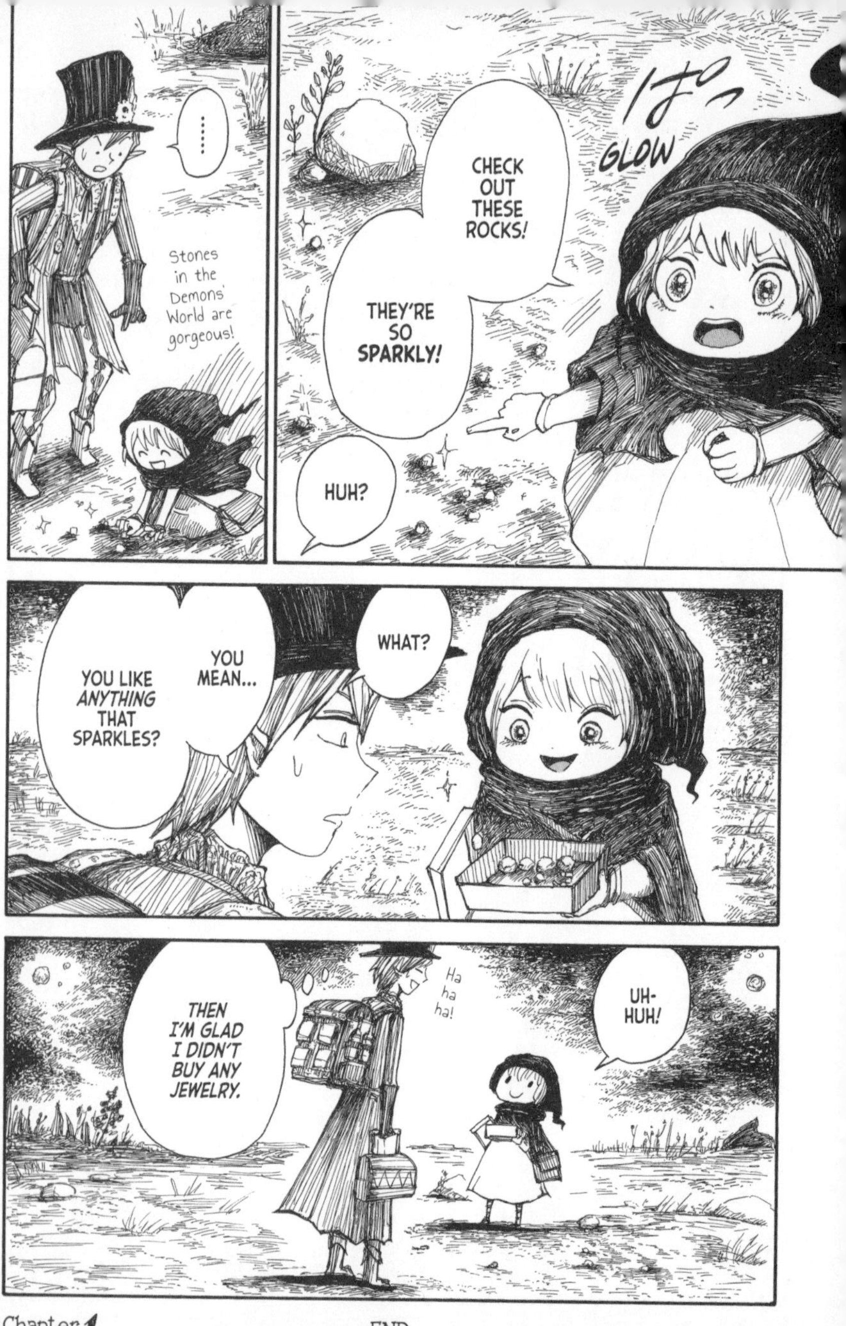
ぱっ
GLOW
CHECK OUT THESE ROCKS!
THEY'RE SO SPARKLY!
HUH?
......
Stones in the Demons' World are gorgeous!
WHAT?
YOU MEAN...
YOU LIKE *ANYTHING* THAT SPARKLES?
UH-HUH!
Ha ha ha!
THEN I'M GLAD I DIDN'T BUY ANY JEWELRY.

Chapter 1 END

After the Visit 1

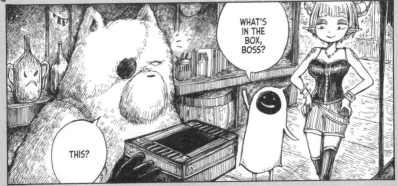

WHAT'S IN THE BOX, BOSS?
THIS?
LETTERS FROM MY GRAND-DAUGHTER.
READING THEM REMINDS ME OF HER.
Aw, it's not candy?
THAT'S HER.
CUTE, ISN'T SHE?
LOOKS JUST LIKE YOU!
YOU'RE NOT USUALLY SO SENTIMENTAL.
YOU WEREN'T CURSED WITH HOMESICK-NESS, WERE YOU?
Hmph!

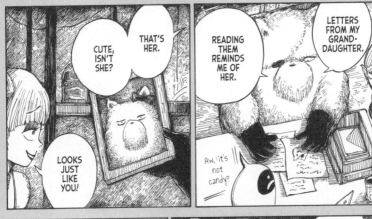

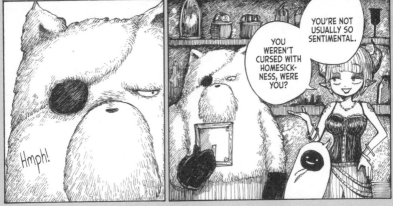

Nicola Traveling Around the Demon's World

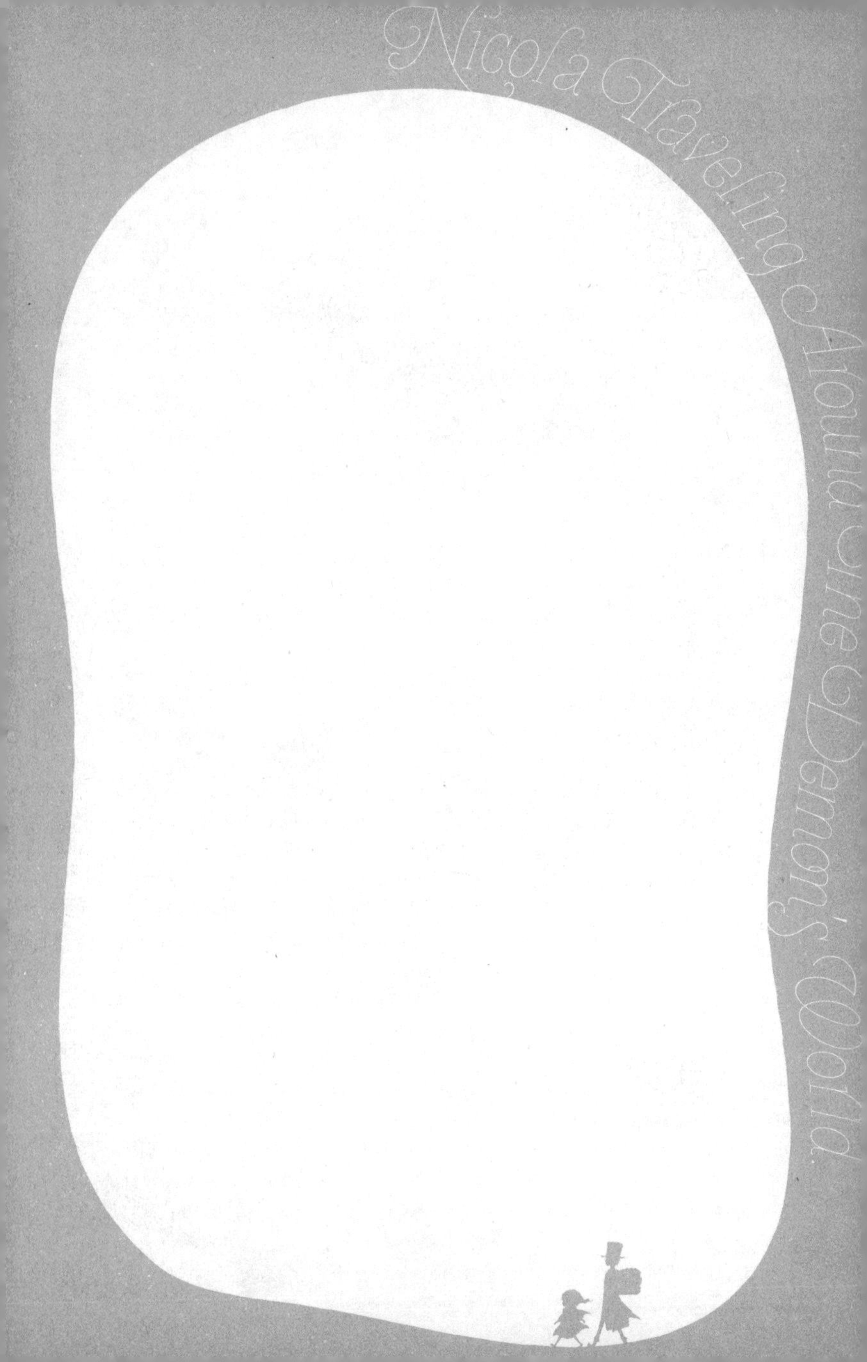

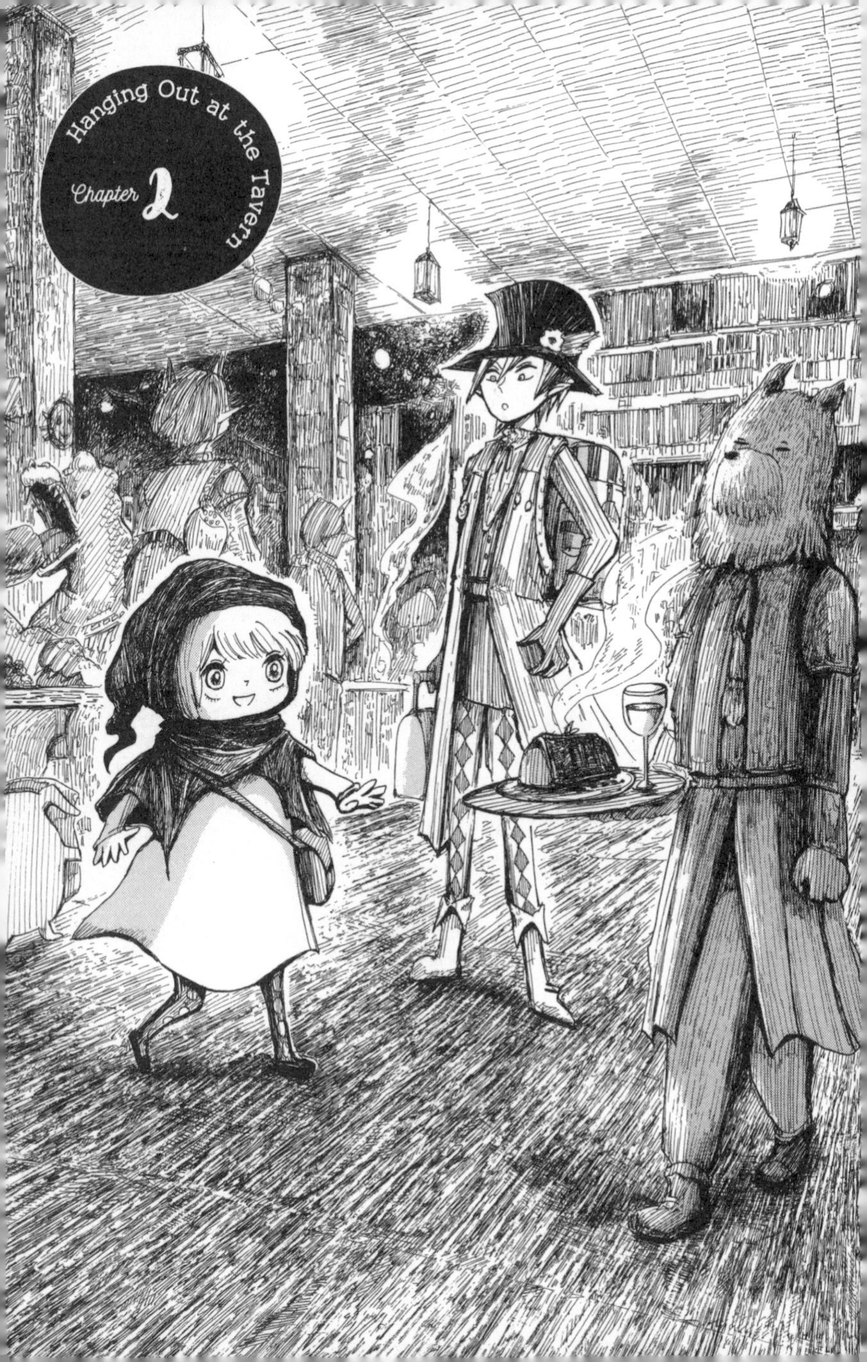
Hanging Out at the Tavern
Chapter 2

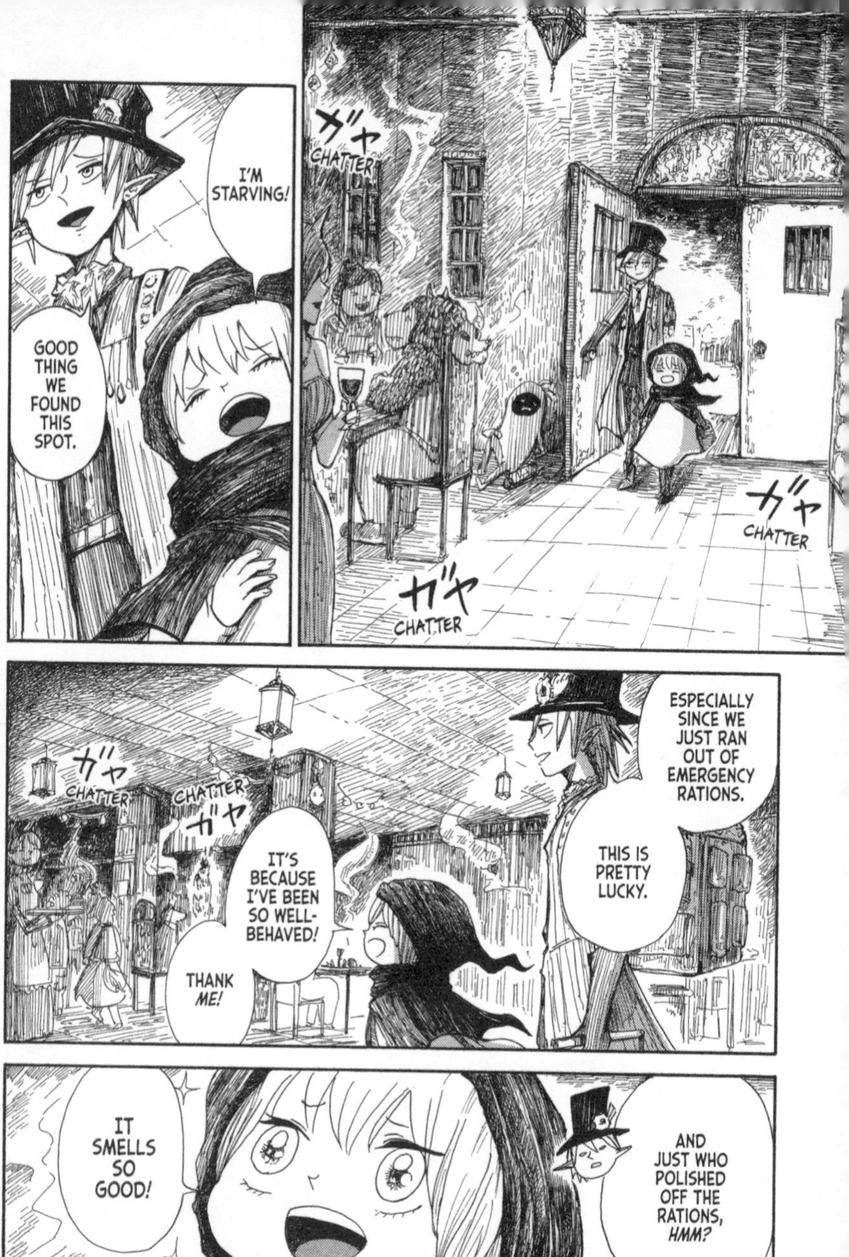
ガヤ
CHATTER
ガヤ
CHATTER
ガヤ
CHATTER
I'M STARVING!
GOOD THING WE FOUND THIS SPOT.
ESPECIALLY SINCE WE JUST RAN OUT OF EMERGENCY RATIONS.
THIS IS PRETTY LUCKY.
IT'S BECAUSE I'VE BEEN SO WELL-BEHAVED!
THANK *ME!*
CHATTER
ガヤ
ガヤ
CHATTER
AND JUST WHO POLISHED OFF THE RATIONS, *HMM?*
IT SMELLS SO GOOD!

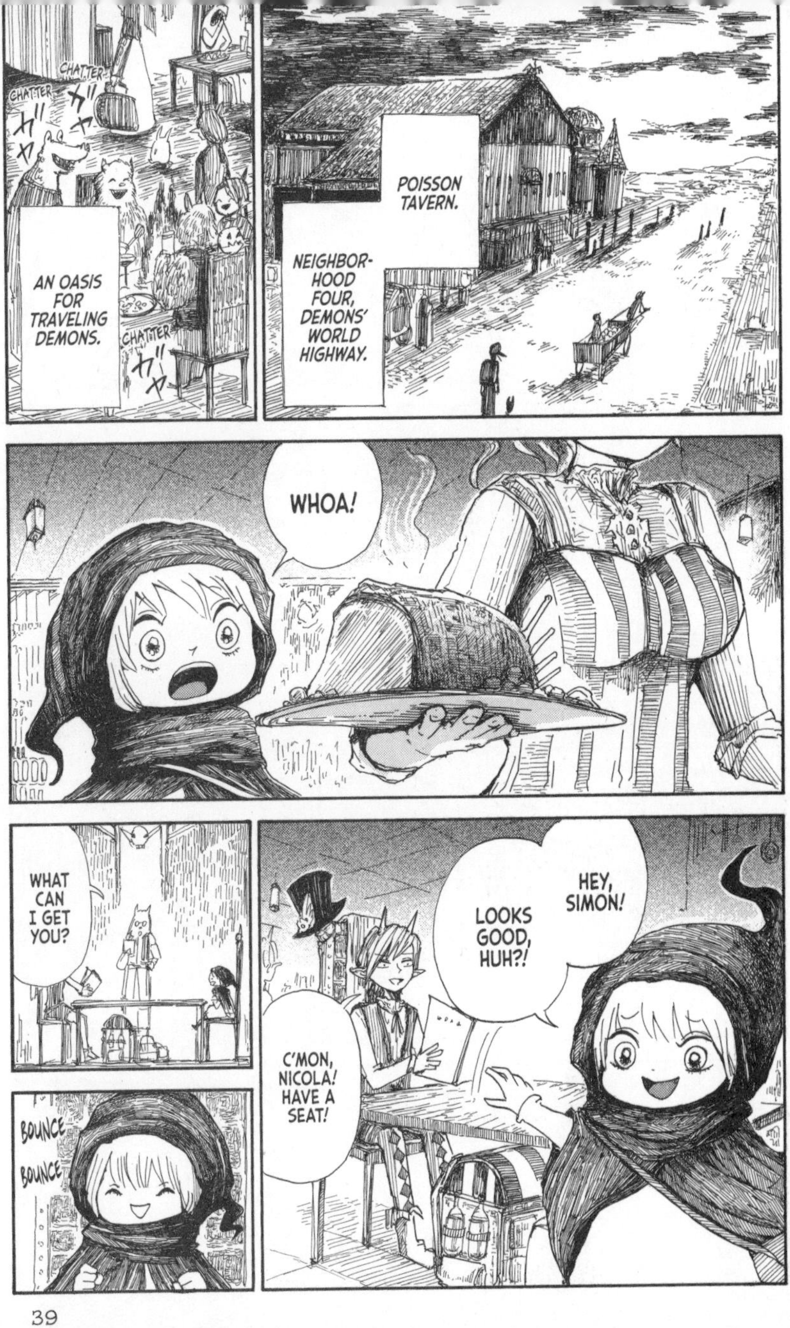
POISSON TAVERN.
NEIGHBORHOOD FOUR, DEMONS' WORLD HIGHWAY.
CHATTER
CHATTER
AN OASIS FOR TRAVELING DEMONS.
CHATTER
WHOA!
HEY, SIMON!
LOOKS GOOD, HUH?!
C'MON, NICOLA! HAVE A SEAT!
WHAT CAN I GET YOU?
BOUNCE
BOUNCE

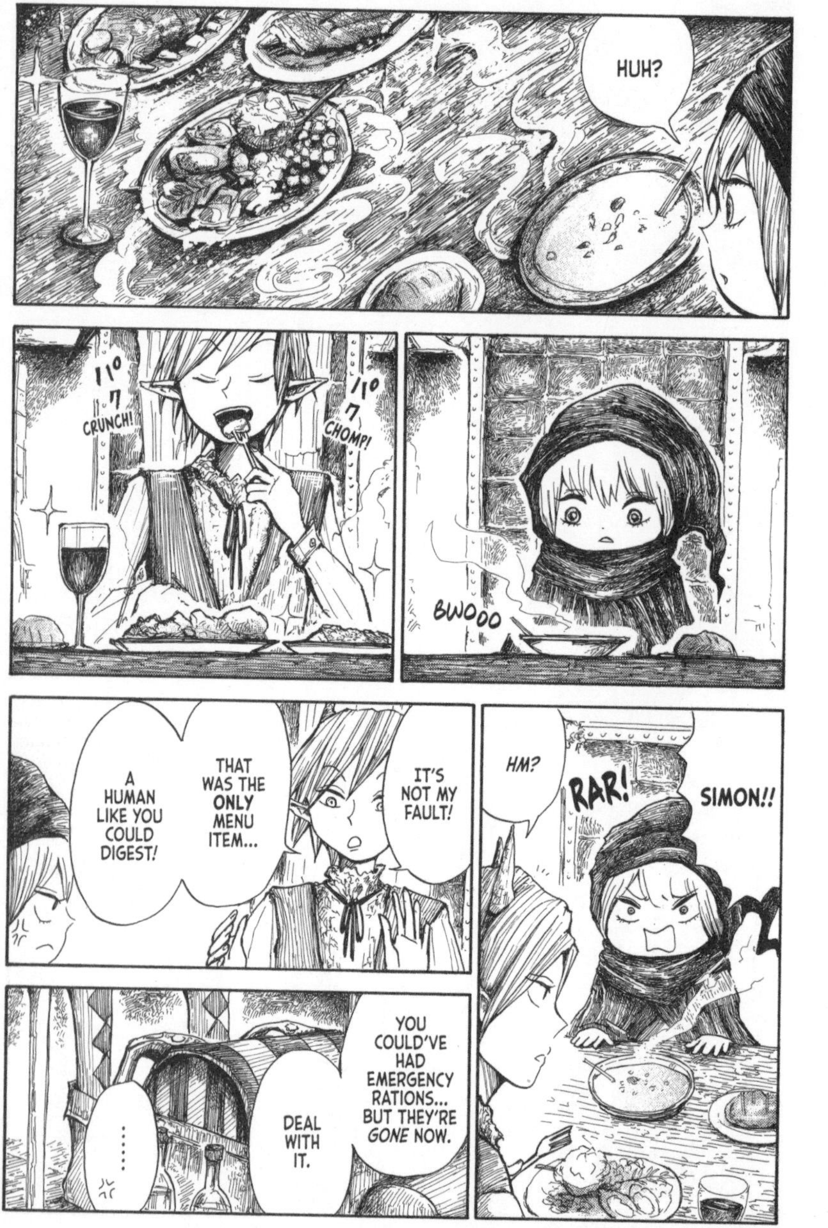

HUH?
BWOOO
パク
CHOMP!
パク
CRUNCH!
SIMON!!
RAR!
HM?
IT'S NOT MY FAULT!
THAT WAS THE **ONLY** MENU ITEM...
A HUMAN LIKE YOU COULD DIGEST!
YOU COULD'VE HAD EMERGENCY RATIONS... BUT THEY'RE *GONE* NOW.
DEAL WITH IT.
......

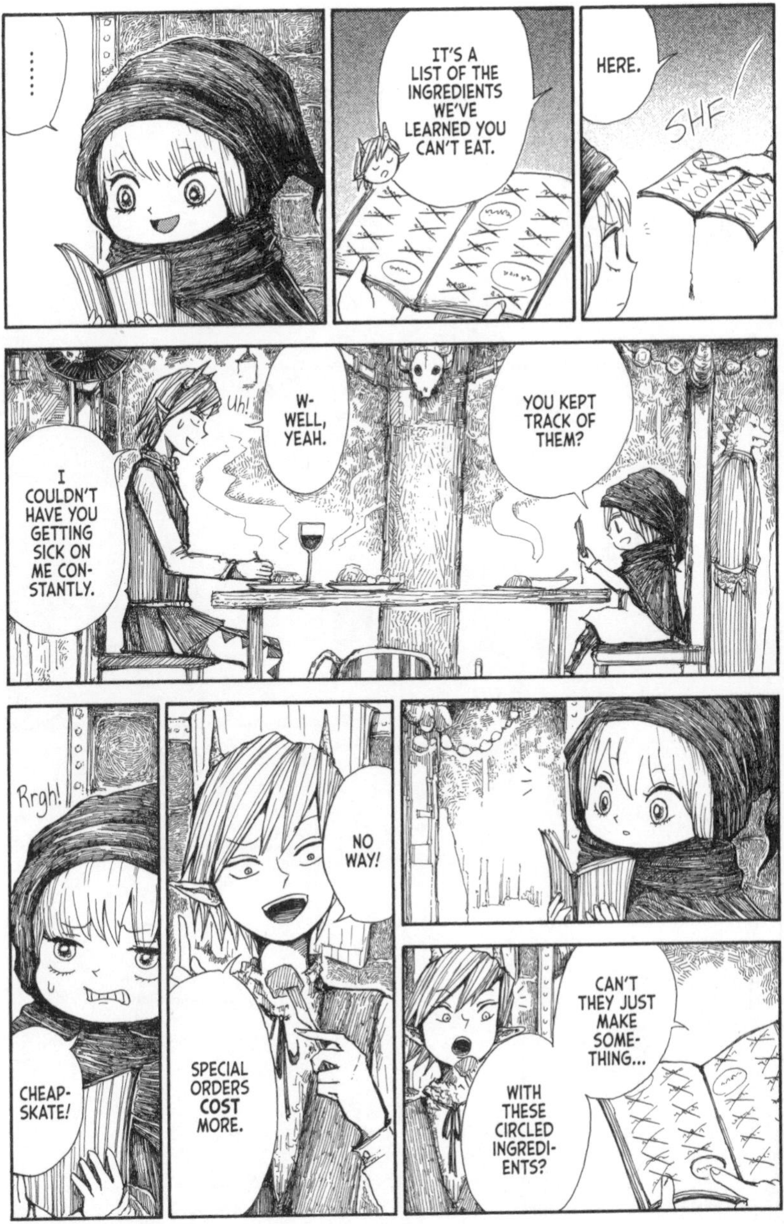
HERE.
SHF
IT'S A LIST OF THE INGREDIENTS WE'VE LEARNED YOU CAN'T EAT.
......
YOU KEPT TRACK OF THEM?
W-WELL, YEAH.
Uh!
I COULDN'T HAVE YOU GETTING SICK ON ME CONSTANTLY.
CAN'T THEY JUST MAKE SOMETHING...
WITH THESE CIRCLED INGREDIENTS?
NO WAY!
SPECIAL ORDERS **COST** MORE.
Rrgh!
CHEAPSKATE!

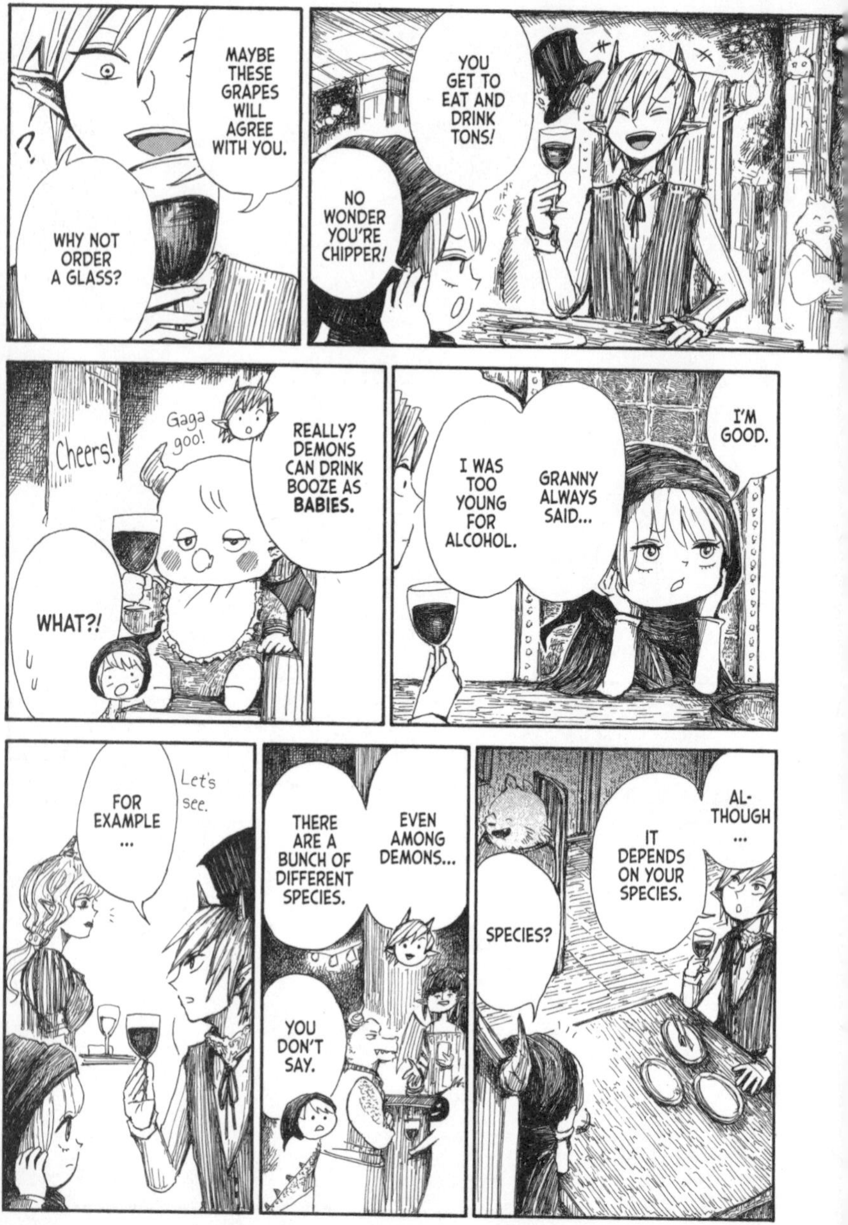
YOU GET TO EAT AND DRINK TONS!
NO WONDER YOU'RE CHIPPER!
MAYBE THESE GRAPES WILL AGREE WITH YOU.
WHY NOT ORDER A GLASS?
I'M GOOD.
GRANNY ALWAYS SAID...
I WAS TOO YOUNG FOR ALCOHOL.
REALLY? DEMONS CAN DRINK BOOZE AS **BABIES.**
Gaga goo!
Cheers!
WHAT?!
AL-THOUGH...
IT DEPENDS ON YOUR SPECIES.
SPECIES?
EVEN AMONG DEMONS...
THERE ARE A BUNCH OF DIFFERENT SPECIES.
YOU DON'T SAY.
Let's see.
FOR EXAMPLE...

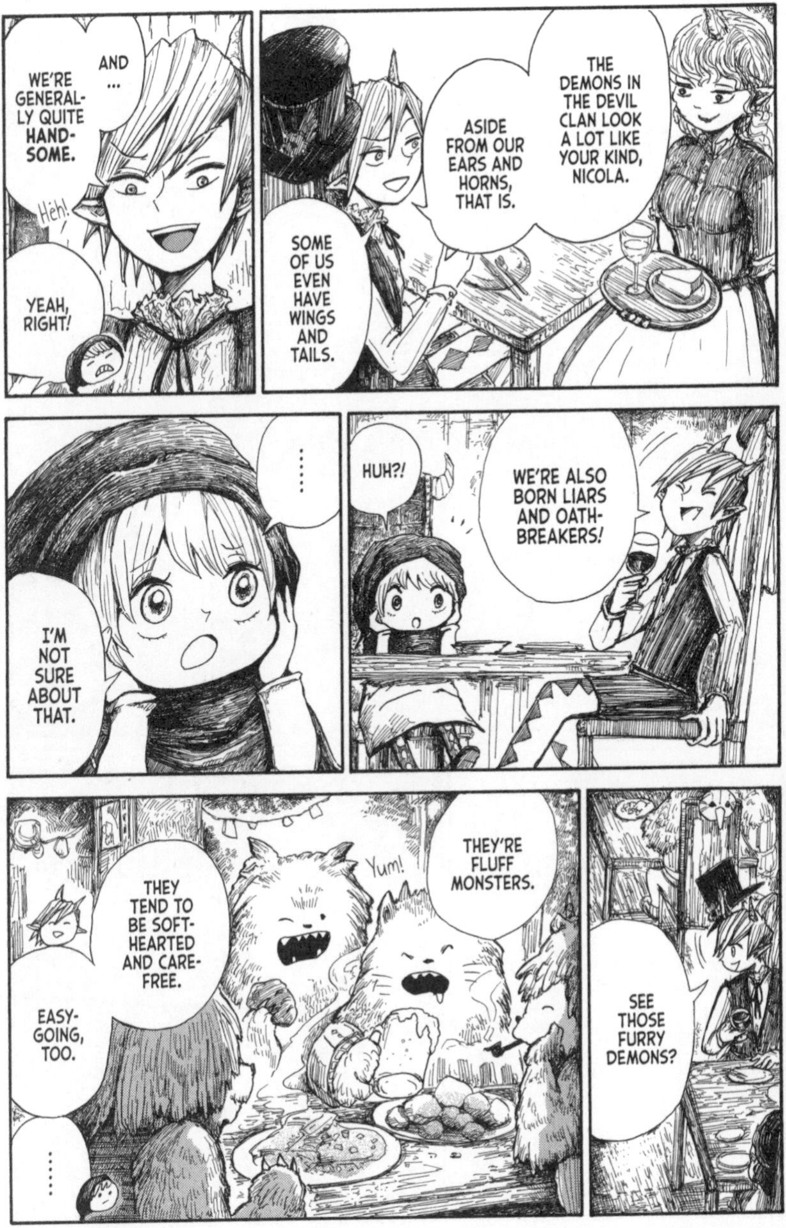
THE DEMONS IN THE DEVIL CLAN LOOK A LOT LIKE YOUR KIND, NICOLA.
ASIDE FROM OUR EARS AND HORNS, THAT IS.
SOME OF US EVEN HAVE WINGS AND TAILS.
AND ...
WE'RE GENERALLY QUITE **HANDSOME.**
Heh!
YEAH, RIGHT!
WE'RE ALSO BORN LIARS AND OATH-BREAKERS!
HUH?!
......
I'M NOT SURE ABOUT THAT.
SEE THOSE FURRY DEMONS?
THEY'RE FLUFF MONSTERS.
Yum!
THEY TEND TO BE SOFT-HEARTED AND CAREFREE.
EASY-GOING, TOO.
......

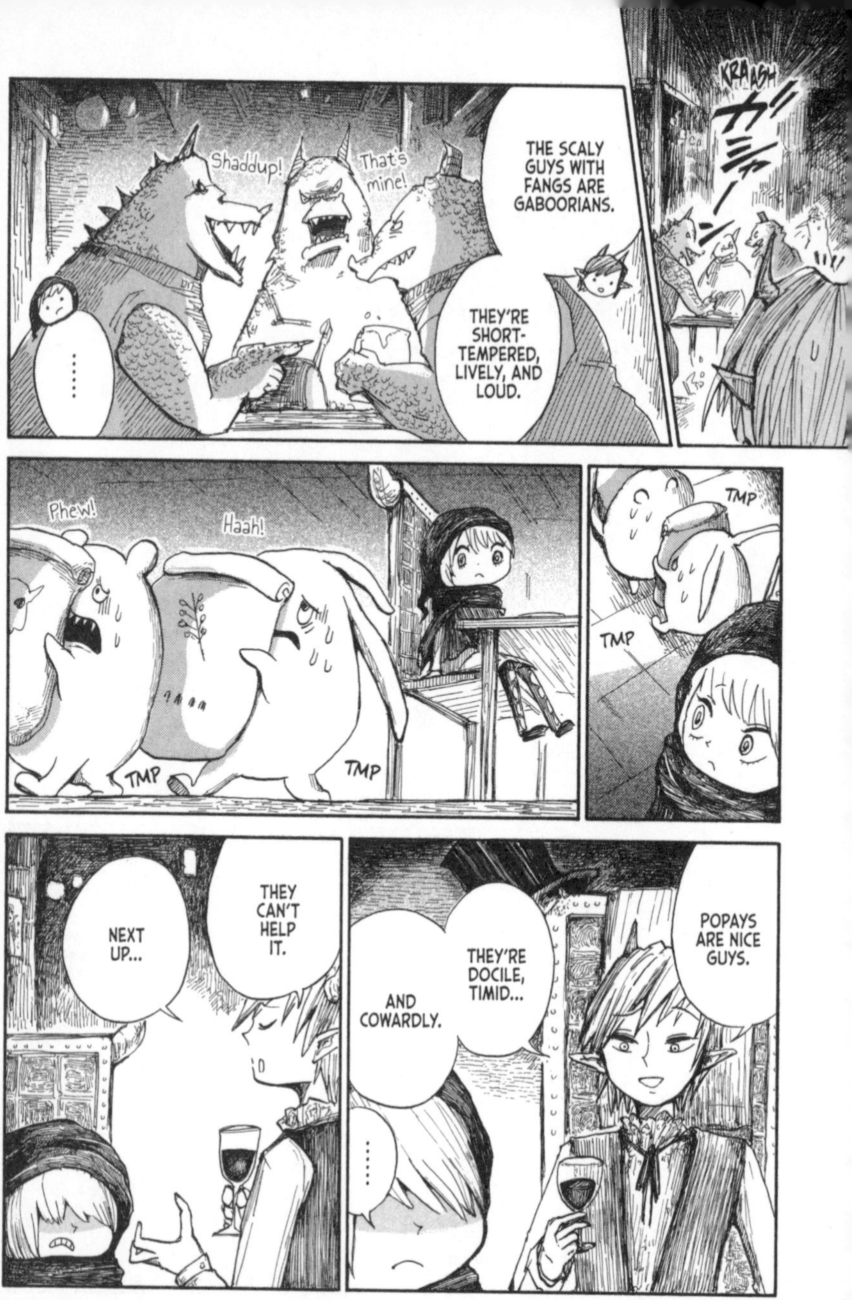
KRAASH
ガシャーン
THE SCALY GUYS WITH FANGS ARE GABOORIANS.
THEY'RE SHORT-TEMPERED, LIVELY, AND LOUD.
That's mine!
Shaddup!
......
TMP
TMP
Haah!
Phew!
TMP
TMP
POPAYS ARE NICE GUYS.
THEY'RE DOCILE, TIMID...
AND COWARDLY.
......
THEY CAN'T HELP IT.
NEXT UP...

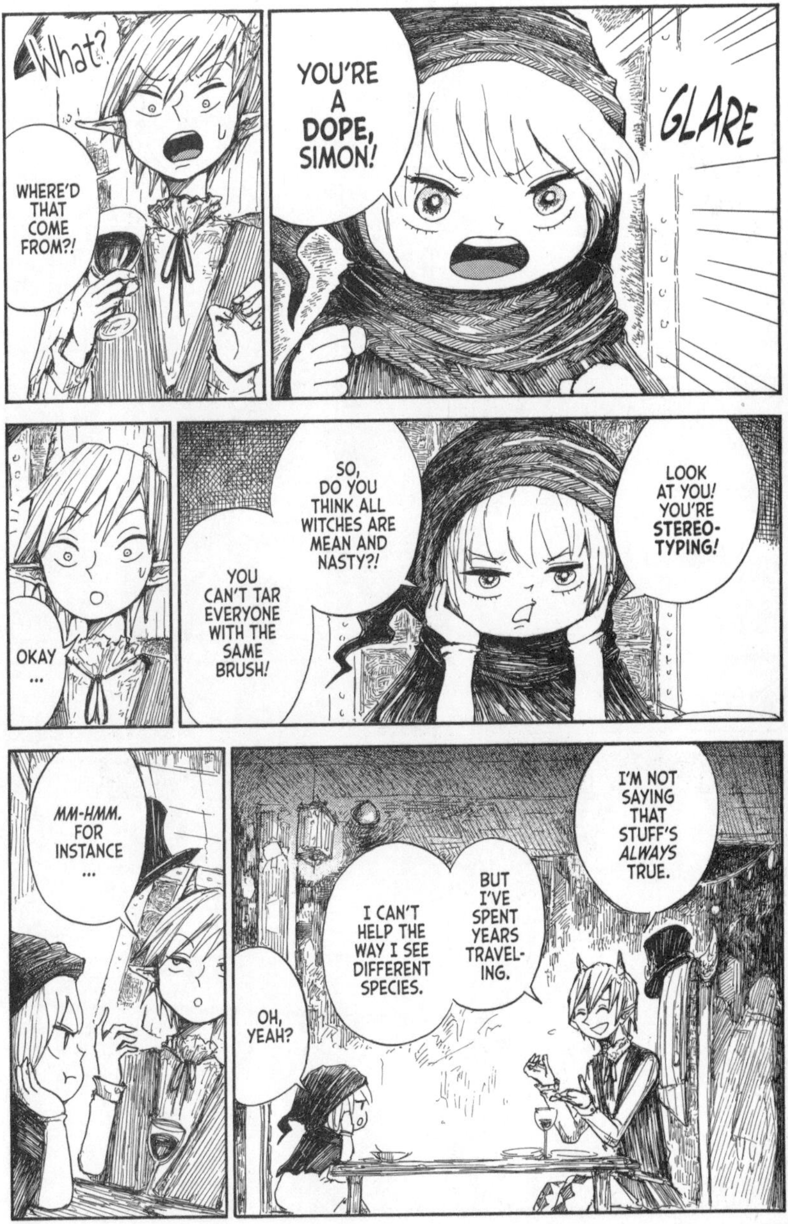

GLARE
YOU'RE A DOPE, SIMON!
What?
WHERE'D THAT COME FROM?!
LOOK AT YOU! YOU'RE STEREO-TYPING!
SO, DO YOU THINK ALL WITCHES ARE MEAN AND NASTY?!
YOU CAN'T TAR EVERYONE WITH THE SAME BRUSH!
OKAY ...
I'M NOT SAYING THAT STUFF'S *ALWAYS* TRUE.
BUT I'VE SPENT YEARS TRAVEL-ING.
I CAN'T HELP THE WAY I SEE DIFFERENT SPECIES.
OH, YEAH?
MM-HMM. FOR INSTANCE ...

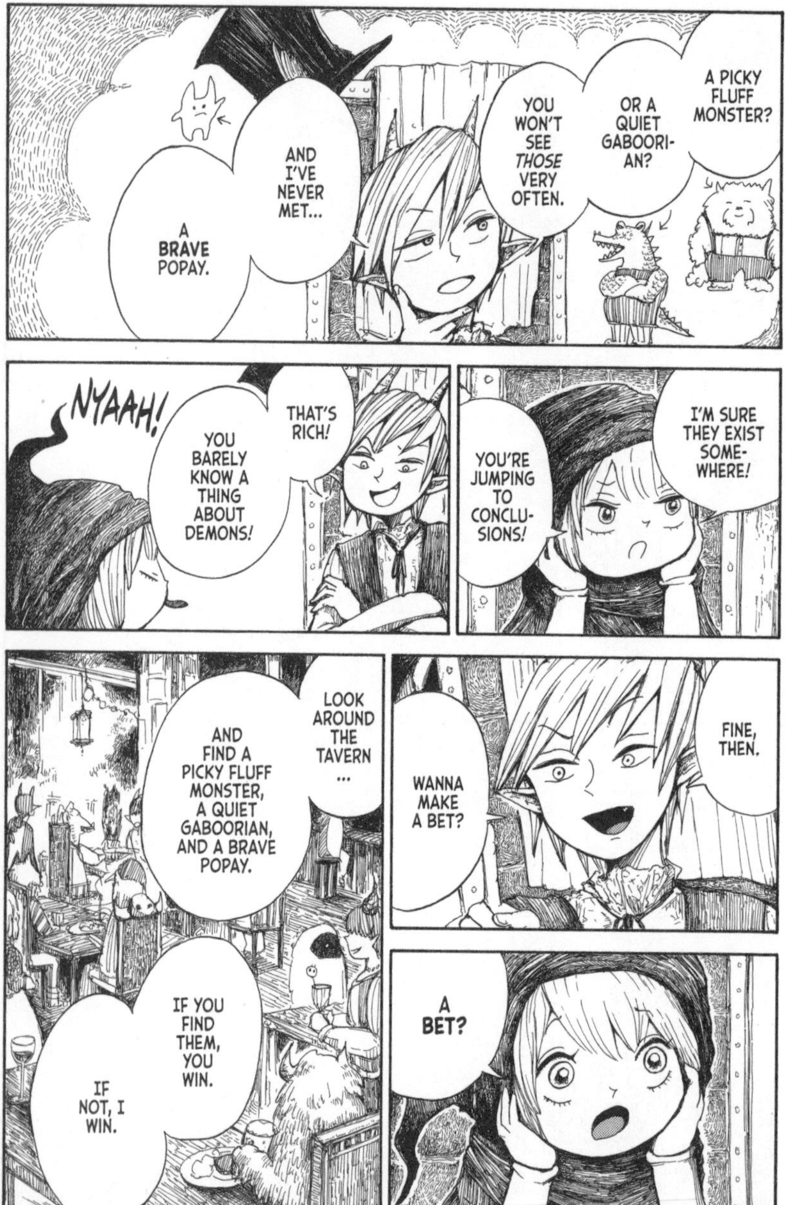
A PICKY FLUFF MONSTER?
OR A QUIET GABOORI-AN?
YOU WON'T SEE *THOSE* VERY OFTEN.
AND I'VE NEVER MET...
A **BRAVE** POPAY.
I'M SURE THEY EXIST SOME-WHERE!
YOU'RE JUMPING TO CONCLU-SIONS!
THAT'S RICH!
YOU BARELY KNOW A THING ABOUT DEMONS!
NYAAH!
FINE, THEN.
WANNA MAKE A BET?
A **BET?**
LOOK AROUND THE TAVERN ...
AND FIND A PICKY FLUFF MONSTER, A QUIET GABOORIAN, AND A BRAVE POPAY.
IF YOU FIND THEM, YOU WIN.
IF NOT, I WIN.

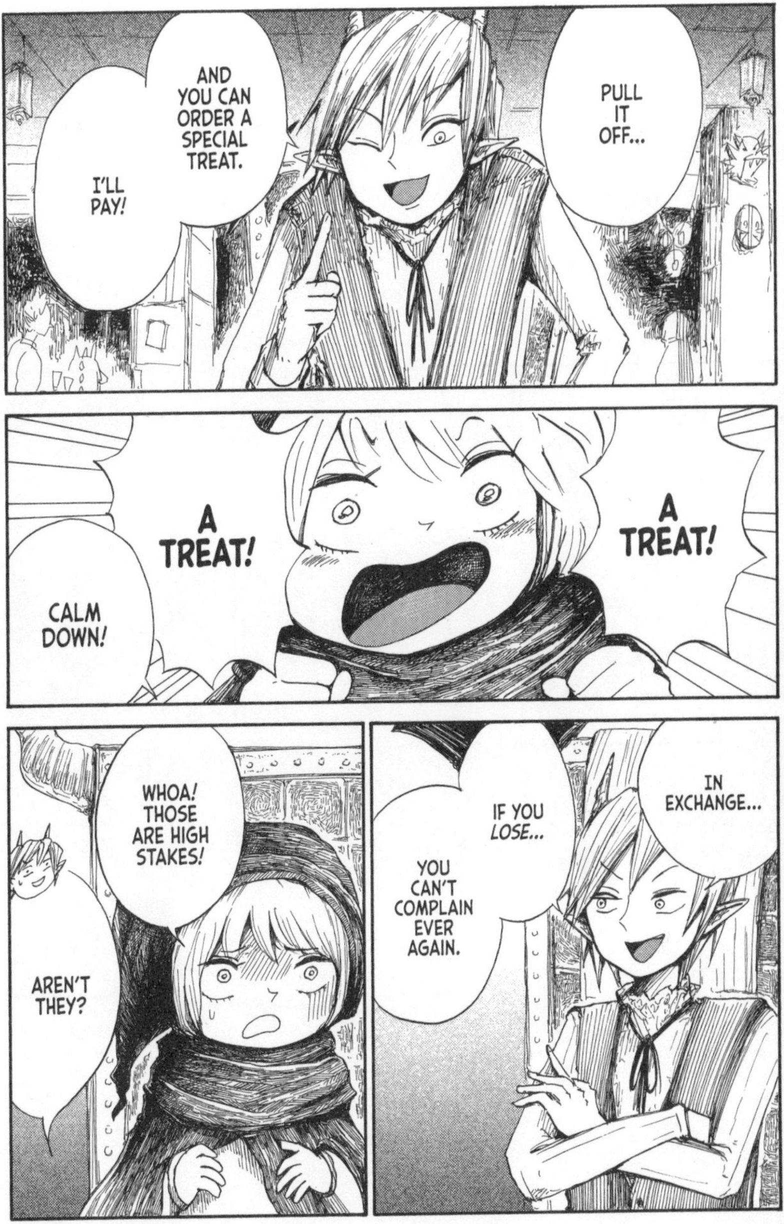
PULL IT OFF...
AND YOU CAN ORDER A SPECIAL TREAT.
I'LL PAY!
A TREAT!
A TREAT!
CALM DOWN!
IN EXCHANGE...
IF YOU *LOSE*...
YOU CAN'T COMPLAIN EVER AGAIN.
WHOA! THOSE ARE HIGH STAKES!
AREN'T THEY?

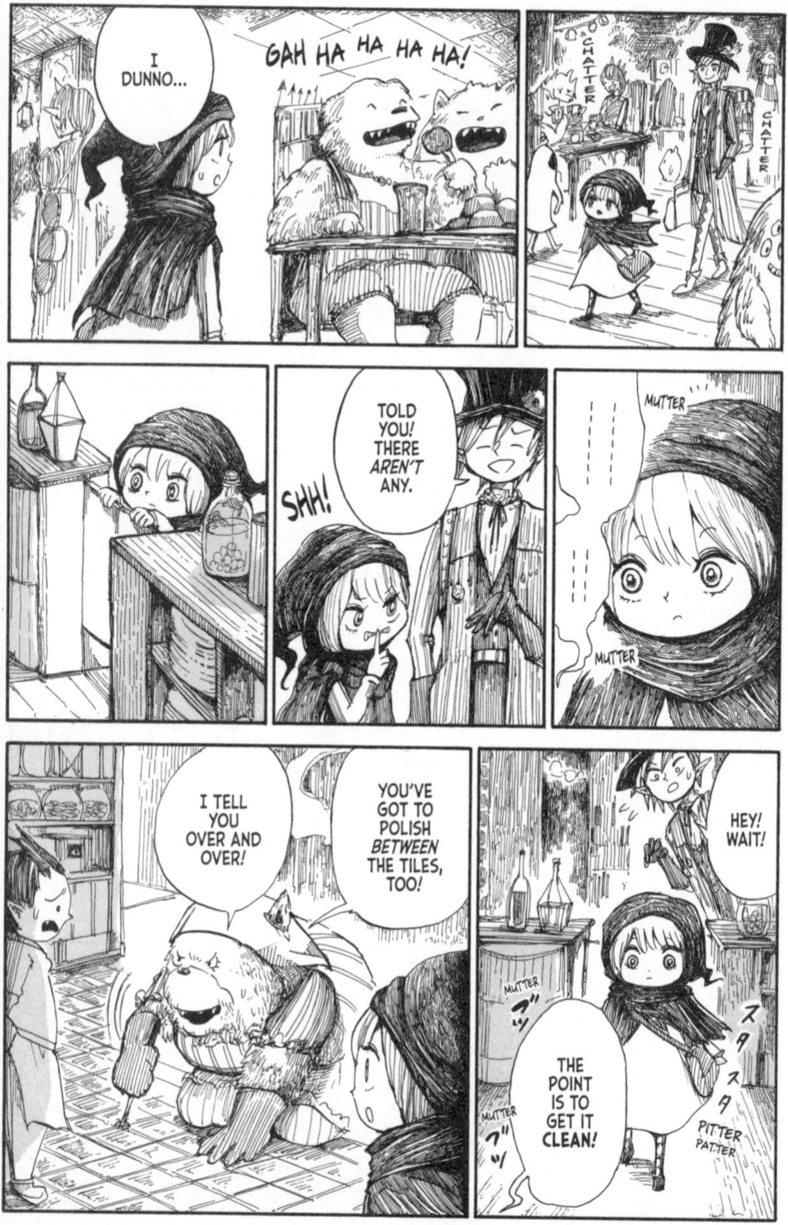
CHATTER
CHATTER
GAH HA HA HA HA!
I DUNNO...
MUTTER
MUTTER
TOLD YOU! THERE *AREN'T* ANY.
SHH!
HEY! WAIT!
スタスタ
PITTER PATTER
MUTTER
ブツ
THE POINT IS TO GET IT CLEAN!
MUTTER
ブツ
YOU'VE GOT TO POLISH *BETWEEN* THE TILES, TOO!
I TELL YOU OVER AND OVER!

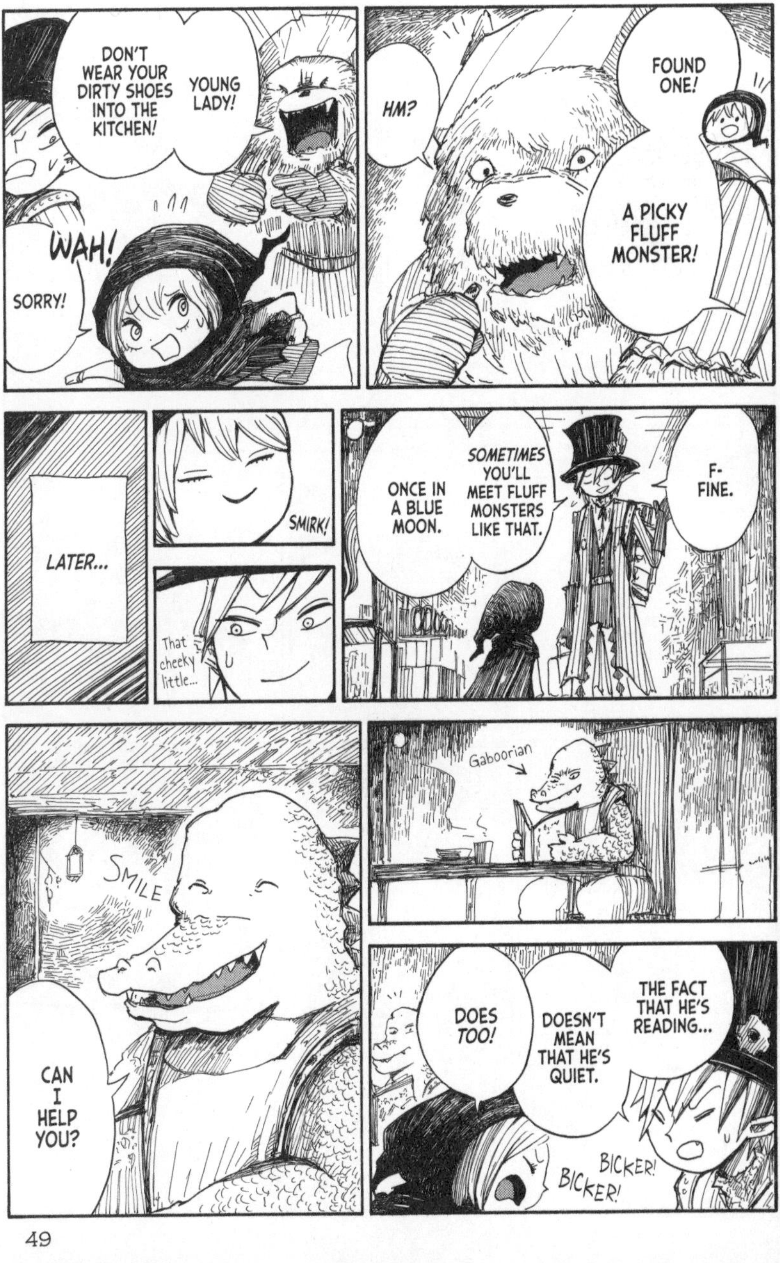
FOUND ONE!
HM?
A PICKY FLUFF MONSTER!
DON'T WEAR YOUR DIRTY SHOES INTO THE KITCHEN! YOUNG LADY!
WAH!
SORRY!
F-FINE.
SOMETIMES YOU'LL MEET FLUFF MONSTERS LIKE THAT.
ONCE IN A BLUE MOON.
SMIRK!
That cheeky little...
LATER...
Gaboorian
THE FACT THAT HE'S READING...
DOESN'T MEAN THAT HE'S QUIET.
DOES TOO!
BICKER!
BICKER!
SMILE
CAN I HELP YOU?

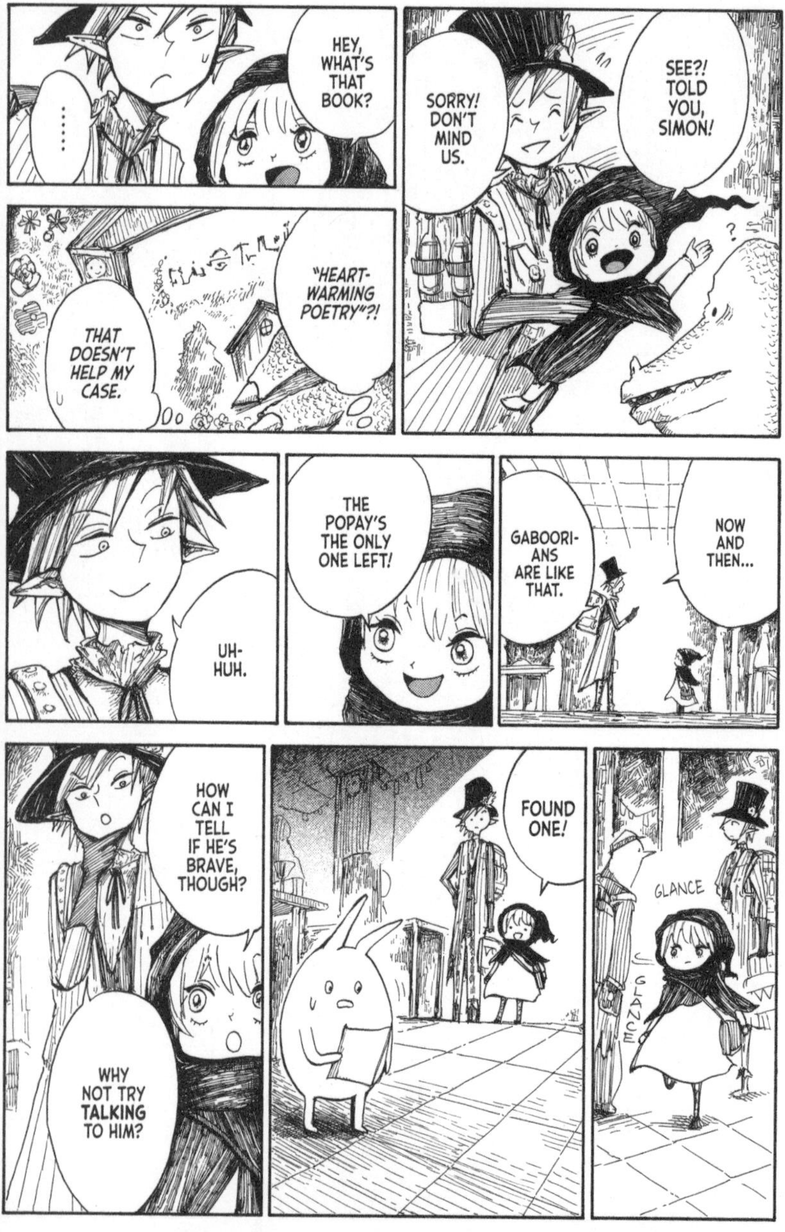
SEE?! TOLD YOU, SIMON!
SORRY! DON'T MIND US.
HEY, WHAT'S THAT BOOK?
......
"HEART-WARMING POETRY"?!
THAT DOESN'T HELP MY CASE.
NOW AND THEN...
GABOORI-ANS ARE LIKE THAT.
THE POPAY'S THE ONLY ONE LEFT!
UH-HUH.
GLANCE
GLANCE
FOUND ONE!
HOW CAN I TELL IF HE'S BRAVE, THOUGH?
WHY NOT TRY TALKING TO HIM?

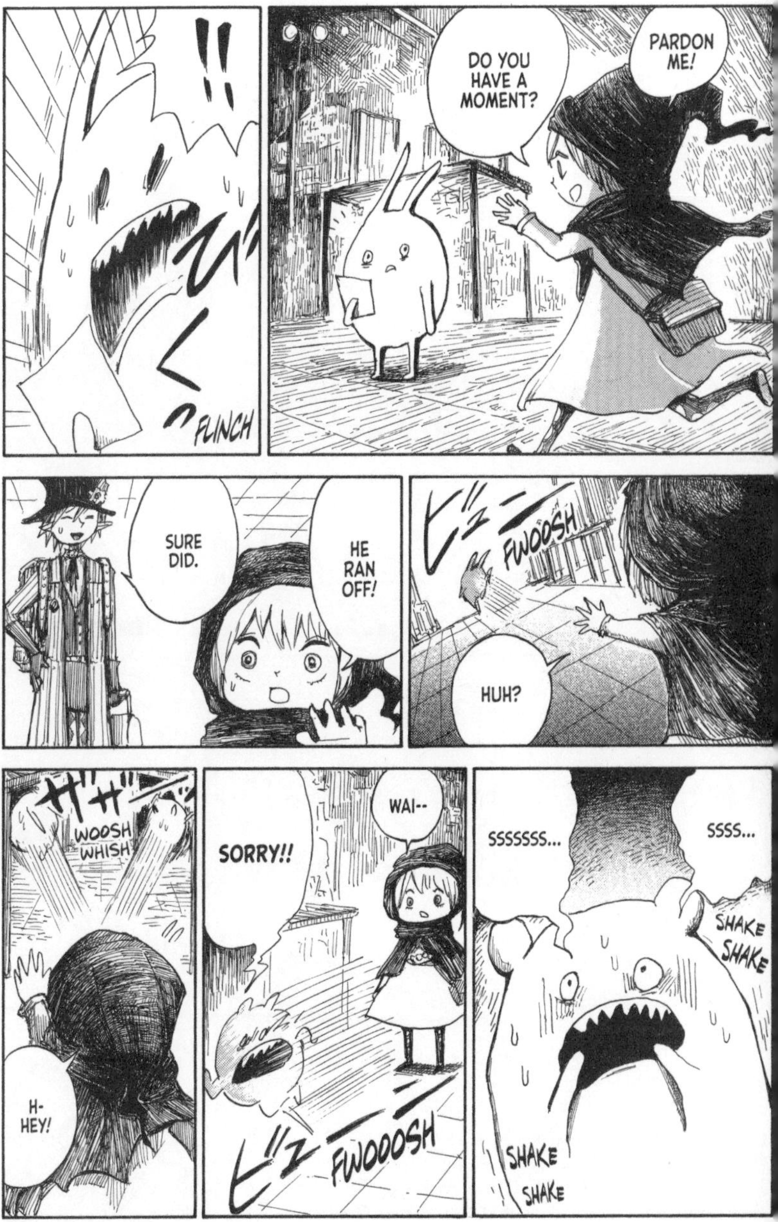
PARDON ME!
DO YOU HAVE A MOMENT?
!!
FLINCH
FWOOSH
HUH?
HE RAN OFF!
SURE DID.
SSSS...
SSSSSSS...
SHAKE SHAKE
SHAKE SHAKE
WAI--
SORRY!!
FWOOOSH
WOOSH WHISH
H-HEY!

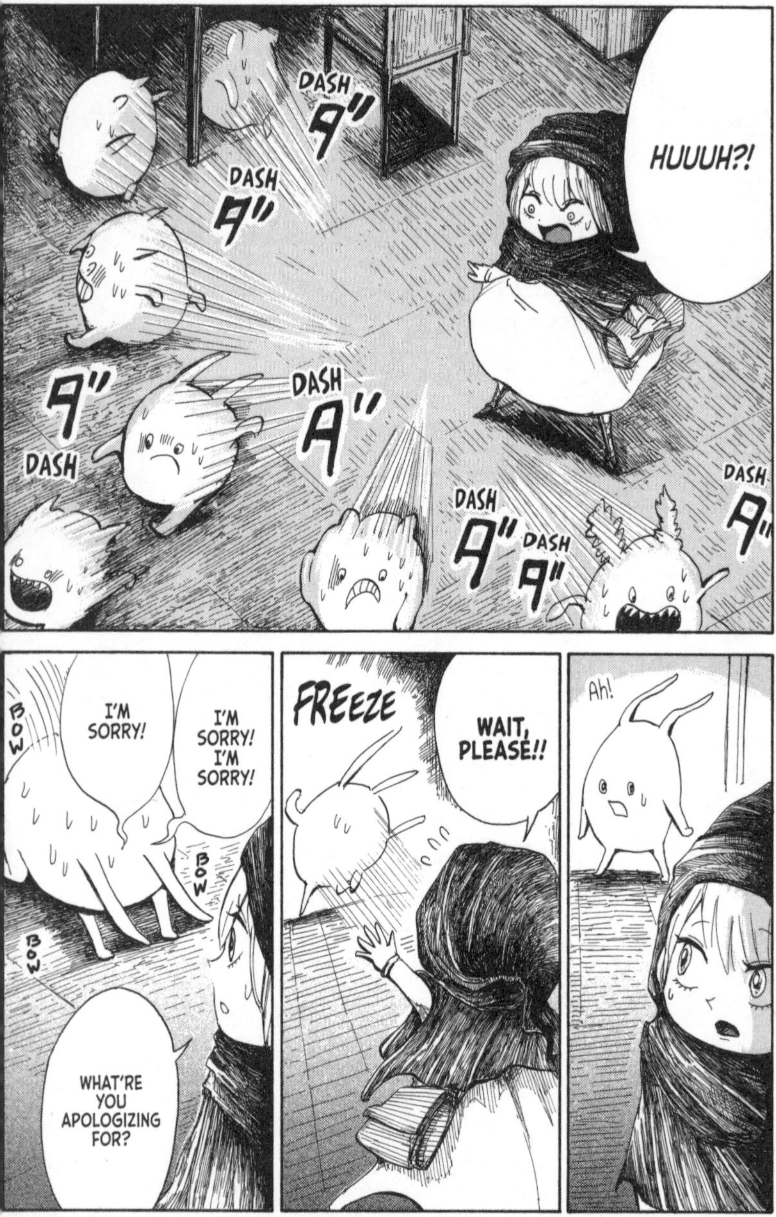
HUUUH?!
DASH ダ
DASH ダ
DASH ダ
DASH ダ
DASH ダ
DASH ダ
ダ DASH
Ah!
WAIT, PLEASE!!
FREEZE
I'M SORRY! I'M SORRY!
BOW
I'M SORRY!
BOW
BOW
WHAT'RE YOU APOLOGIZING FOR?

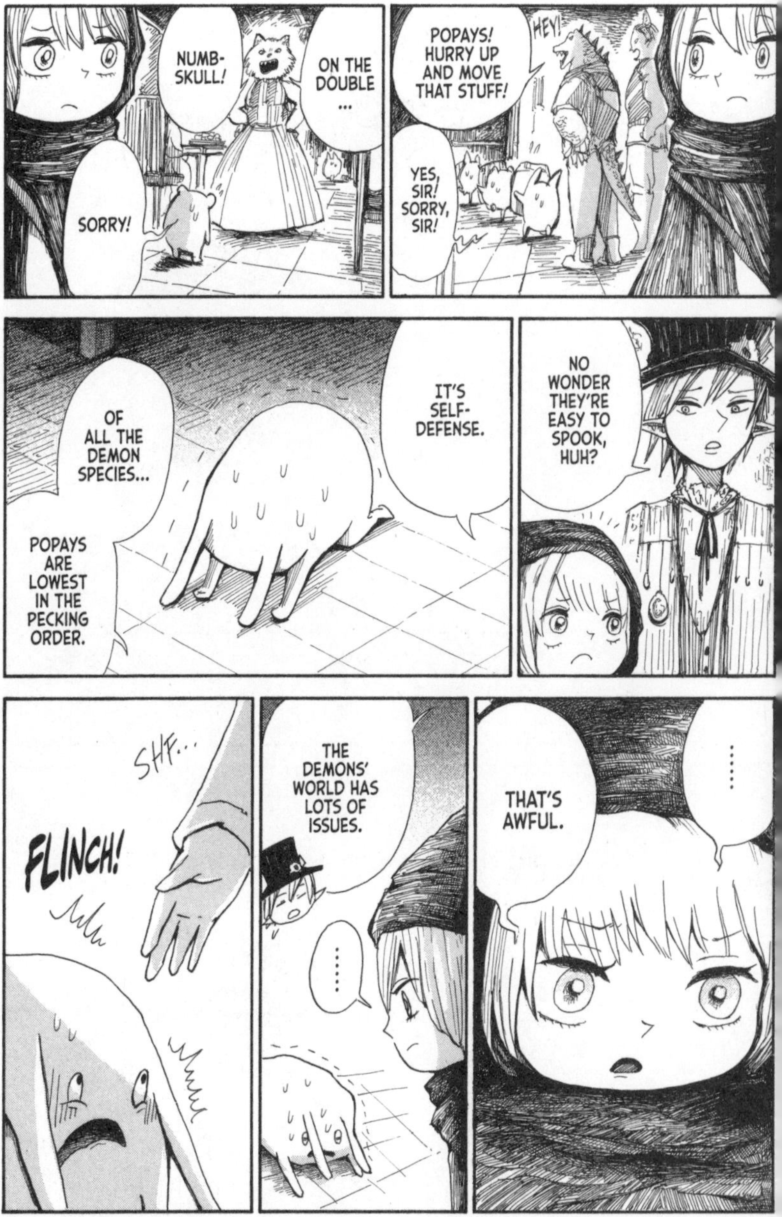
HEY!
POPAYS! HURRY UP AND MOVE THAT STUFF!
YES, SIR! SORRY, SIR!
ON THE DOUBLE ...
NUMB-SKULL!
SORRY!
NO WONDER THEY'RE EASY TO SPOOK, HUH?
IT'S SELF-DEFENSE.
OF ALL THE DEMON SPECIES...
POPAYS ARE LOWEST IN THE PECKING ORDER.
......
THAT'S AWFUL.
THE DEMONS' WORLD HAS LOTS OF ISSUES.
......
SHF...
FLINCH!

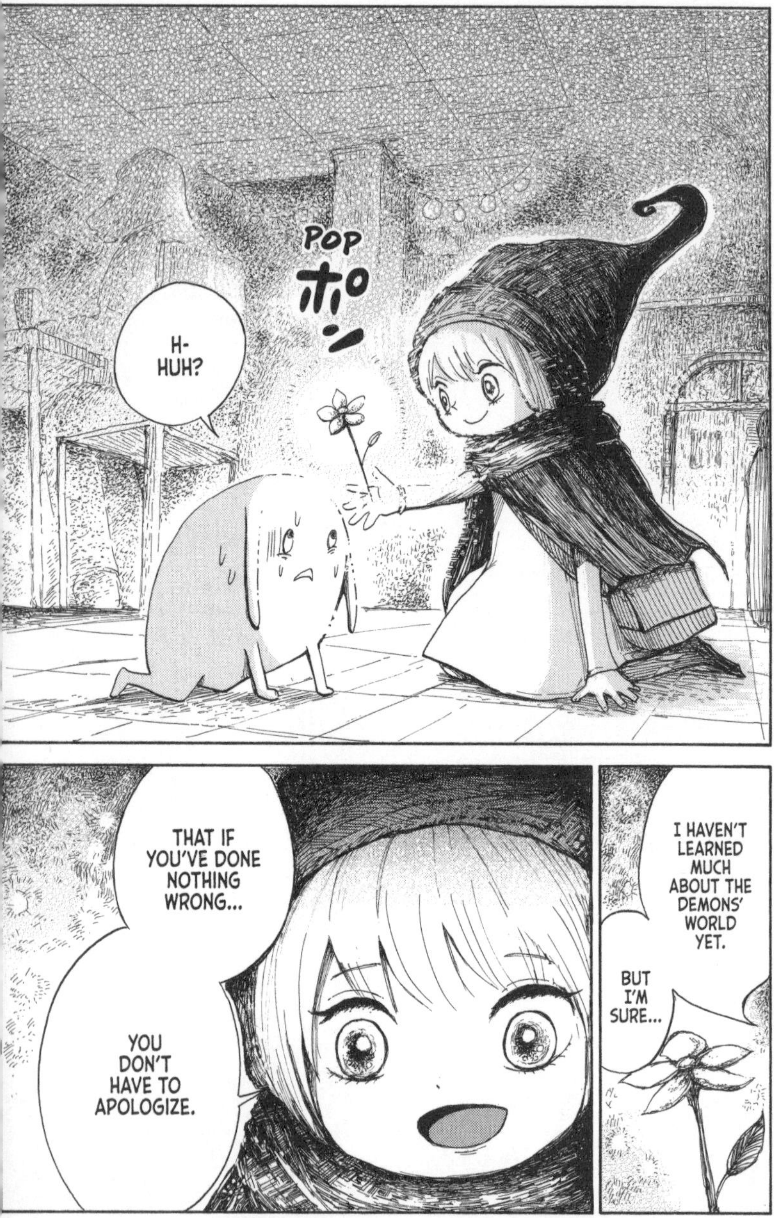
POP
ポン
H-HUH?
I HAVEN'T LEARNED MUCH ABOUT THE DEMONS' WORLD YET.
BUT I'M SURE...
THAT IF YOU'VE DONE NOTHING WRONG...
YOU DON'T HAVE TO APOLOGIZE.

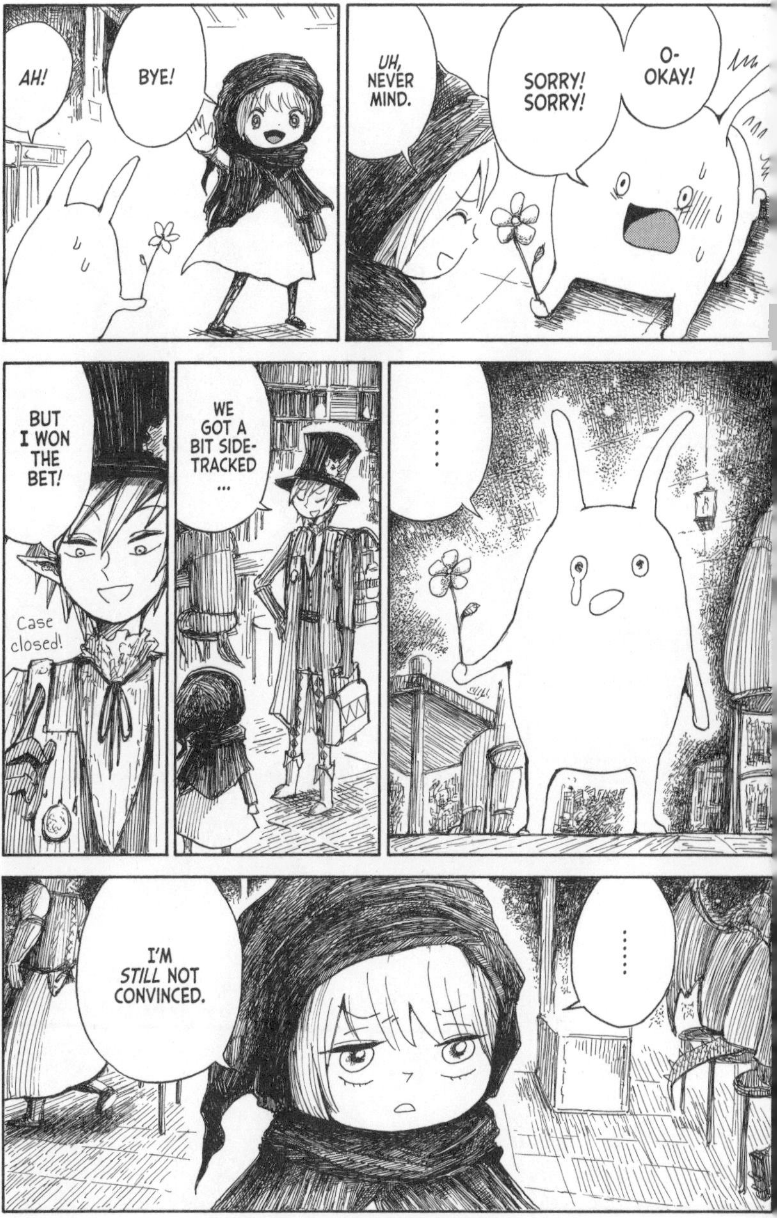
O-OKAY!
SORRY! SORRY!
UH, NEVER MIND.
BYE!
AH!
......
WE GOT A BIT SIDE-TRACKED ...
BUT I WON THE BET!
Case closed!
......
I'M *STILL* NOT CONVINCED.

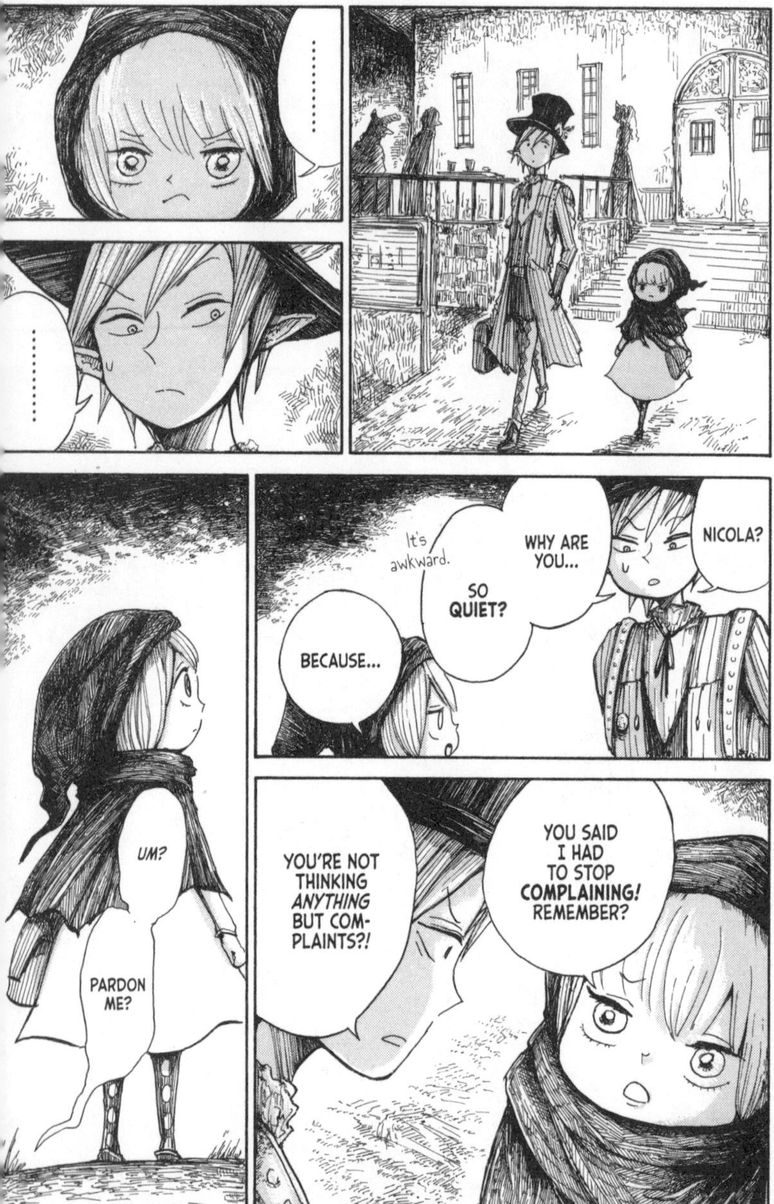
......
......
NICOLA?
WHY ARE YOU... SO QUIET?
It's awkward.
BECAUSE...
YOU SAID I HAD TO STOP COMPLAINING! REMEMBER?
YOU'RE NOT THINKING ANYTHING BUT COMPLAINTS?!
UM?
PARDON ME?

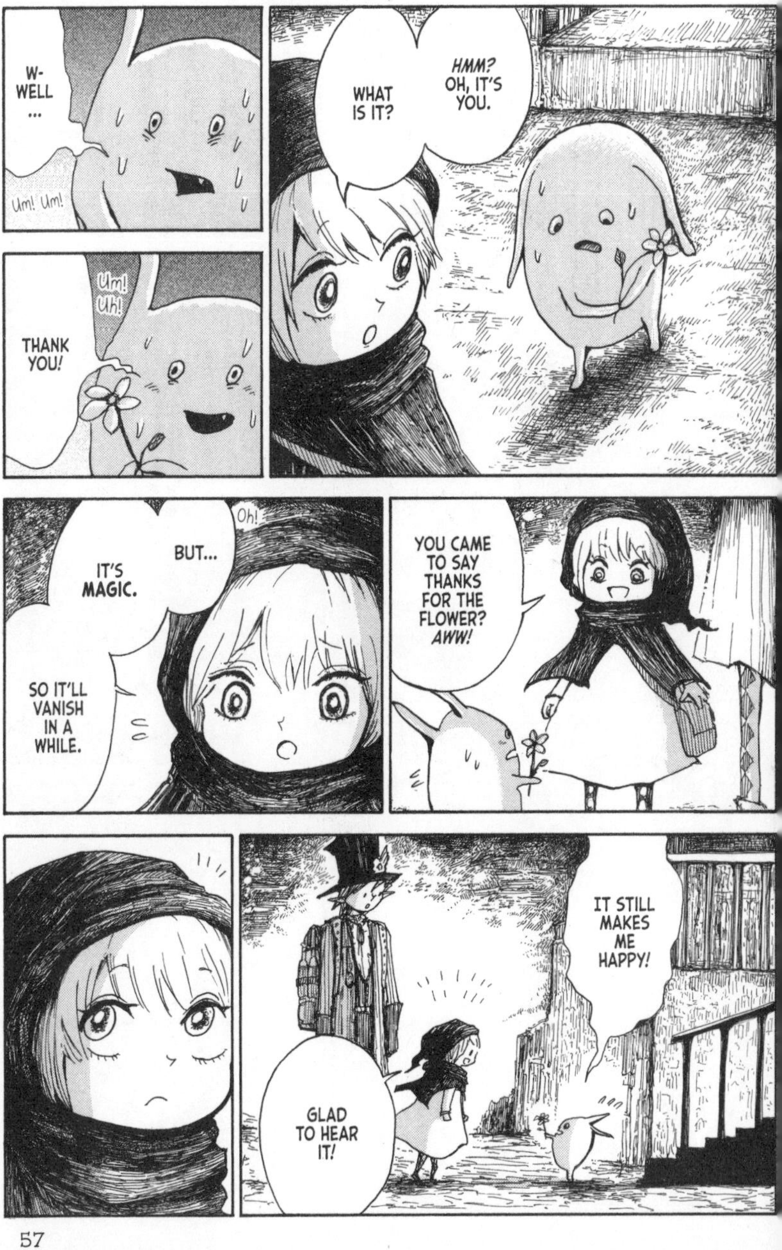
HMM? OH, IT'S YOU.
WHAT IS IT?
W-WELL...
Um! Um!
Um! Uh!
THANK YOU!
YOU CAME TO SAY THANKS FOR THE FLOWER? AWW!
Oh!
BUT...
IT'S MAGIC.
SO IT'LL VANISH IN A WHILE.
IT STILL MAKES ME HAPPY!
GLAD TO HEAR IT!

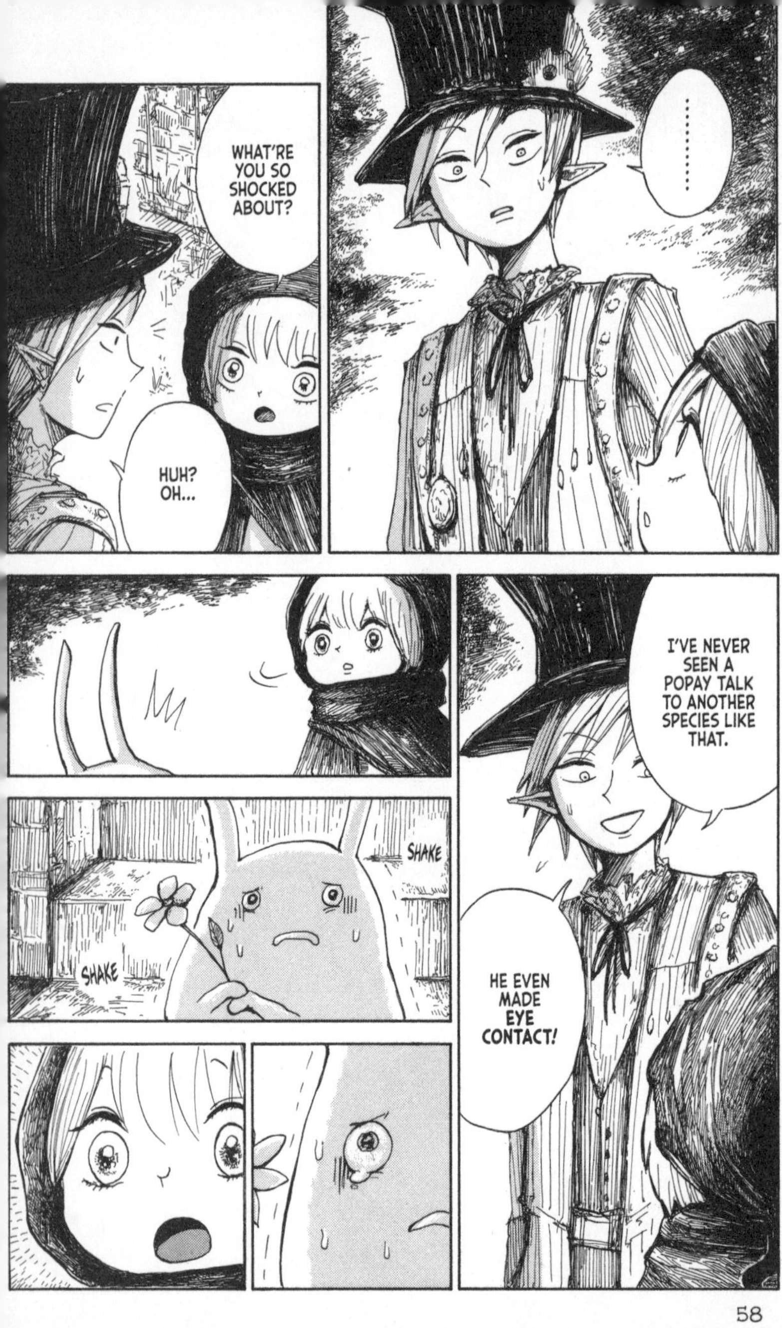
......
WHAT'RE YOU SO SHOCKED ABOUT?
HUH? OH...
I'VE NEVER SEEN A POPAY TALK TO ANOTHER SPECIES LIKE THAT.
HE EVEN MADE EYE CONTACT!
SHAKE
SHAKE

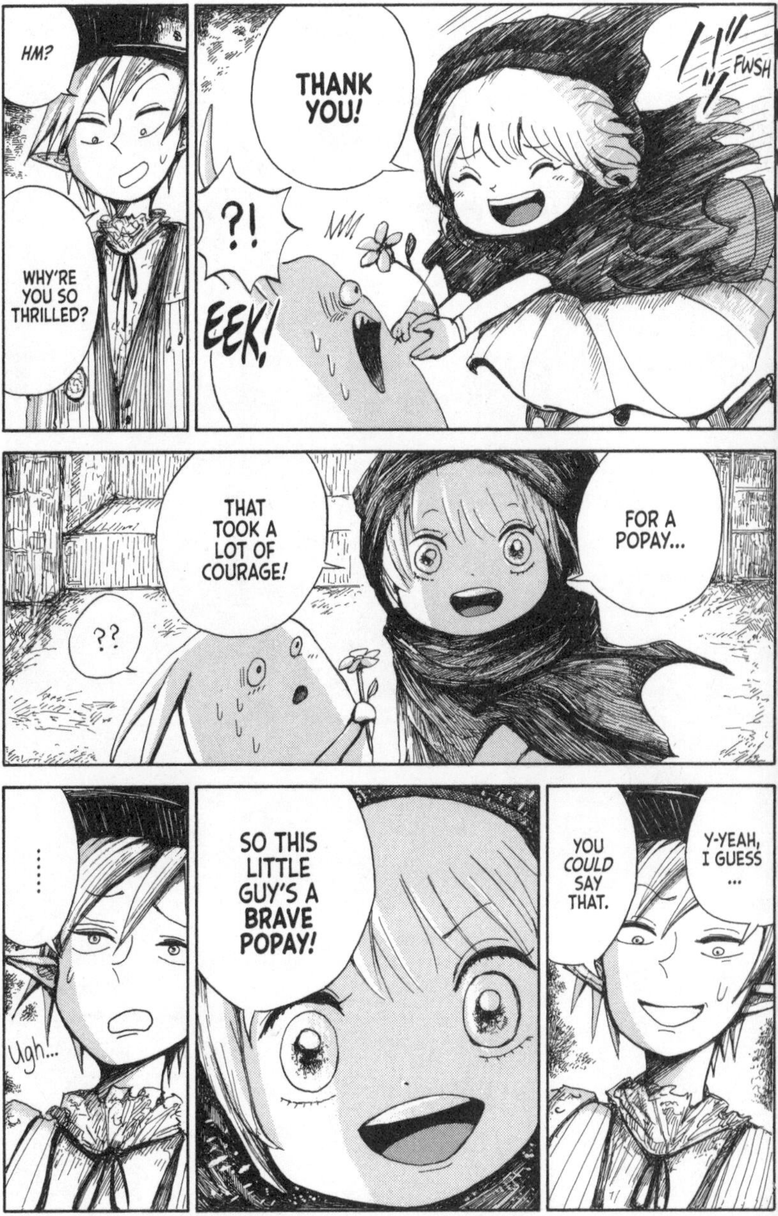
FWSH
THANK YOU!
?!
EEK!
HM?
WHY'RE YOU SO THRILLED?
FOR A POPAY...
THAT TOOK A LOT OF COURAGE!
??
Y-YEAH, I GUESS ...
YOU *COULD* SAY THAT.
SO THIS LITTLE GUY'S A **BRAVE** POPAY!
......
Ugh...

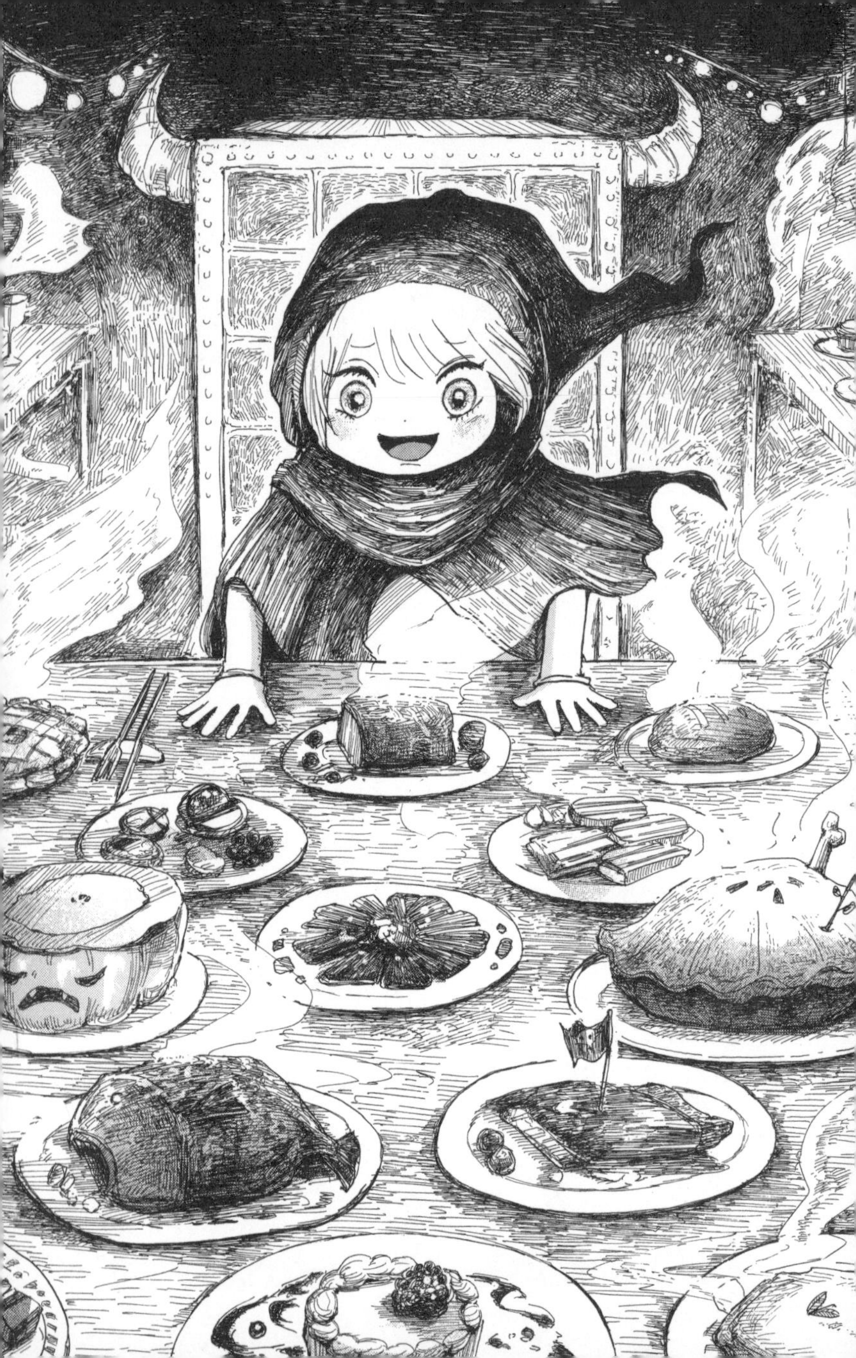

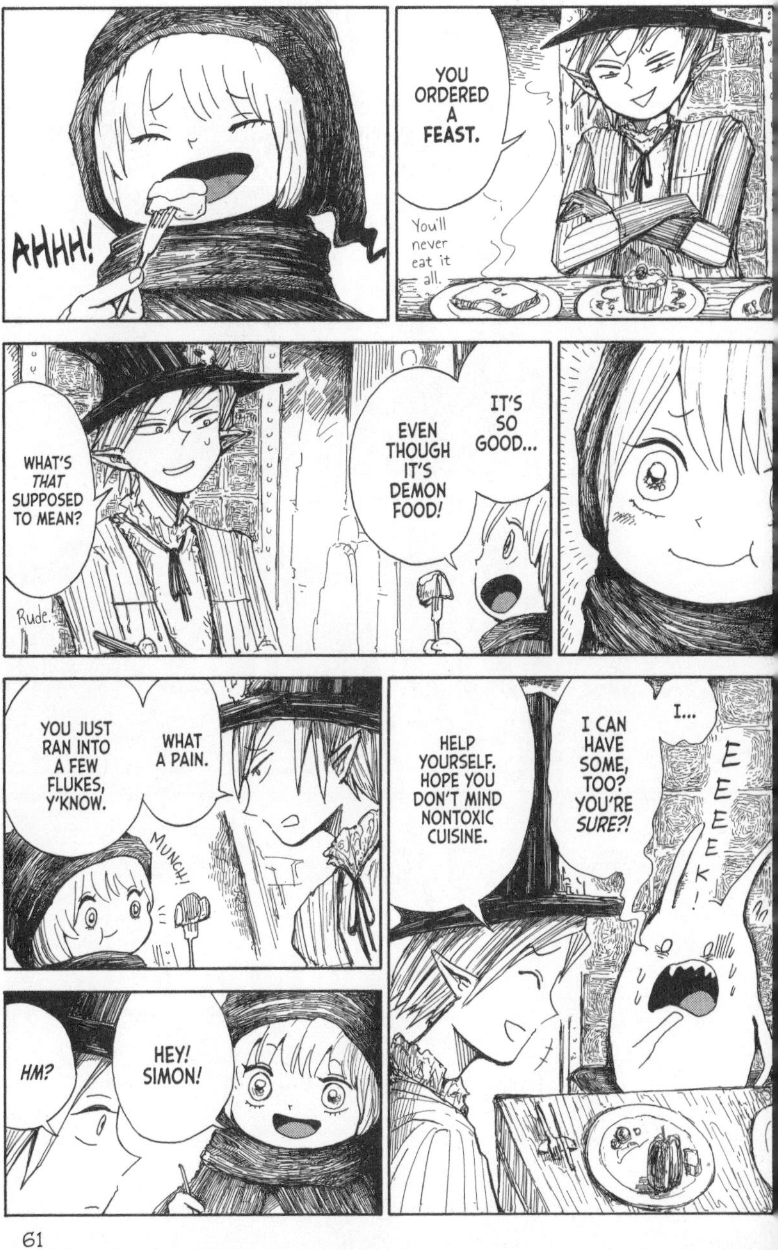
YOU ORDERED A FEAST.
You'll never eat it all.
AHHH!
IT'S SO GOOD...
EVEN THOUGH IT'S DEMON FOOD!
WHAT'S *THAT* SUPPOSED TO MEAN?
Rude.
I...
I CAN HAVE SOME, TOO? YOU'RE *SURE?!*
EEEEEK!
HELP YOURSELF. HOPE YOU DON'T MIND NONTOXIC CUISINE.
WHAT A PAIN.
YOU JUST RAN INTO A FEW FLUKES, Y'KNOW.
MUNCH!
HEY! SIMON!
HM?

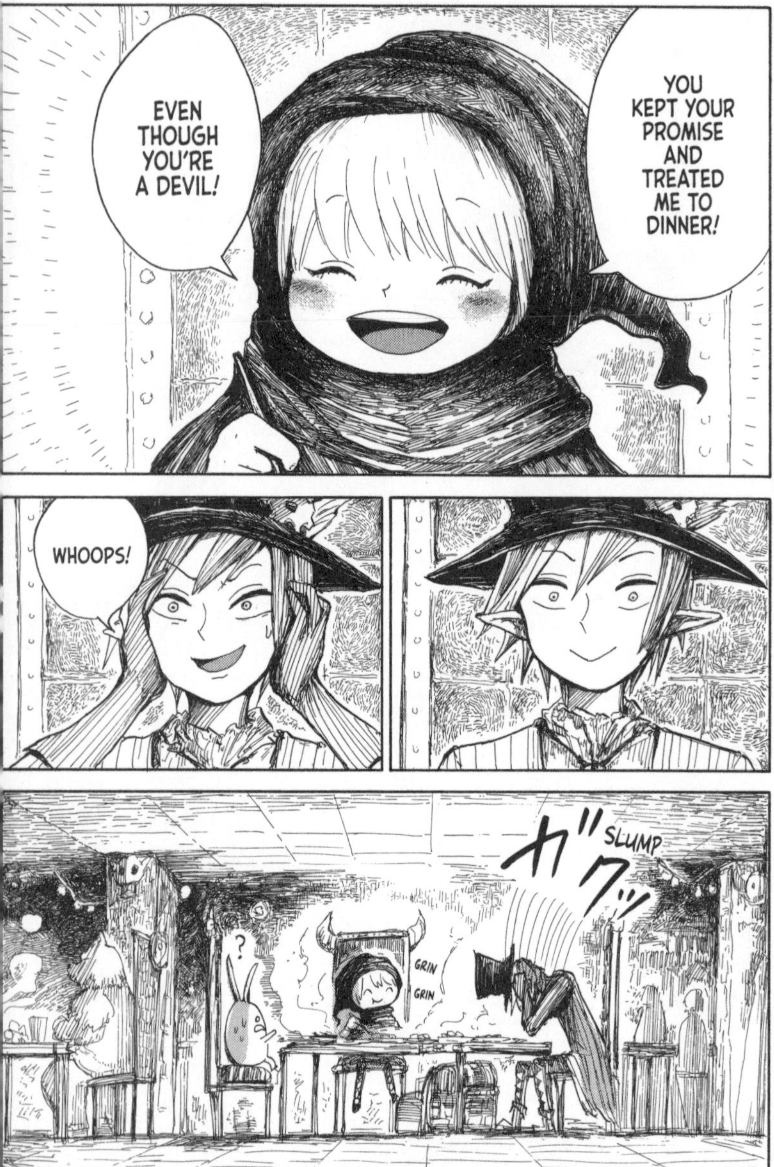
YOU KEPT YOUR PROMISE AND TREATED ME TO DINNER!
EVEN THOUGH YOU'RE A DEVIL!
WHOOPS!
ガクッ
SLUMP
GRIN GRIN

Chapter 2 END

After the Visit 2

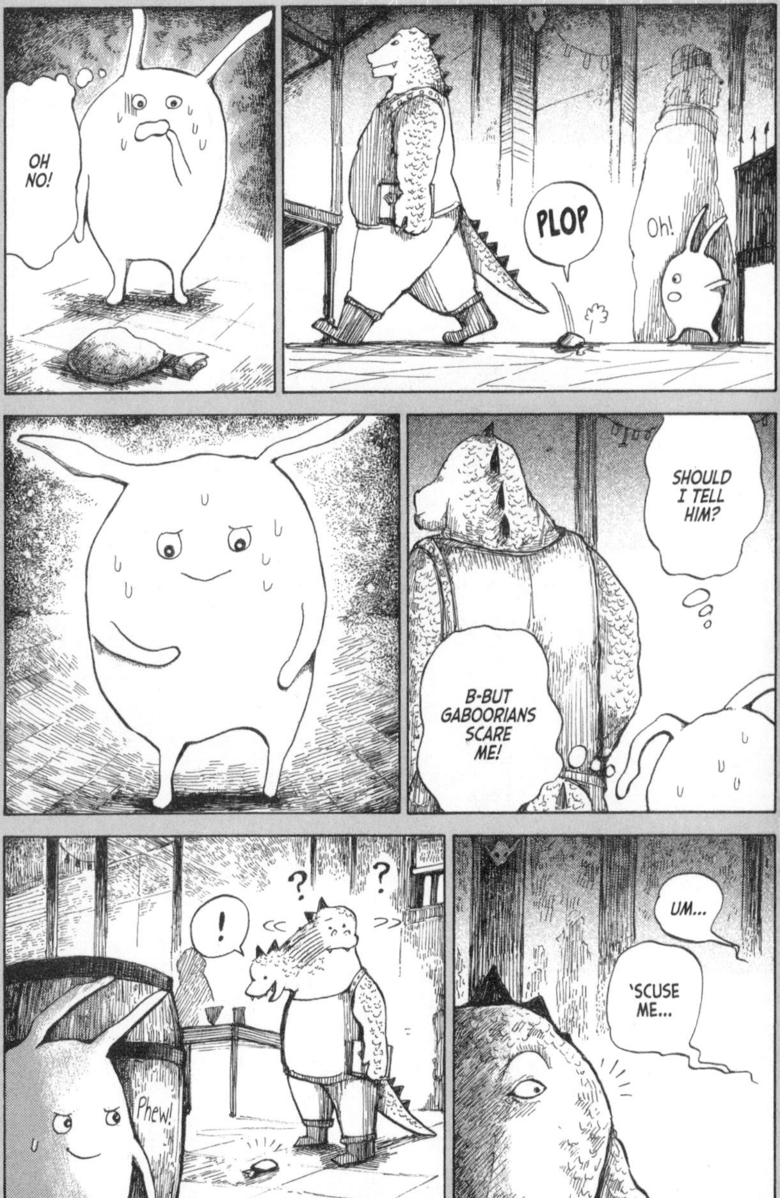
PLOP
Oh!
OH NO!
SHOULD I TELL HIM?
B-BUT GABOORIANS SCARE ME!
UM...
'SCUSE ME...
!
?
?
Phew!

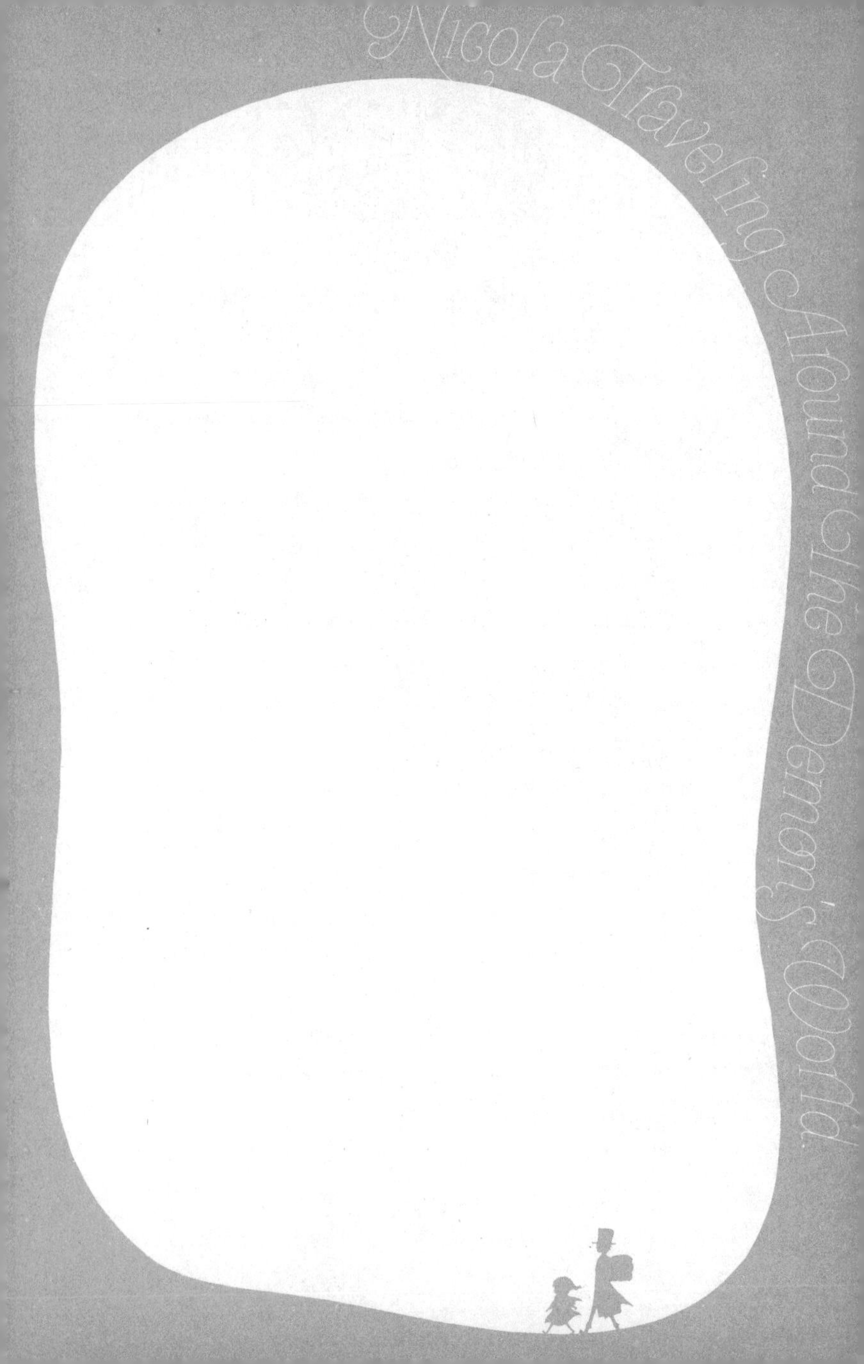
Nicola Traveling Around the Demon's World

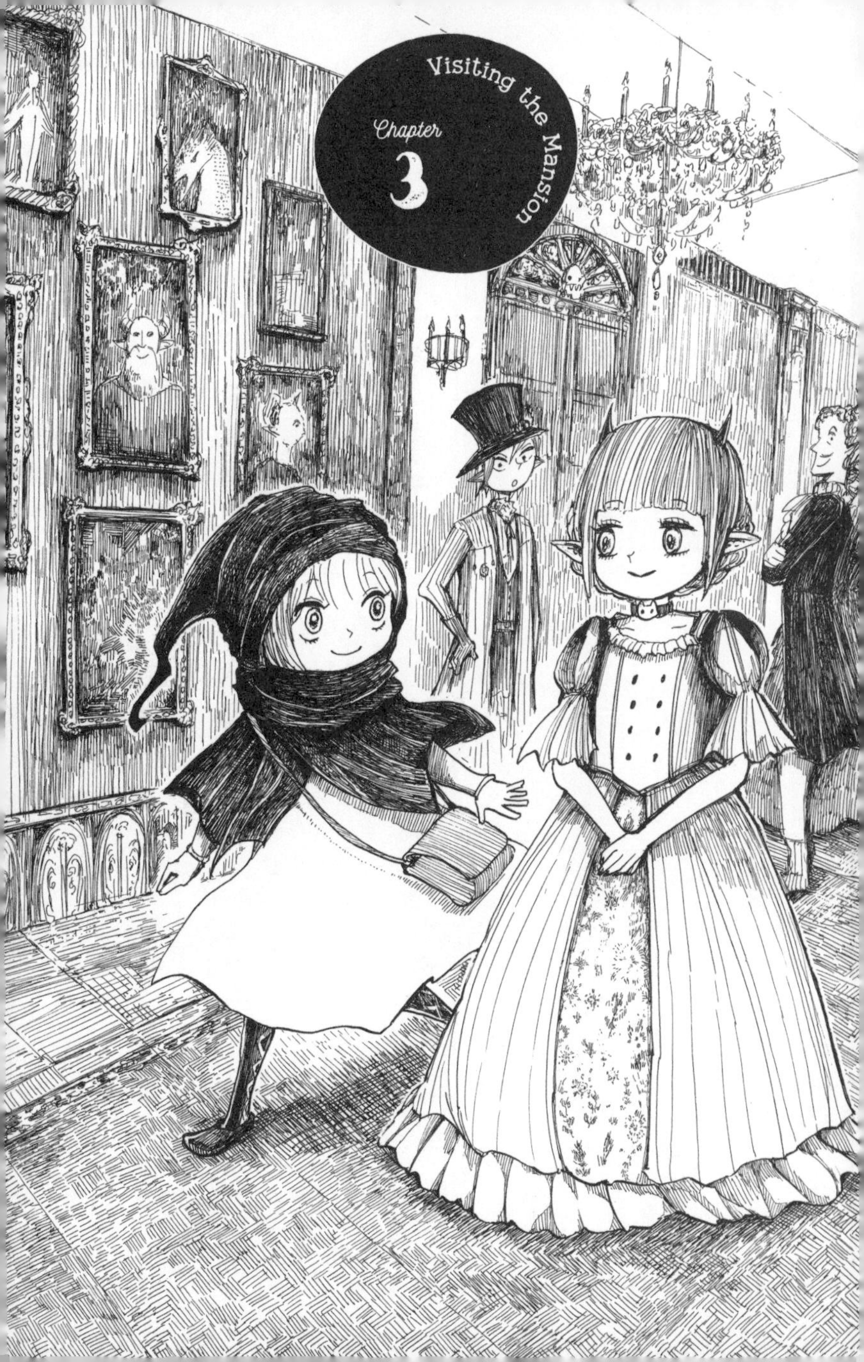
Chapter 3
Visiting the Mansion

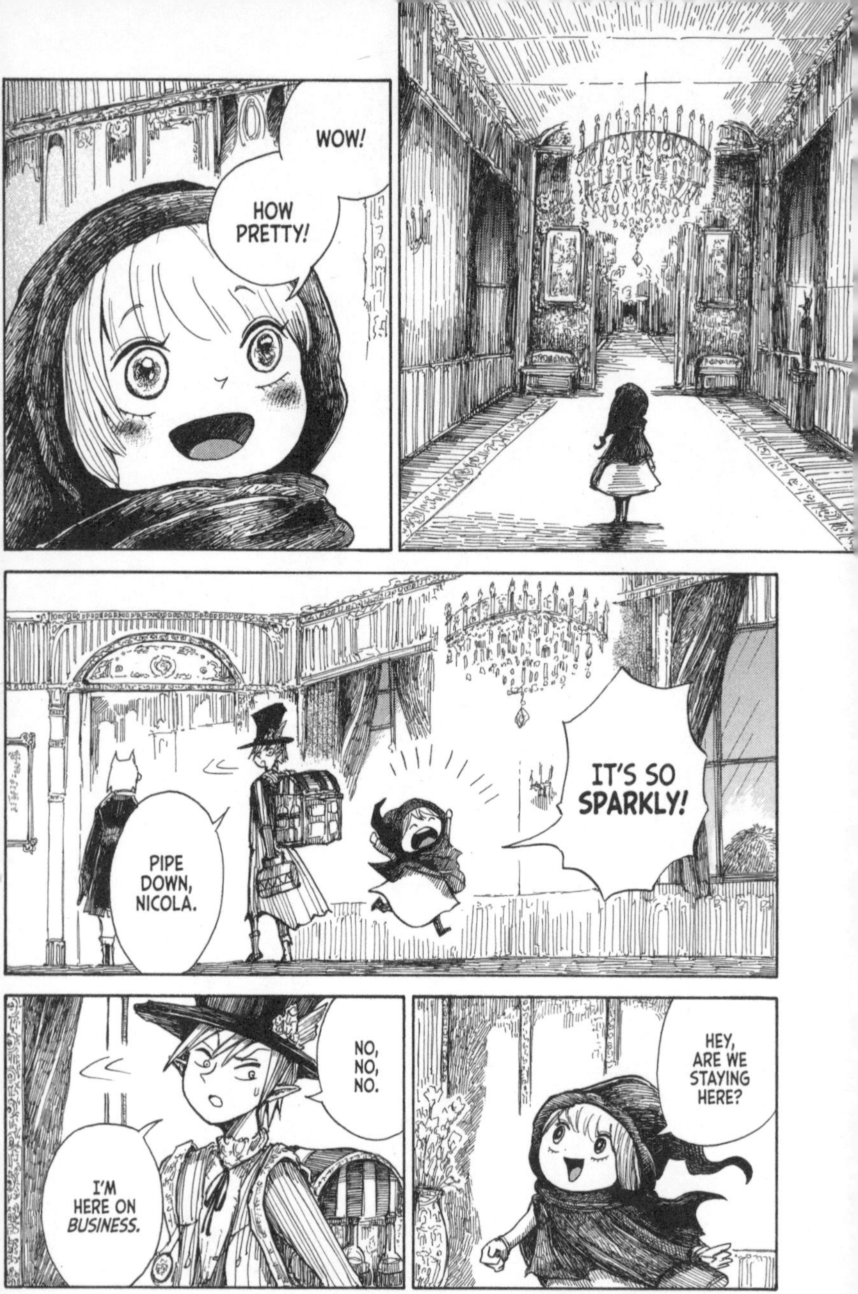
WOW!
HOW PRETTY!
IT'S SO SPARKLY!
PIPE DOWN, NICOLA.
HEY, ARE WE STAYING HERE?
NO, NO, NO.
I'M HERE ON *BUSINESS.*

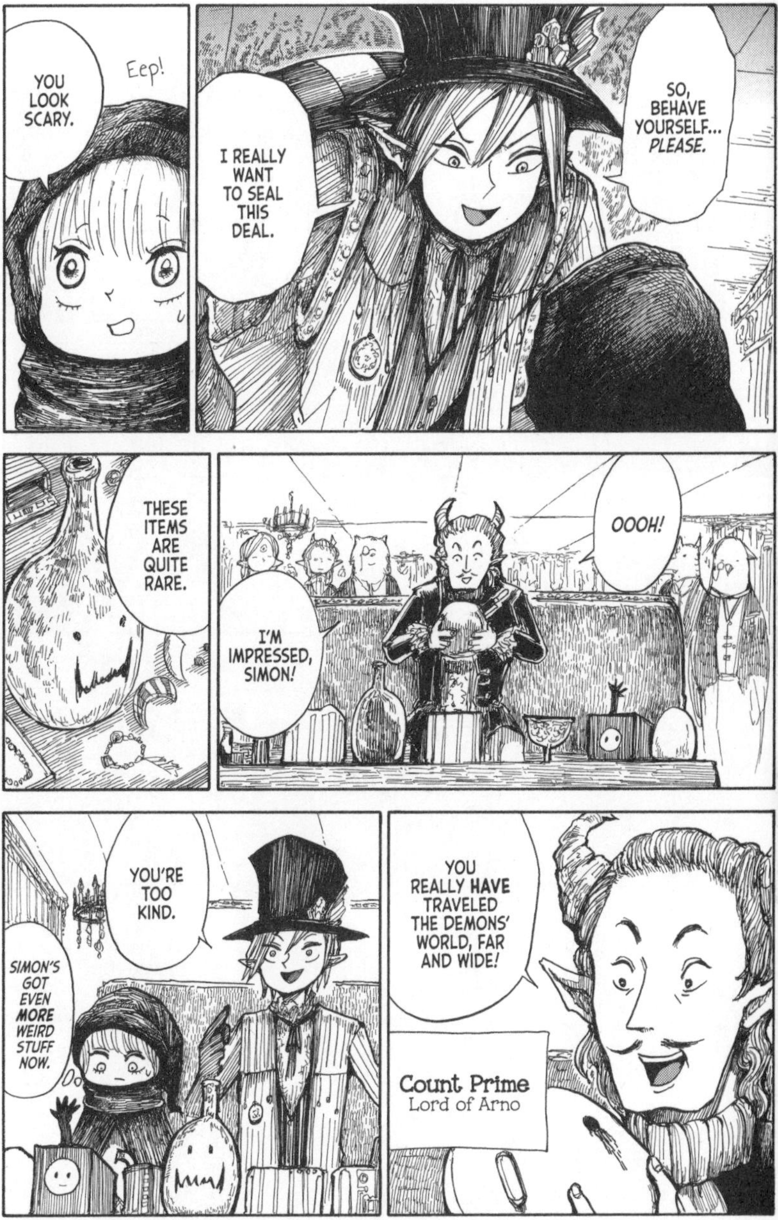
SO, BEHAVE YOURSELF... *PLEASE.*
I REALLY WANT TO SEAL THIS DEAL.
Eep!
YOU LOOK SCARY.
OOOH!
I'M IMPRESSED, SIMON!
THESE ITEMS ARE QUITE RARE.
YOU REALLY **HAVE** TRAVELED THE DEMONS' WORLD, FAR AND WIDE!
Count Prime
Lord of Arno
YOU'RE TOO KIND.
SIMON'S GOT EVEN **MORE** WEIRD STUFF NOW.

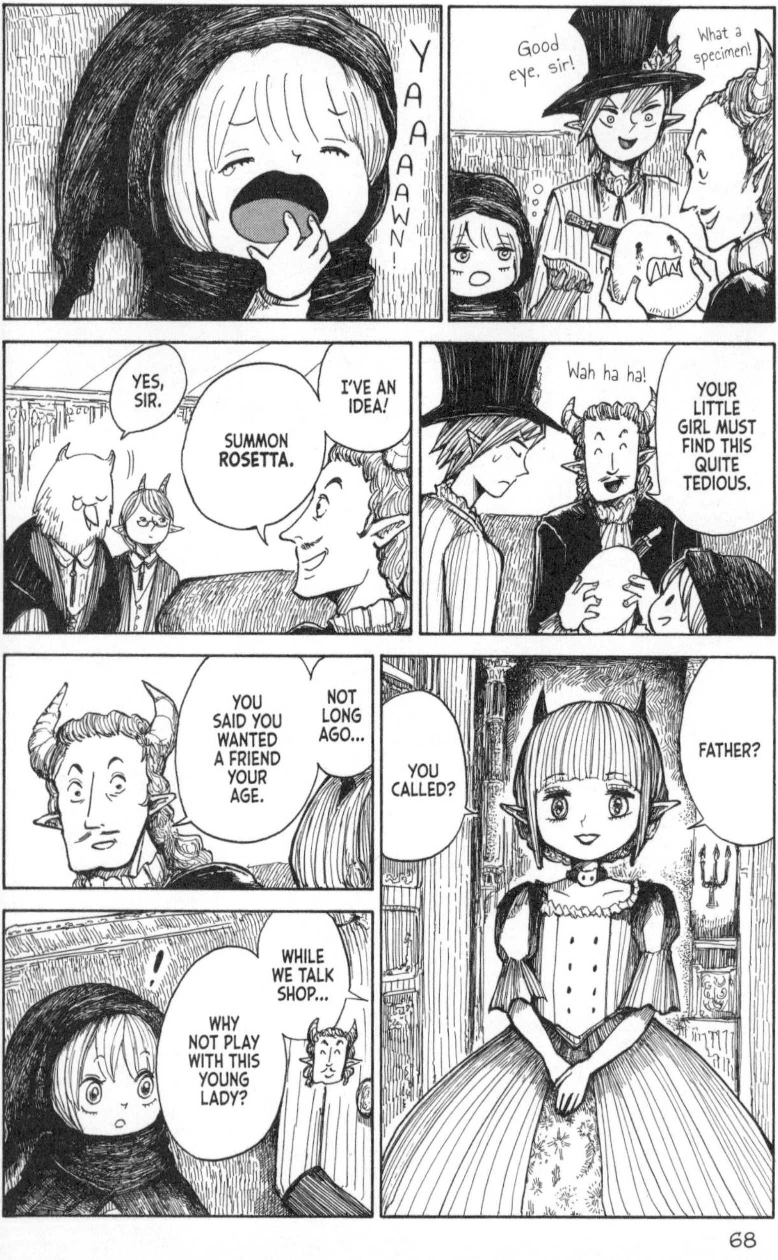
What a specimen!
Good eye, sir!
YAAAAAWN!
YOUR LITTLE GIRL MUST FIND THIS QUITE TEDIOUS.
Wah ha ha!
I'VE AN IDEA!
SUMMON ROSETTA.
YES, SIR.
FATHER?
YOU CALLED?
NOT LONG AGO...
YOU SAID YOU WANTED A FRIEND YOUR AGE.
WHILE WE TALK SHOP...
WHY NOT PLAY WITH THIS YOUNG LADY?
!

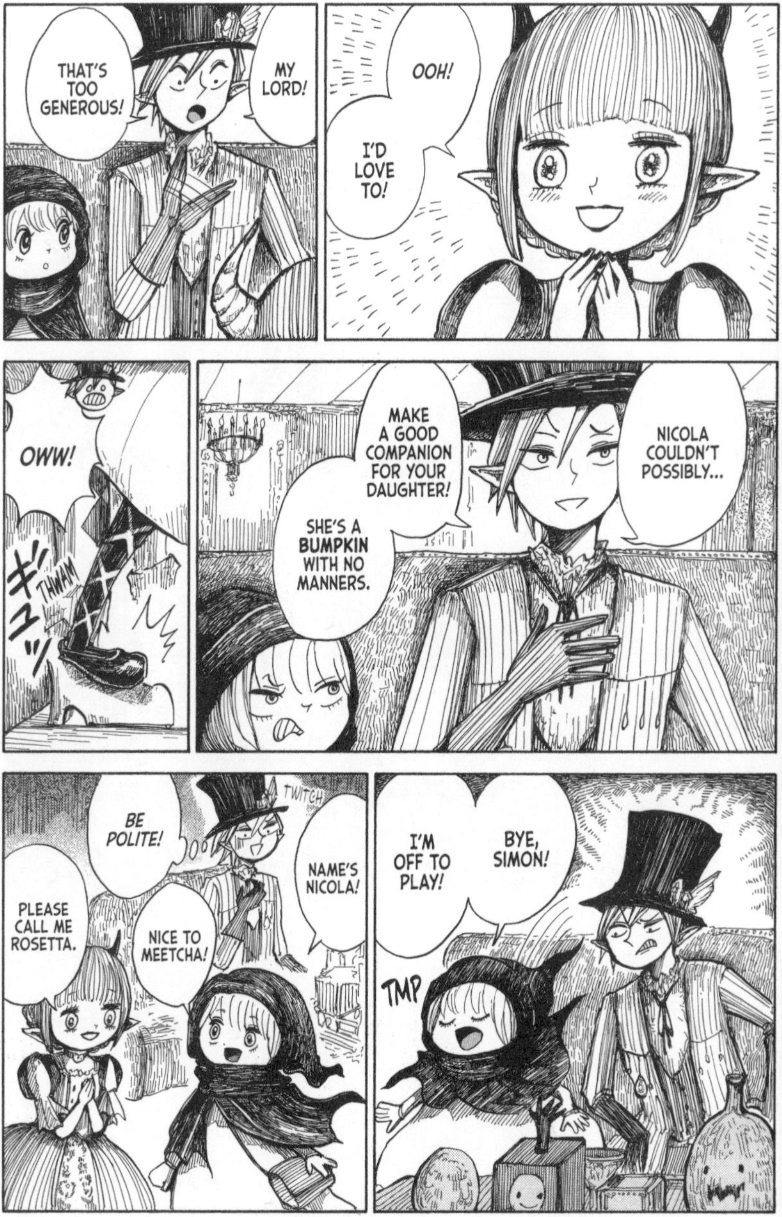
OOH!
I'D LOVE TO!
MY LORD!
THAT'S TOO GENEROUS!
NICOLA COULDN'T POSSIBLY...
MAKE A GOOD COMPANION FOR YOUR DAUGHTER!
SHE'S A **BUMPKIN** WITH NO MANNERS.
OWW!
ギュッ
THWAM
BYE, SIMON!
I'M OFF TO PLAY!
TMP
TWITCH
NAME'S NICOLA!
BE POLITE!
NICE TO MEETCHA!
PLEASE CALL ME ROSETTA.

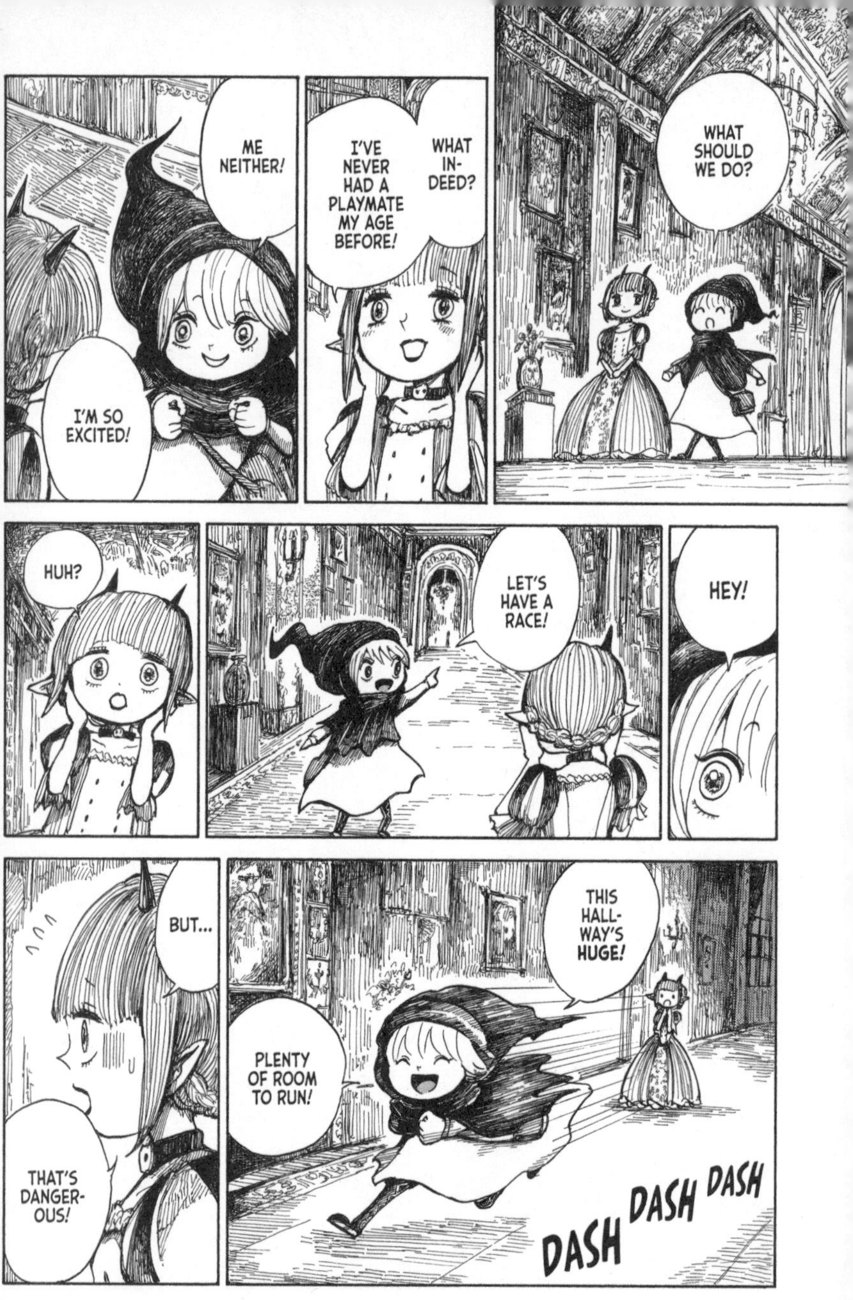
WHAT SHOULD WE DO?
WHAT IN-DEED?
I'VE NEVER HAD A PLAYMATE MY AGE BEFORE!
ME NEITHER!
I'M SO EXCITED!
HEY!
LET'S HAVE A RACE!
HUH?
THIS HALL-WAY'S HUGE!
PLENTY OF ROOM TO RUN!
DASH DASH DASH
BUT...
THAT'S DANGER-OUS!

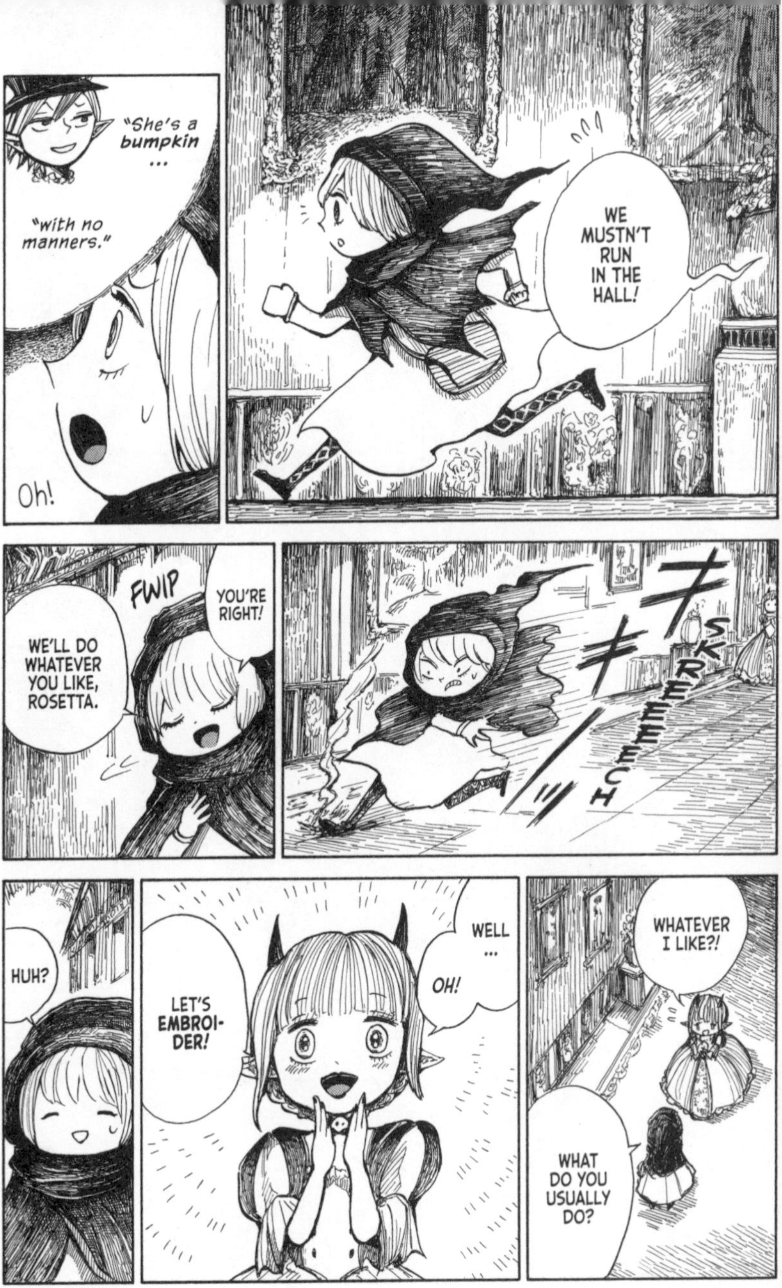
WE MUSTN'T RUN IN THE HALL!
"She's a bumpkin ...
"with no manners."
Oh!
SKREEEEECH
YOU'RE RIGHT!
FWIP
WE'LL DO WHATEVER YOU LIKE, ROSETTA.
WHATEVER I LIKE?!
WHAT DO YOU USUALLY DO?
WELL ...
OH!
LET'S EMBROIDER!
HUH?

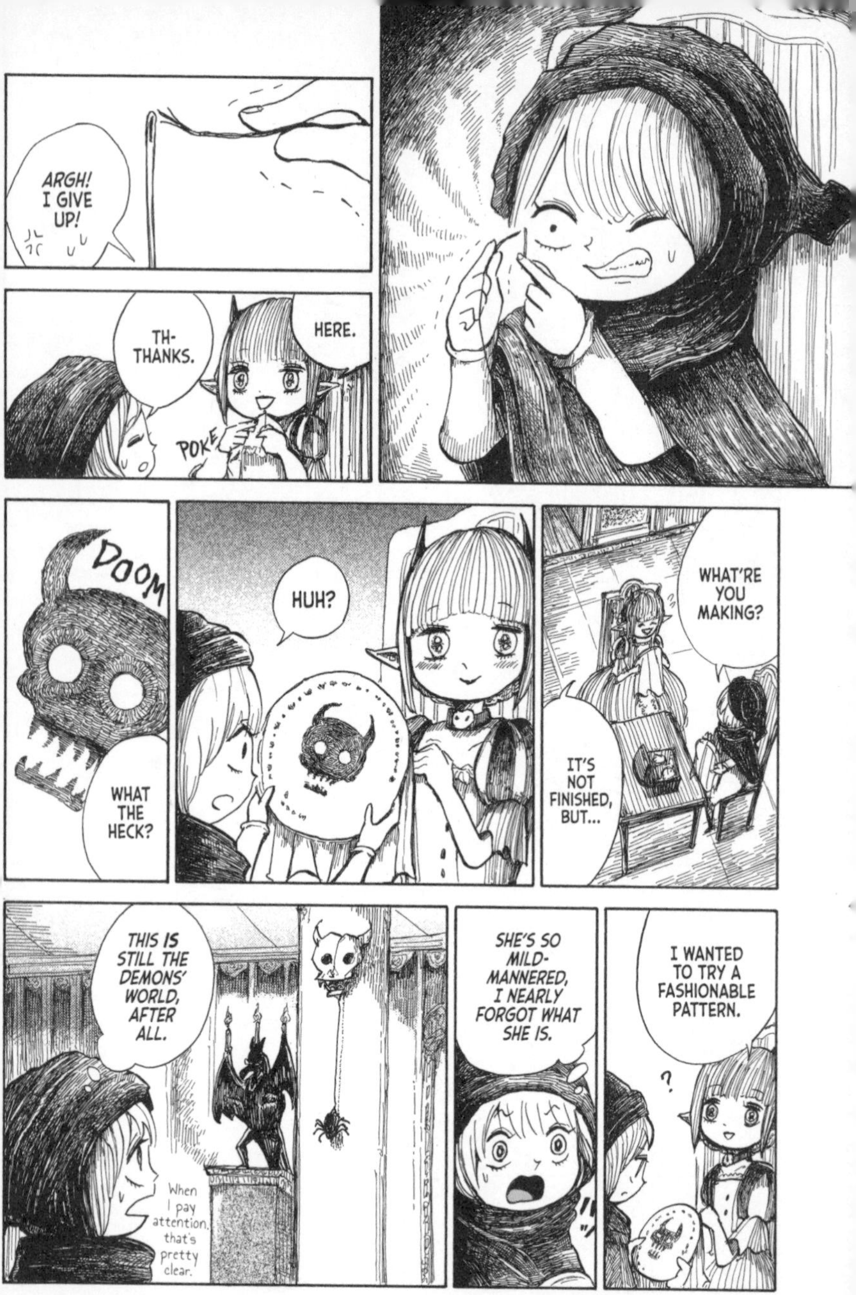
ARGH! I GIVE UP!
HERE.
TH- THANKS.
POKE
WHAT'RE YOU MAKING?
IT'S NOT FINISHED, BUT...
HUH?
DOOM
WHAT THE HECK?
I WANTED TO TRY A FASHIONABLE PATTERN.
?
SHE'S SO MILD-MANNERED, I NEARLY FORGOT WHAT SHE IS.
THIS *IS* STILL THE DEMONS' WORLD, AFTER ALL.
When I pay attention, that's pretty clear.

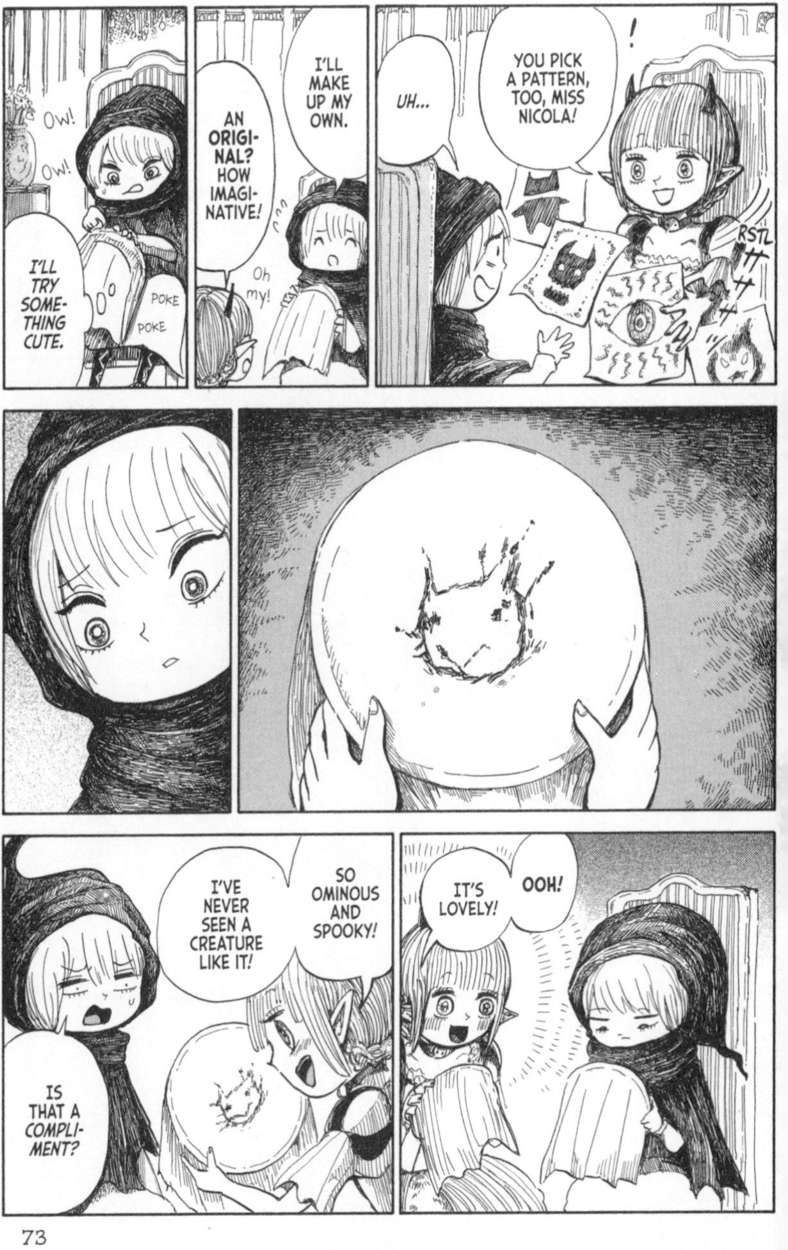
!
YOU PICK A PATTERN, TOO, MISS NICOLA!
RSTL
UH...
I'LL MAKE UP MY OWN.
AN ORIGINAL? HOW IMAGINATIVE!
Oh my!
Ow!
Ow!
POKE
POKE
I'LL TRY SOMETHING CUTE.
OOH!
IT'S LOVELY!
SO OMINOUS AND SPOOKY!
I'VE NEVER SEEN A CREATURE LIKE IT!
IS THAT A COMPLIMENT?

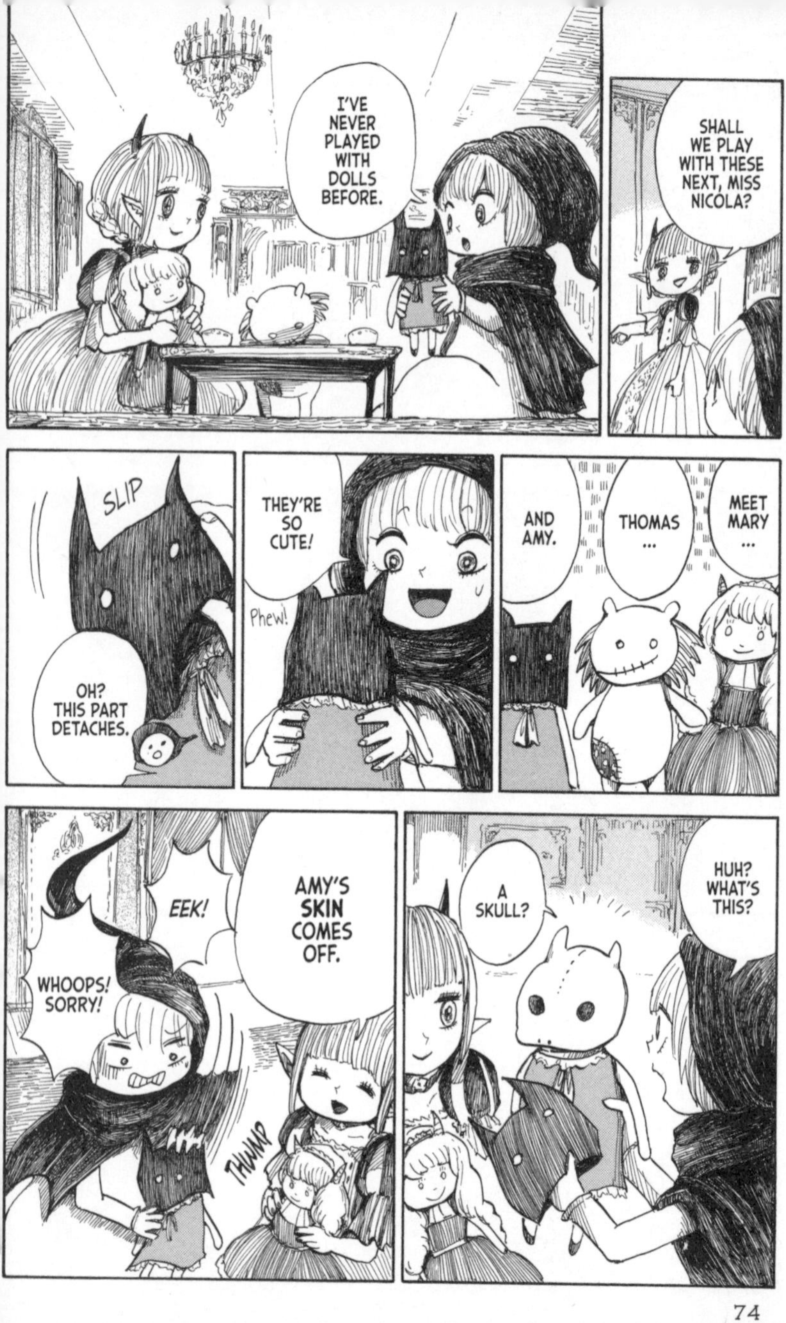
SHALL WE PLAY WITH THESE NEXT, MISS NICOLA?
I'VE NEVER PLAYED WITH DOLLS BEFORE.
MEET MARY ...
THOMAS ...
AND AMY.
THEY'RE SO CUTE!
Phew!
SLIP
OH? THIS PART DETACHES.
HUH? WHAT'S THIS?
A SKULL?
AMY'S **SKIN** COMES OFF.
EEK!
WHOOPS! SORRY!
THWMP

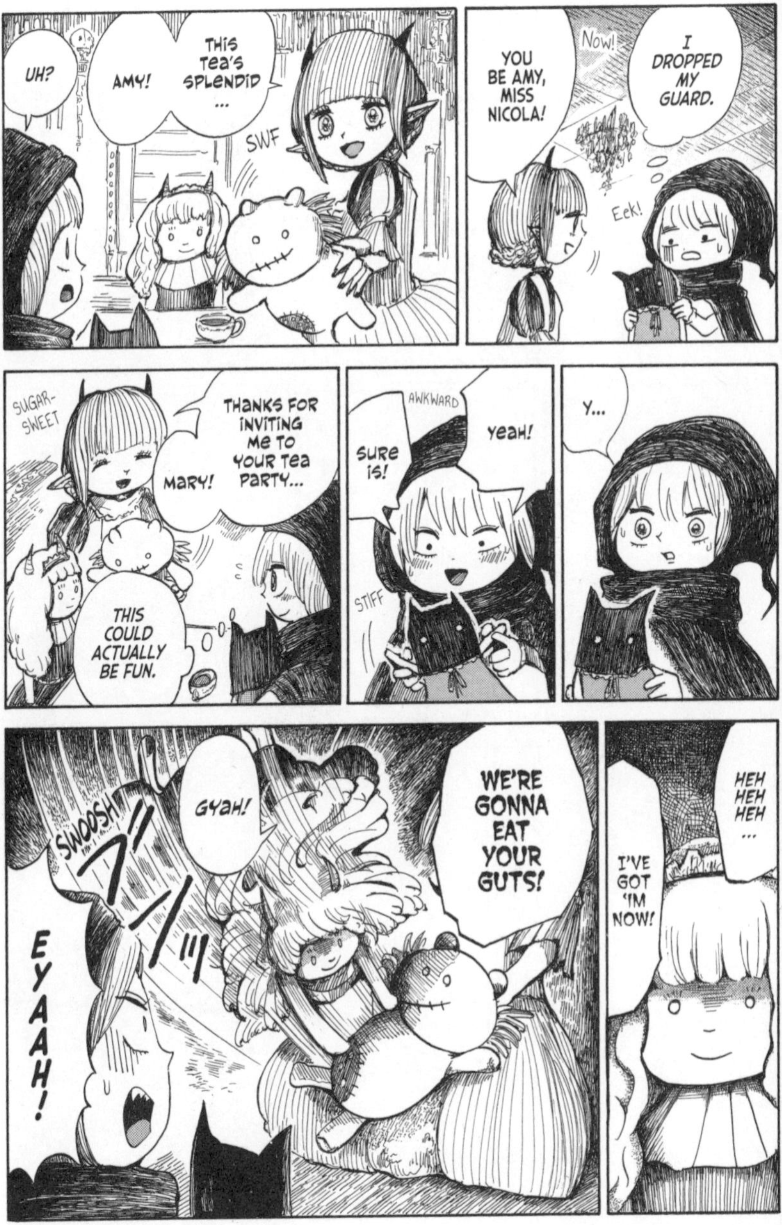
I DROPPED MY GUARD.
Now!
YOU BE AMY, MISS NICOLA!
Eek!
THIS Tea's SPLENDID ...
AMY!
UH?
SWF
Y...
AWKWARD
Yeah!
Sure is!
STIFF
THANKS FOR INVITING ME TO YOUR TEA PARTY...
MARY!
SUGAR-SWEET
THIS COULD ACTUALLY BE FUN.
HEH HEH HEH ...
I'VE GOT 'IM NOW!
WE'RE GONNA EAT YOUR GUTS!
GYAH!
SWOOSH
EYAAAH!

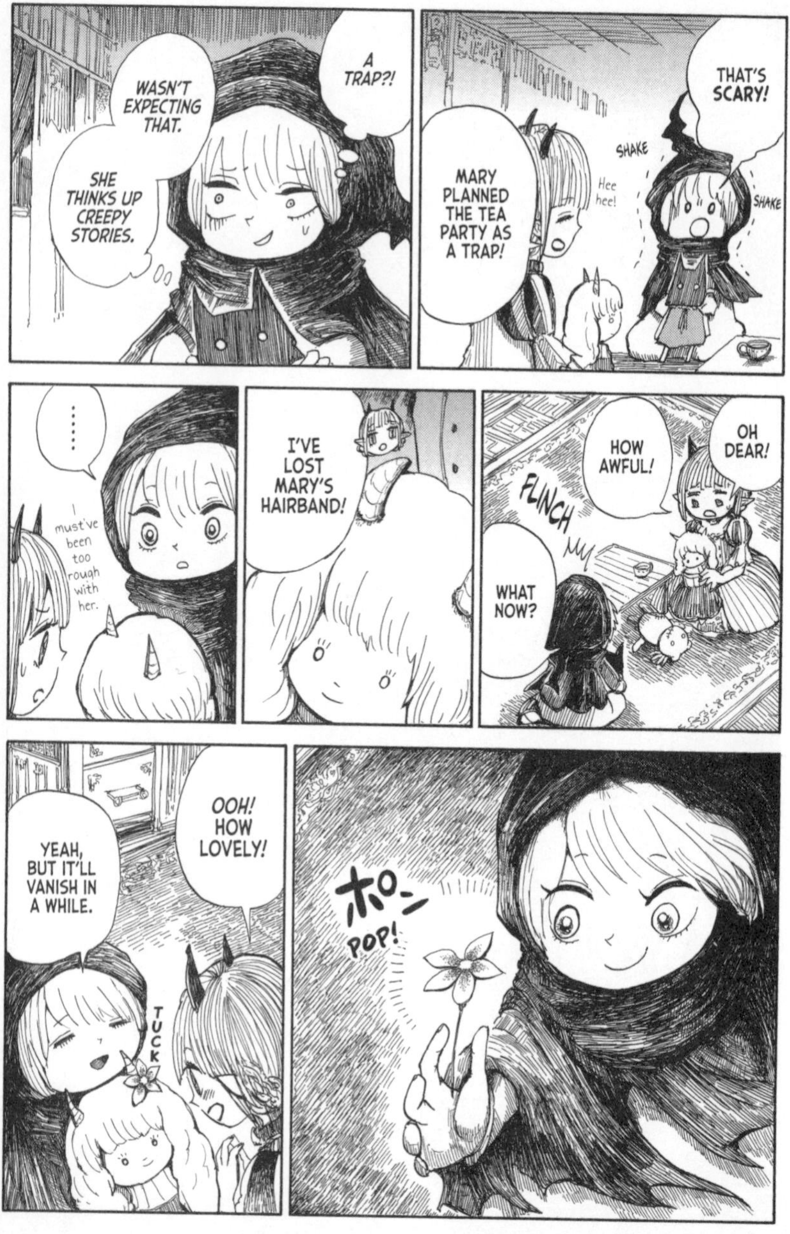
MARY PLANNED THE TEA PARTY AS A TRAP!
Hee hee!
THAT'S SCARY!
SHAKE
SHAKE
A TRAP?!
WASN'T EXPECTING THAT.
SHE THINKS UP CREEPY STORIES.
OH DEAR!
HOW AWFUL!
FLINCH
WHAT NOW?
I'VE LOST MARY'S HAIRBAND!
......
I must've been too rough with her.
ホロ~
POP!
OOH! HOW LOVELY!
YEAH, BUT IT'LL VANISH IN A WHILE.
TUCK

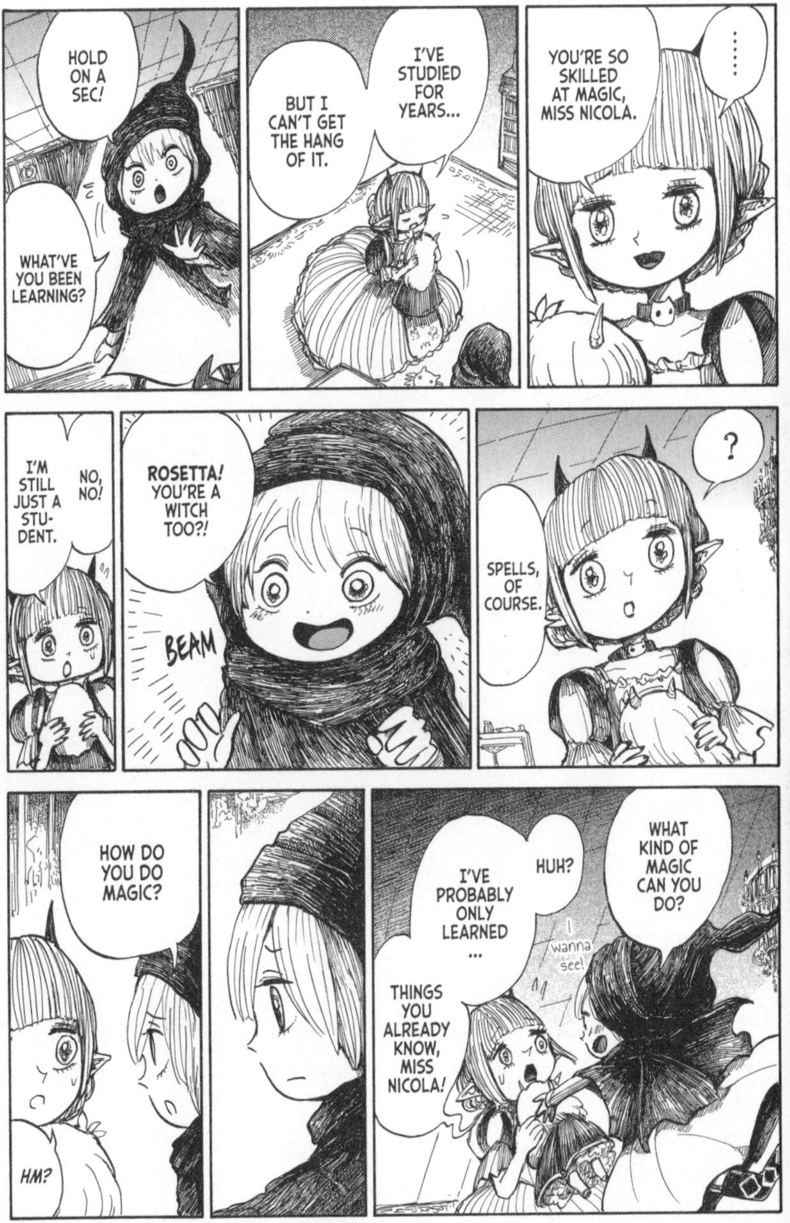
……
YOU'RE SO SKILLED AT MAGIC, MISS NICOLA.
I'VE STUDIED FOR YEARS...
BUT I CAN'T GET THE HANG OF IT.
HOLD ON A SEC!
WHAT'VE YOU BEEN LEARNING?
?
SPELLS, OF COURSE.
ROSETTA! YOU'RE A WITCH TOO?!
BEAM
NO, NO!
I'M STILL JUST A STU-DENT.
WHAT KIND OF MAGIC CAN YOU DO?
I wanna see!
HUH?
I'VE PROBABLY ONLY LEARNED ...
THINGS YOU ALREADY KNOW, MISS NICOLA!
HOW DO YOU DO MAGIC?
HM?

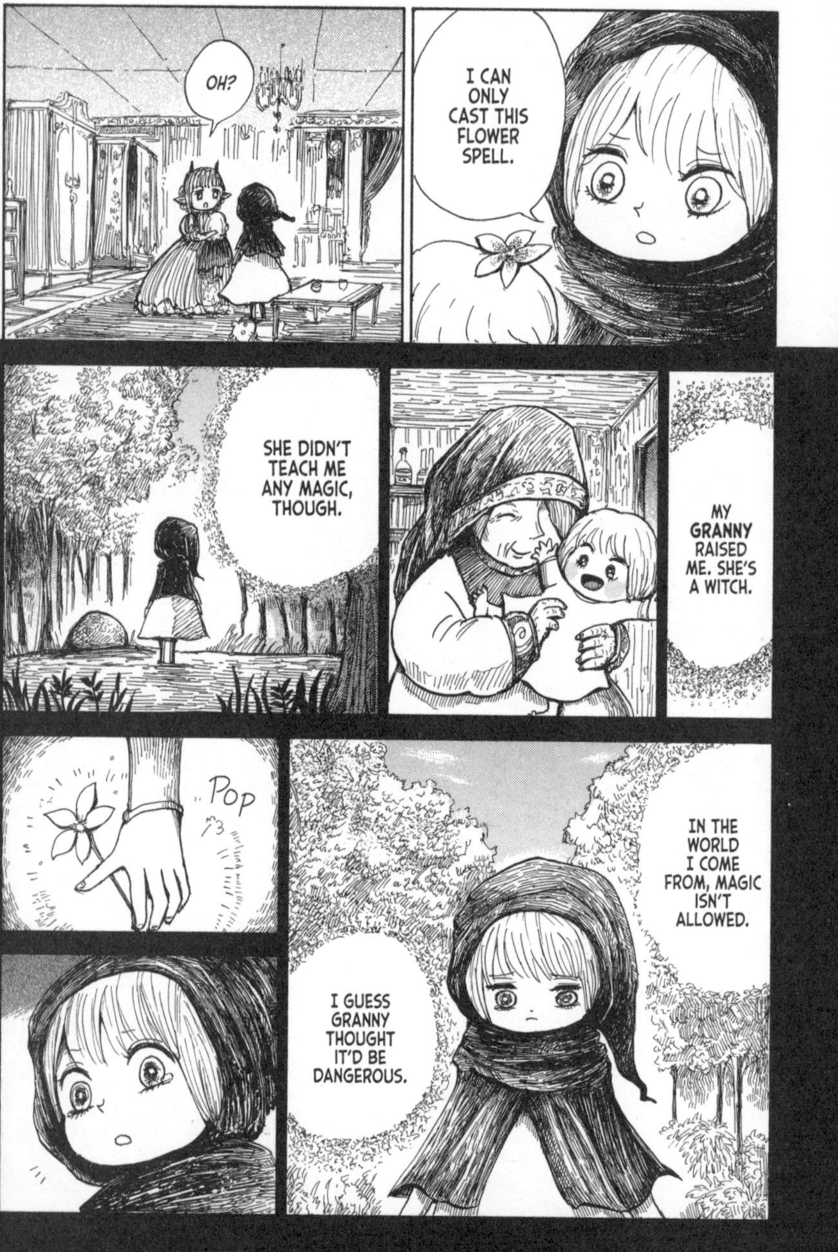
I CAN ONLY CAST THIS FLOWER SPELL.
OH?
MY GRANNY RAISED ME. SHE'S A WITCH.
SHE DIDN'T TEACH ME ANY MAGIC, THOUGH.
IN THE WORLD I COME FROM, MAGIC ISN'T ALLOWED.
I GUESS GRANNY THOUGHT IT'D BE DANGEROUS.
Pop

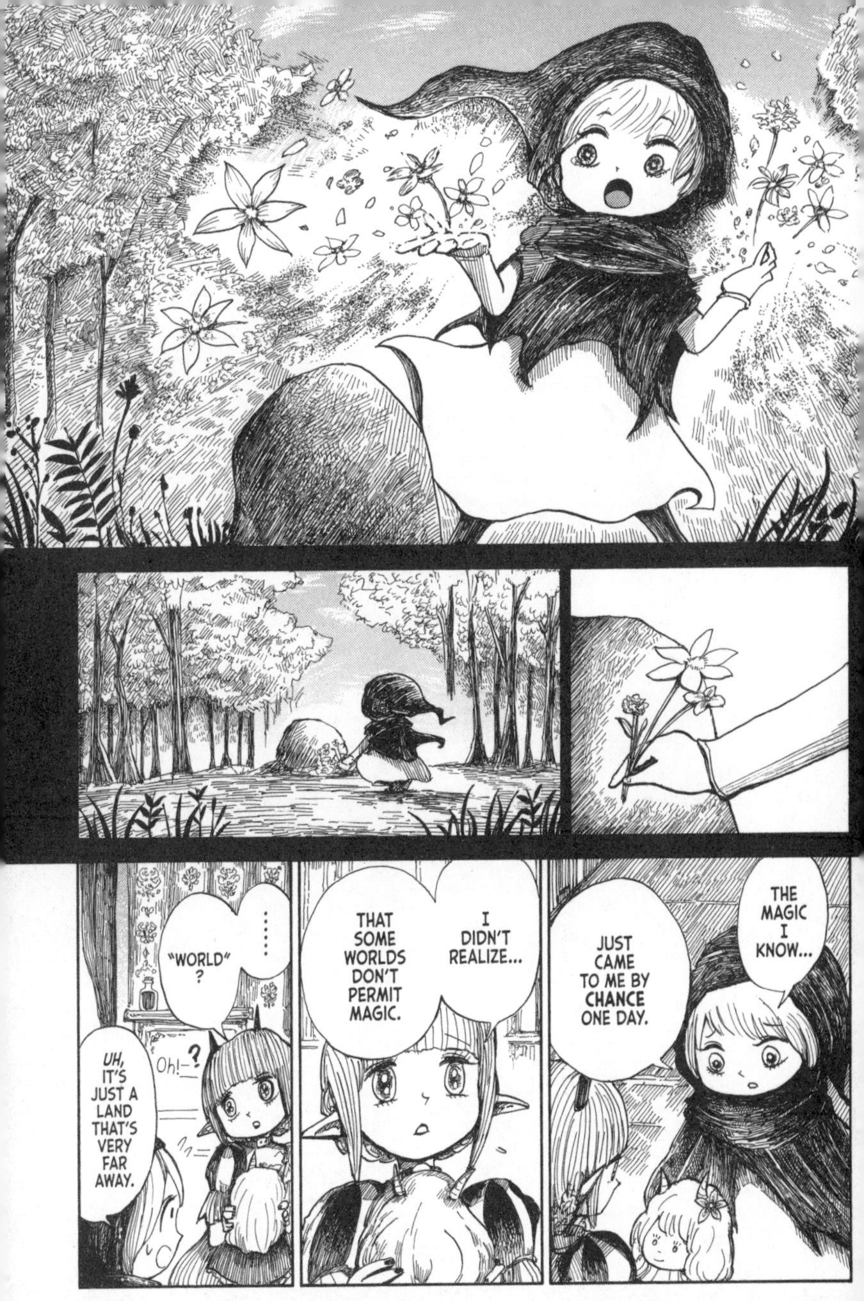
THE MAGIC I KNOW...
JUST CAME TO ME BY CHANCE ONE DAY.
I DIDN'T REALIZE...
THAT SOME WORLDS DON'T PERMIT MAGIC.
......
"WORLD"?
Oh!—?
UH, IT'S JUST A LAND THAT'S VERY FAR AWAY.

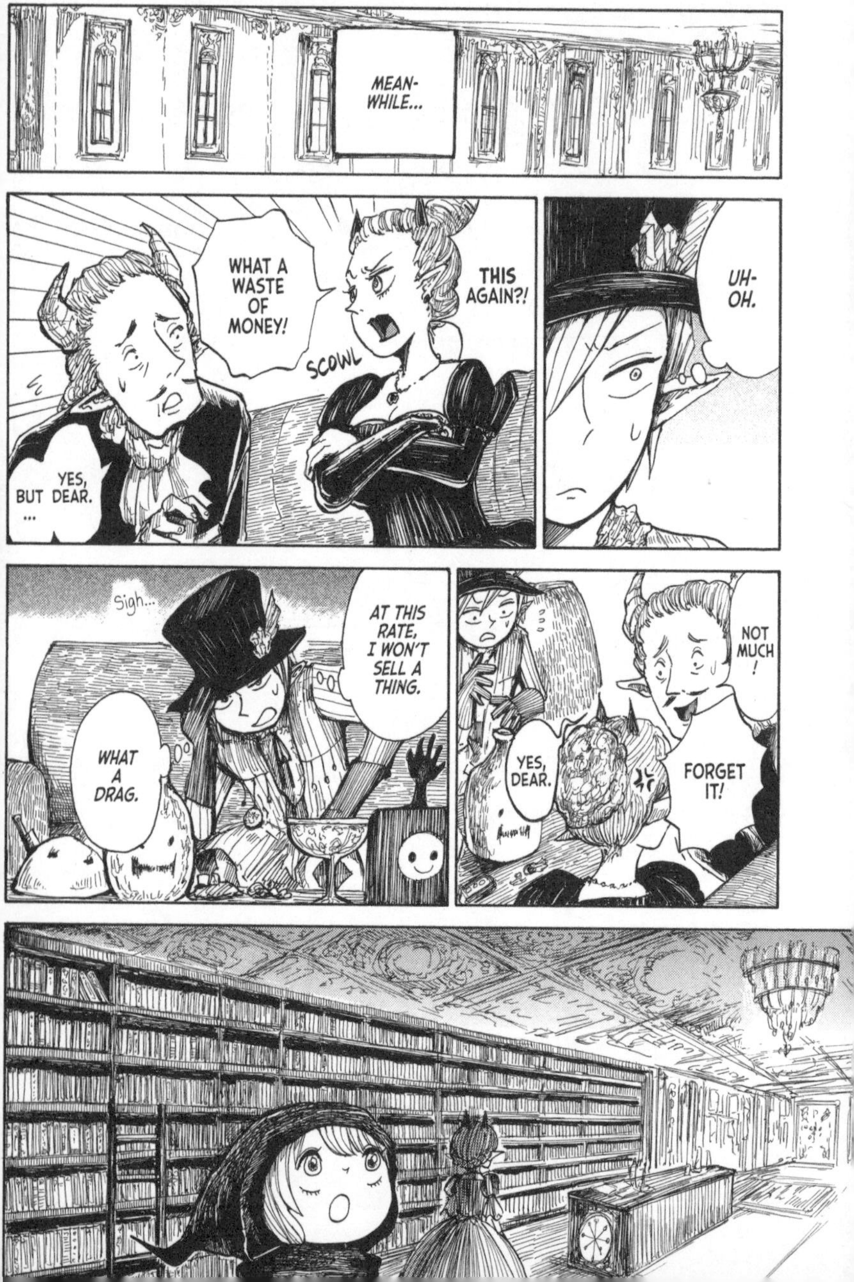
MEAN-WHILE...
UH-OH.
THIS AGAIN?!
WHAT A WASTE OF MONEY!
SCOWL
YES, DEAR.
BUT...
NOT MUCH!
FORGET IT!
YES, DEAR.
AT THIS RATE, I WON'T SELL A THING.
Sigh...
WHAT A DRAG.

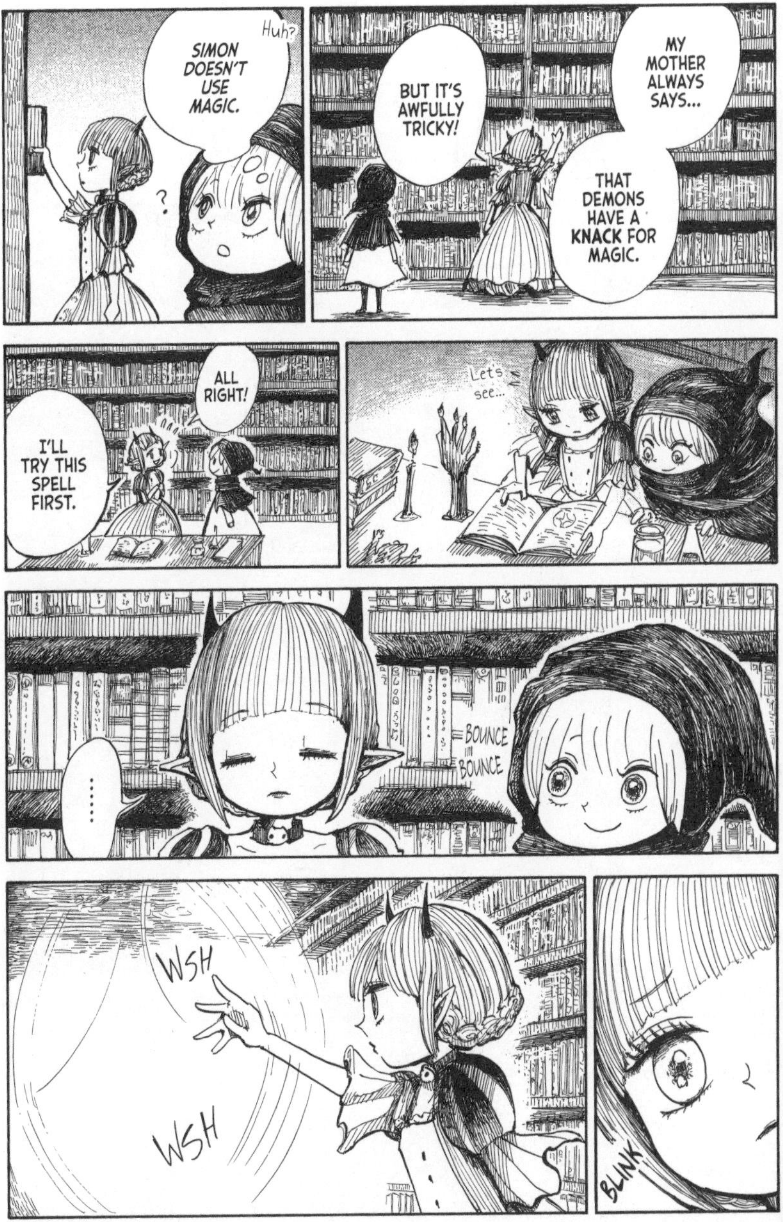
MY MOTHER ALWAYS SAYS...
THAT DEMONS HAVE A KNACK FOR MAGIC.
BUT IT'S AWFULLY TRICKY!
Huh?
SIMON DOESN'T USE MAGIC.
?
Let's see...
ALL RIGHT!
I'LL TRY THIS SPELL FIRST.
BOUNCE BOUNCE
......
BLINK
WSH
WSH

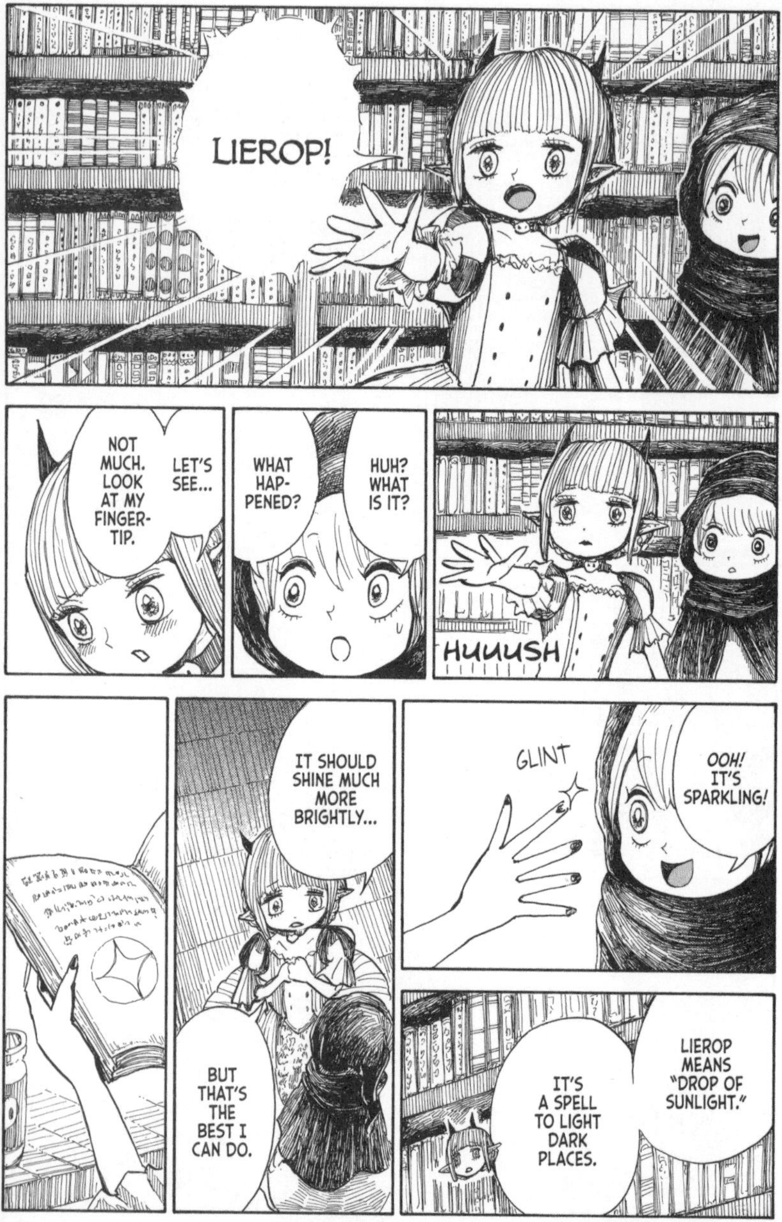
LIEROP!
HUUUSH
HUH? WHAT IS IT?
WHAT HAP-PENED?
LET'S SEE...
NOT MUCH. LOOK AT MY FINGER-TIP.
OOH! IT'S SPARKLING!
GLINT
LIEROP MEANS "DROP OF SUNLIGHT."
IT'S A SPELL TO LIGHT DARK PLACES.
IT SHOULD SHINE MUCH MORE BRIGHTLY...
BUT THAT'S THE BEST I CAN DO.

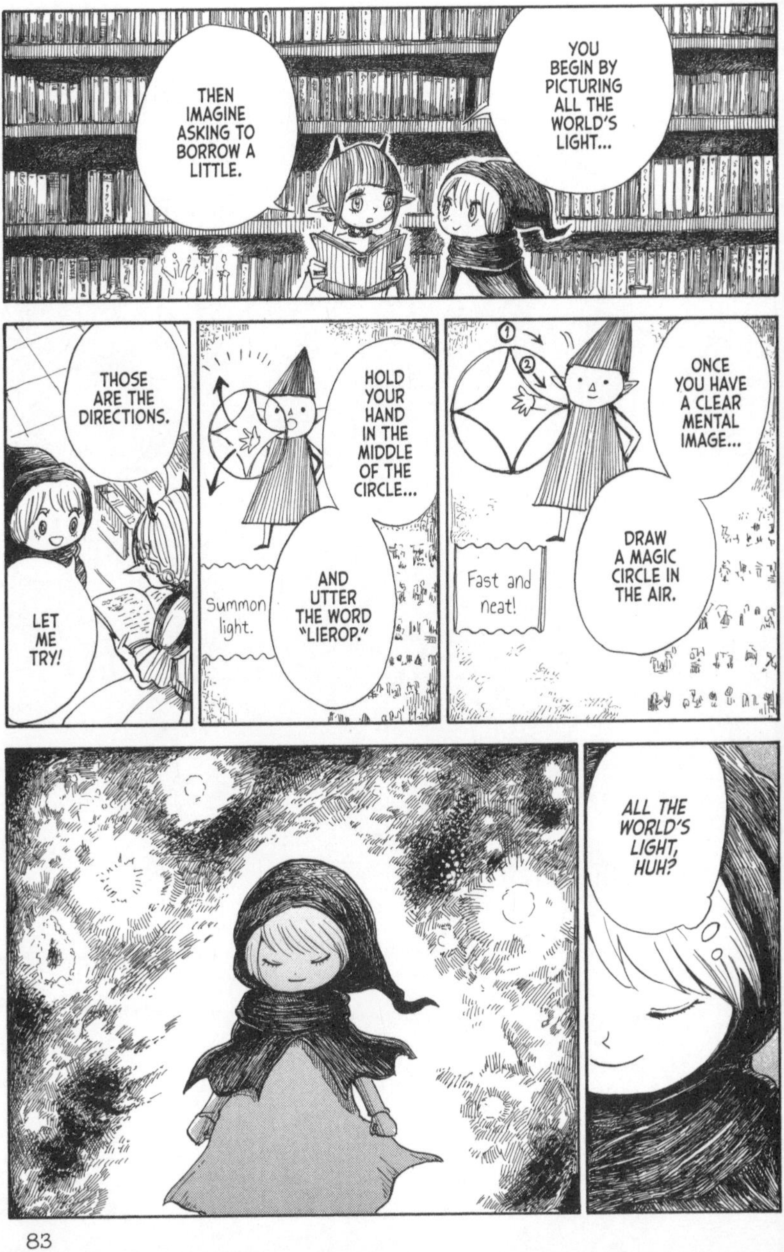
YOU BEGIN BY PICTURING ALL THE WORLD'S LIGHT...
THEN IMAGINE ASKING TO BORROW A LITTLE.
ONCE YOU HAVE A CLEAR MENTAL IMAGE...
DRAW A MAGIC CIRCLE IN THE AIR.
Fast and neat!
HOLD YOUR HAND IN THE MIDDLE OF THE CIRCLE...
AND UTTER THE WORD "LIEROP."
Summon light.
THOSE ARE THE DIRECTIONS.
LET ME TRY!
ALL THE WORLD'S LIGHT, HUH?

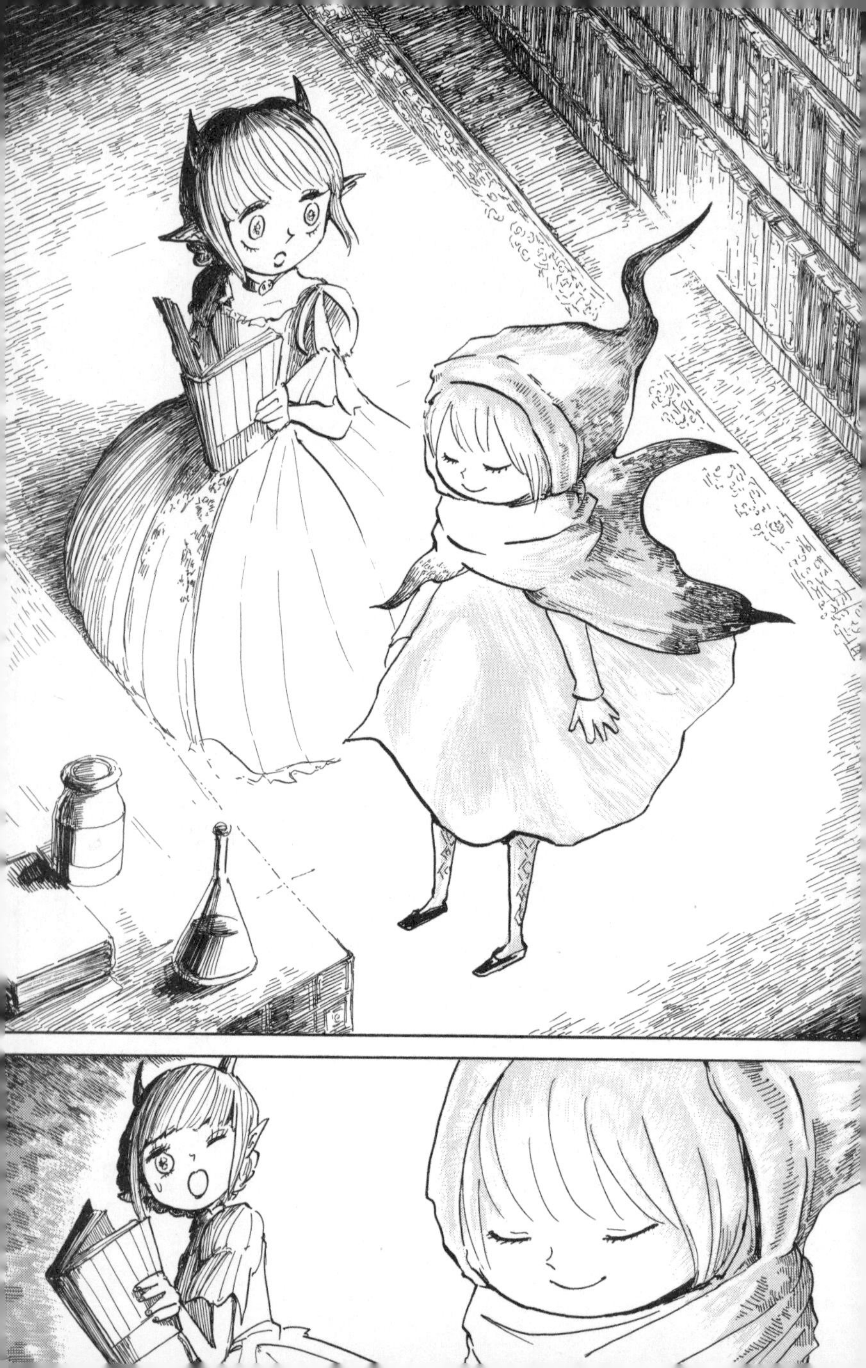

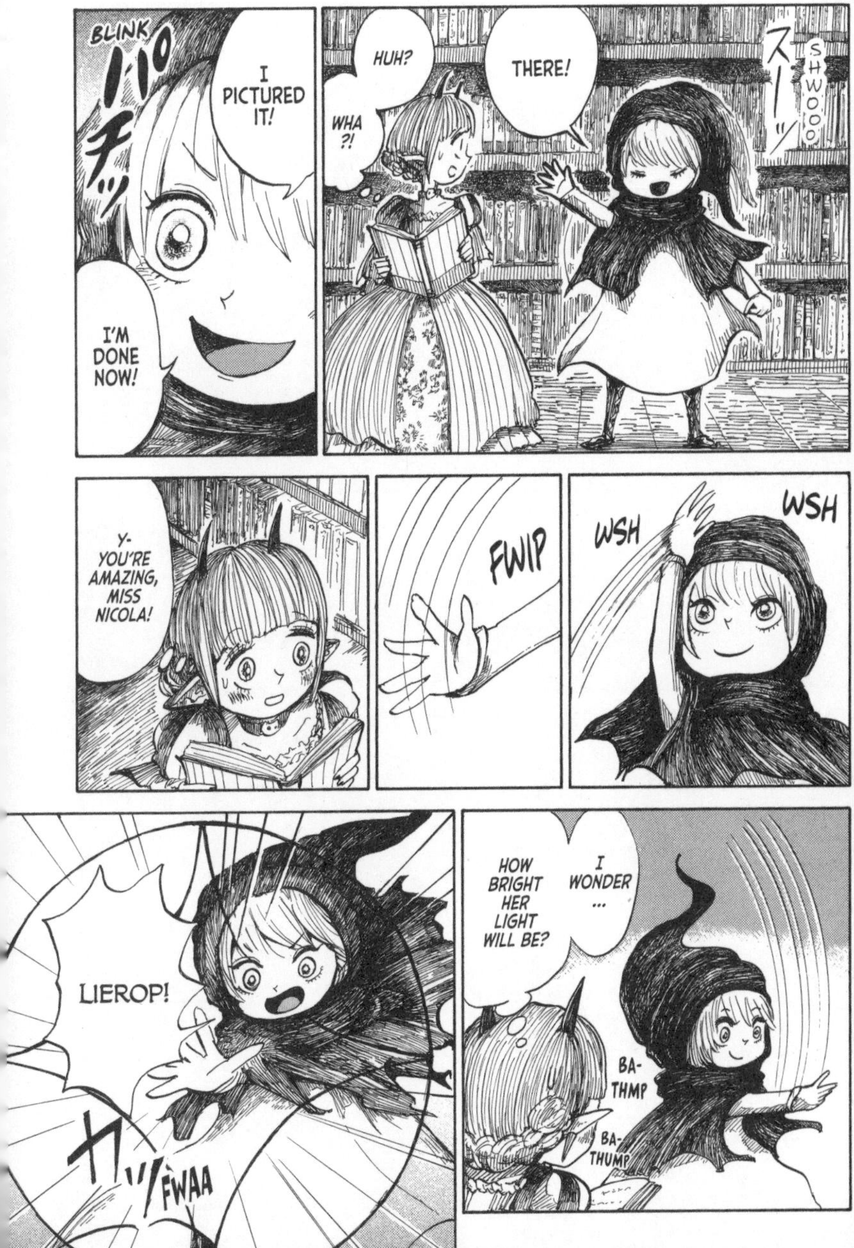
スーッ
SHWOOO
THERE!
HUH?
WHA ?!
BLINK
パチッ
I PICTURED IT!
I'M DONE NOW!
WSH
WSH
FWIP
Y- YOU'RE AMAZING, MISS NICOLA!
I WONDER ...
HOW BRIGHT HER LIGHT WILL BE?
BA-THUMP
BA-THUMP
LIEROP!
カッ!
FWAA

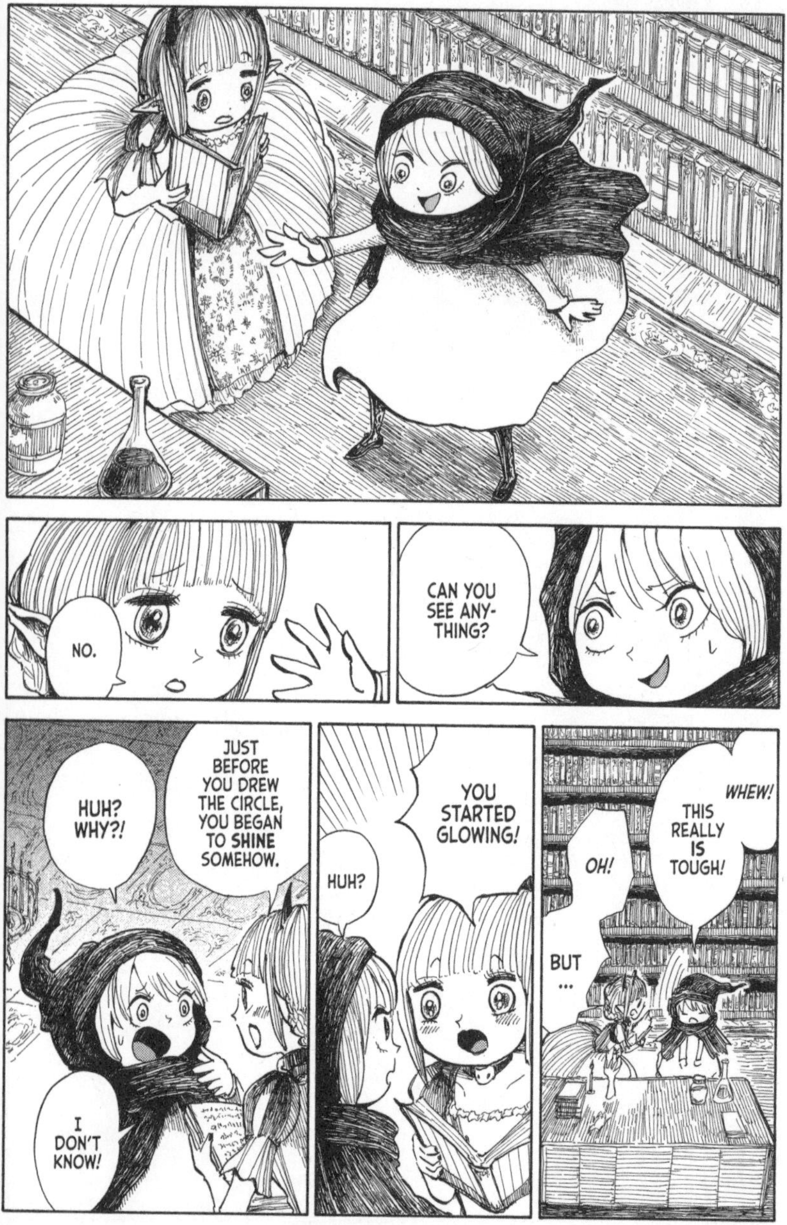
CAN YOU SEE ANYTHING?
NO.
WHEW! THIS REALLY IS TOUGH!
OH!
BUT ...
YOU STARTED GLOWING!
HUH?
JUST BEFORE YOU DREW THE CIRCLE, YOU BEGAN TO SHINE SOMEHOW.
HUH? WHY?!
I DON'T KNOW!

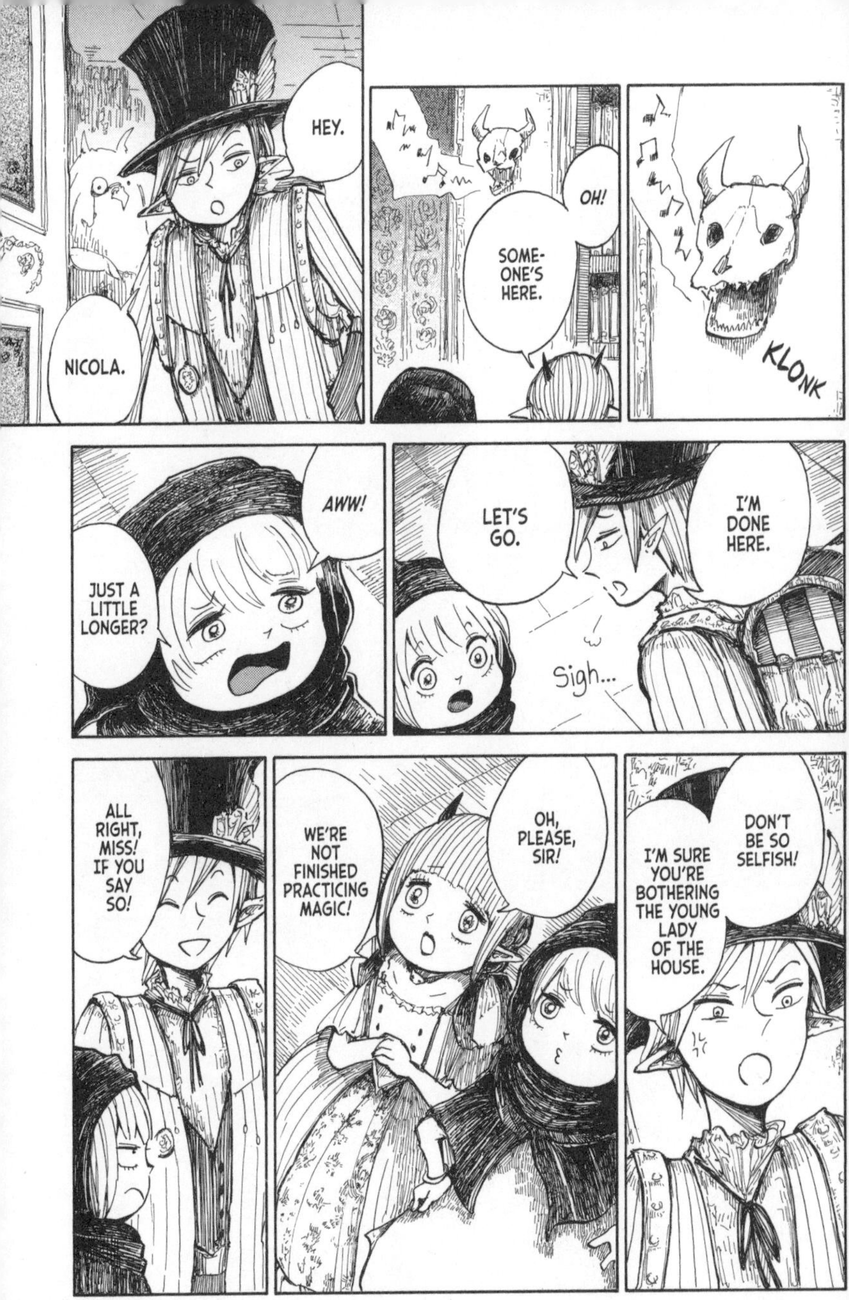
KLONK
OH!
SOMEONE'S HERE.
HEY.
NICOLA.
I'M DONE HERE.
LET'S GO.
Sigh...
AWW!
JUST A LITTLE LONGER?
DON'T BE SO SELFISH!
I'M SURE YOU'RE BOTHERING THE YOUNG LADY OF THE HOUSE.
OH, PLEASE, SIR!
WE'RE NOT FINISHED PRACTICING MAGIC!
ALL RIGHT, MISS! IF YOU SAY SO!

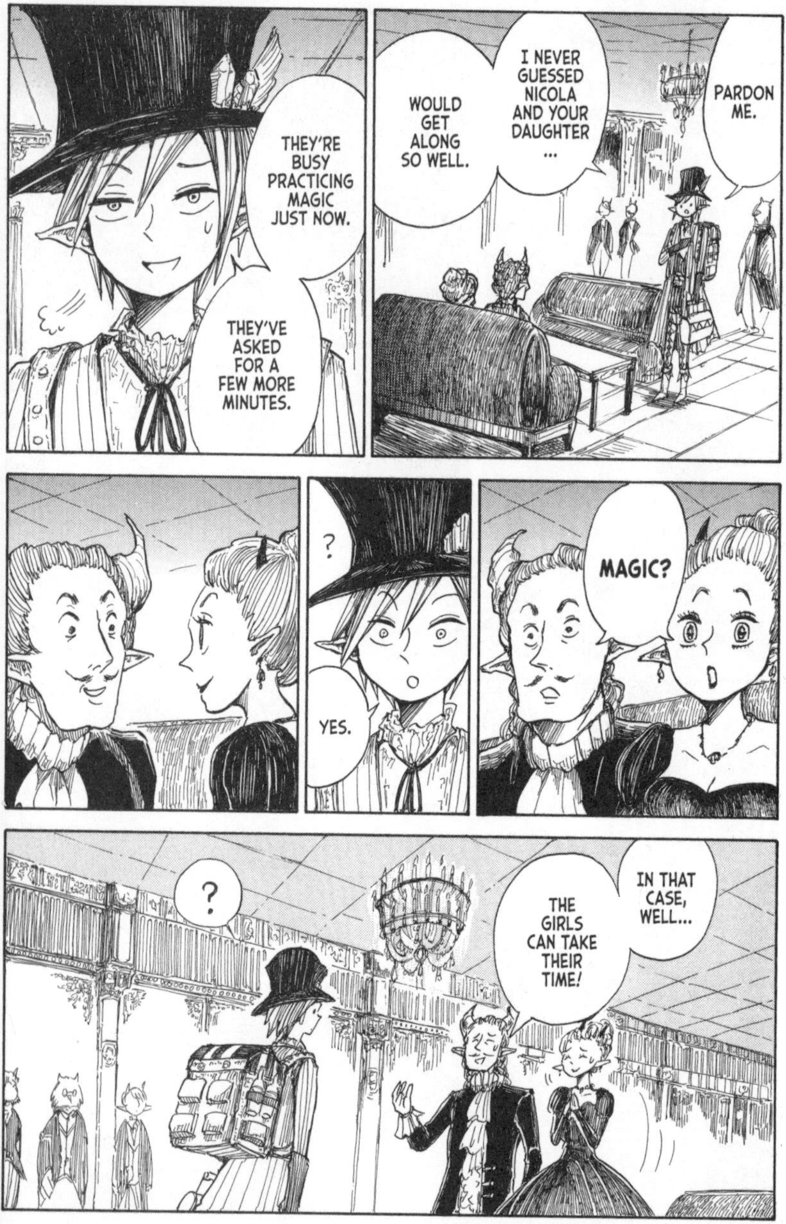
PARDON ME.
I NEVER GUESSED NICOLA AND YOUR DAUGHTER ...
WOULD GET ALONG SO WELL.
THEY'RE BUSY PRACTICING MAGIC JUST NOW.
THEY'VE ASKED FOR A FEW MORE MINUTES.
MAGIC?
?
YES.
IN THAT CASE, WELL...
THE GIRLS CAN TAKE THEIR TIME!
?

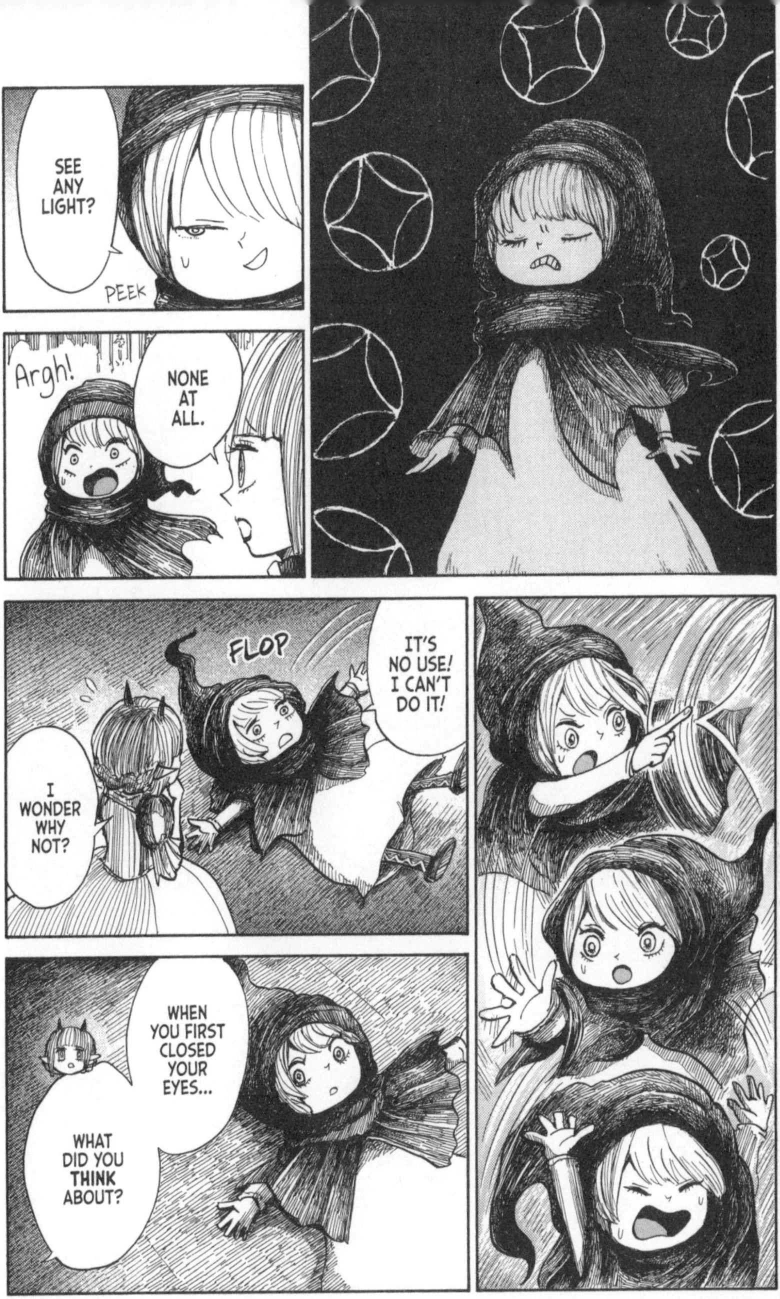
SEE ANY LIGHT?
PEEK
NONE AT ALL.
Argh!
IT'S NO USE! I CAN'T DO IT!
FLOP
I WONDER WHY NOT?
WHEN YOU FIRST CLOSED YOUR EYES...
WHAT DID YOU **THINK** ABOUT?

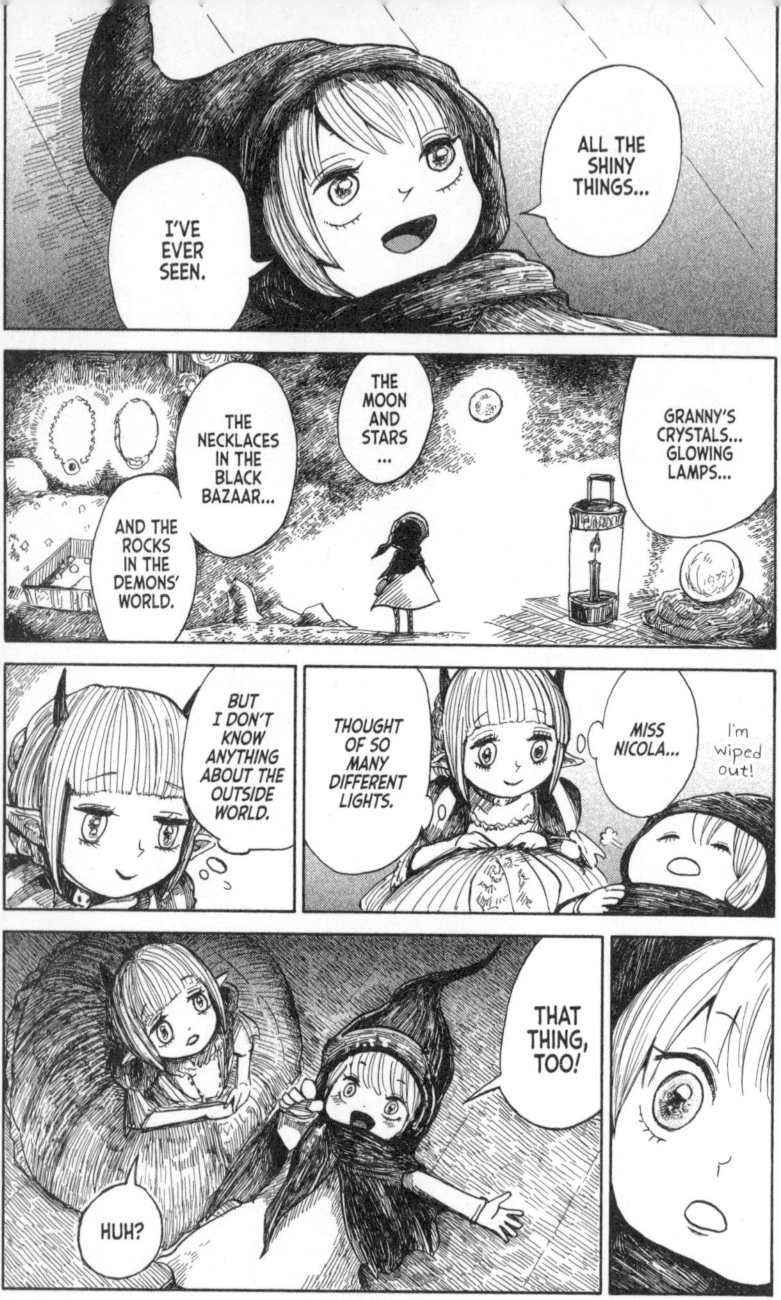
ALL THE SHINY THINGS...
I'VE EVER SEEN.
GRANNY'S CRYSTALS... GLOWING LAMPS...
THE MOON AND STARS ...
THE NECKLACES IN THE BLACK BAZAAR...
AND THE ROCKS IN THE DEMONS' WORLD.
I'm wiped out!
MISS NICOLA...
THOUGHT OF SO MANY DIFFERENT LIGHTS.
BUT I DON'T KNOW ANYTHING ABOUT THE OUTSIDE WORLD.
THAT THING, TOO!
HUH?

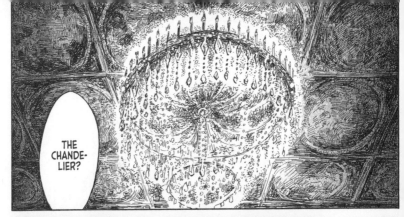

THE CHANDE-LIER?

IT'S SO PRETTY!

. . . . .

FWIP

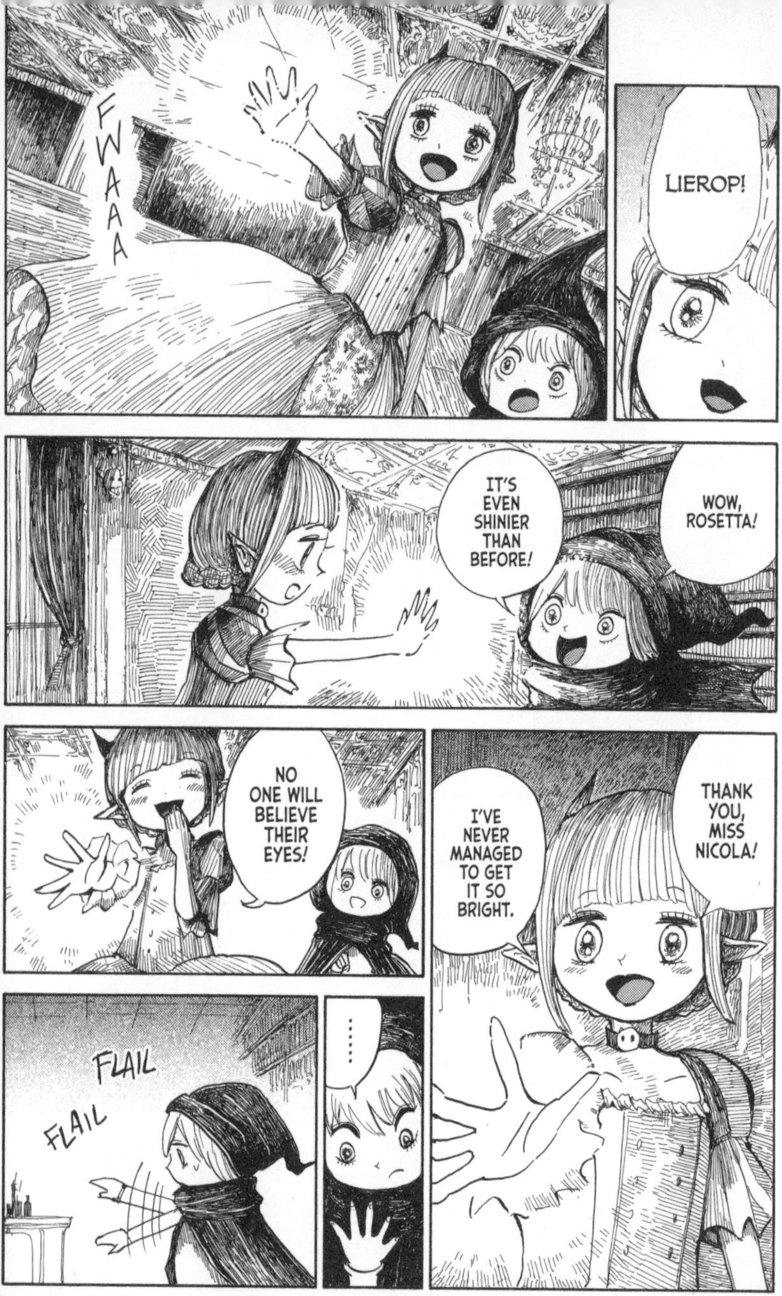
LIEROP!
FWAAA
WOW, ROSETTA!
IT'S EVEN SHINIER THAN BEFORE!
THANK YOU, MISS NICOLA!
I'VE NEVER MANAGED TO GET IT SO BRIGHT.
NO ONE WILL BELIEVE THEIR EYES!
......
FLAIL
FLAIL

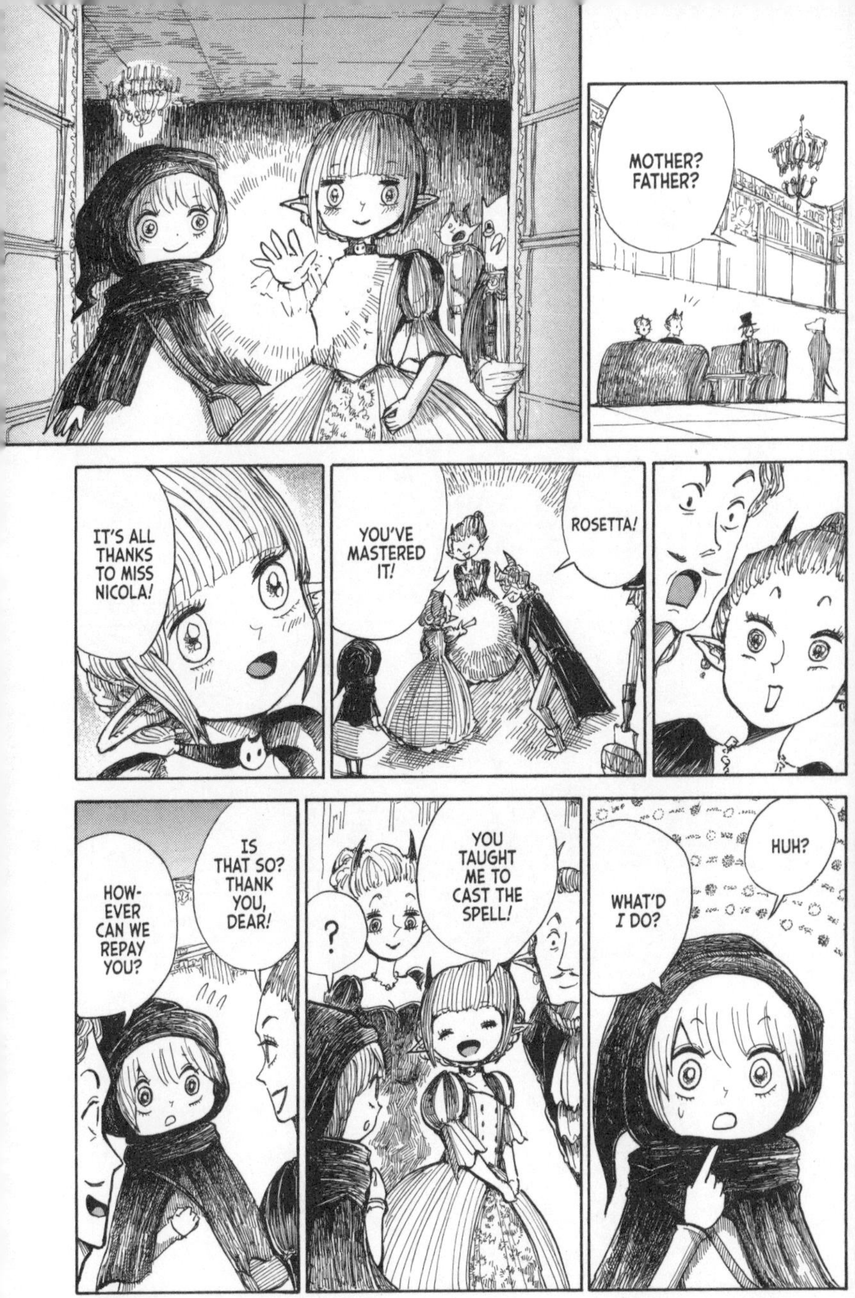
MOTHER? FATHER?
ROSETTA!
YOU'VE MASTERED IT!
IT'S ALL THANKS TO MISS NICOLA!
HUH?
WHAT'D *I* DO?
YOU TAUGHT ME TO CAST THE SPELL!
?
IS THAT SO? THANK YOU, DEAR!
HOW-EVER CAN WE REPAY YOU?

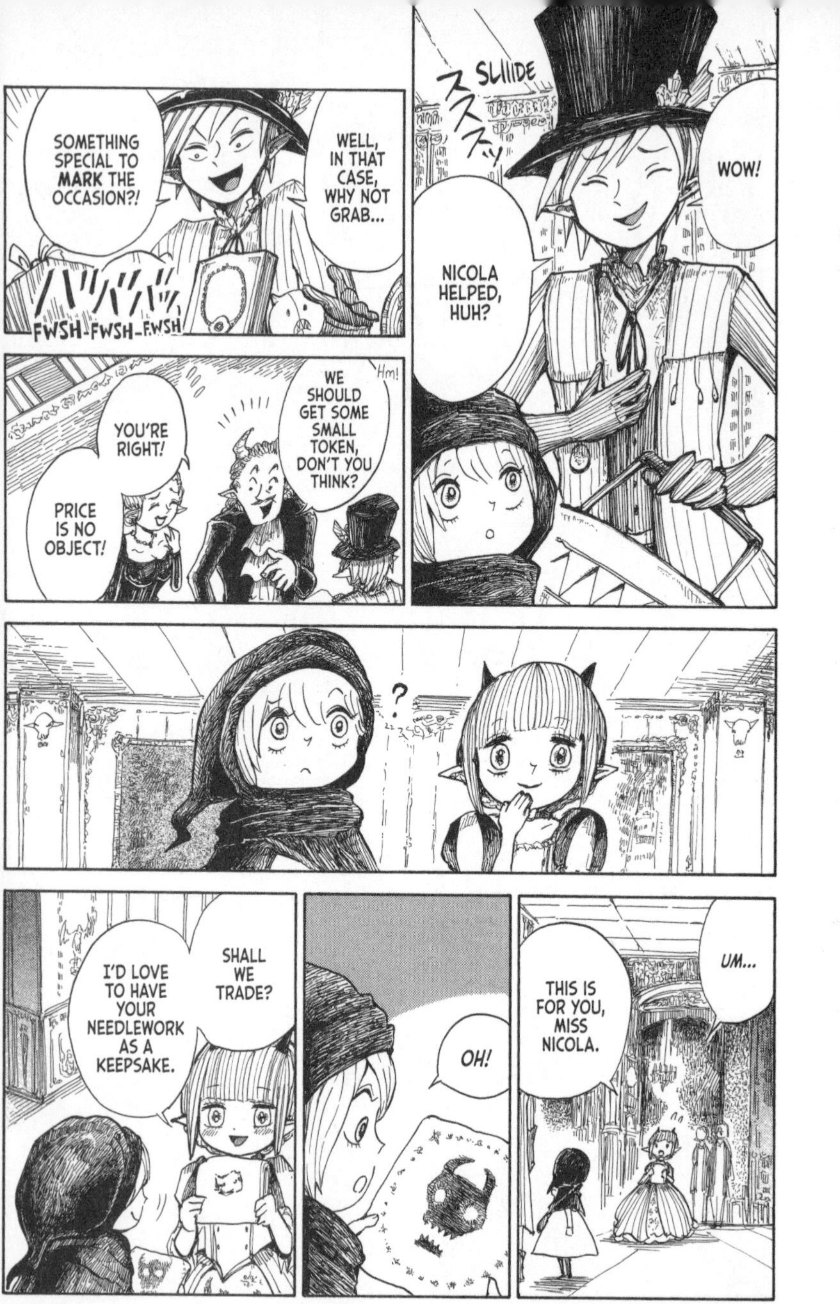
SLIIIDE
スススッ
WOW!
NICOLA HELPED, HUH?
WELL, IN THAT CASE, WHY NOT GRAB...
SOMETHING SPECIAL TO MARK THE OCCASION?!
バババッ
FWSH-FWSH-FWSH
Hm!
WE SHOULD GET SOME SMALL TOKEN, DON'T YOU THINK?
YOU'RE RIGHT!
PRICE IS NO OBJECT!
?
UM...
THIS IS FOR YOU, MISS NICOLA.
OH!
SHALL WE TRADE?
I'D LOVE TO HAVE YOUR NEEDLEWORK AS A KEEPSAKE.

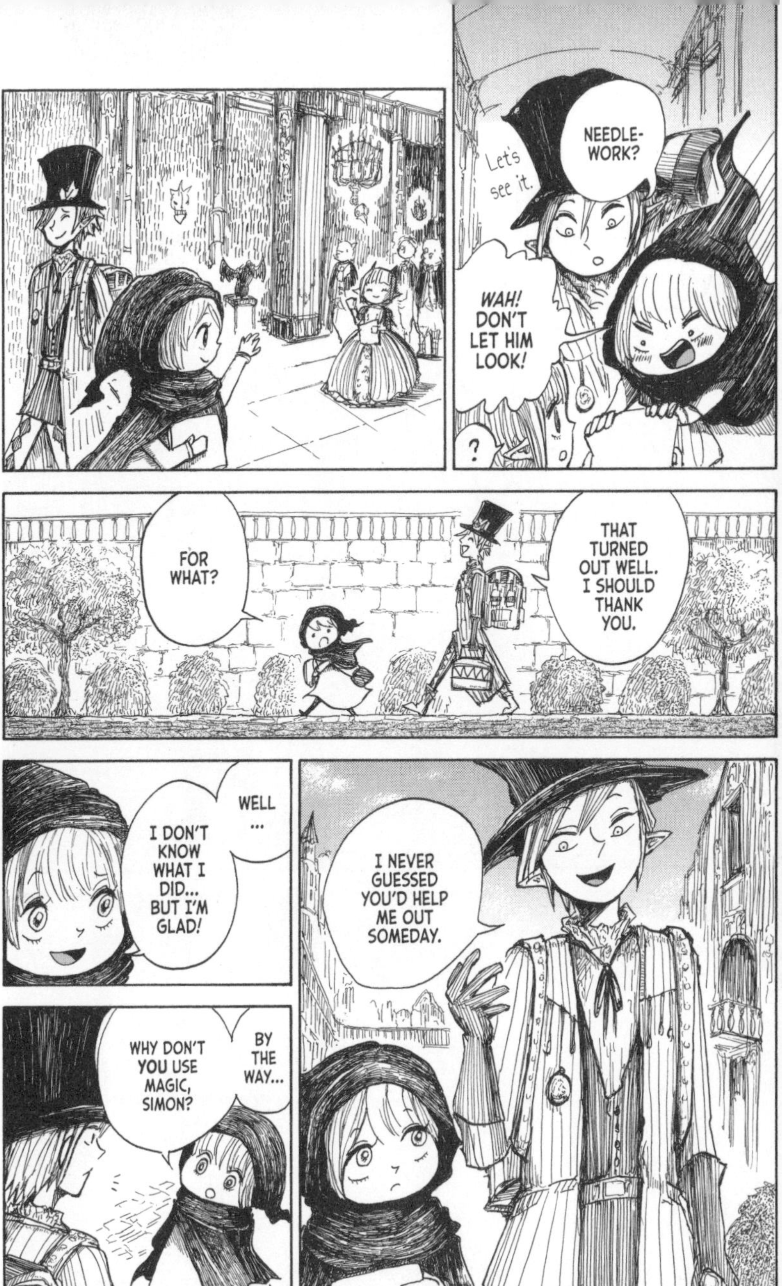

NEEDLE-WORK?
Let's see it.
WAH! DON'T LET HIM LOOK!
?
THAT TURNED OUT WELL. I SHOULD THANK YOU.
FOR WHAT?
I NEVER GUESSED YOU'D HELP ME OUT SOMEDAY.
WELL ...
I DON'T KNOW WHAT I DID... BUT I'M GLAD!
BY THE WAY...
WHY DON'T YOU USE MAGIC, SIMON?

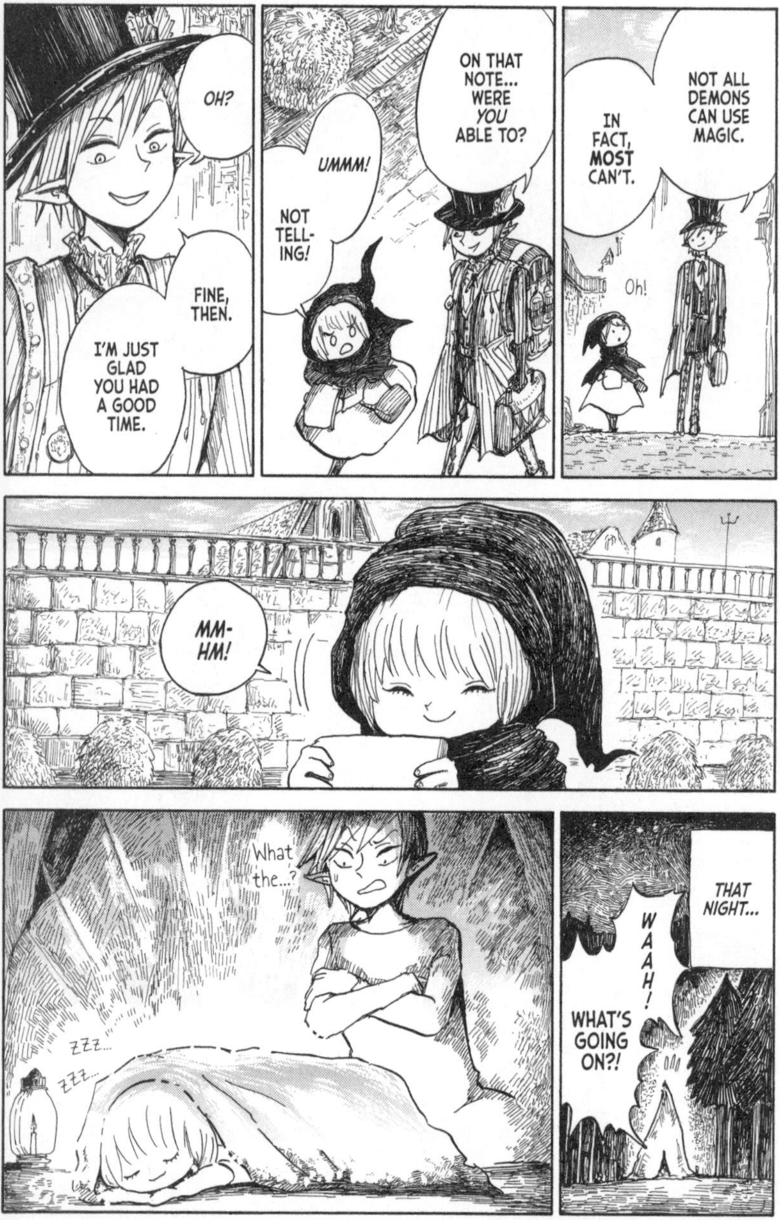
NOT ALL DEMONS CAN USE MAGIC.
IN FACT, MOST CAN'T.
Oh!
ON THAT NOTE... WERE YOU ABLE TO?
UMMM!
NOT TELLING!
OH?
FINE, THEN.
I'M JUST GLAD YOU HAD A GOOD TIME.
MM-HM!
THAT NIGHT...
WAAAH!
WHAT'S GOING ON?!
What the...?
ZZZ...
ZZZ...

Chapter 3 END

After the Visit 3

after that

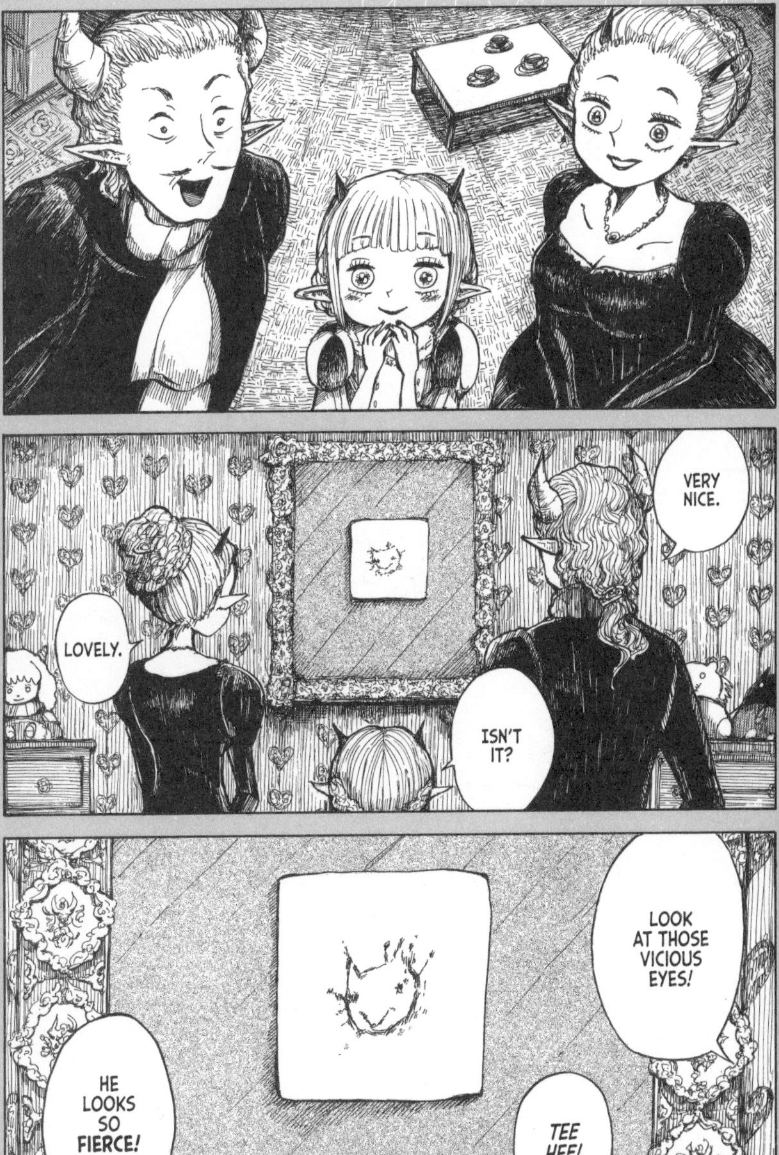
VERY NICE.
LOVELY.
ISN'T IT?
LOOK AT THOSE VICIOUS EYES!
HE LOOKS SO FIERCE!
TEE HEE!

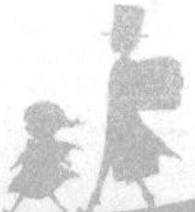

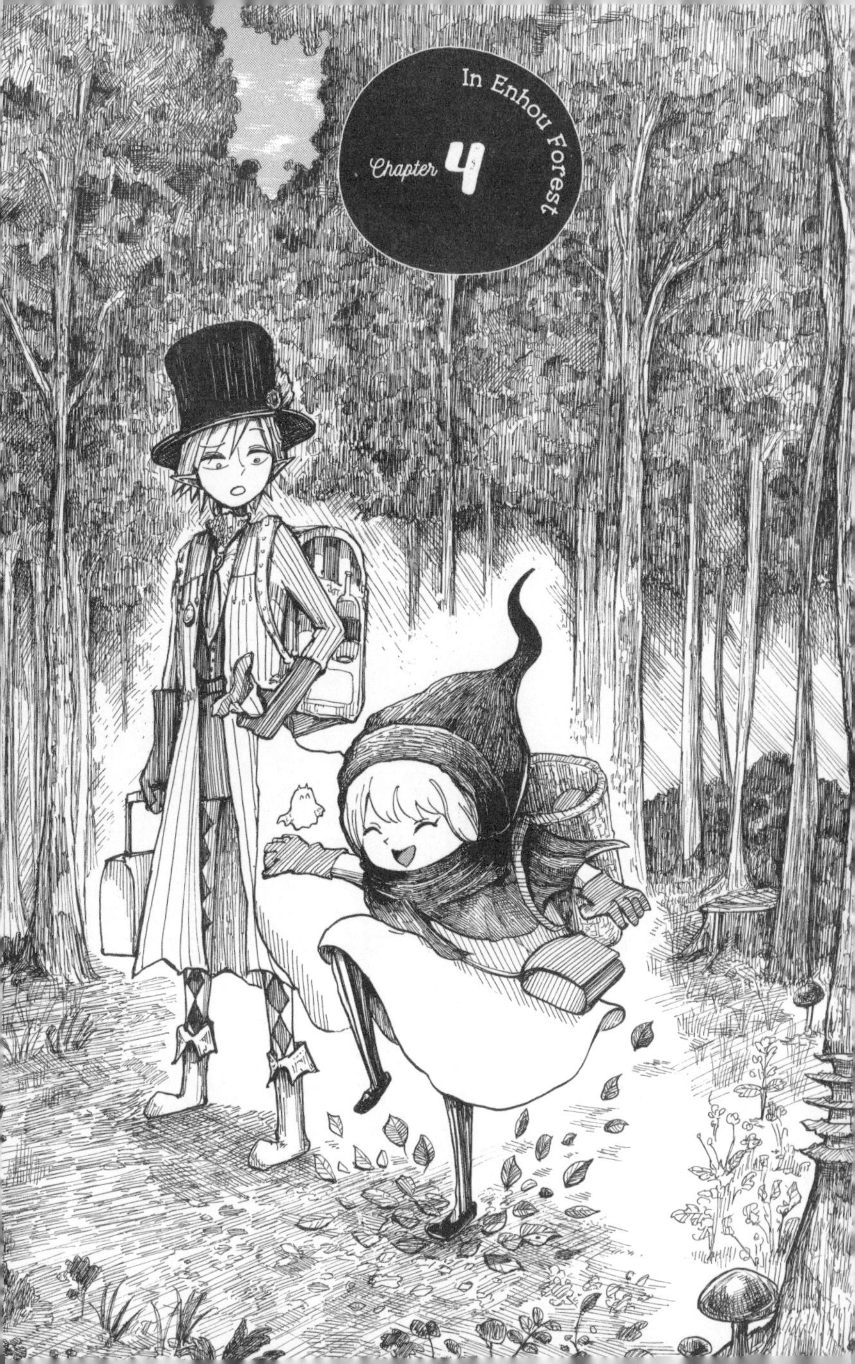
Chapter 4
In Enhou Forest

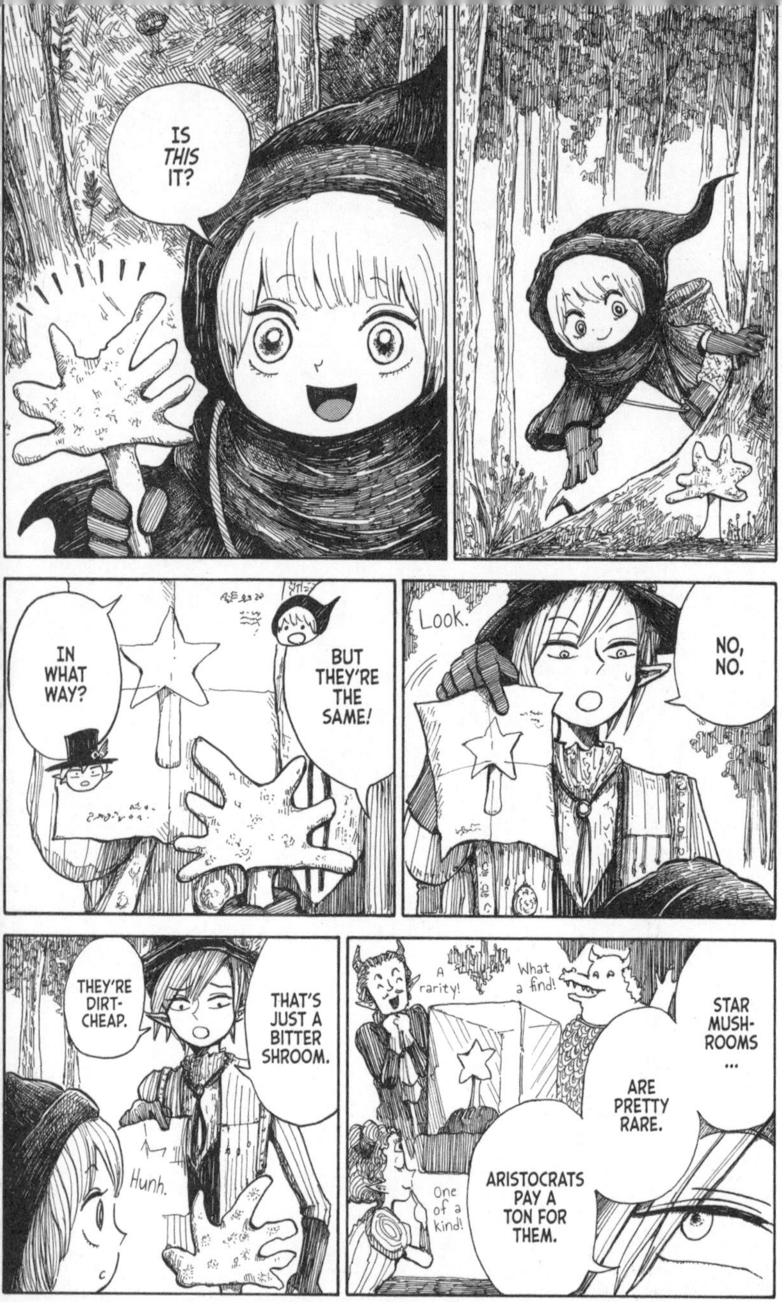
IS THIS IT?
NO, NO.
Look.
BUT THEY'RE THE SAME!
IN WHAT WAY?
STAR MUSH-ROOMS ...
What a find!
A rarity!
ARE PRETTY RARE.
ARISTOCRATS PAY A TON FOR THEM.
One of a kind!
THAT'S JUST A BITTER SHROOM.
THEY'RE DIRT-CHEAP.
Hunh.

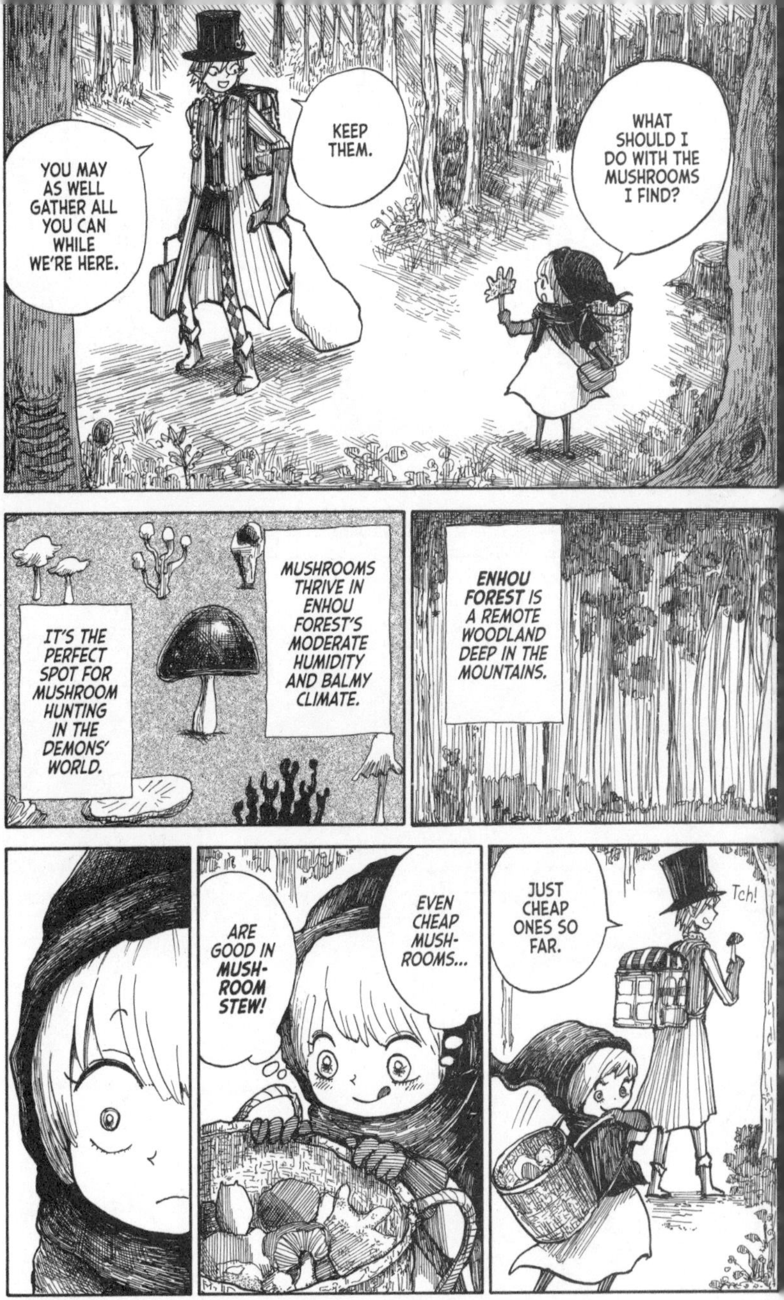
WHAT SHOULD I DO WITH THE MUSHROOMS I FIND?
KEEP THEM.
YOU MAY AS WELL GATHER ALL YOU CAN WHILE WE'RE HERE.
ENHOU FOREST IS A REMOTE WOODLAND DEEP IN THE MOUNTAINS.
MUSHROOMS THRIVE IN ENHOU FOREST'S MODERATE HUMIDITY AND BALMY CLIMATE.
IT'S THE PERFECT SPOT FOR MUSHROOM HUNTING IN THE DEMONS' WORLD.
JUST CHEAP ONES SO FAR.
Tch!
EVEN CHEAP MUSH-ROOMS...
ARE GOOD IN MUSH-ROOM STEW!

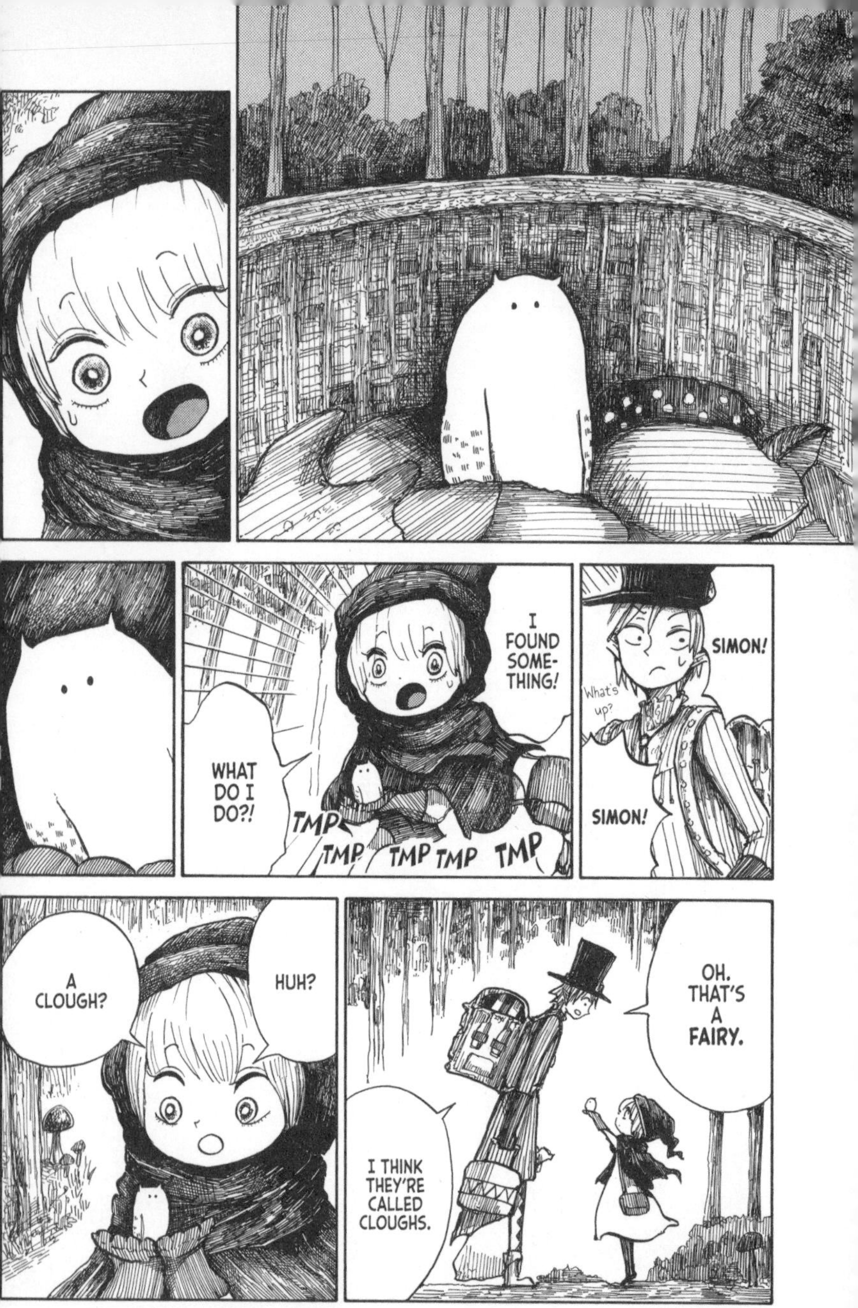
SIMON!
What's up?
SIMON!
I FOUND SOME-THING!
WHAT DO I DO?!
TMP
TMP TMP TMP TMP
OH. THAT'S A FAIRY.
I THINK THEY'RE CALLED CLOUGHS.
HUH?
A CLOUGH?

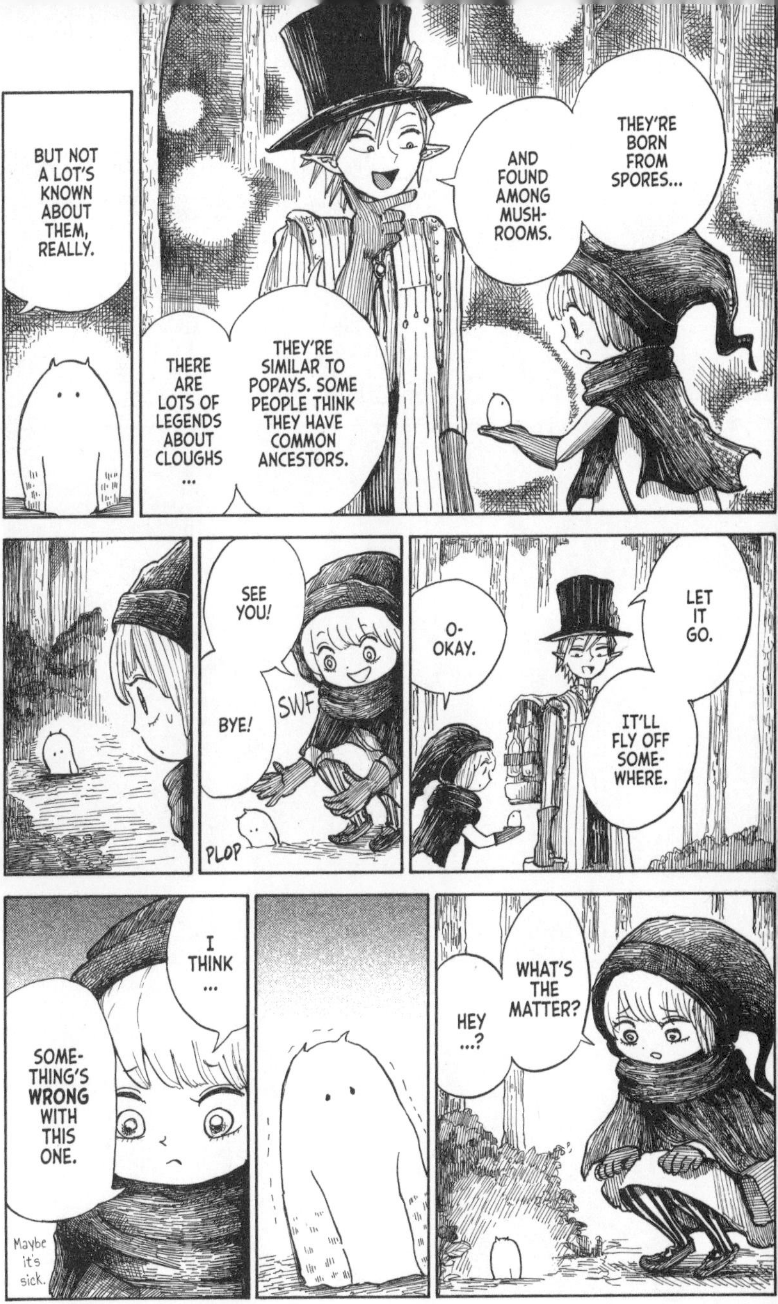
THEY'RE BORN FROM SPORES...
AND FOUND AMONG MUSHROOMS.
THEY'RE SIMILAR TO POPAYS. SOME PEOPLE THINK THEY HAVE COMMON ANCESTORS.
THERE ARE LOTS OF LEGENDS ABOUT CLOUGHS ...
BUT NOT A LOT'S KNOWN ABOUT THEM, REALLY.
LET IT GO.
O-OKAY.
IT'LL FLY OFF SOMEWHERE.
SEE YOU!
SWF
BYE!
PLOP
WHAT'S THE MATTER?
HEY ...?
I THINK ...
SOMETHING'S **WRONG** WITH THIS ONE.
Maybe it's sick.

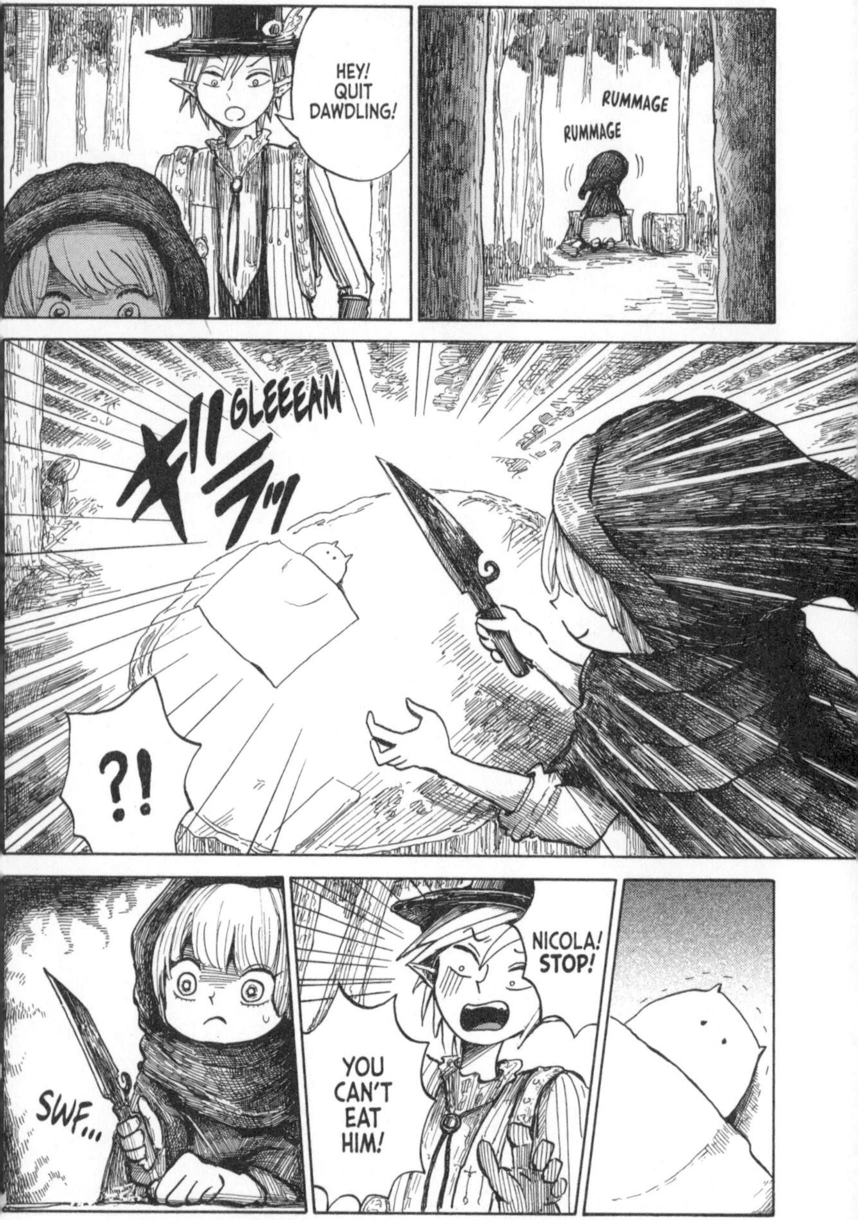
RUMMAGE
RUMMAGE
HEY! QUIT DAWDLING!
GLEEEAM
ギラッ
?!
NICOLA! STOP!
YOU CAN'T EAT HIM!
SWF...

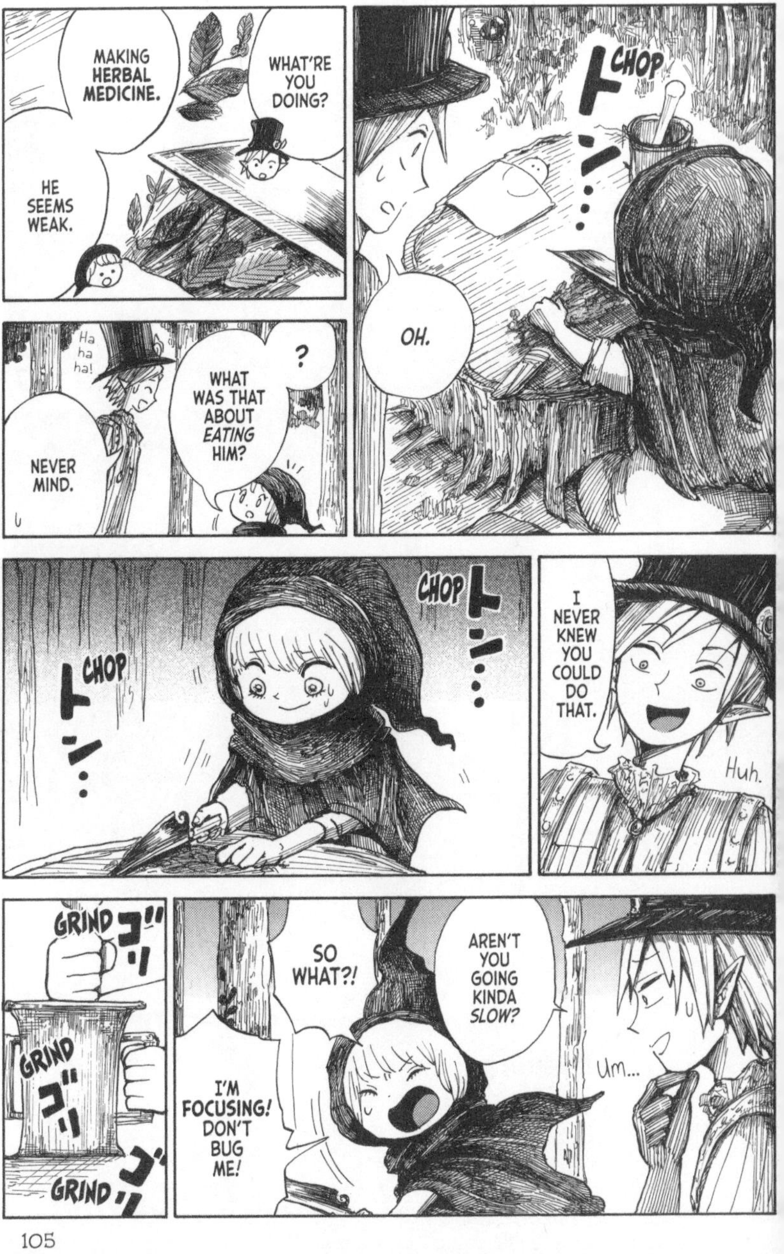
CHOP
OH.
WHAT'RE YOU DOING?
MAKING HERBAL MEDICINE.
HE SEEMS WEAK.
?
WHAT WAS THAT ABOUT *EATING* HIM?
Ha ha ha!
NEVER MIND.
I NEVER KNEW YOU COULD DO THAT.
Huh.
CHOP
CHOP
Um...
AREN'T YOU GOING KINDA *SLOW*?
SO WHAT?!
I'M FOCUSING! DON'T BUG ME!
GRIND
GRIND
GRIND

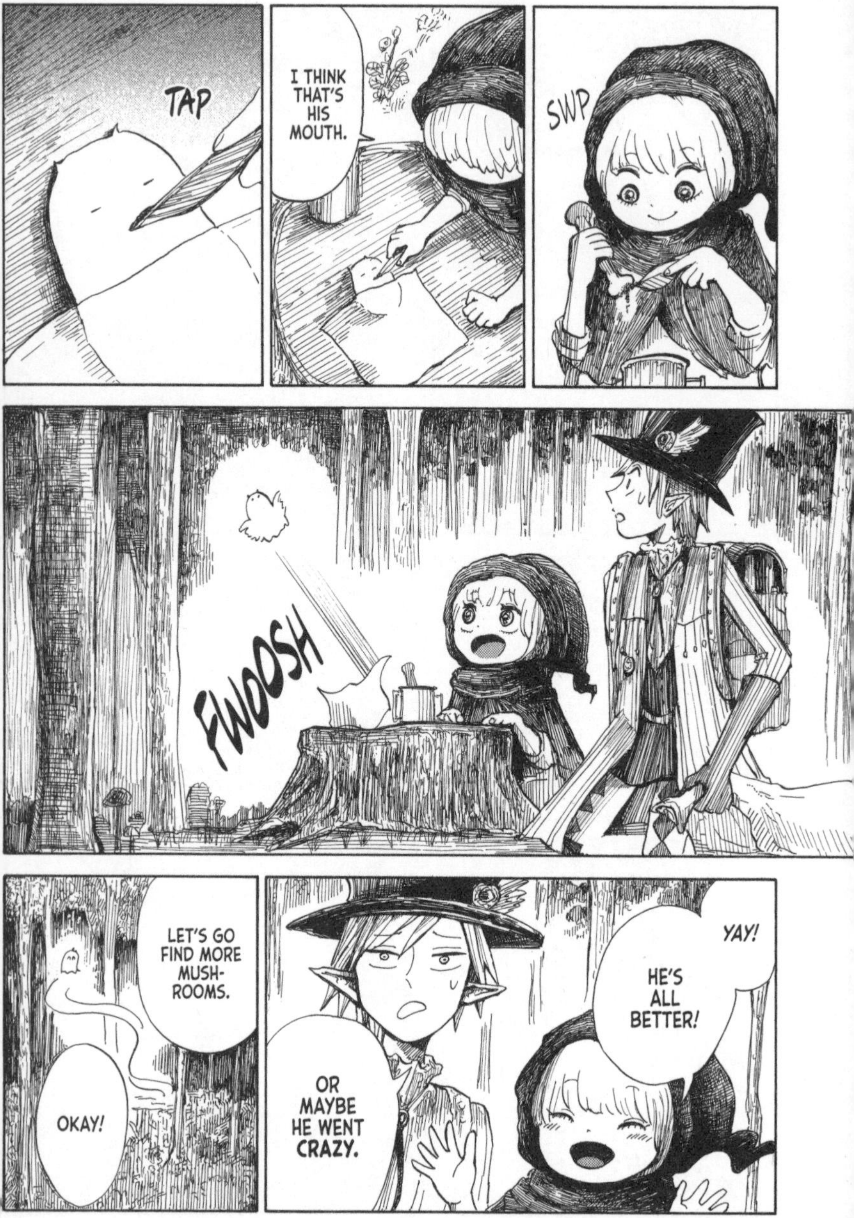
SWP
I THINK THAT'S HIS MOUTH.
TAP
FWOOSH
YAY!
HE'S ALL BETTER!
OR MAYBE HE WENT CRAZY.
LET'S GO FIND MORE MUSH-ROOMS.
OKAY!

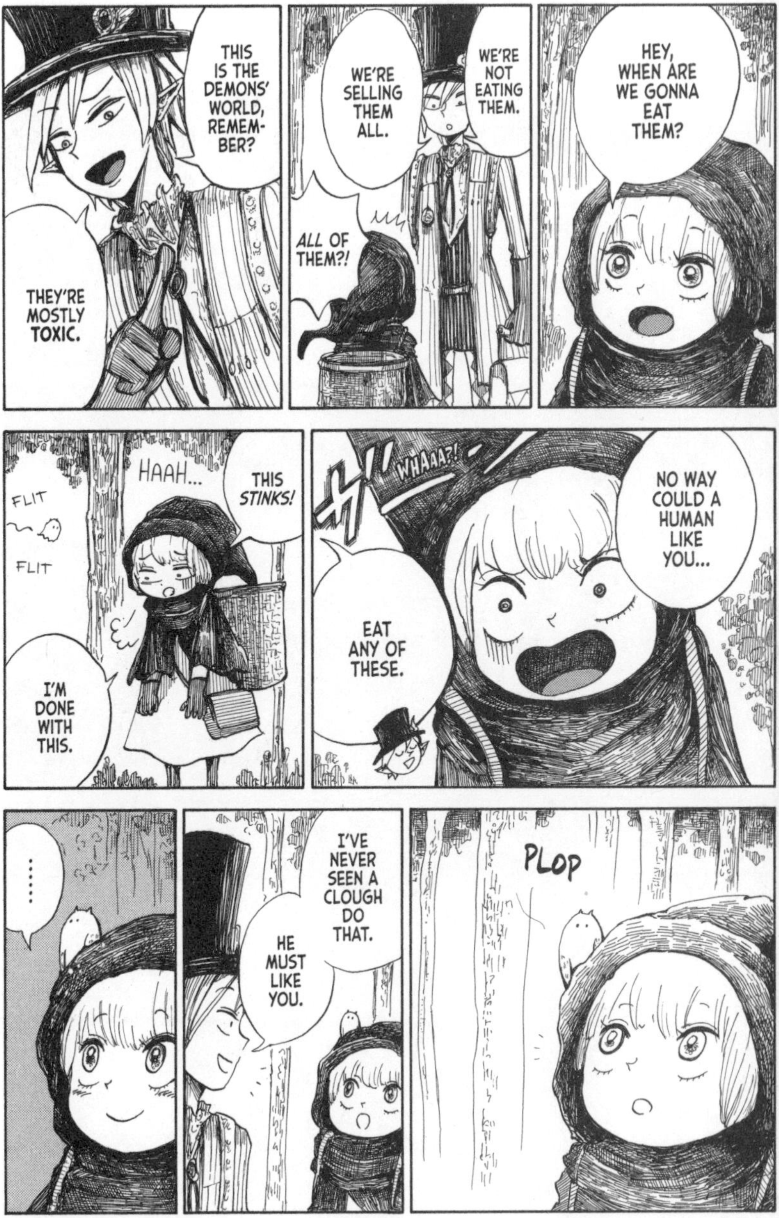
HEY, WHEN ARE WE GONNA EAT THEM?
WE'RE NOT EATING THEM.
WE'RE SELLING THEM ALL.
ALL OF THEM?!
THIS IS THE DEMONS' WORLD, REMEMBER?
THEY'RE MOSTLY TOXIC.
WHAAA?!
NO WAY COULD A HUMAN LIKE YOU...
EAT ANY OF THESE.
THIS *STINKS!*
HAAH...
FLIT
FLIT
I'M DONE WITH THIS.
PLOP
I'VE NEVER SEEN A CLOUGH DO THAT.
HE MUST LIKE YOU.
......

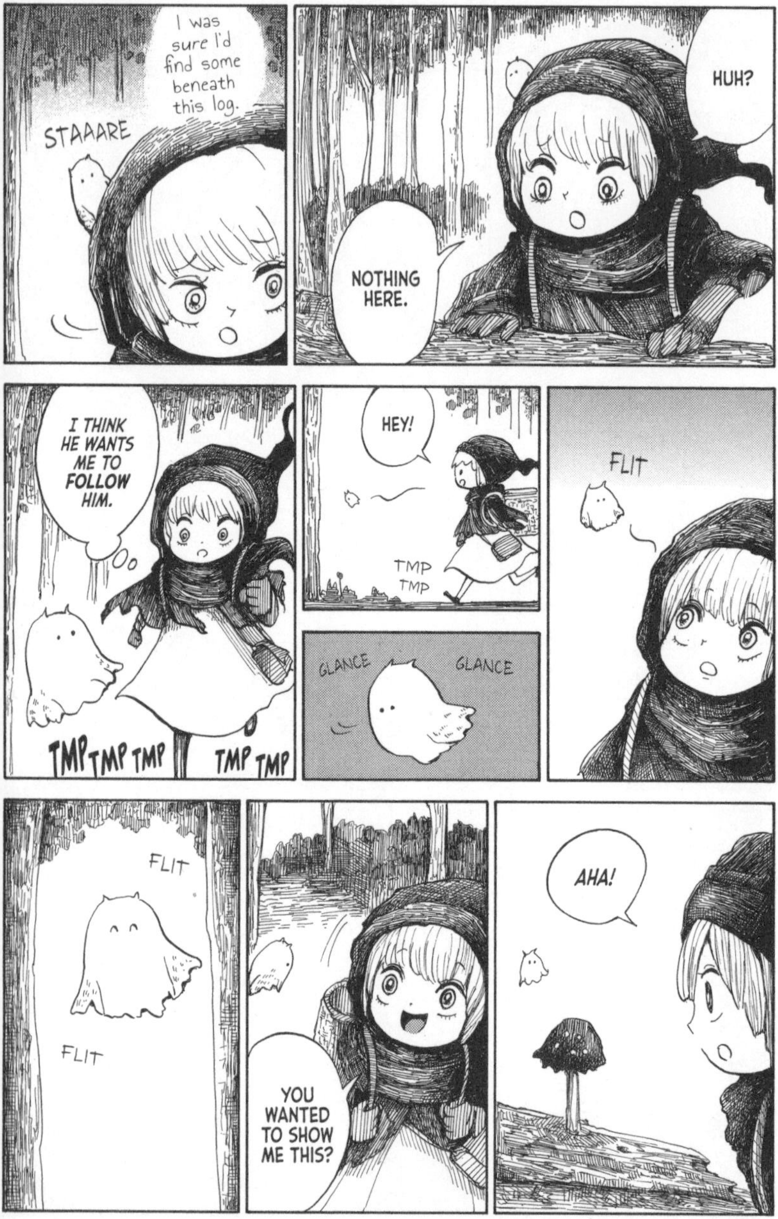
HUH?
NOTHING HERE.
I was sure I'd find some beneath this log.
STAAARE
FLIT
HEY!
TMP TMP
GLANCE GLANCE
I THINK HE WANTS ME TO FOLLOW HIM.
TMP TMP TMP TMP TMP
AHA!
YOU WANTED TO SHOW ME THIS?
FLIT
FLIT

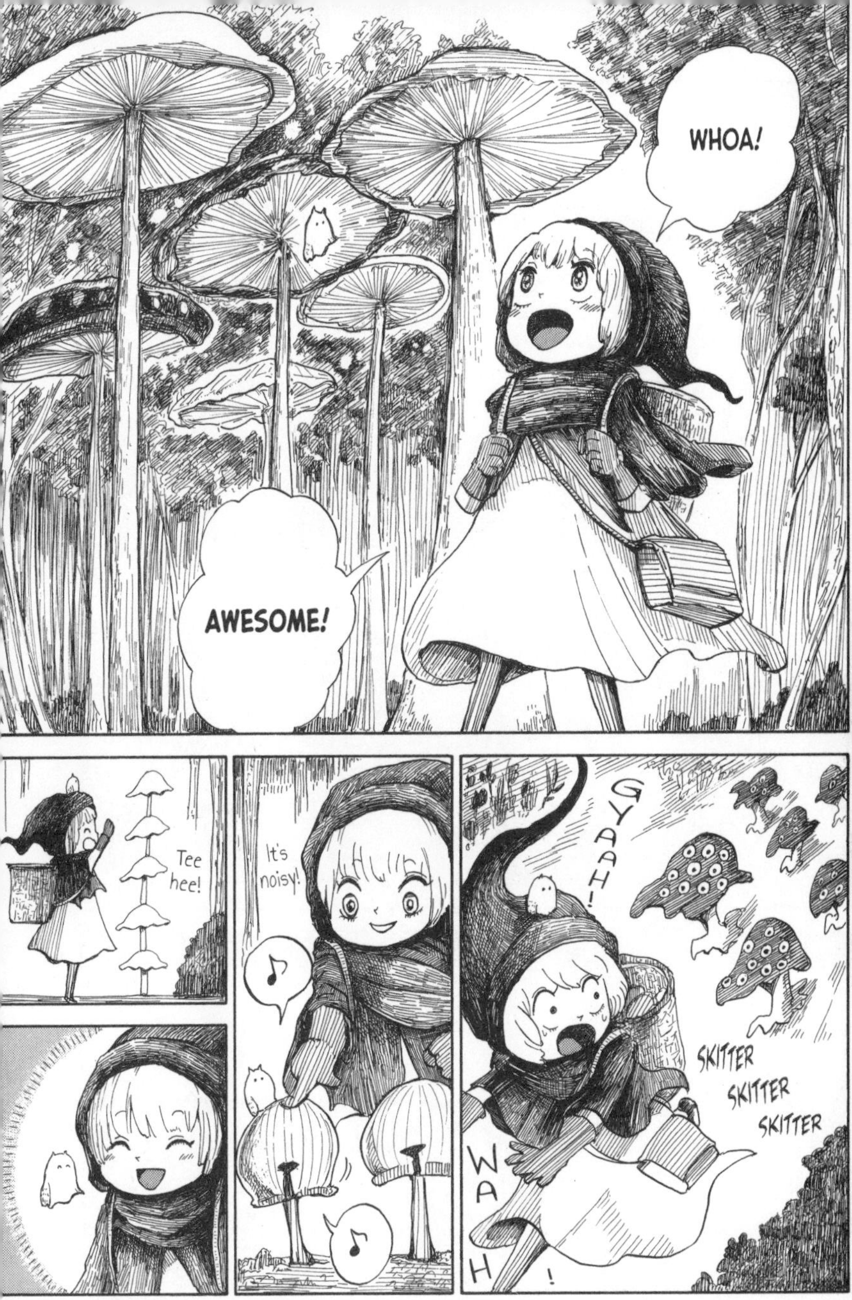
WHOA!
AWESOME!
GYAAAH!
SKITTER
SKITTER
SKITTER
WAH!
It's noisy!
♪
♪
Tee hee!

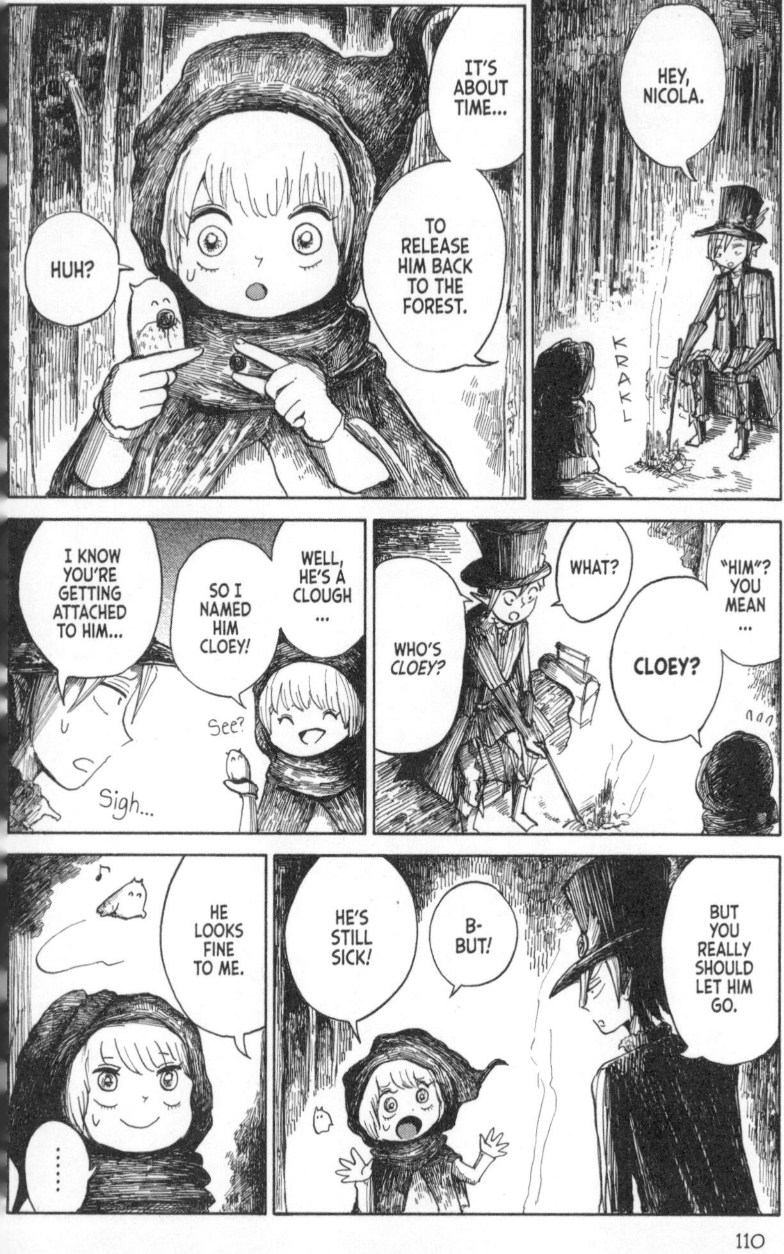
HEY, NICOLA.
KRAKL
IT'S ABOUT TIME...
TO RELEASE HIM BACK TO THE FOREST.
HUH?
"HIM"? YOU MEAN ...
CLOEY?
WHAT?
WHO'S *CLOEY?*
WELL, HE'S A CLOUGH ...
SO I NAMED HIM CLOEY!
See?
I KNOW YOU'RE GETTING ATTACHED TO HIM...
Sigh...
BUT YOU REALLY SHOULD LET HIM GO.
B-BUT!
HE'S STILL SICK!
HE LOOKS FINE TO ME.
......

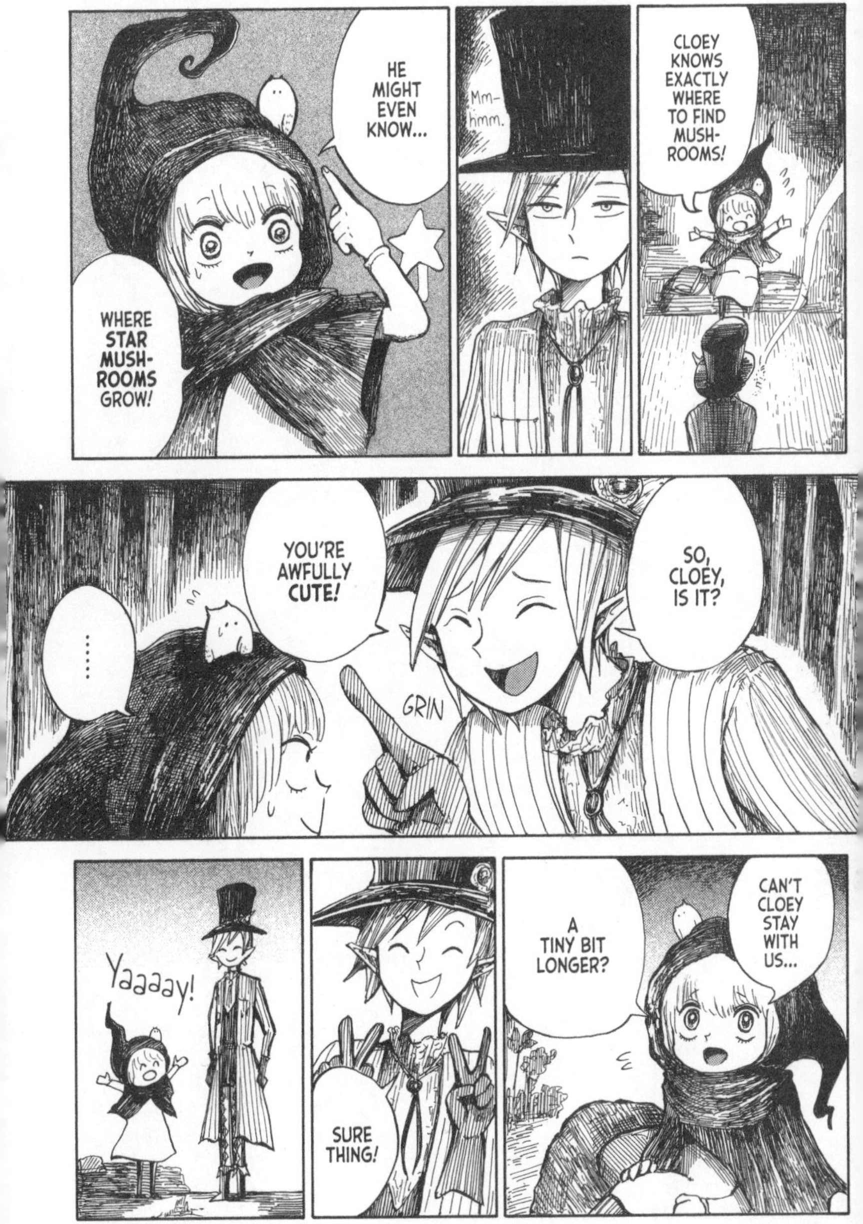
CLOEY KNOWS EXACTLY WHERE TO FIND MUSH-ROOMS!
Mm-hmm.
HE MIGHT EVEN KNOW...
WHERE STAR MUSH-ROOMS GROW!
SO, CLOEY, IS IT?
YOU'RE AWFULLY CUTE!
GRIN
......
CAN'T CLOEY STAY WITH US...
A TINY BIT LONGER?
SURE THING!
Yaaaay!

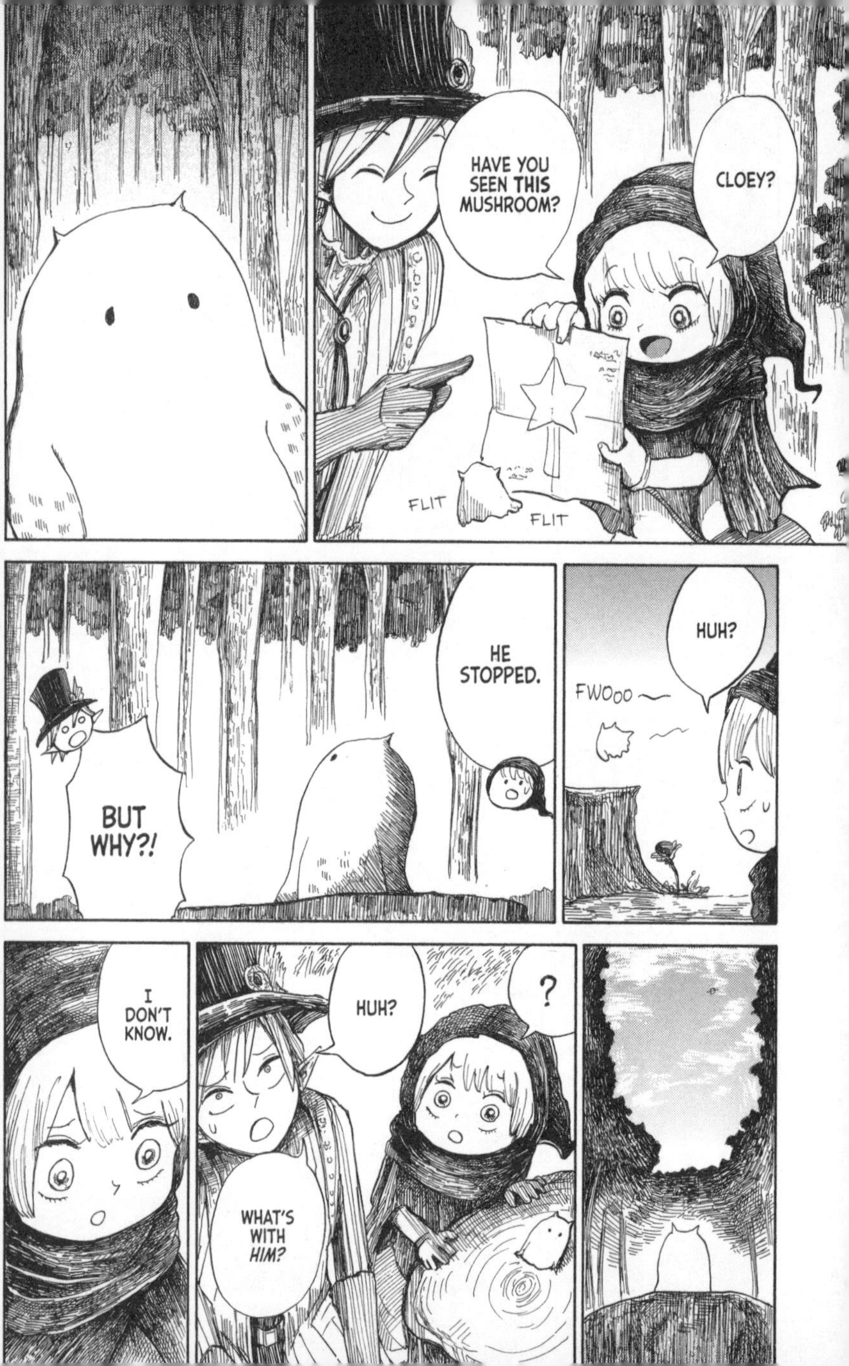
CLOEY?
HAVE YOU SEEN THIS MUSHROOM?
FLIT
FLIT
HUH?
FWOooo~
HE STOPPED.
BUT WHY?!
?
HUH?
WHAT'S WITH *HIM*?
I DON'T KNOW.

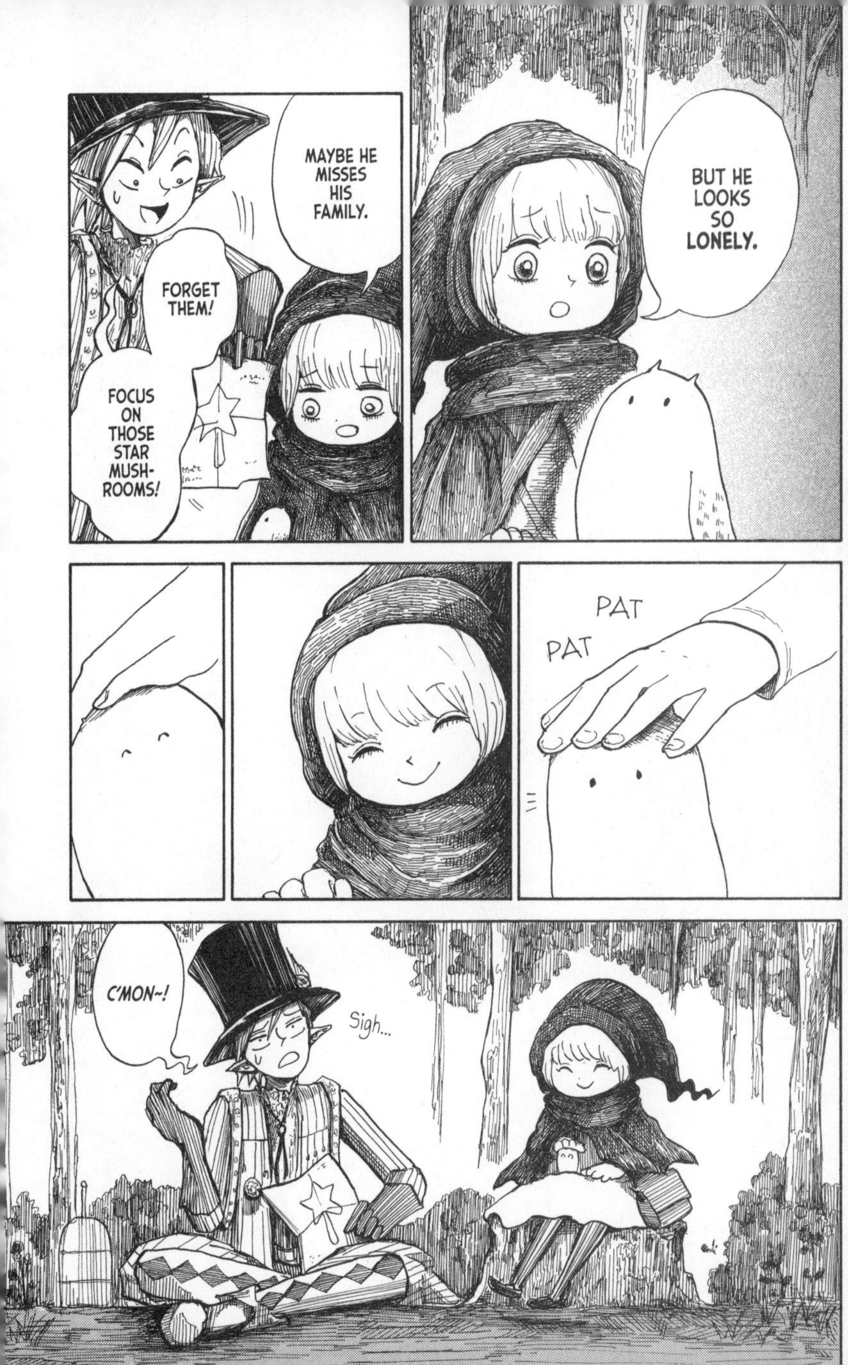
BUT HE LOOKS SO LONELY.
MAYBE HE MISSES HIS FAMILY.
FORGET THEM!
FOCUS ON THOSE STAR MUSH-ROOMS!
PAT
PAT
Sigh...
C'MON~!

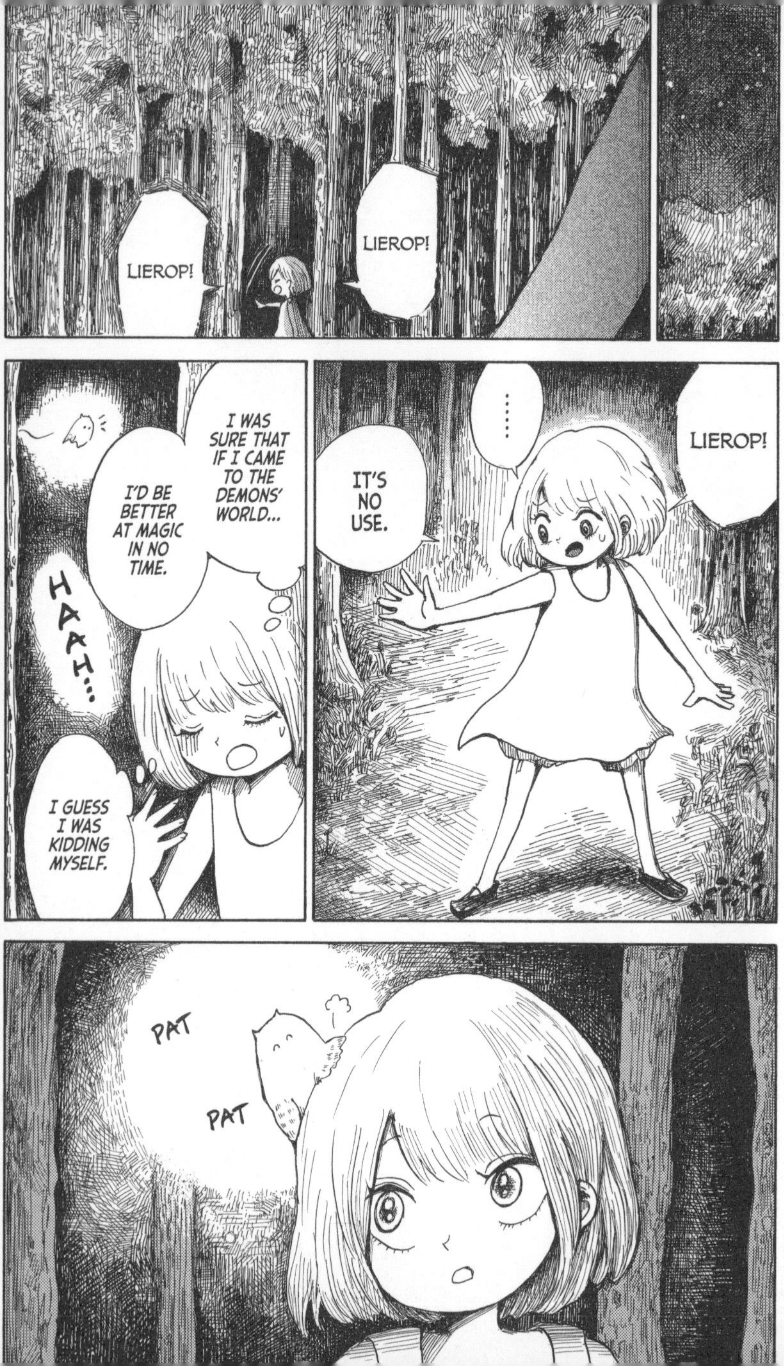
LIEROP!
LIEROP!
LIEROP!
......
IT'S NO USE.
I WAS SURE THAT IF I CAME TO THE DEMONS' WORLD...
I'D BE BETTER AT MAGIC IN NO TIME.
HAAAH...
I GUESS I WAS KIDDING MYSELF.
PAT
PAT

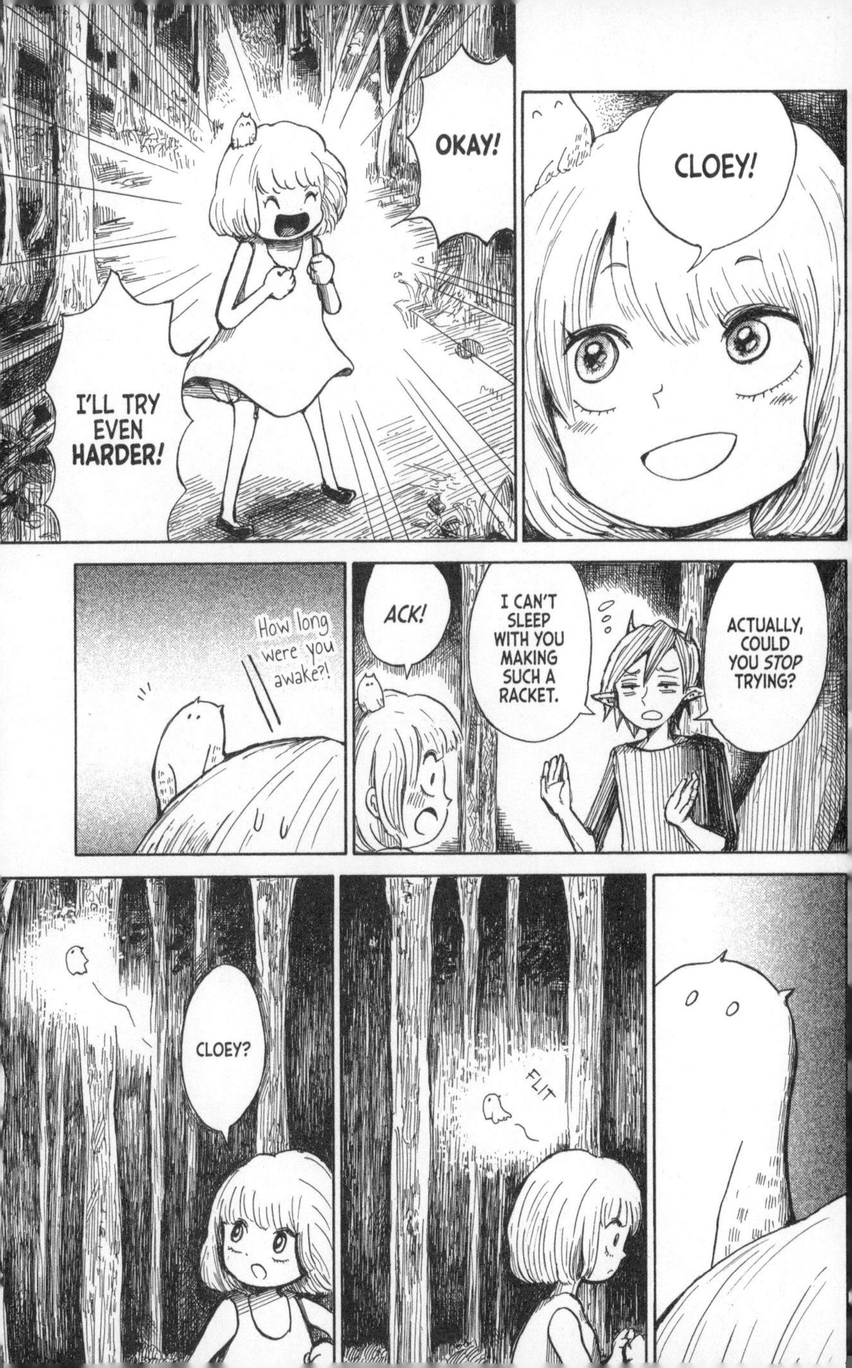
CLOEY!
OKAY!
I'LL TRY EVEN HARDER!
ACTUALLY, COULD YOU *STOP* TRYING?
I CAN'T SLEEP WITH YOU MAKING SUCH A RACKET.
ACK!
How long were you awake?!
FLIT
CLOEY?

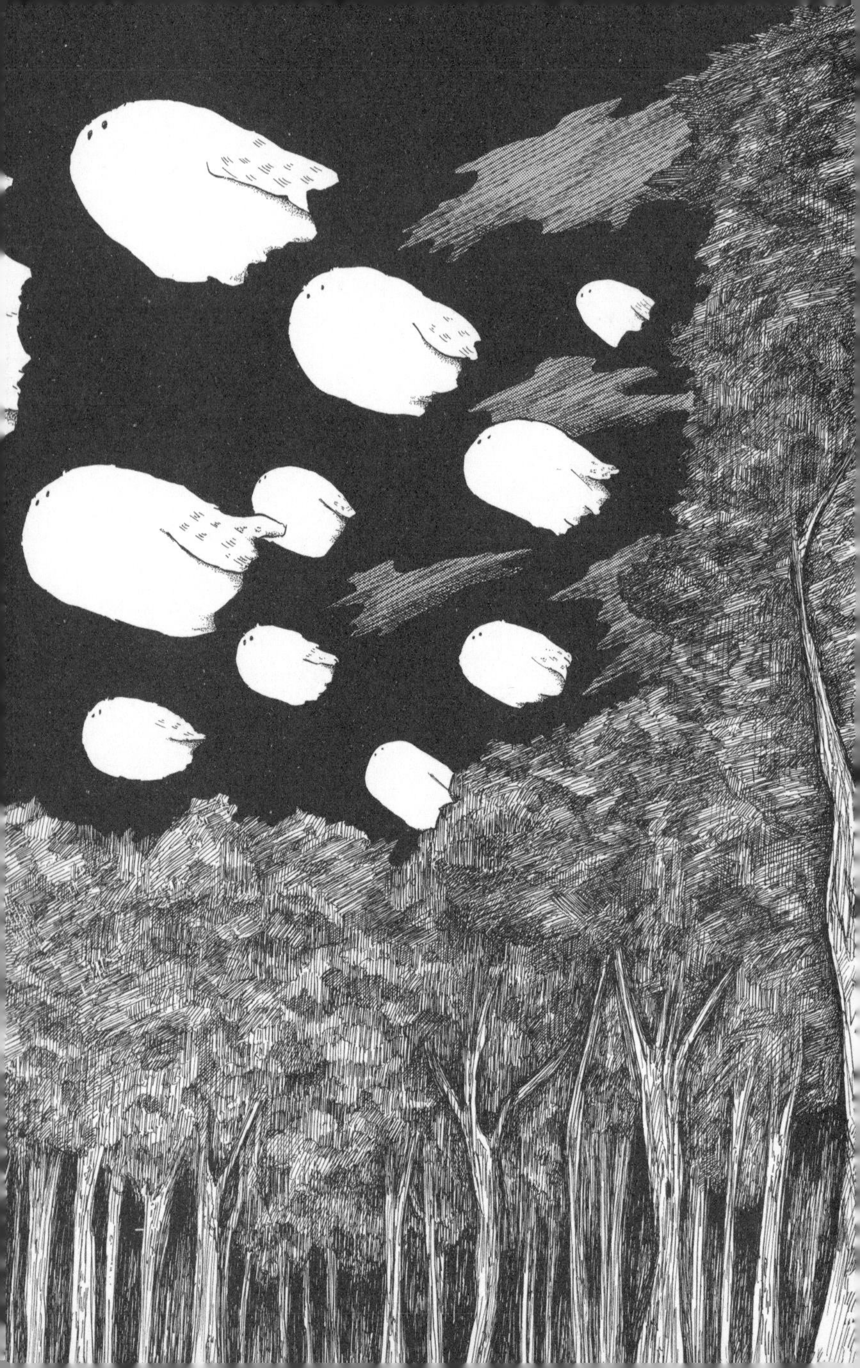

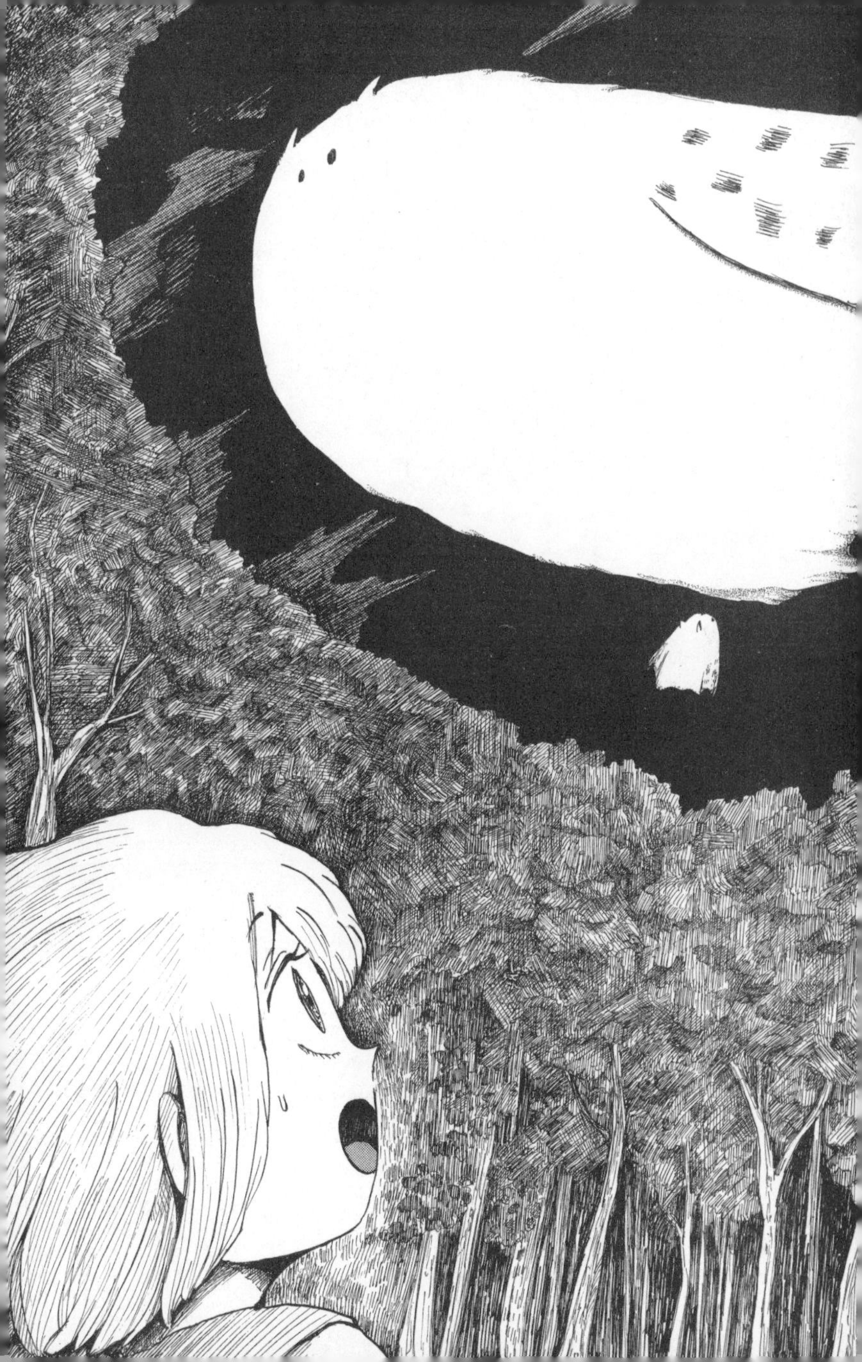

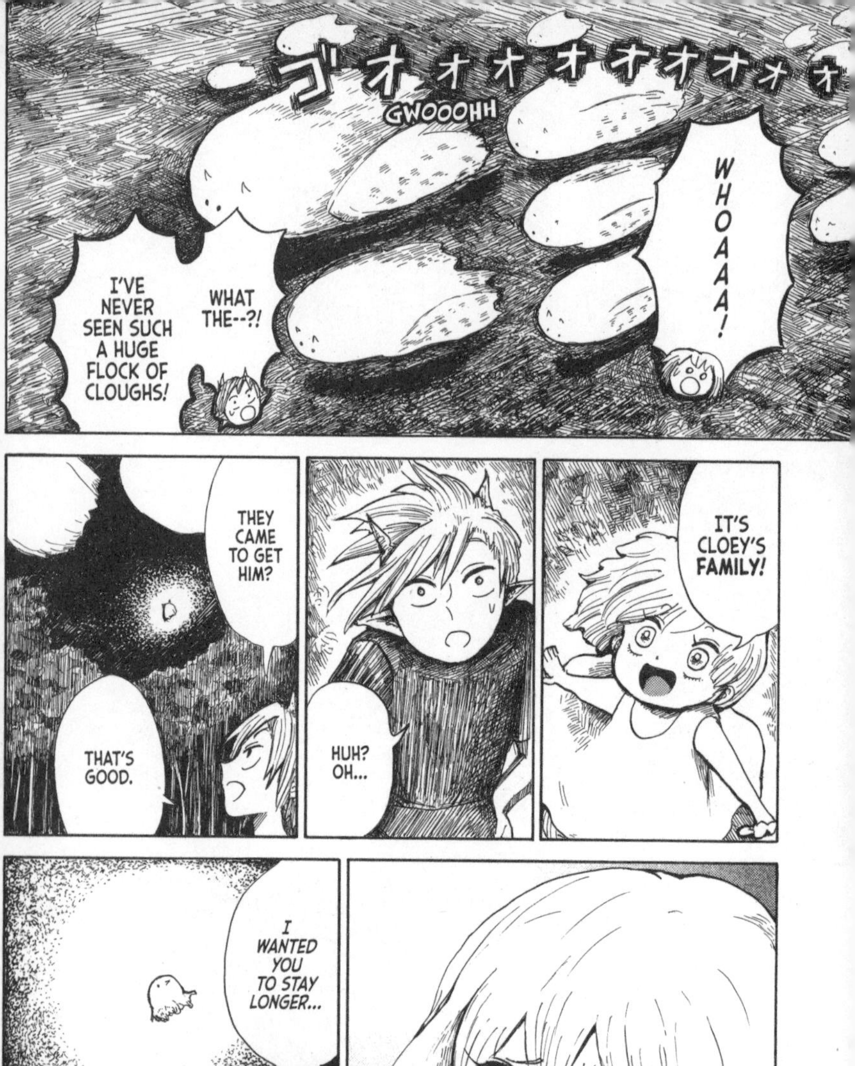
ゴオオオオオオオオオオ
GWOOOHH
WHOAAAA!
WHAT THE--?!
I'VE NEVER SEEN SUCH A HUGE FLOCK OF CLOUGHS!
IT'S CLOEY'S FAMILY!
HUH? OH...
THEY CAME TO GET HIM?
THAT'S GOOD.
I WANTED YOU TO STAY LONGER...
CLOEY.

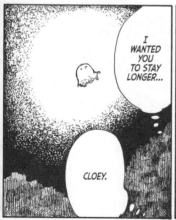

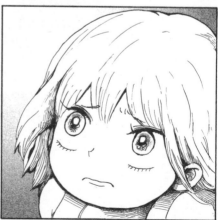

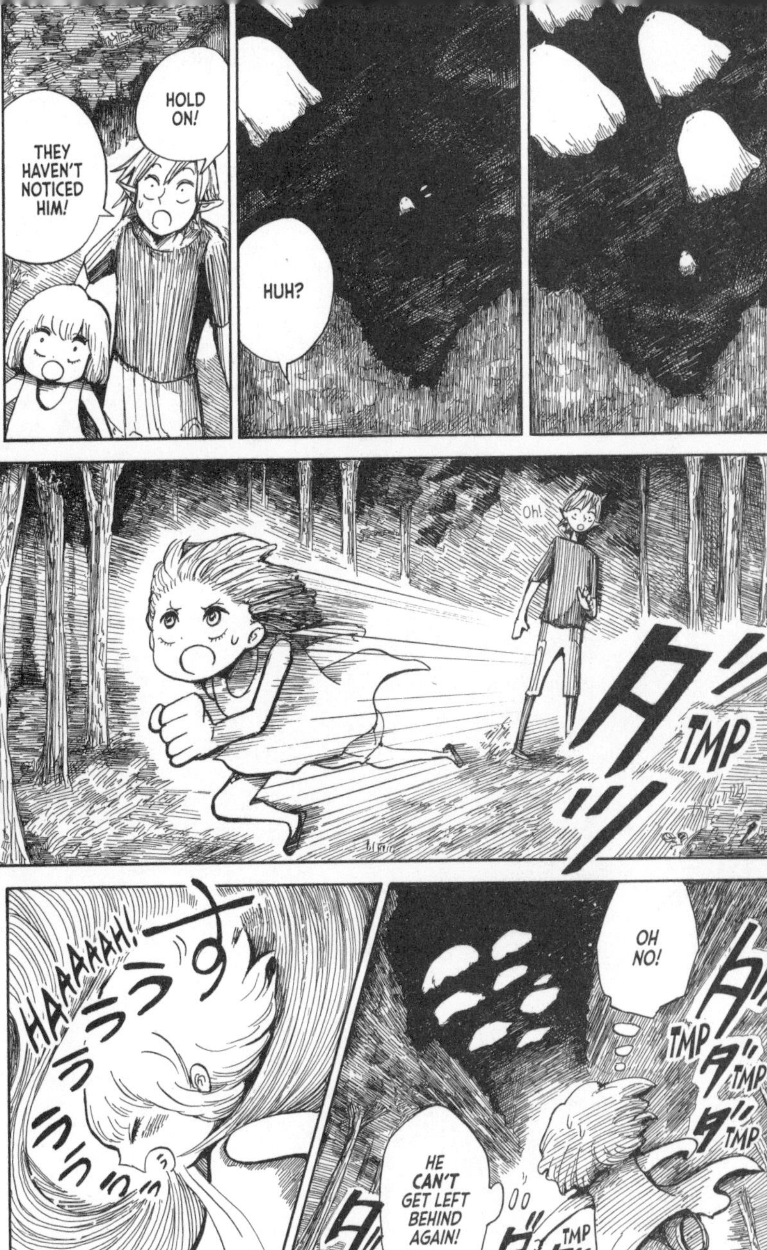
HUH?
HOLD ON!
THEY HAVEN'T NOTICED HIM!
Oh!
TMP
OH NO!
TMP
TMP
TMP
TMP
HE CAN'T GET LEFT BEHIND AGAIN!
TMP
TMP
TMP
HAAAAAH!

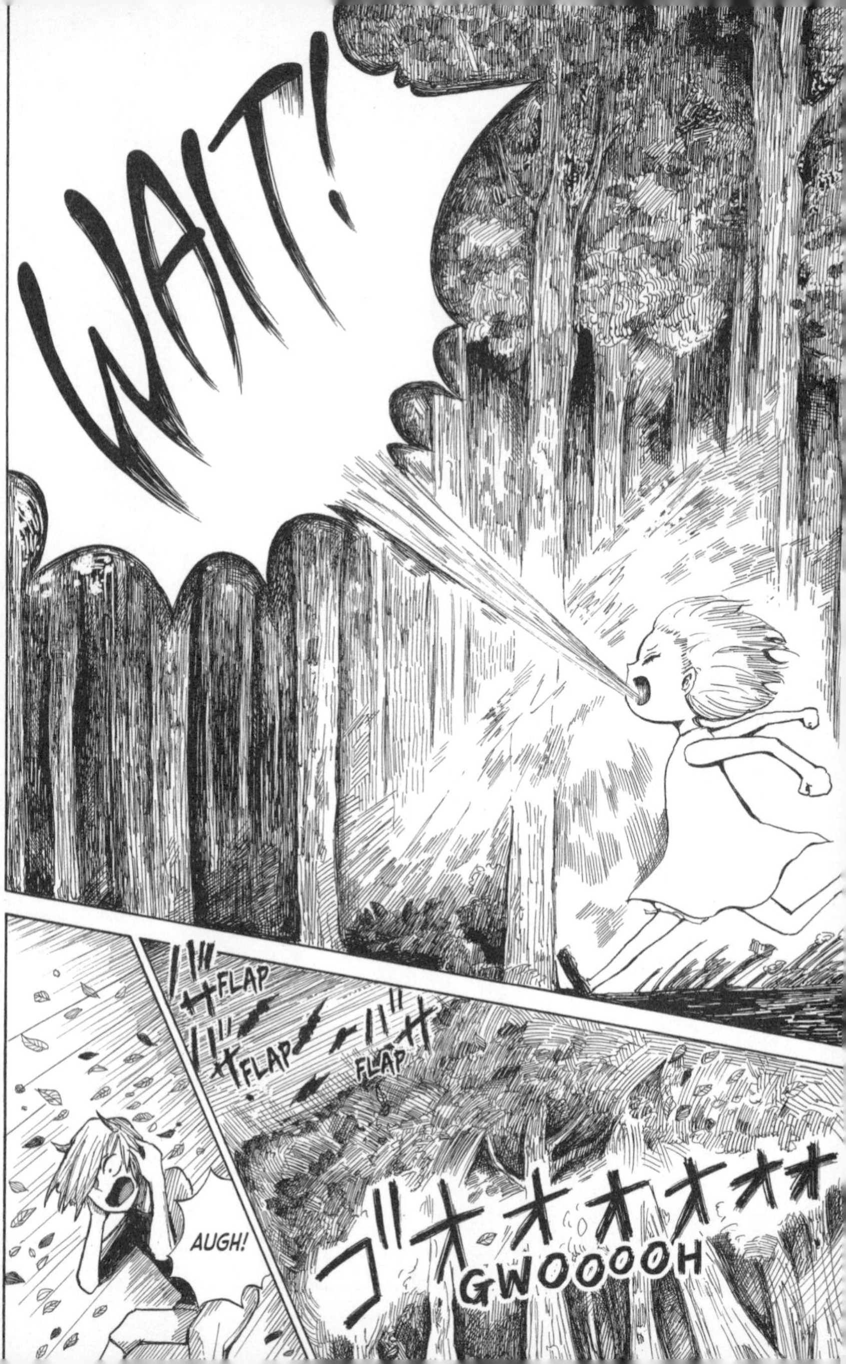
WAIT!
FLAP
FLAP
FLAP
ゴオオオオオ
GWOOOOH
AUGH!

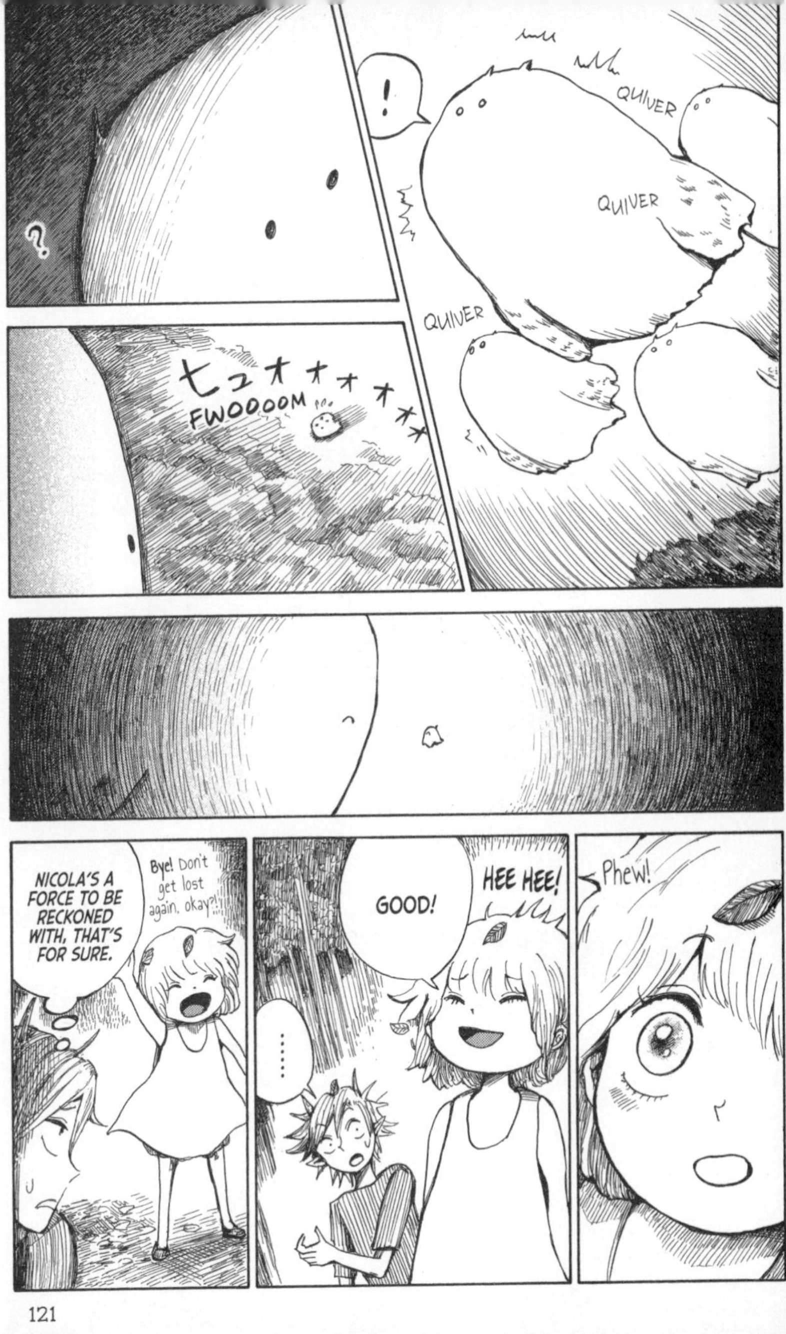

!
QUIVER
QUIVER
QUIVER
?
ヒュオォォォォォ
FWOOOOM
Phew!
HEE HEE!
GOOD!
......
Bye! Don't get lost again, okay?!
NICOLA'S A FORCE TO BE RECKONED WITH, THAT'S FOR SURE.

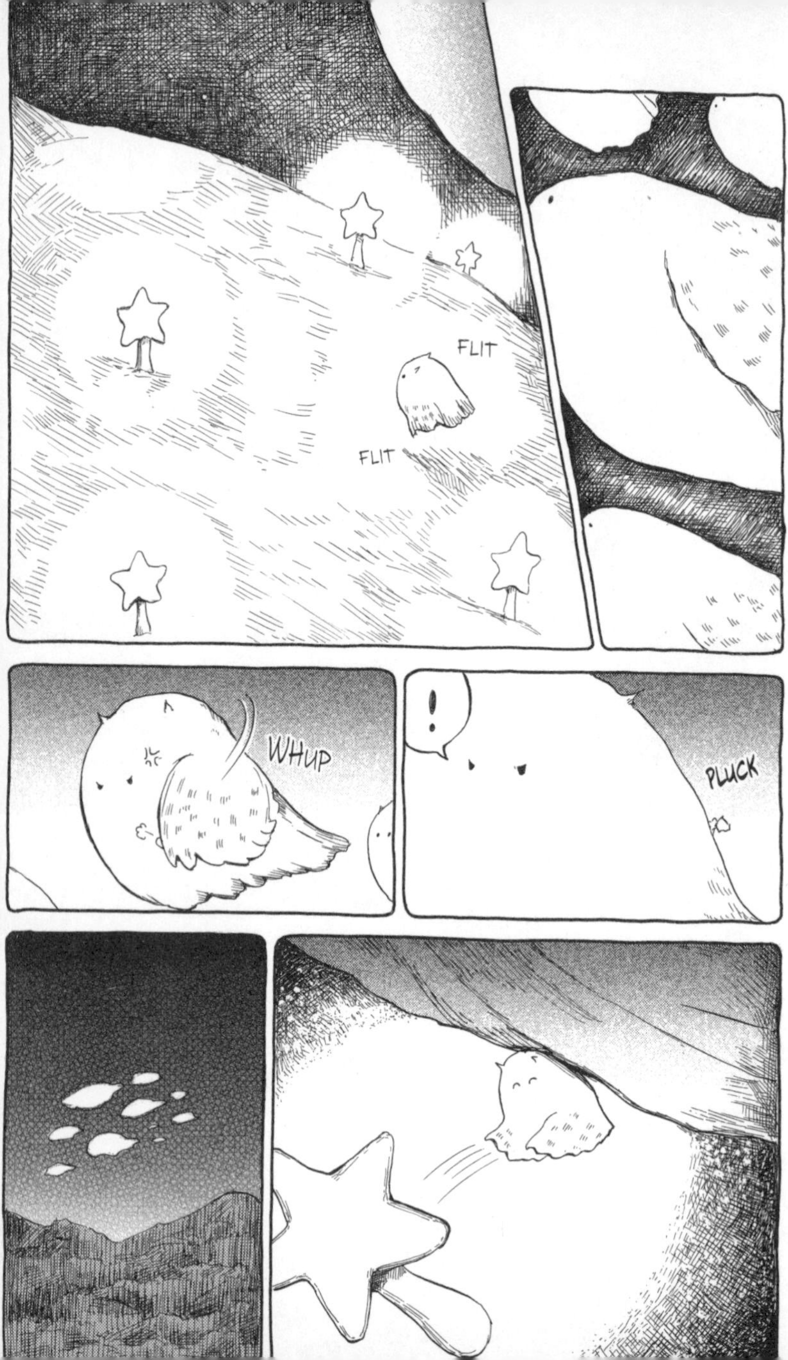
FLIT
FLIT
!
PLUCK
WHUP

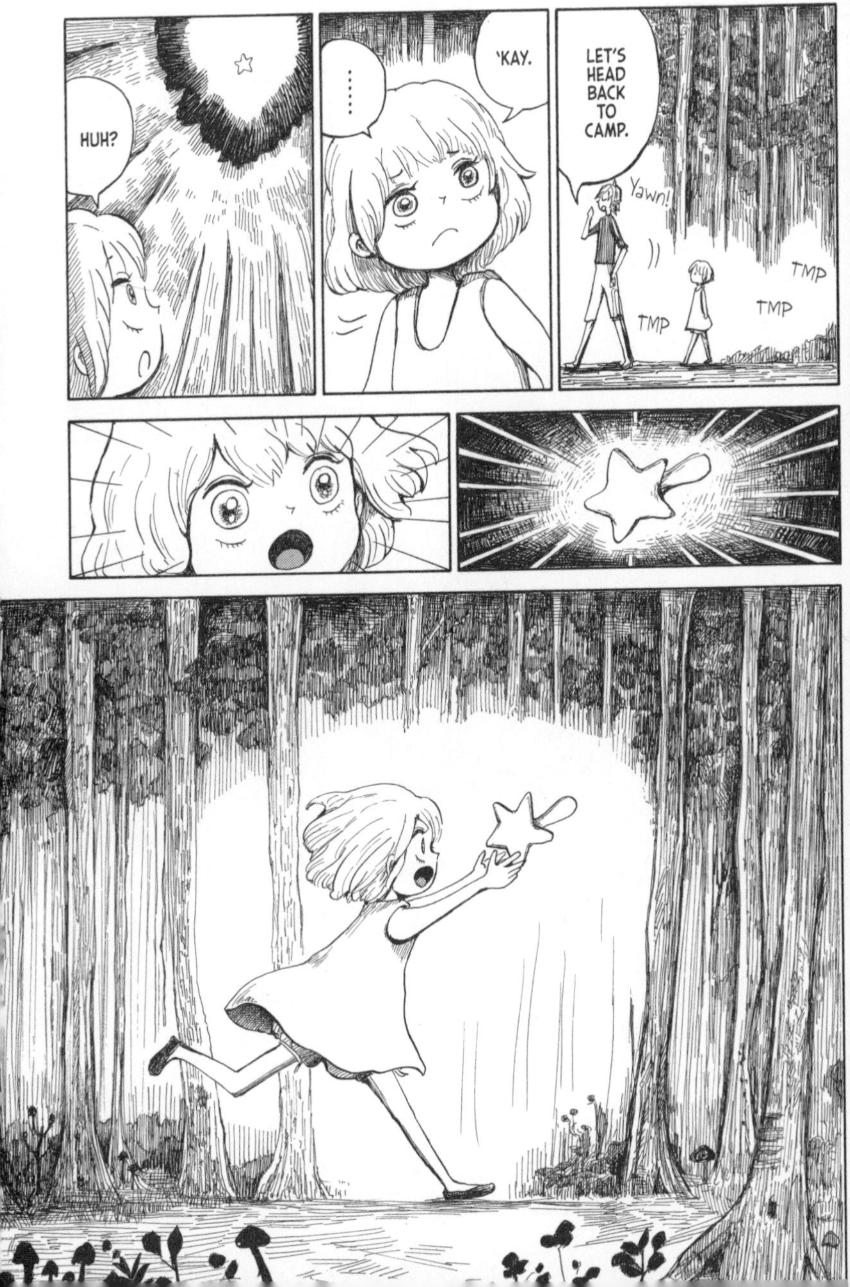
LET'S HEAD BACK TO CAMP.
Yawn!
TMP
TMP
TMP
'KAY.
......
HUH?

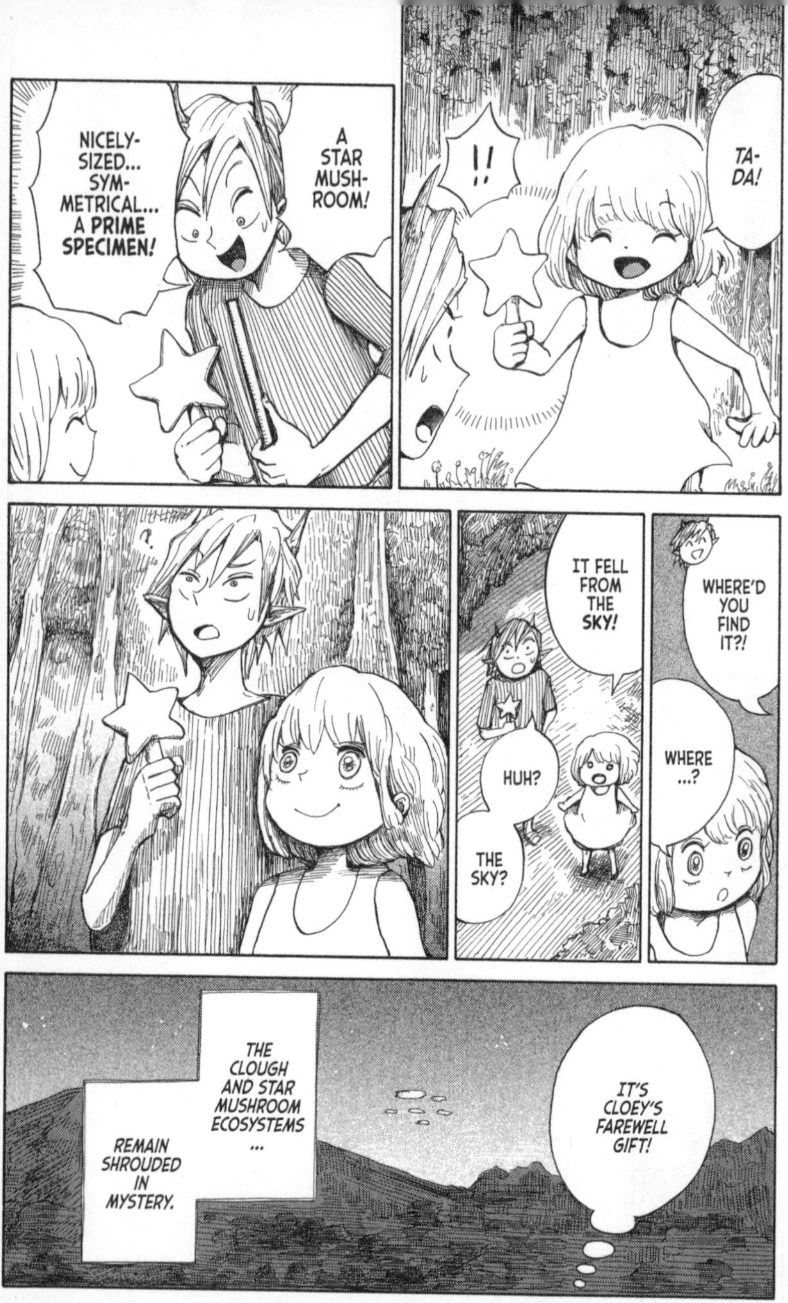
TA-DA!
!!
A STAR MUSH-ROOM!
NICELY-SIZED... SYM-METRICAL... A PRIME SPECIMEN!
WHERE'D YOU FIND IT?!
WHERE ...?
IT FELL FROM THE SKY!
HUH?
THE SKY?
?
IT'S CLOEY'S FAREWELL GIFT!
THE CLOUGH AND STAR MUSHROOM ECOSYSTEMS ...
REMAIN SHROUDED IN MYSTERY.

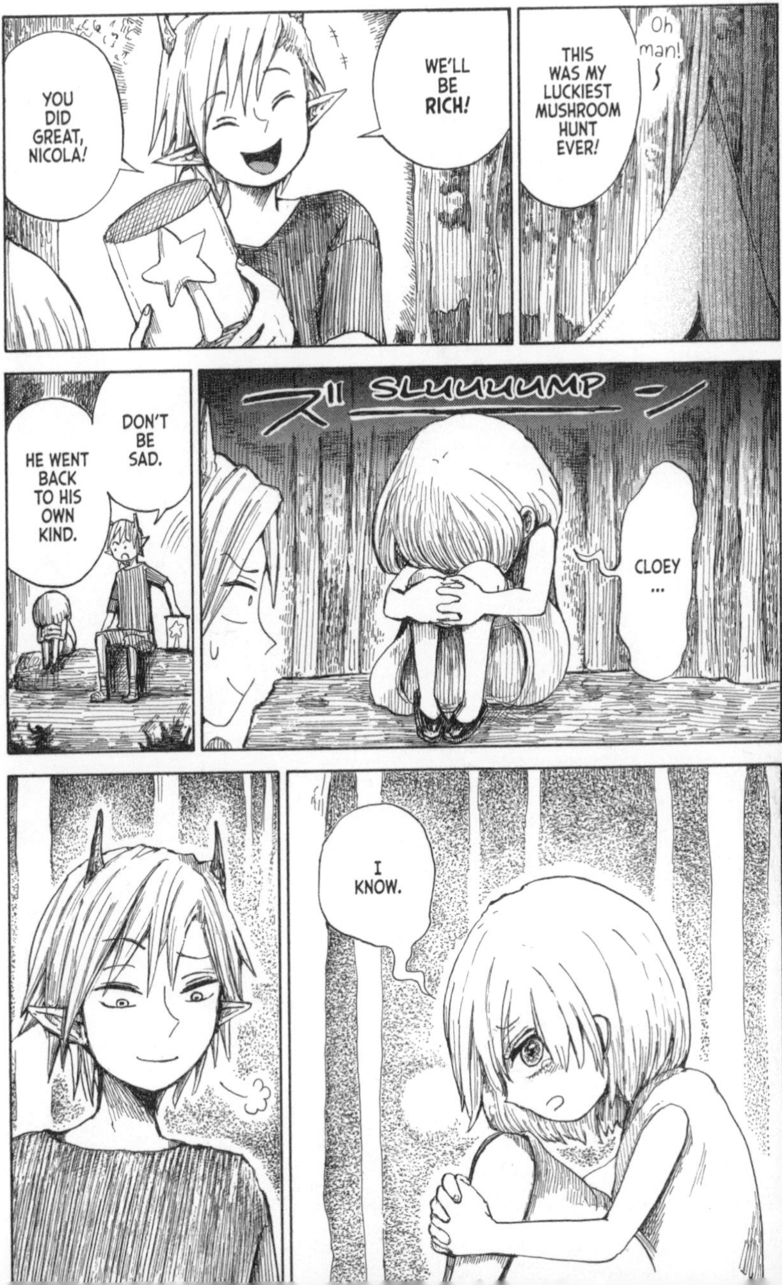
Oh man!
THIS WAS MY LUCKIEST MUSHROOM HUNT EVER!
WE'LL BE RICH!
YOU DID GREAT, NICOLA!
SLUUUUUMP
CLOEY ...
DON'T BE SAD.
HE WENT BACK TO HIS OWN KIND.
I KNOW.

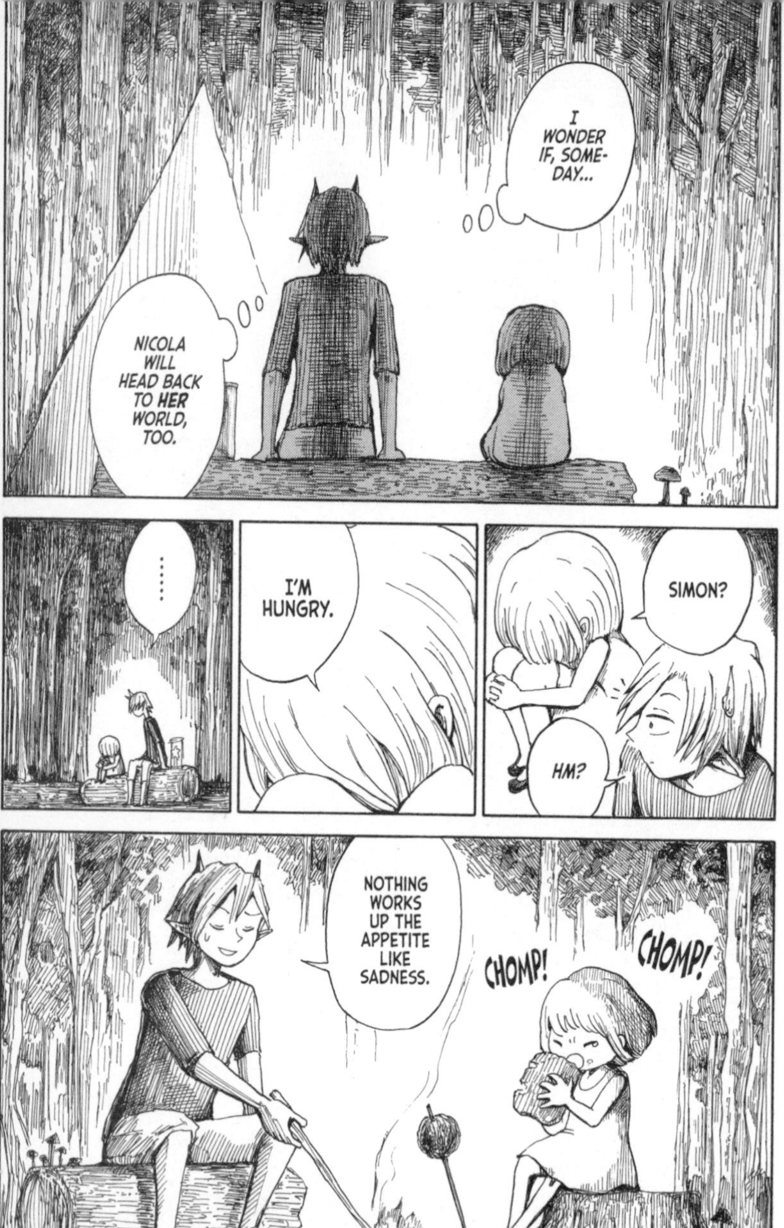
I WONDER IF, SOME-DAY...
NICOLA WILL HEAD BACK TO HER WORLD, TOO.
SIMON?
HM?
I'M HUNGRY.
......
NOTHING WORKS UP THE APPETITE LIKE SADNESS.
CHOMP!
CHOMP!

Chapter 4 END

After the Visit 4

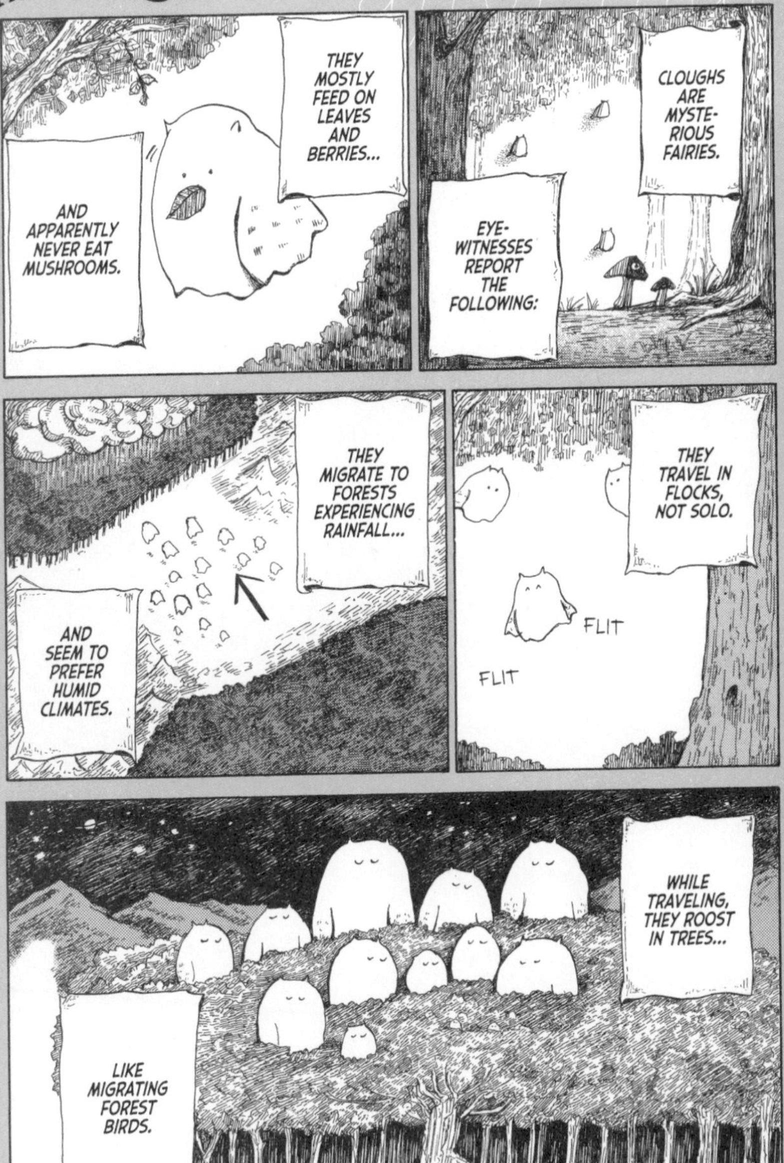
after that
CLOUGHS ARE MYSTERIOUS FAIRIES.
EYE-WITNESSES REPORT THE FOLLOWING:
THEY MOSTLY FEED ON LEAVES AND BERRIES...
AND APPARENTLY NEVER EAT MUSHROOMS.
THEY TRAVEL IN FLOCKS, NOT SOLO.
FLIT
FLIT
THEY MIGRATE TO FORESTS EXPERIENCING RAINFALL...
AND SEEM TO PREFER HUMID CLIMATES.
WHILE TRAVELING, THEY ROOST IN TREES...
LIKE MIGRATING FOREST BIRDS.
EXCERPTS FROM A REPORT ON CLOUGHS

Nicola Traveling Around the Demon's World

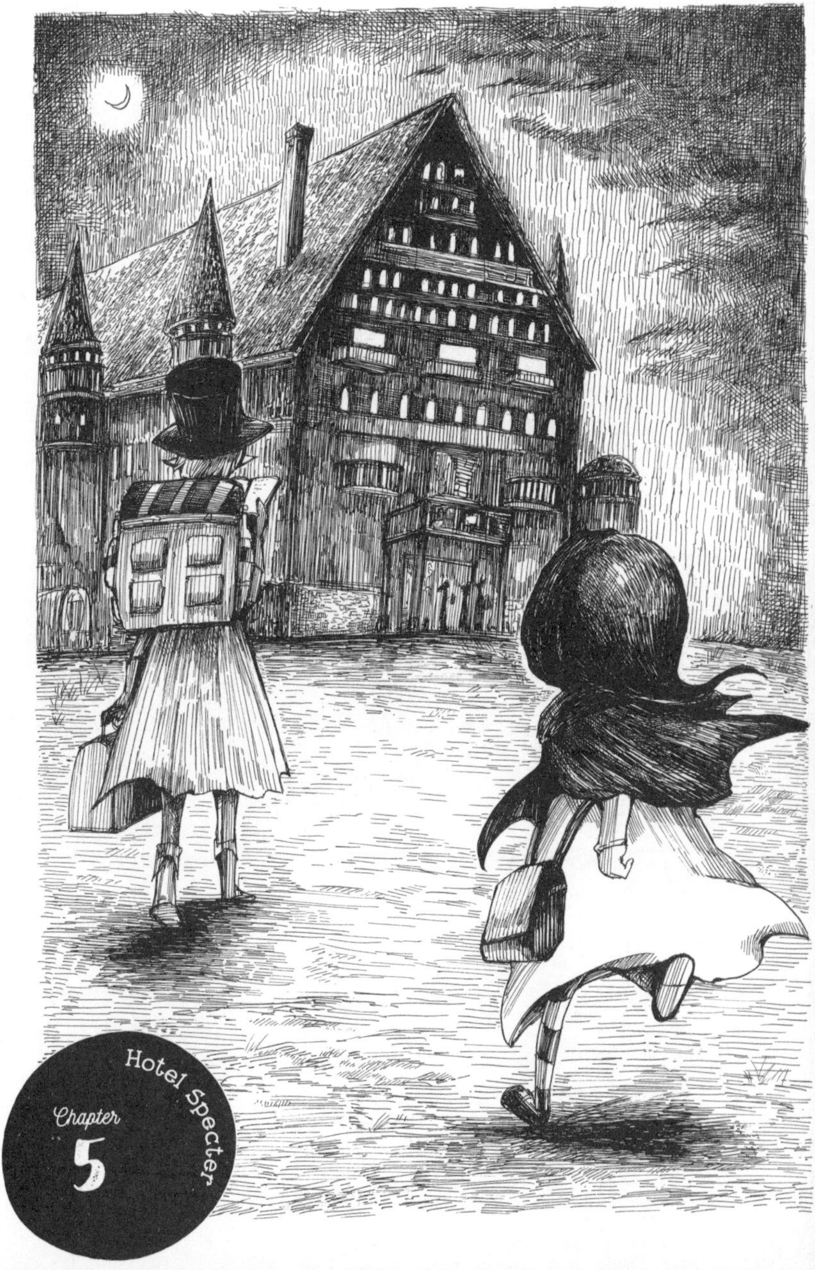
Chapter
5
Hotel Specter

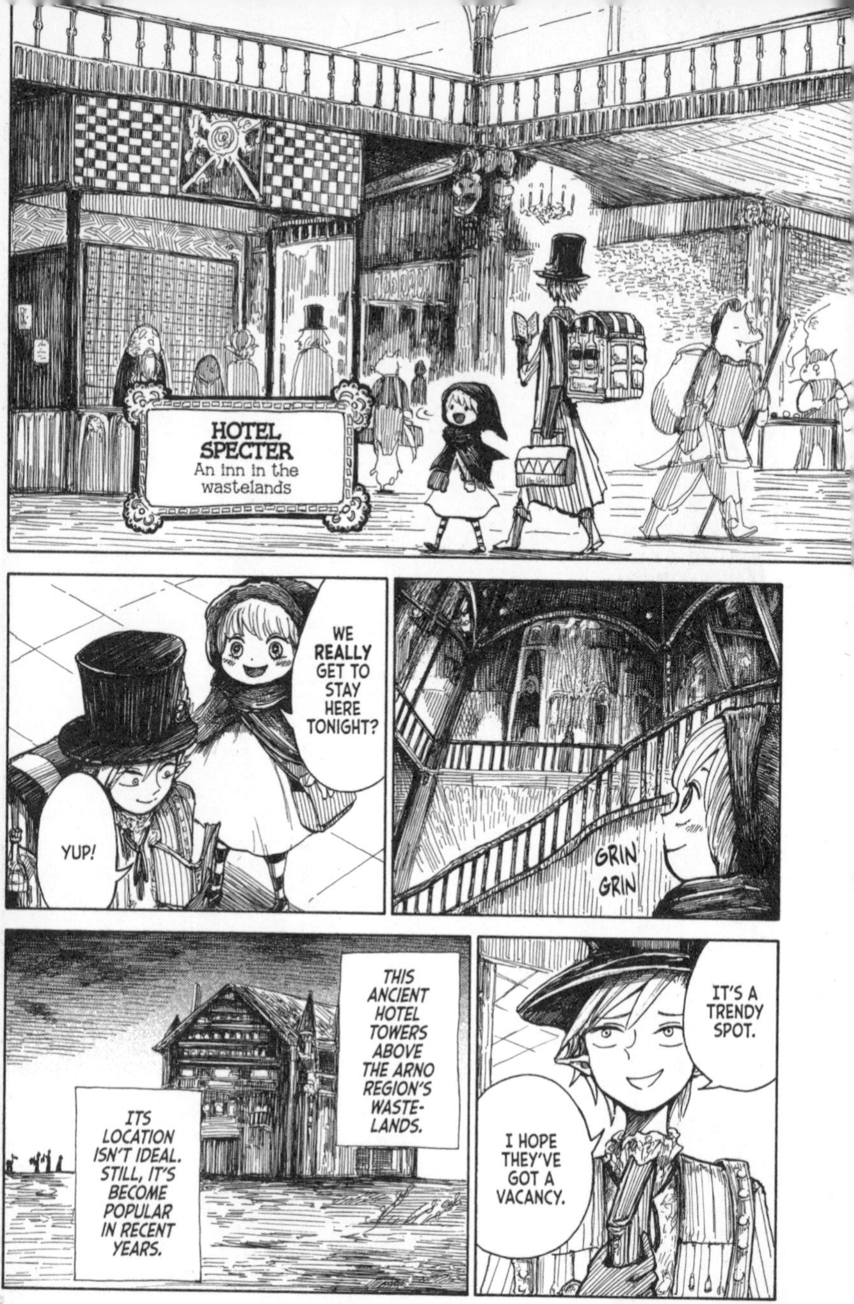
HOTEL SPECTER
An inn in the wastelands
GRIN GRIN
WE REALLY GET TO STAY HERE TONIGHT?
YUP!
IT'S A TRENDY SPOT.
I HOPE THEY'VE GOT A VACANCY.
THIS ANCIENT HOTEL TOWERS ABOVE THE ARNO REGION'S WASTE-LANDS.
ITS LOCATION ISN'T IDEAL. STILL, IT'S BECOME POPULAR IN RECENT YEARS.

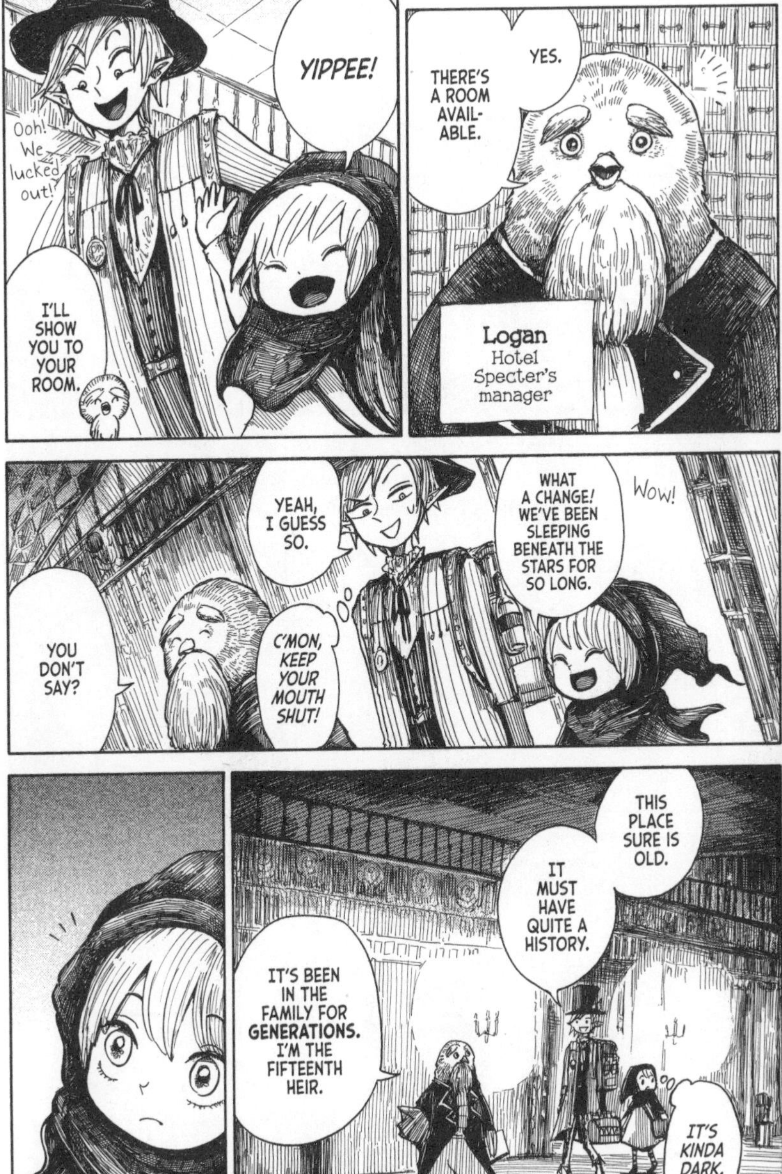
YES.
THERE'S A ROOM AVAIL-ABLE.
Logan Hotel Specter's manager
YIPPEE!
Ooh! We lucked out!
I'LL SHOW YOU TO YOUR ROOM.
Wow!
WHAT A CHANGE! WE'VE BEEN SLEEPING BENEATH THE STARS FOR SO LONG.
YEAH, I GUESS SO.
C'MON, KEEP YOUR MOUTH SHUT!
YOU DON'T SAY?
THIS PLACE SURE IS OLD.
IT MUST HAVE QUITE A HISTORY.
IT'S BEEN IN THE FAMILY FOR GENERATIONS. I'M THE FIFTEENTH HEIR.
IT'S KINDA DARK.

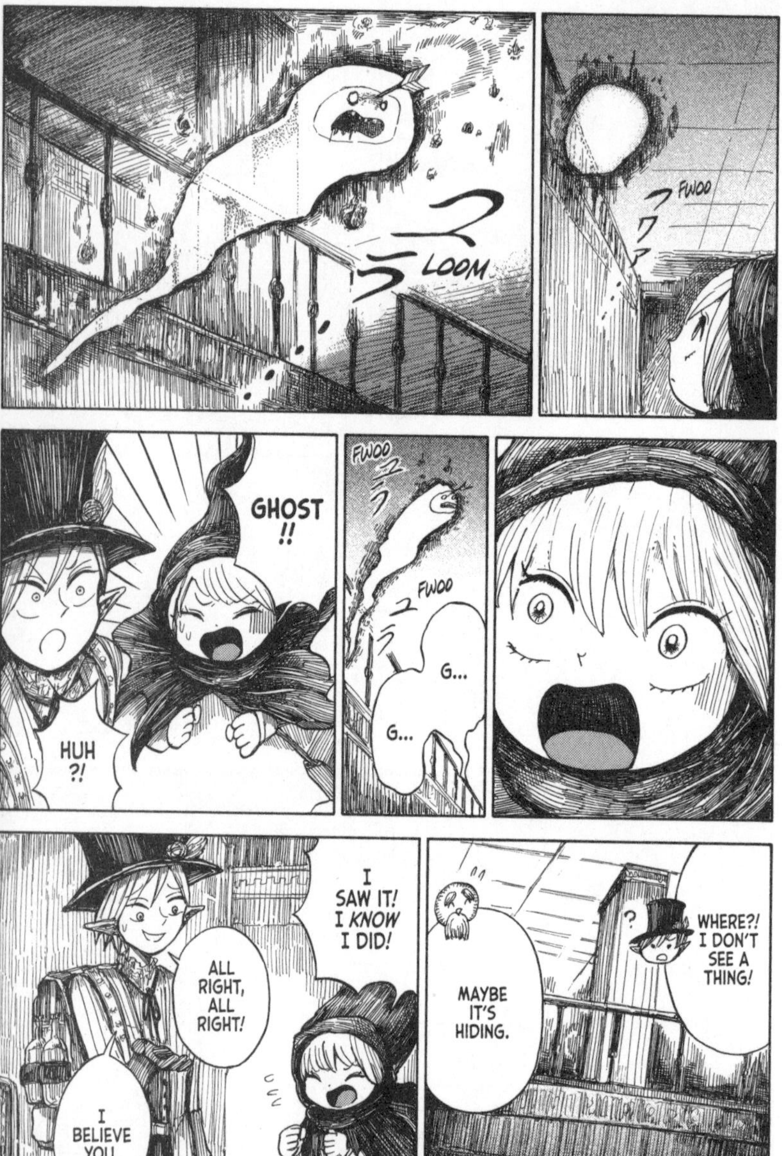
FWOO
LOOM
FWOO
FWOO
G...
G...
GHOST !!
HUH ?!
WHERE?! I DON'T SEE A THING!
MAYBE IT'S HIDING.
I SAW IT! I *KNOW* I DID!
ALL RIGHT, ALL RIGHT!
I BELIEVE YOU.

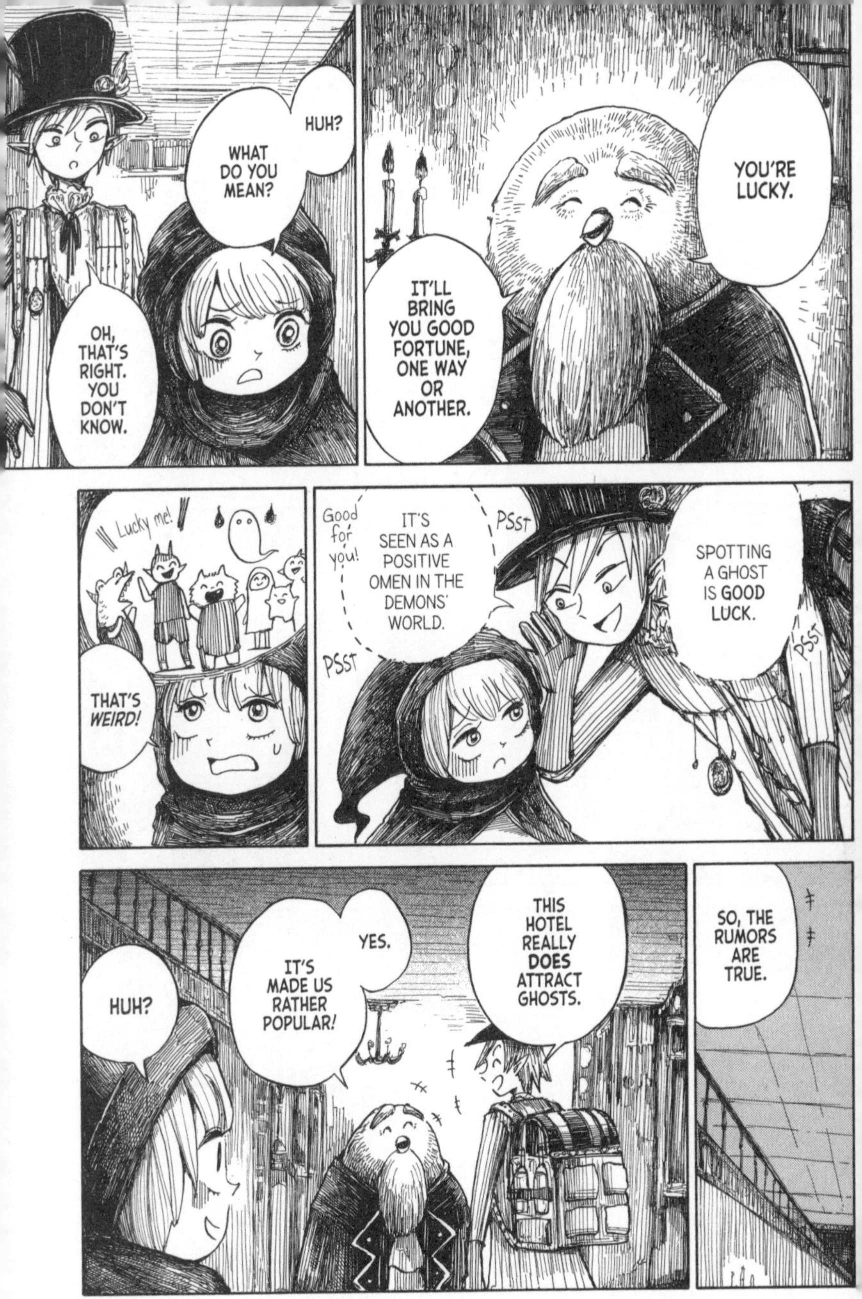
YOU'RE LUCKY.
IT'LL BRING YOU GOOD FORTUNE, ONE WAY OR ANOTHER.
HUH?
WHAT DO YOU MEAN?
OH, THAT'S RIGHT. YOU DON'T KNOW.
SPOTTING A GHOST IS **GOOD** LUCK.
PSST
PSST
IT'S SEEN AS A POSITIVE OMEN IN THE DEMONS' WORLD.
Good for you!
PSST
Lucky me!
THAT'S *WEIRD!*
SO, THE RUMORS ARE TRUE.
THIS HOTEL REALLY **DOES** ATTRACT GHOSTS.
YES.
IT'S MADE US RATHER POPULAR!
HUH?

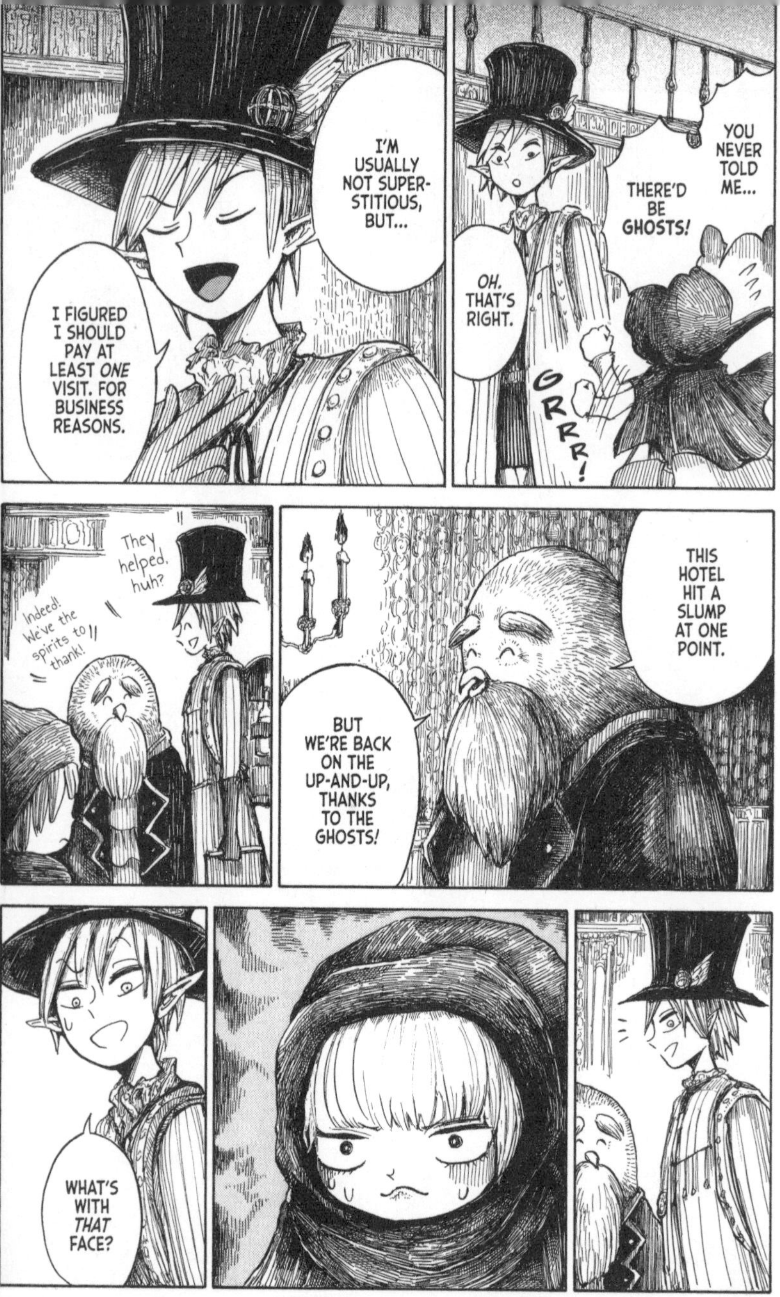
YOU NEVER TOLD ME...
THERE'D BE *GHOSTS!*
OH. THAT'S RIGHT.
GRRR!
I'M USUALLY NOT SUPER-STITIOUS, BUT...
I FIGURED I SHOULD PAY AT LEAST *ONE* VISIT. FOR BUSINESS REASONS.
THIS HOTEL HIT A SLUMP AT ONE POINT.
BUT WE'RE BACK ON THE UP-AND-UP, THANKS TO THE GHOSTS!
They helped, huh?
Indeed! We've the spirits to thank!
WHAT'S WITH *THAT* FACE?

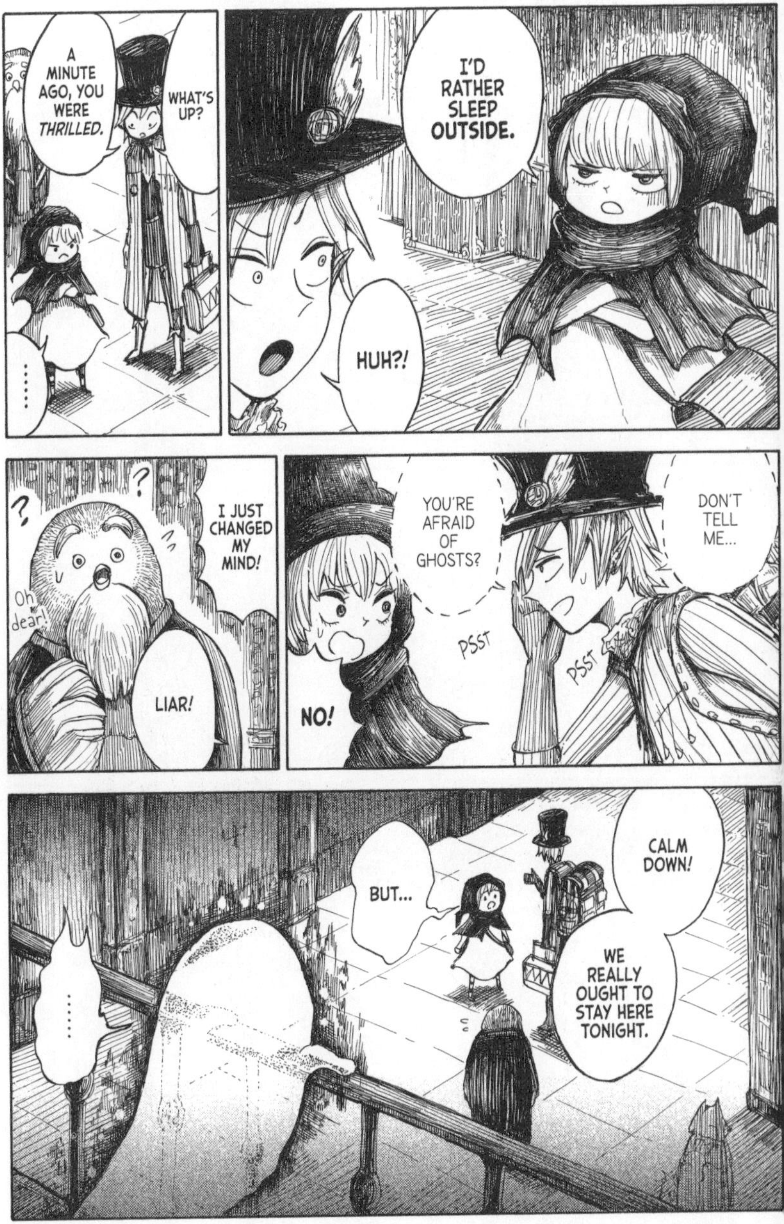
I'D RATHER SLEEP OUTSIDE.
HUH?!
WHAT'S UP?
A MINUTE AGO, YOU WERE *THRILLED.*
......
DON'T TELL ME...
YOU'RE AFRAID OF GHOSTS?
PSST
PSST
NO!
I JUST CHANGED MY MIND!
Oh dear!
LIAR!
CALM DOWN!
WE REALLY OUGHT TO STAY HERE TONIGHT.
BUT...
......

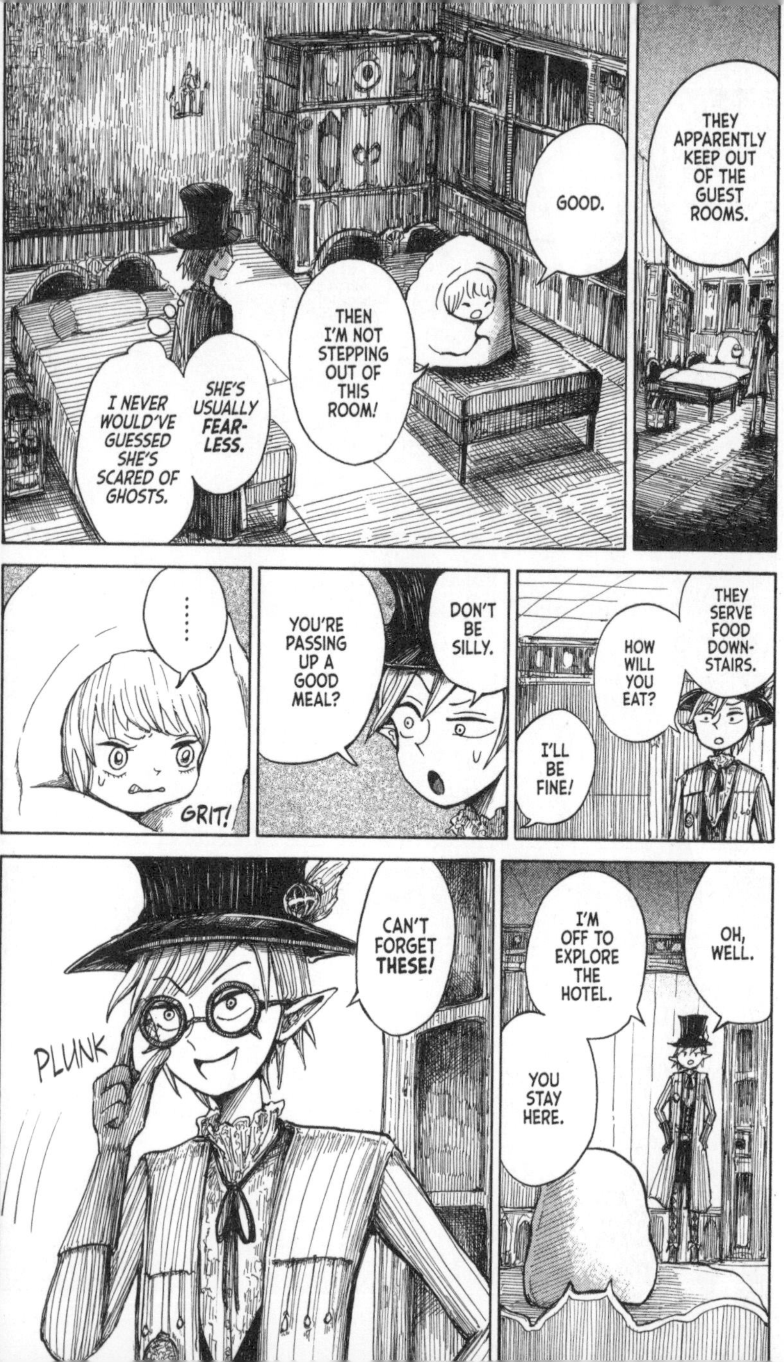
THEY APPARENTLY KEEP OUT OF THE GUEST ROOMS.
GOOD.
THEN I'M NOT STEPPING OUT OF THIS ROOM!
SHE'S USUALLY FEAR-LESS.
I NEVER WOULD'VE GUESSED SHE'S SCARED OF GHOSTS.
THEY SERVE FOOD DOWN-STAIRS.
HOW WILL YOU EAT?
I'LL BE FINE!
DON'T BE SILLY.
YOU'RE PASSING UP A GOOD MEAL?
......
GRIT!
OH, WELL.
I'M OFF TO EXPLORE THE HOTEL.
YOU STAY HERE.
CAN'T FORGET THESE!
PLUNK

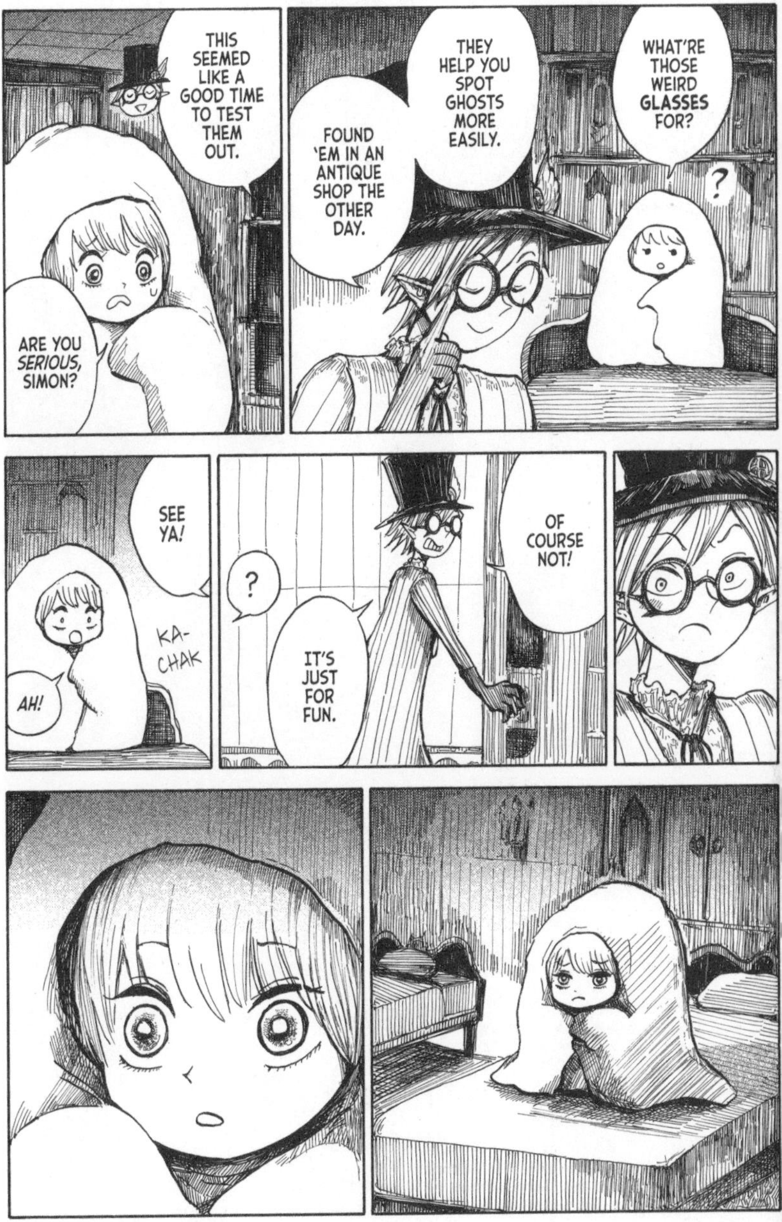
WHAT'RE THOSE WEIRD GLASSES FOR?
?
THEY HELP YOU SPOT GHOSTS MORE EASILY.
FOUND 'EM IN AN ANTIQUE SHOP THE OTHER DAY.
THIS SEEMED LIKE A GOOD TIME TO TEST THEM OUT.
ARE YOU *SERIOUS*, SIMON?
OF COURSE NOT!
?
IT'S JUST FOR FUN.
SEE YA!
KA-CHAK
AH!

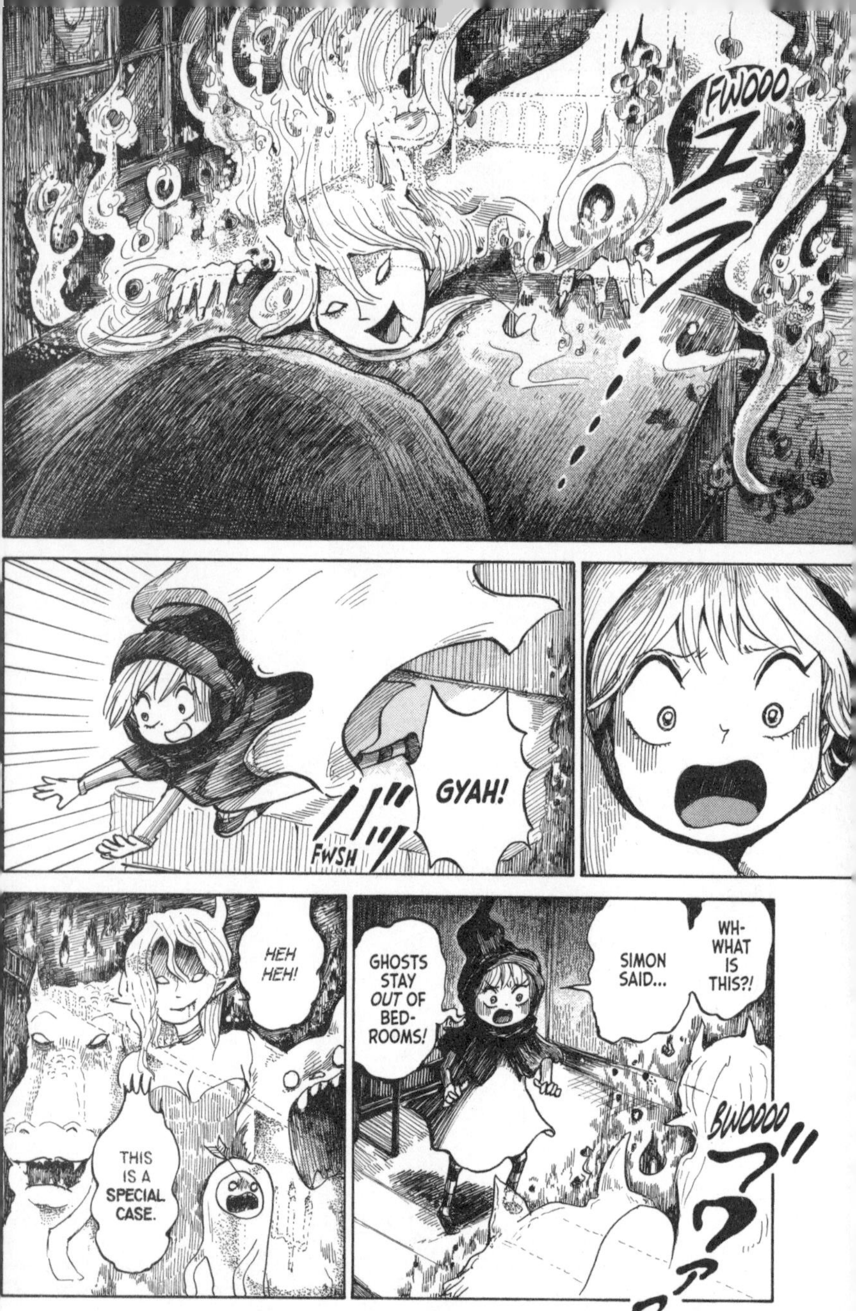
FWOOO
GYAH!
FWSH
WH-WHAT IS THIS?!
SIMON SAID...
GHOSTS STAY OUT OF BED-ROOMS!
BWOOOO
HEH HEH!
THIS IS A SPECIAL CASE.

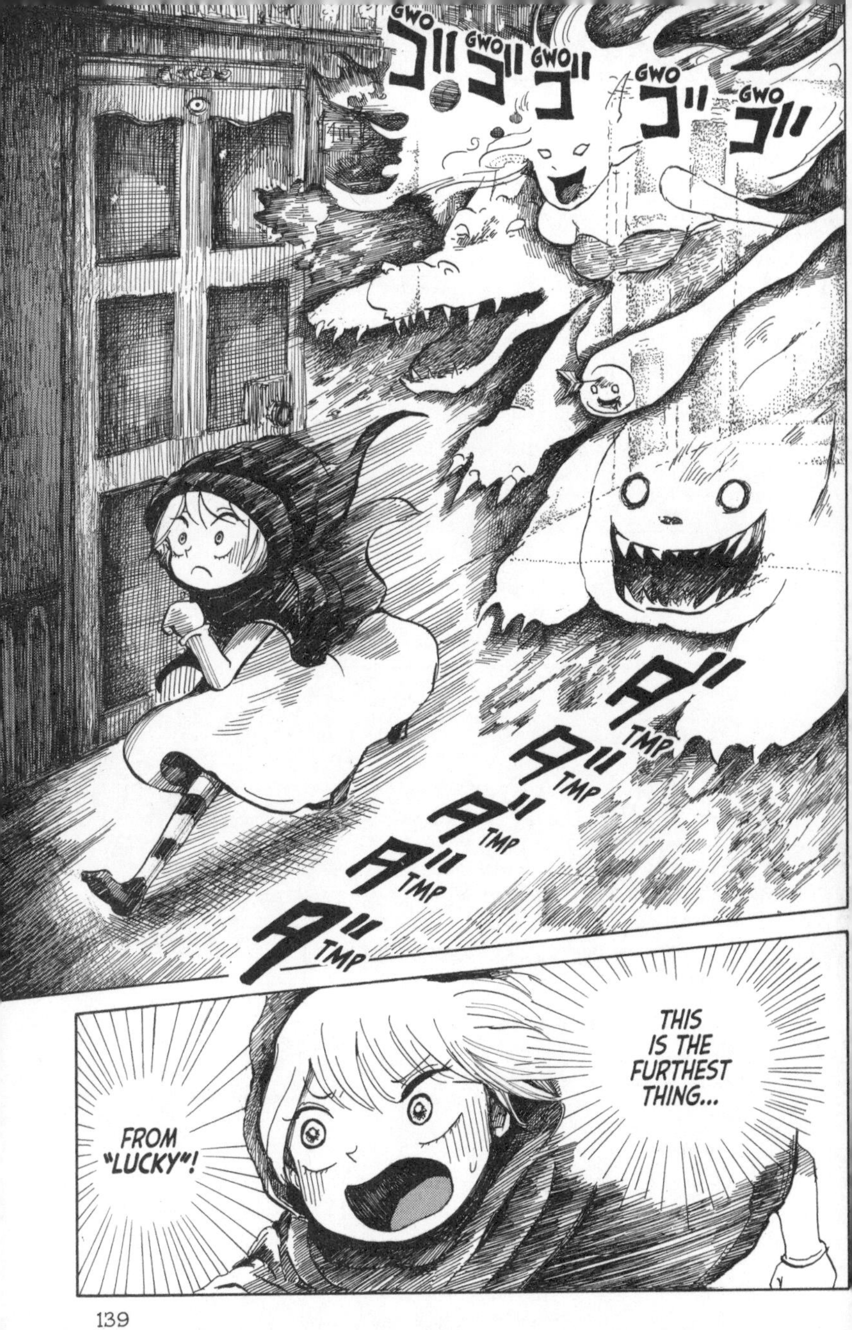
GWO ゴ"
GWO ゴ"
GWO ゴ"
GWO ゴ"
GWO ゴ"
ダ" TMP
ダ" TMP
ダ" TMP
ダ" TMP
ダ" TMP
THIS IS THE FURTHEST THING...
FROM "LUCKY"!

GWO GWO GWO GWO GWO GWO

OOH!

SHE SURE LUCKED OUT!

WOW!

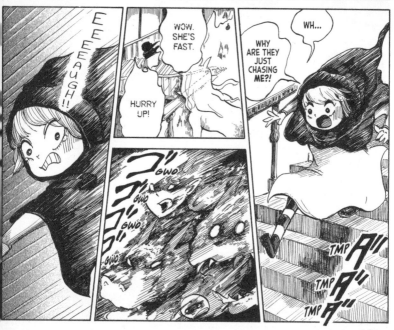

EEEEAUGH!!

WOW. SHE'S FAST.

HURRY UP!

WH...

WHY ARE THEY JUST CHASING ME?!

GWO GWO GWO GWO

TMP TMP TMP

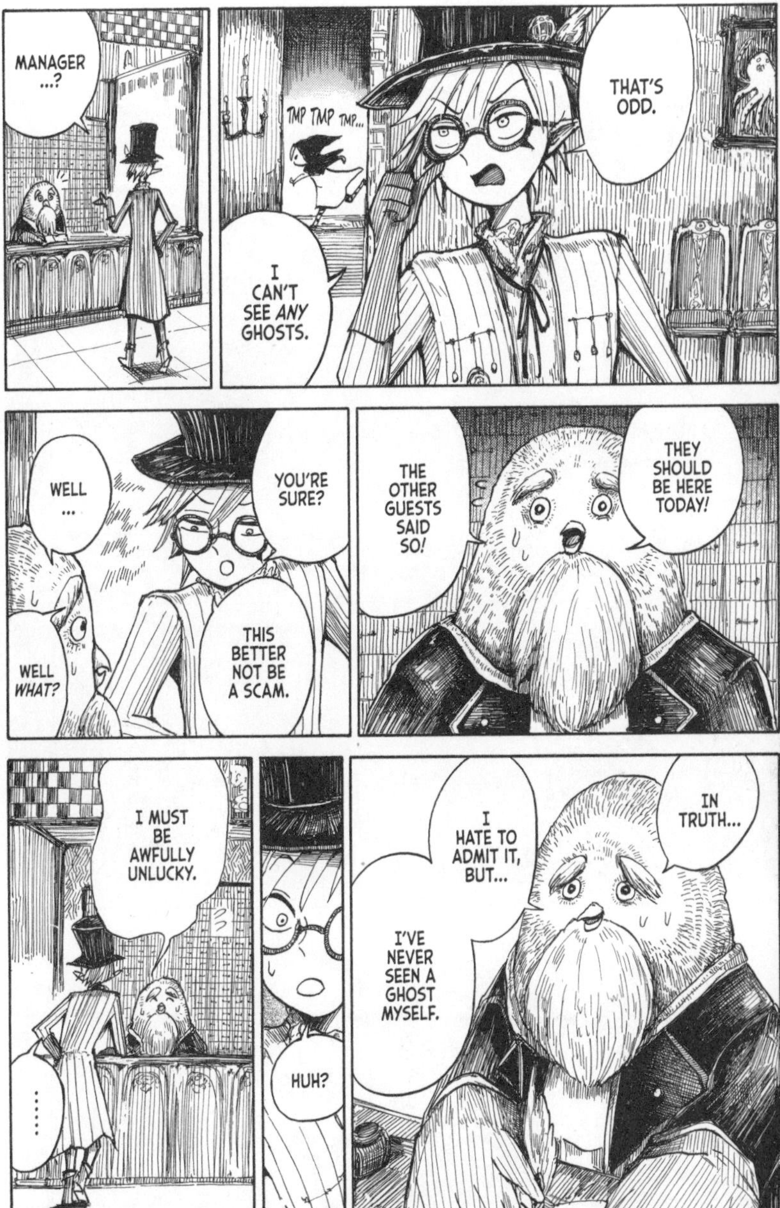
THAT'S ODD.
TMP TMP TMP...
I CAN'T SEE *ANY* GHOSTS.
MANAGER ...?
THEY SHOULD BE HERE TODAY!
THE OTHER GUESTS SAID SO!
YOU'RE SURE?
THIS BETTER NOT BE A SCAM.
WELL ...
WELL *WHAT?*
IN TRUTH...
I HATE TO ADMIT IT, BUT...
I'VE NEVER SEEN A GHOST MYSELF.
HUH?
I MUST BE AWFULLY UNLUCKY.
......

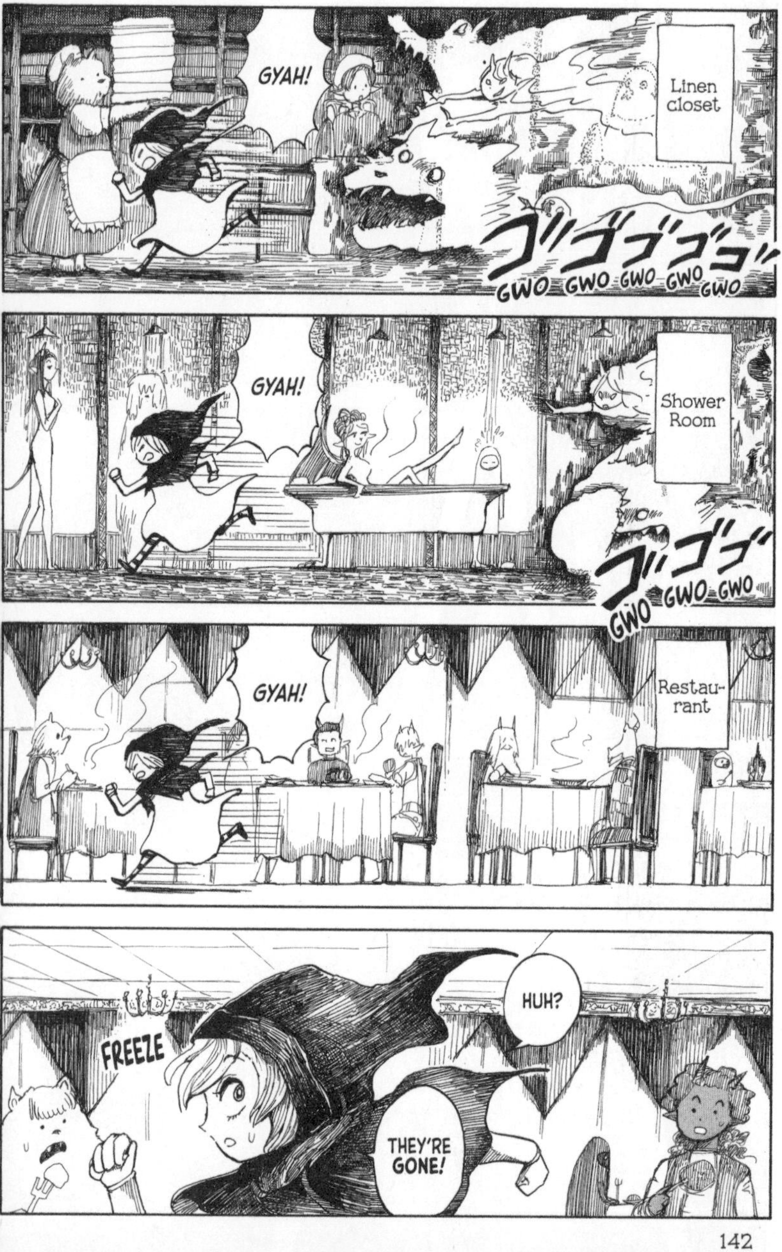
Linen closet
GYAH!
ゴゴゴゴゴ
GWO GWO GWO GWO GWO
Shower Room
GYAH!
ゴゴゴ
GWO GWO GWO
Restau-rant
GYAH!
HUH?
THEY'RE GONE!
FREEZE

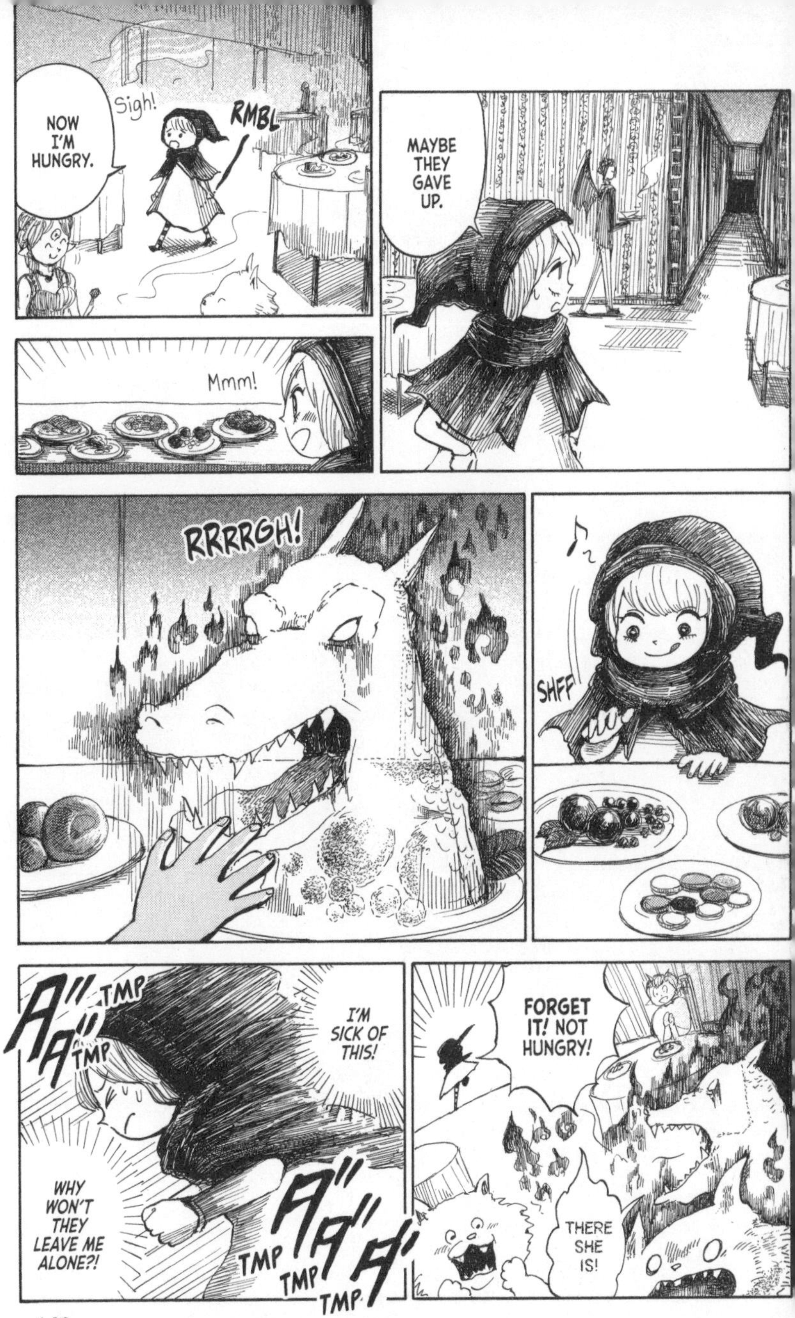
MAYBE THEY GAVE UP.
NOW I'M HUNGRY.
Sigh!
RMBL
Mmm!
SHFF
RRRRGH!
FORGET IT! NOT HUNGRY!
THERE SHE IS!
I'M SICK OF THIS!
TMP
TMP
WHY WON'T THEY LEAVE ME ALONE?!
TMP
TMP
TMP

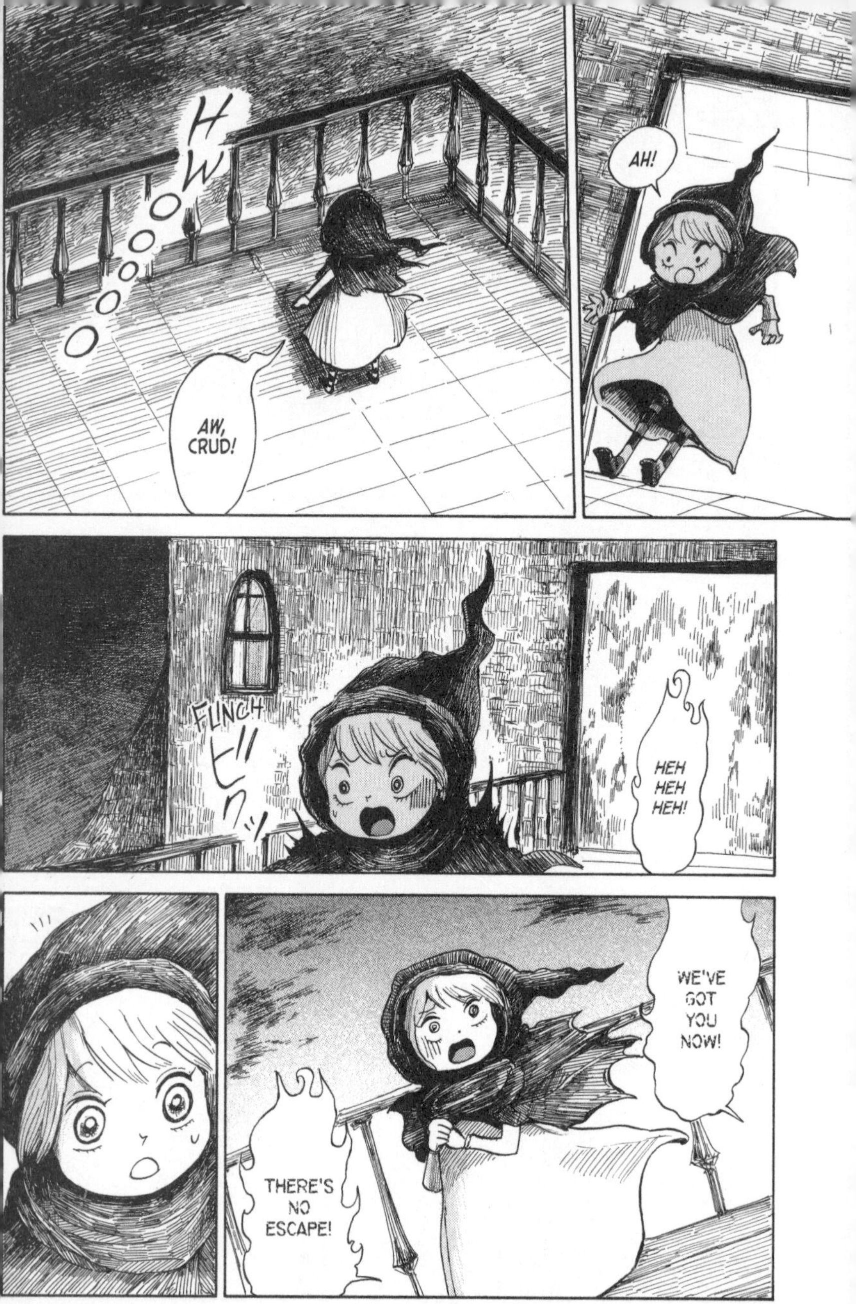
AH!
HWOOOOOOO
AW, CRUD!
HEH HEH HEH!
FLINCH
ビクッ
WE'VE GOT YOU NOW!
THERE'S NO ESCAPE!

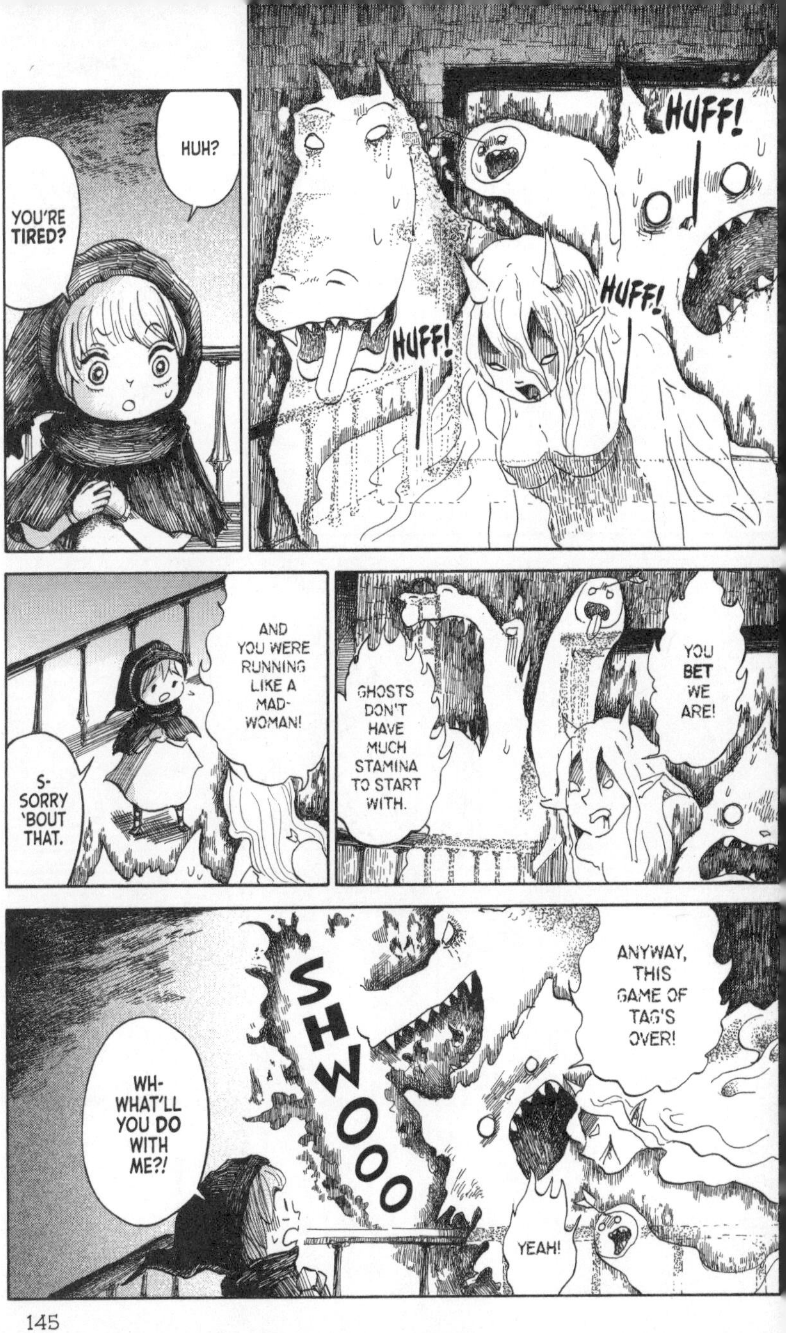
HUFF!
HUFF!
HUFF!
HUH?
YOU'RE TIRED?
YOU BET WE ARE!
GHOSTS DON'T HAVE MUCH STAMINA TO START WITH.
AND YOU WERE RUNNING LIKE A MAD-WOMAN!
S-SORRY 'BOUT THAT.
ANYWAY, THIS GAME OF TAG'S OVER!
SHWOOO
YEAH!
WH-WHAT'LL YOU DO WITH ME?!

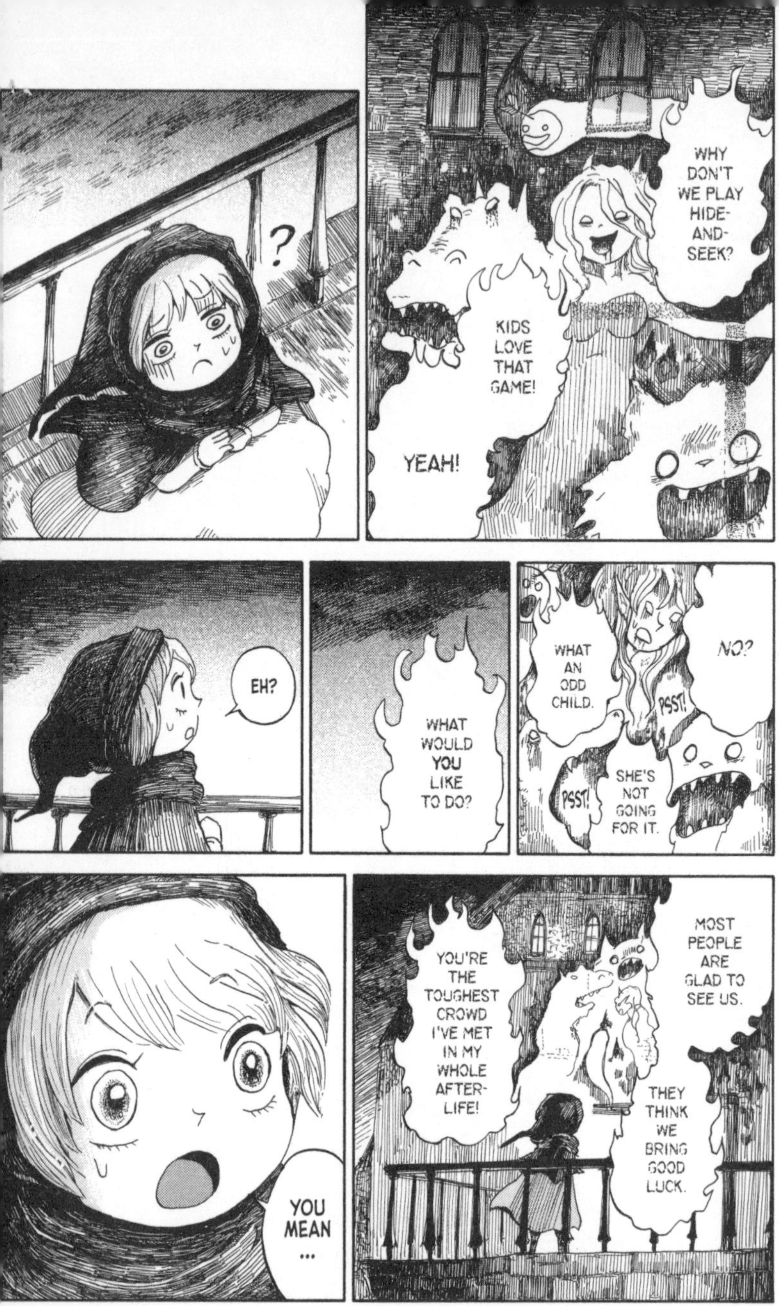
WHY DON'T WE PLAY HIDE-AND-SEEK?
KIDS LOVE THAT GAME!
YEAH!
?
NO?
WHAT AN ODD CHILD.
PSST!
SHE'S NOT GOING FOR IT.
PSST!
WHAT WOULD YOU LIKE TO DO?
EH?
MOST PEOPLE ARE GLAD TO SEE US.
YOU'RE THE TOUGHEST CROWD I'VE MET IN MY WHOLE AFTER-LIFE!
THEY THINK WE BRING GOOD LUCK.
YOU MEAN ...

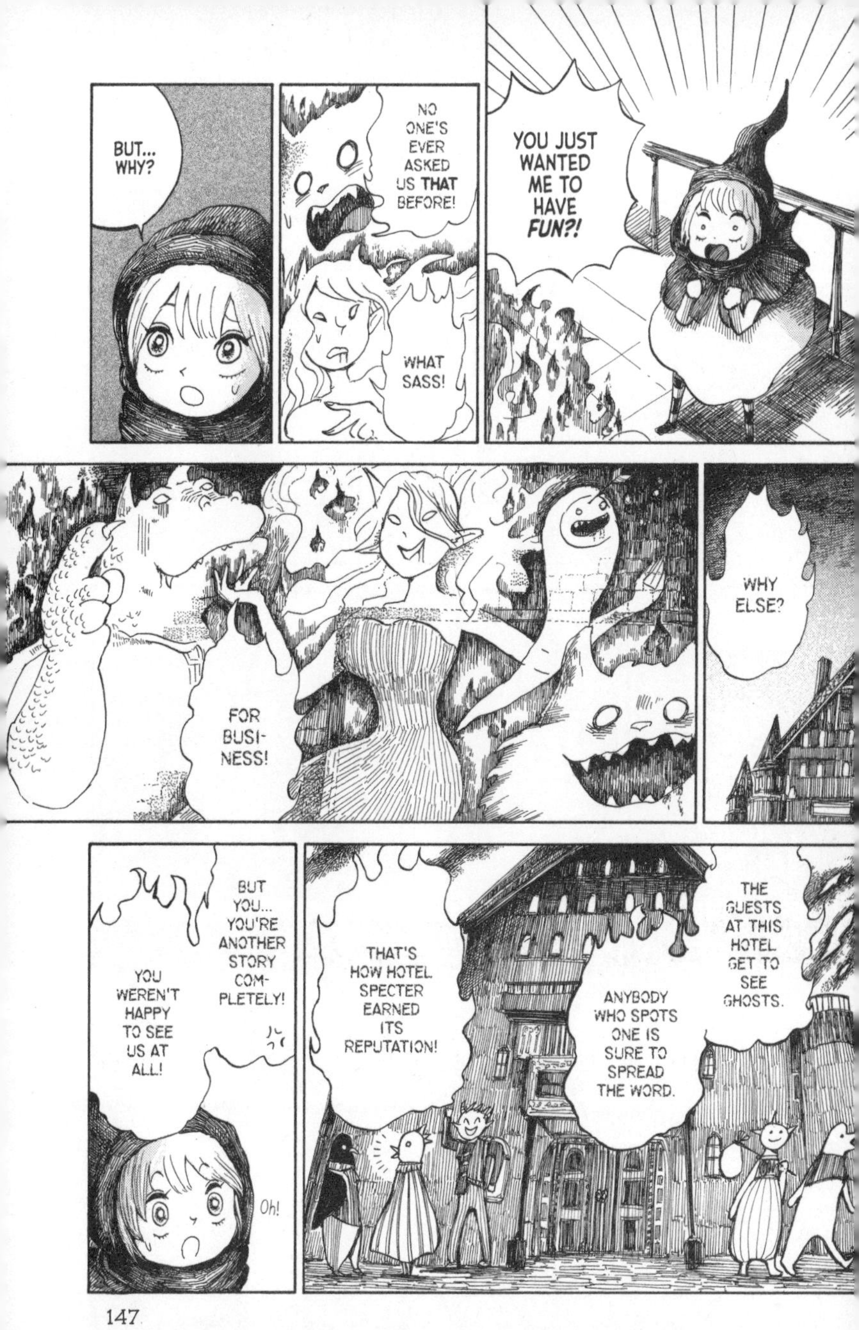
YOU JUST WANTED ME TO HAVE ***FUN?!***
NO ONE'S EVER ASKED US **THAT** BEFORE!
WHAT SASS!
BUT... WHY?
WHY ELSE?
FOR BUSI-NESS!
THE GUESTS AT THIS HOTEL GET TO SEE GHOSTS.
ANYBODY WHO SPOTS ONE IS SURE TO SPREAD THE WORD.
THAT'S HOW HOTEL SPECTER EARNED ITS REPUTATION!
BUT YOU... YOU'RE ANOTHER STORY COM-PLETELY!
YOU WEREN'T HAPPY TO SEE US AT ALL!
Oh!

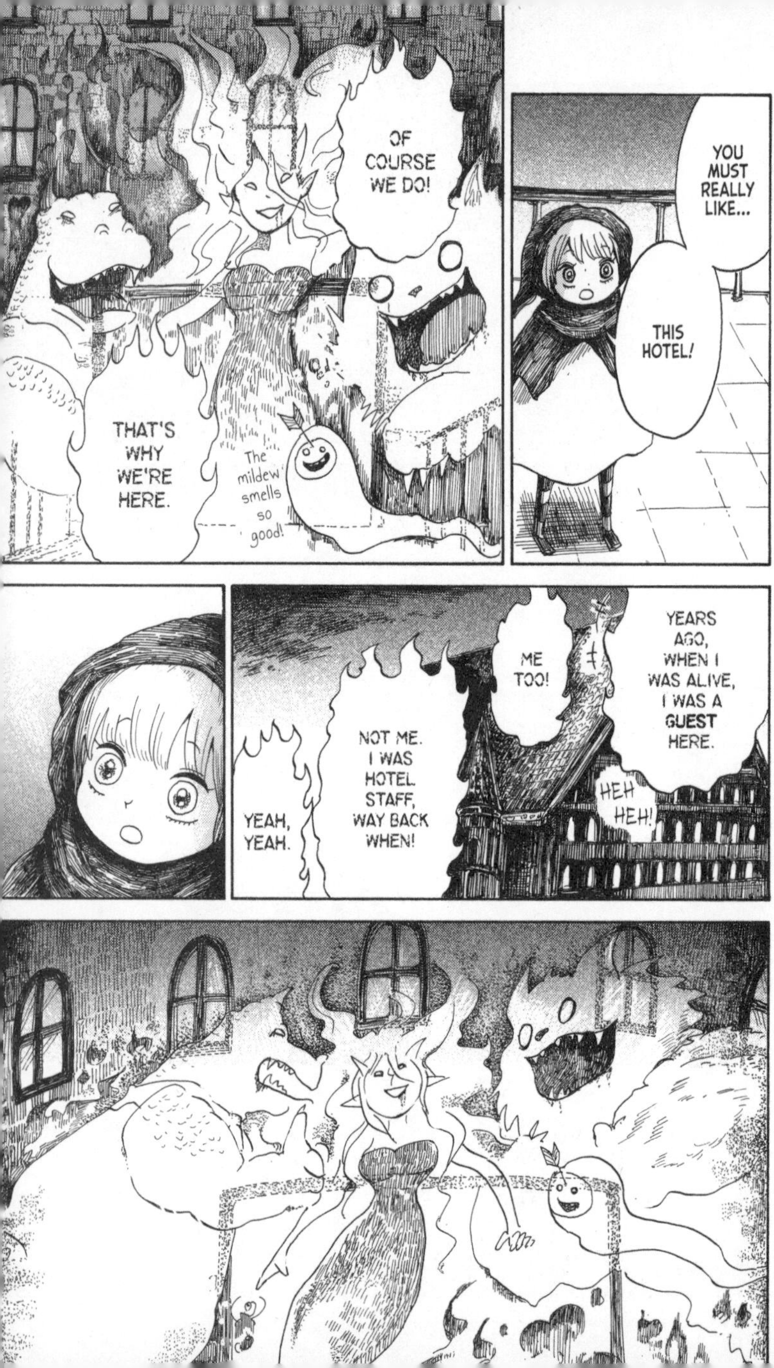
YOU MUST REALLY LIKE...
THIS HOTEL!
OF COURSE WE DO!
THAT'S WHY WE'RE HERE.
The mildew smells so good!
YEARS AGO, WHEN I WAS ALIVE, I WAS A **GUEST** HERE.
HEH HEH!
ME TOO!
NOT ME. I WAS HOTEL STAFF, WAY BACK WHEN!
YEAH, YEAH.

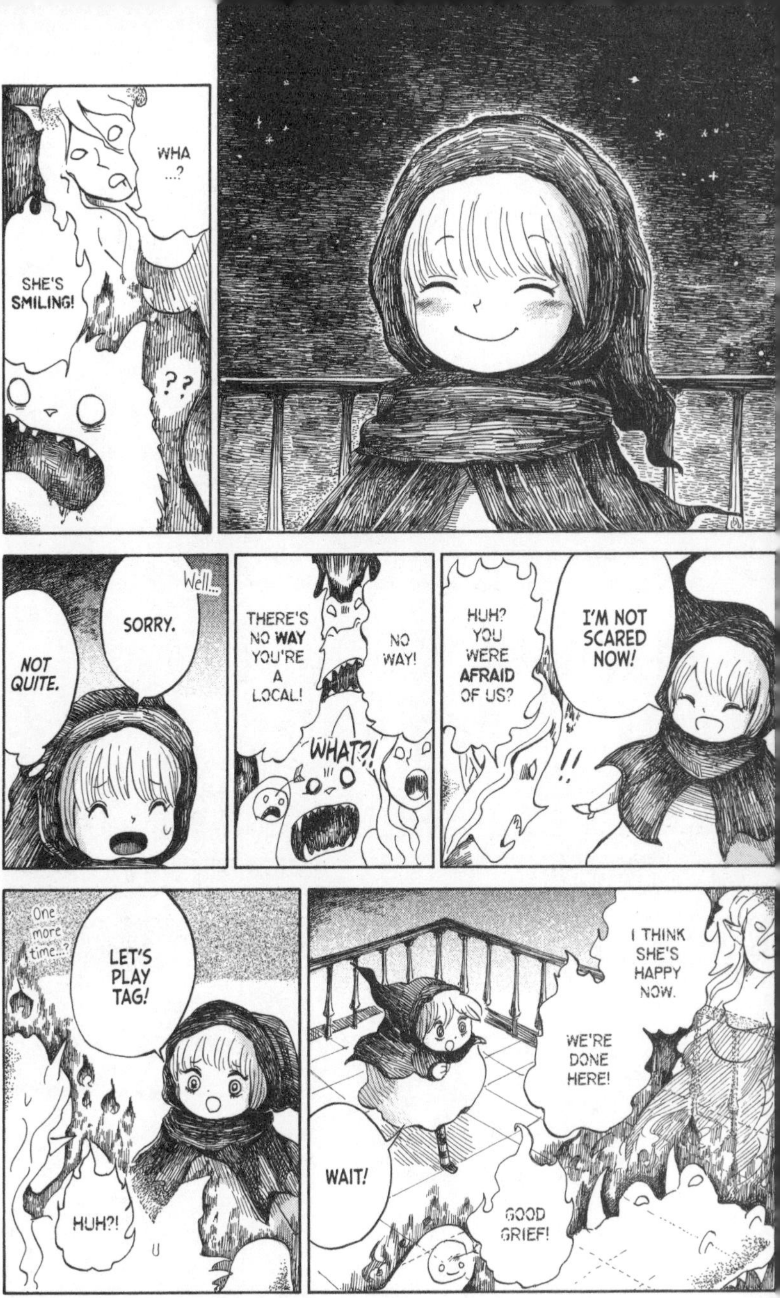
WHA ...?
SHE'S SMILING!
??
I'M NOT SCARED NOW!
HUH? YOU WERE AFRAID OF US?
!!
NO WAY!
THERE'S NO WAY YOU'RE A LOCAL!
WHAT?!
Well...
SORRY.
NOT QUITE.
I THINK SHE'S HAPPY NOW.
WE'RE DONE HERE!
WAIT!
GOOD GRIEF!
One more time...?
LET'S PLAY TAG!
HUH?!

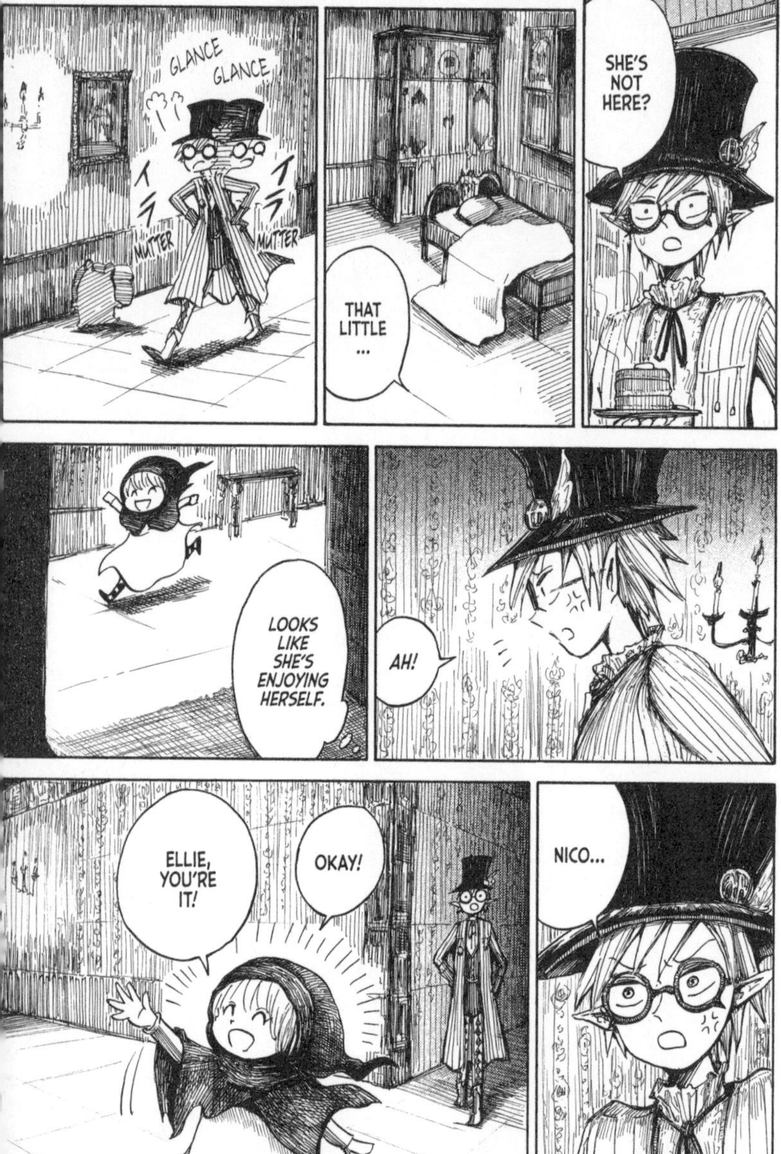
SHE'S NOT HERE?
THAT LITTLE ...
GLANCE
GLANCE
イラ
MUTTER
イラ
MUTTER
AH!
LOOKS LIKE SHE'S ENJOYING HERSELF.
NICO...
OKAY!
ELLIE, YOU'RE IT!

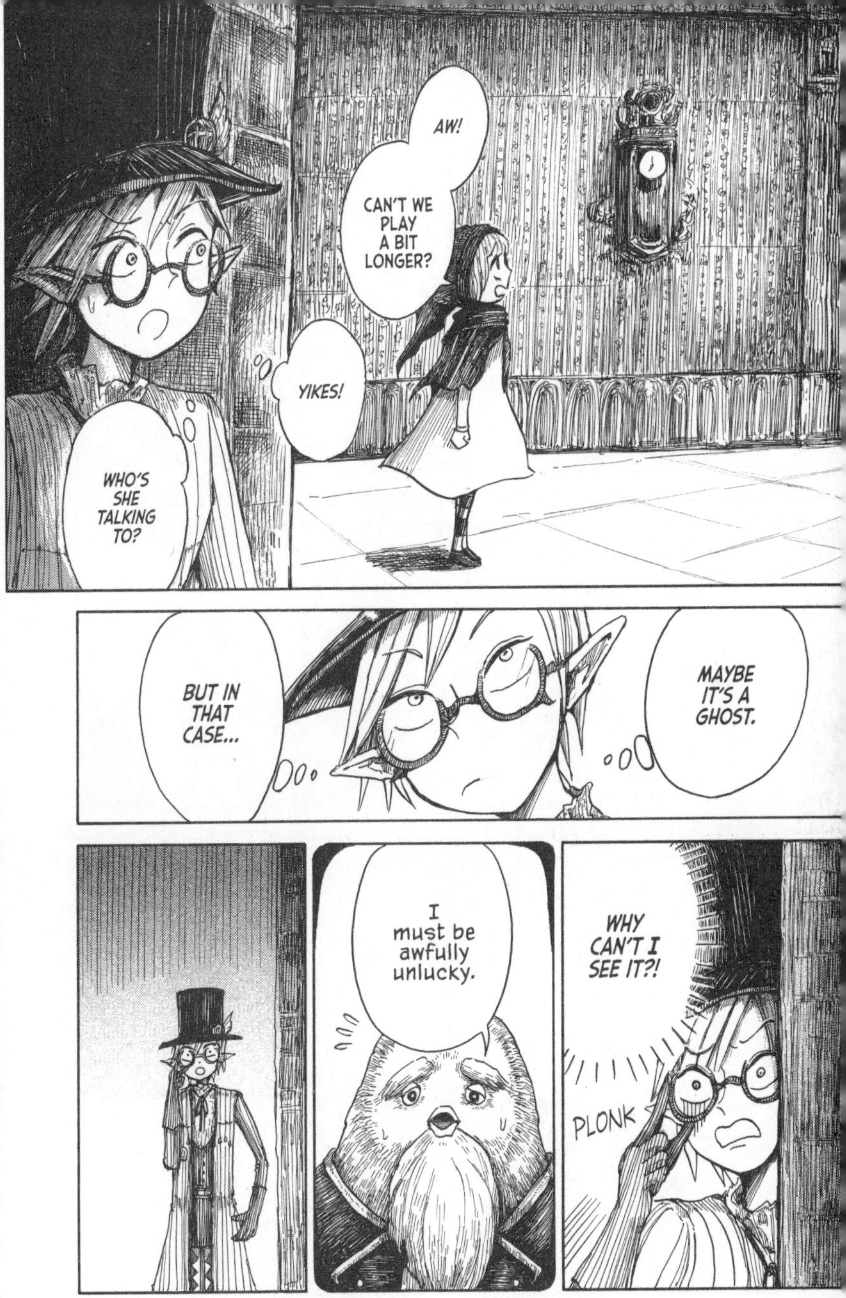
AW!
CAN'T WE PLAY A BIT LONGER?
YIKES!
WHO'S SHE TALKING TO?
MAYBE IT'S A GHOST.
BUT IN THAT CASE...
WHY CAN'T I SEE IT?!
PLONK
I must be awfully unlucky.

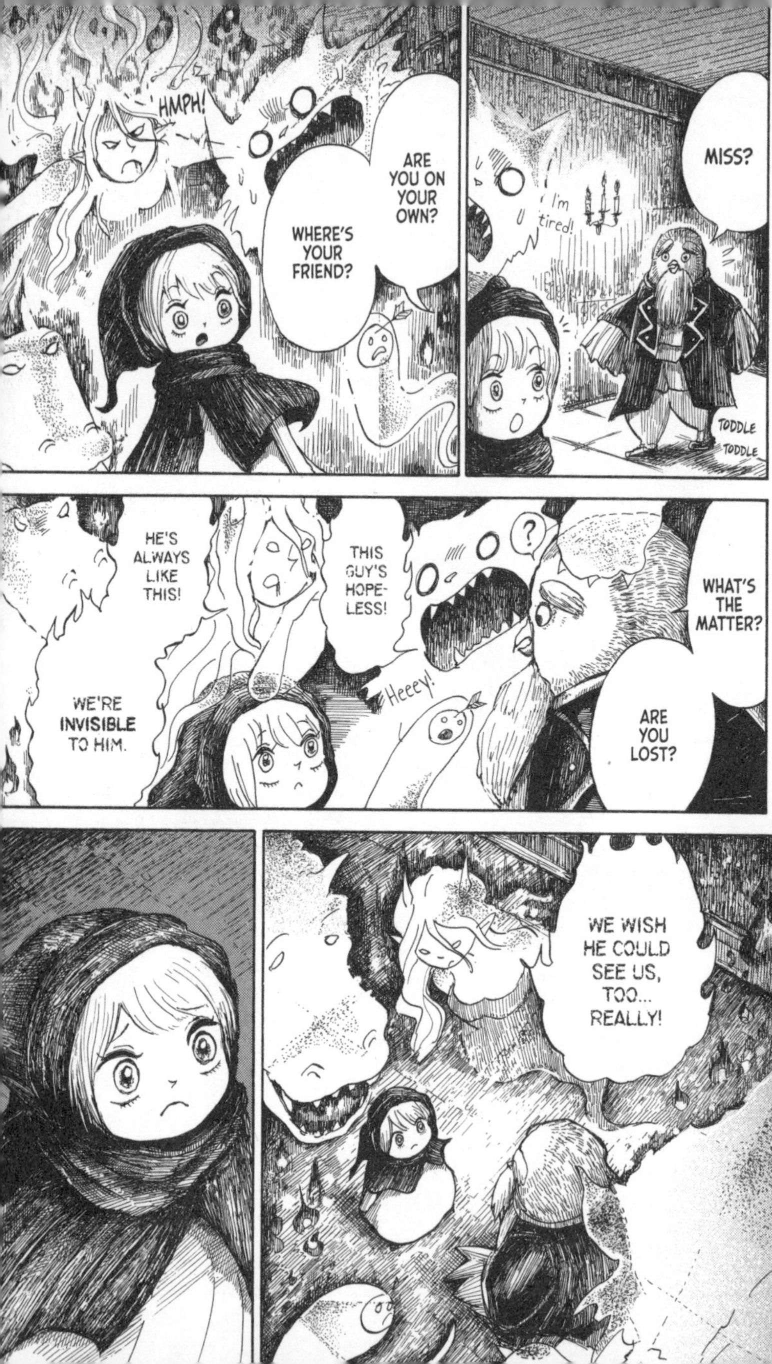
MISS?
I'm tired!
TODDLE
TODDLE
HMPH!
ARE YOU ON YOUR OWN?
WHERE'S YOUR FRIEND?
WHAT'S THE MATTER?
ARE YOU LOST?
?
Heeey!
THIS GUY'S HOPE-LESS!
HE'S ALWAYS LIKE THIS!
WE'RE INVISIBLE TO HIM.
WE WISH HE COULD SEE US, TOO... REALLY!

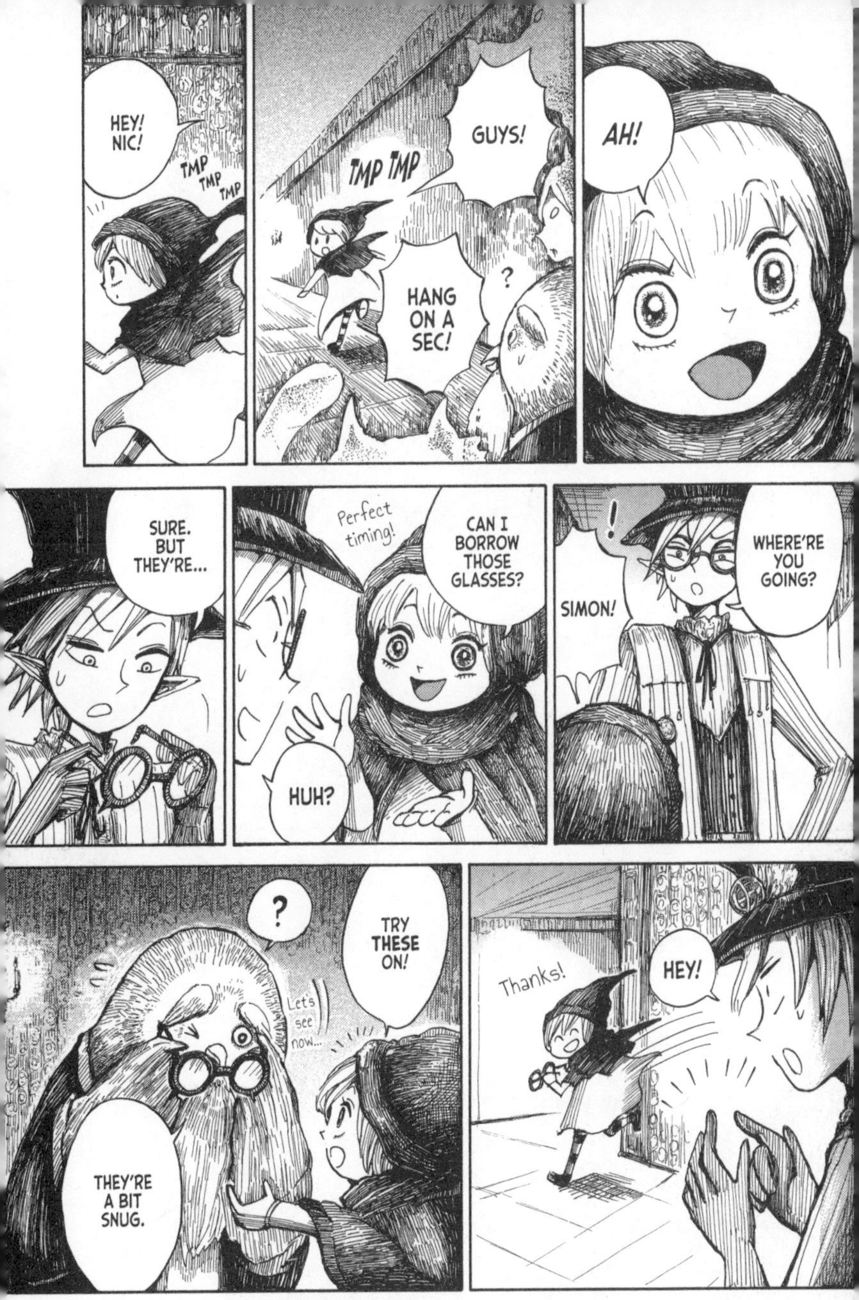
AH!
GUYS!
TMP TMP
?
HANG ON A SEC!
HEY! NIC!
TMP TMP TMP
WHERE'RE YOU GOING?
!
SIMON!
CAN I BORROW THOSE GLASSES?
Perfect timing!
HUH?
SURE. BUT THEY'RE...
HEY!
Thanks!
TRY THESE ON!
?
Let's see now...
THEY'RE A BIT SNUG.

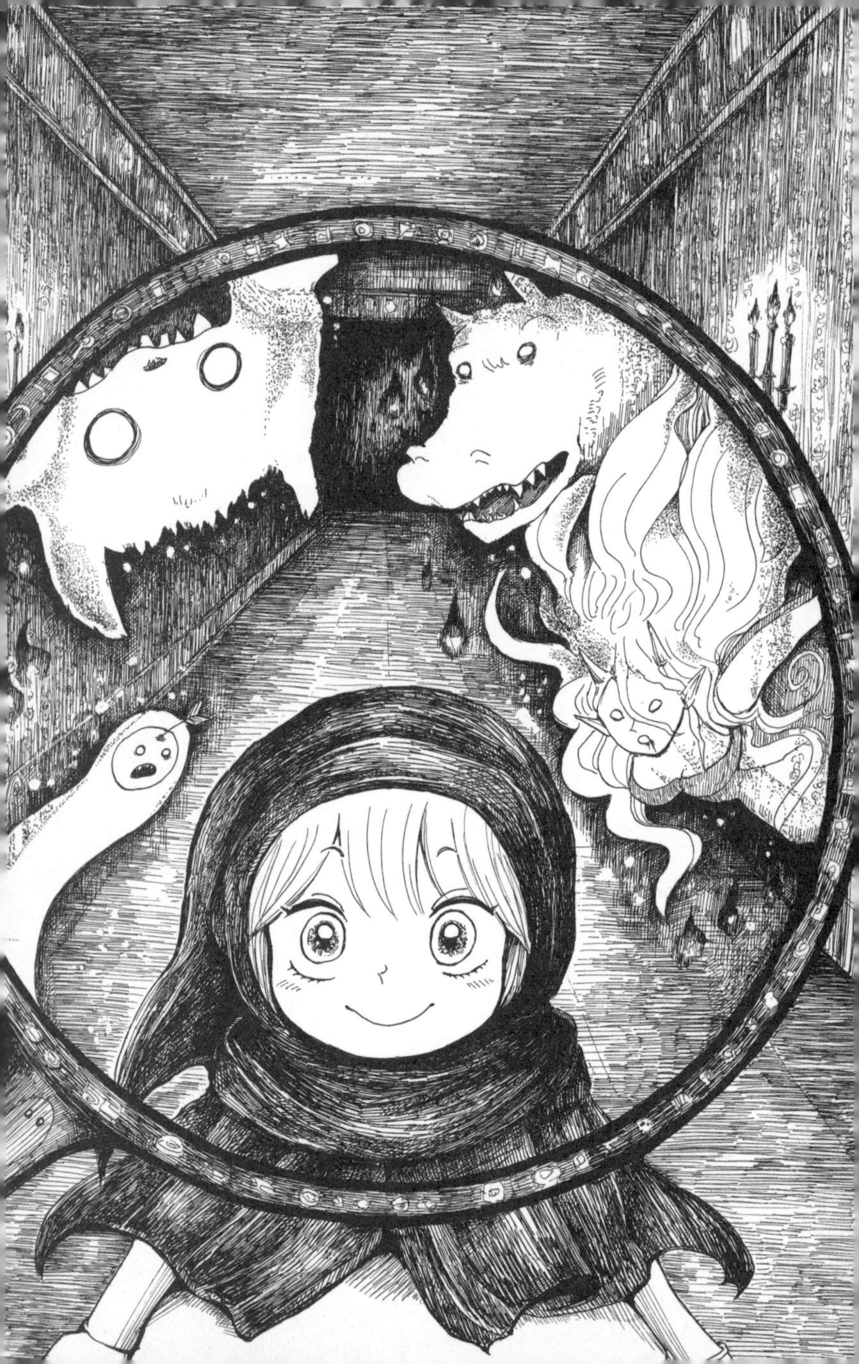

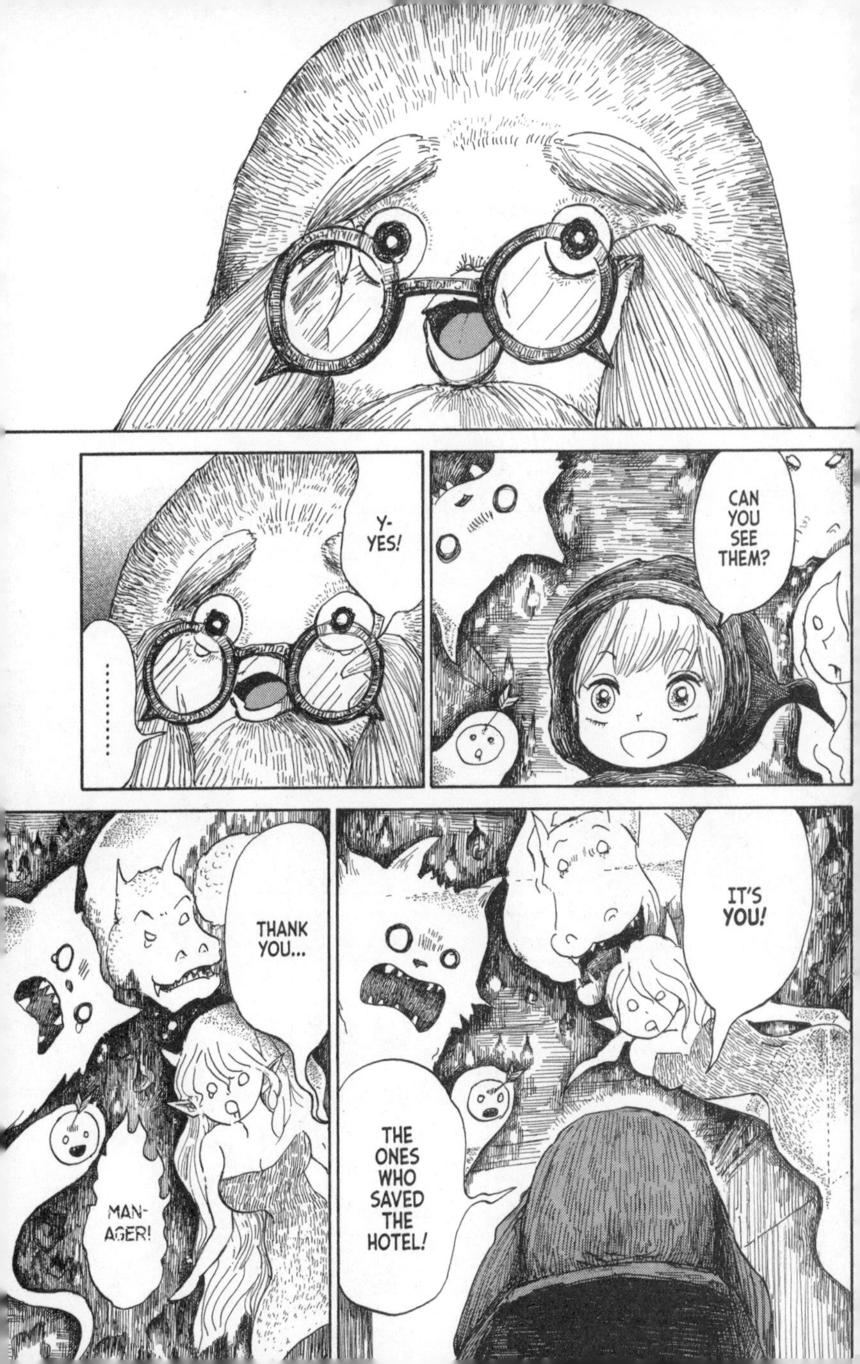
CAN YOU SEE THEM?
Y- YES!
......
IT'S YOU!
THE ONES WHO SAVED THE HOTEL!
THANK YOU...
MAN- AGER!

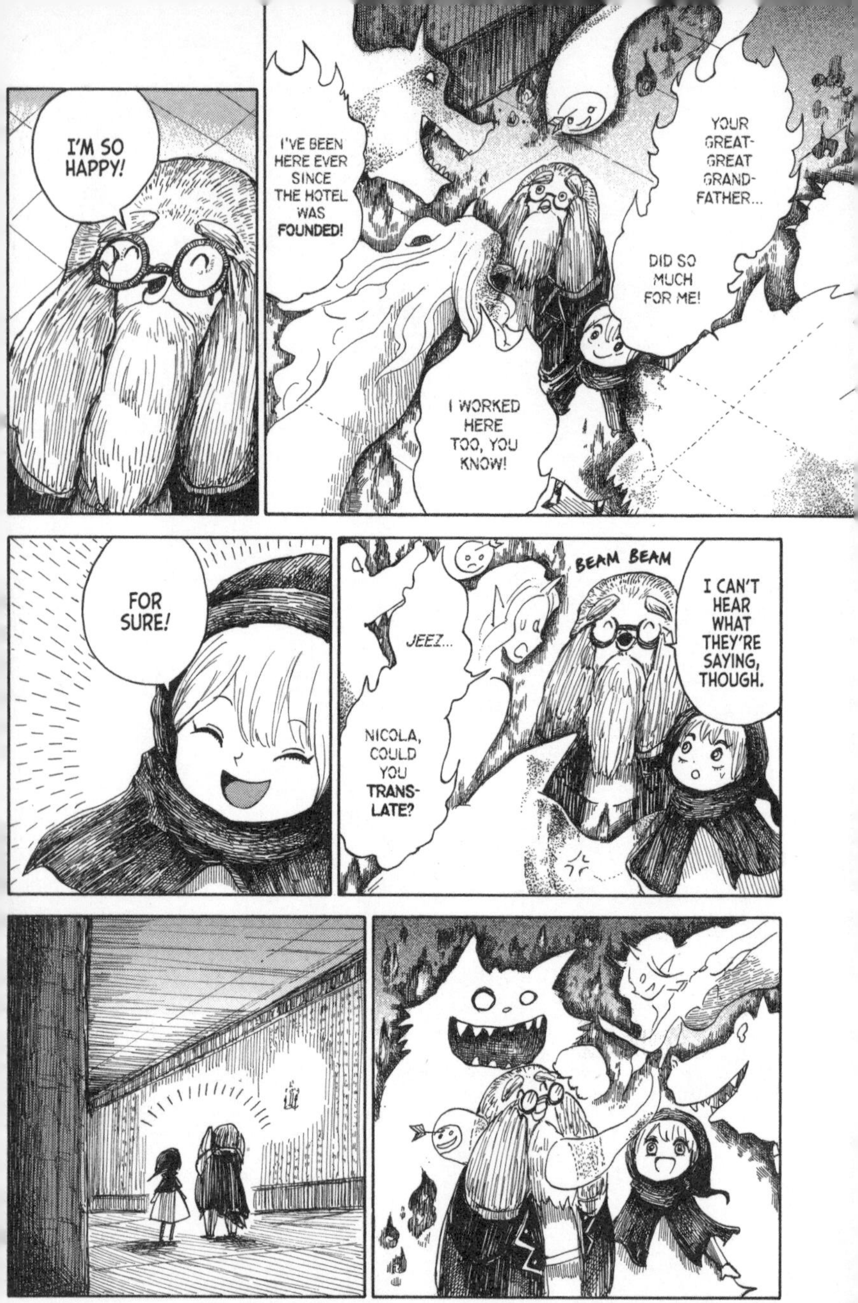
YOUR GREAT-GREAT GRAND-FATHER...
DID SO MUCH FOR ME!
I'VE BEEN HERE EVER SINCE THE HOTEL WAS **FOUNDED!**
I WORKED HERE TOO, YOU KNOW!
I'M SO HAPPY!
BEAM BEAM
I CAN'T HEAR WHAT THEY'RE SAYING, THOUGH.
JEEZ...
NICOLA, COULD YOU **TRANS-LATE?**
FOR SURE!

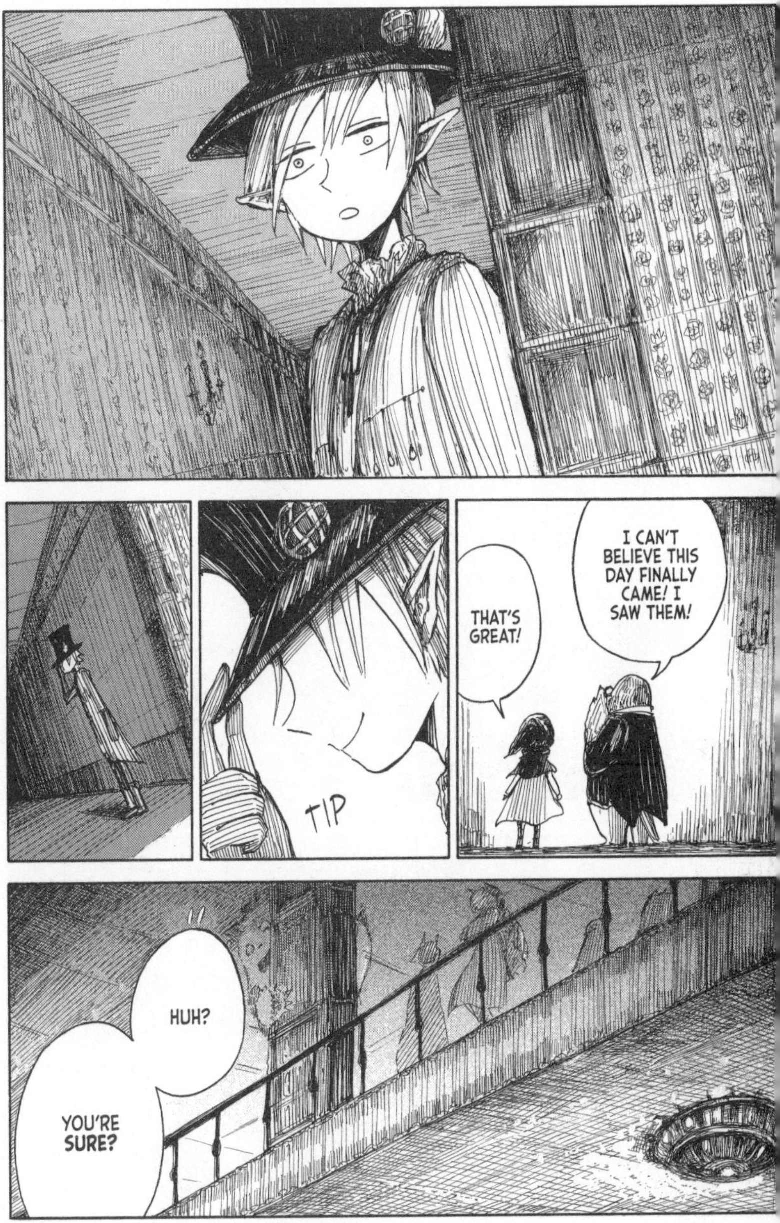
I CAN'T BELIEVE THIS DAY FINALLY CAME! I SAW THEM!
THAT'S GREAT!
TIP
HUH?
YOU'RE SURE?

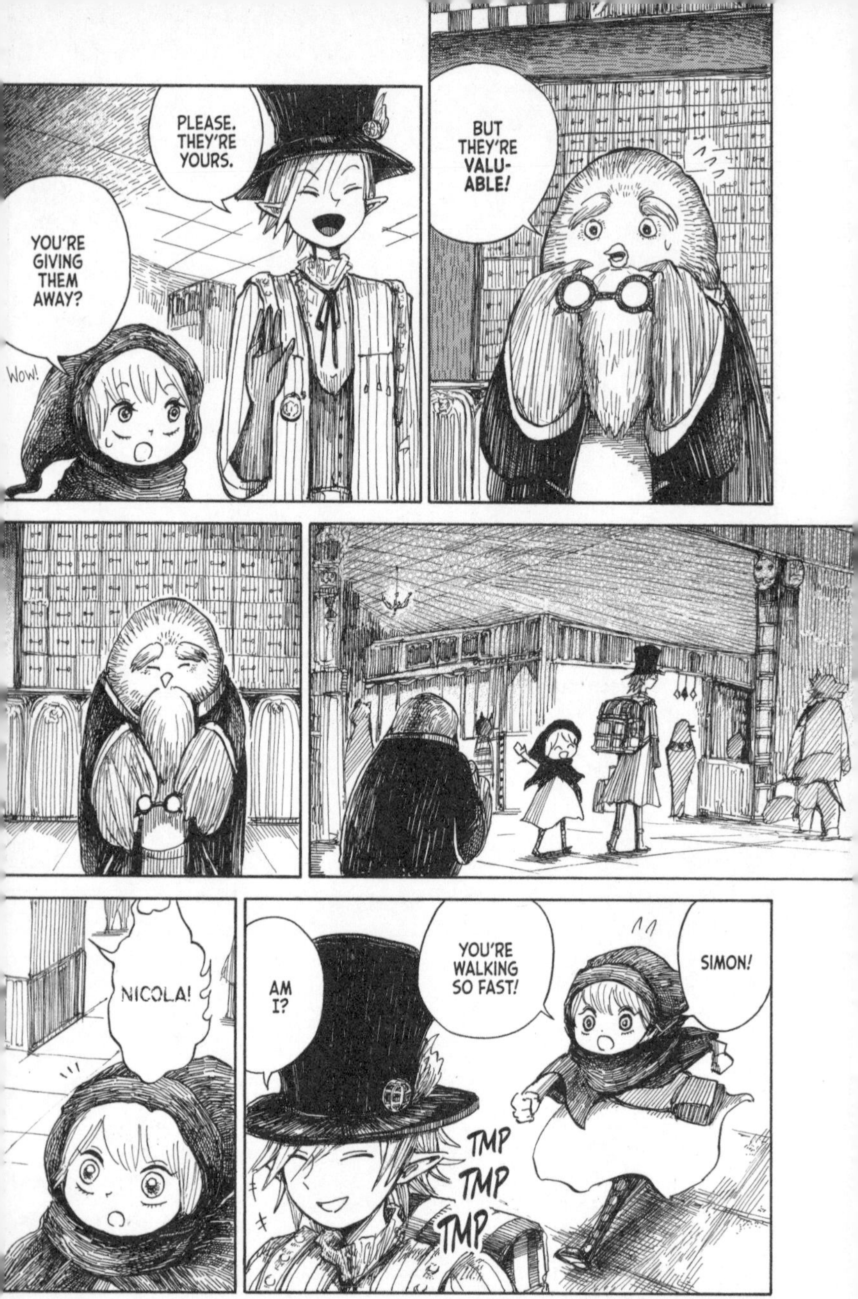
BUT THEY'RE VALU-ABLE!
PLEASE. THEY'RE YOURS.
YOU'RE GIVING THEM AWAY?
Wow!
SIMON!
YOU'RE WALKING SO FAST!
AM I?
TMP TMP TMP
NICOLA!

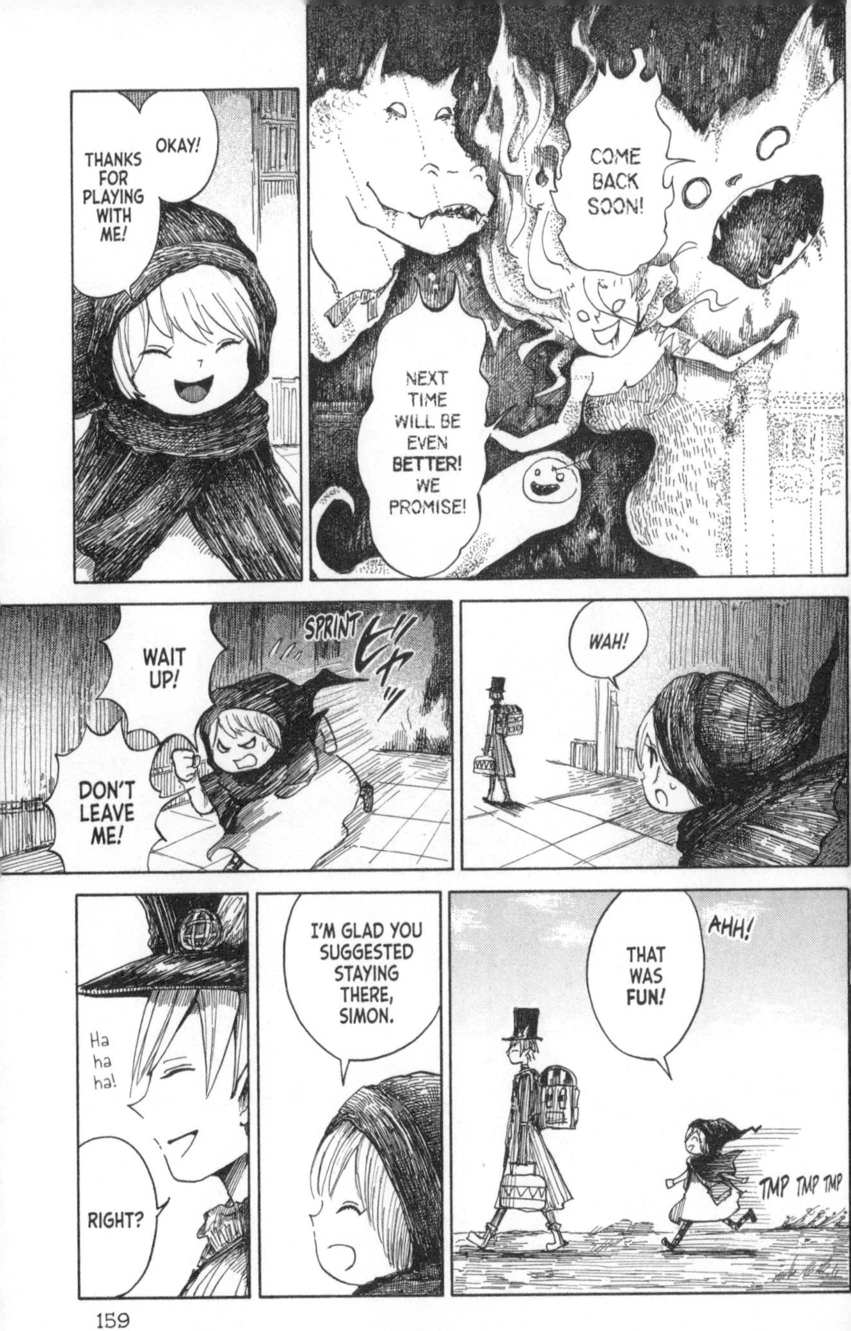
COME BACK SOON!
NEXT TIME WILL BE EVEN BETTER! WE PROMISE!
OKAY!
THANKS FOR PLAYING WITH ME!
WAH!
SPRINT
WAIT UP!
DON'T LEAVE ME!
AHH!
THAT WAS FUN!
TMP TMP TMP
I'M GLAD YOU SUGGESTED STAYING THERE, SIMON.
Ha ha ha!
RIGHT?

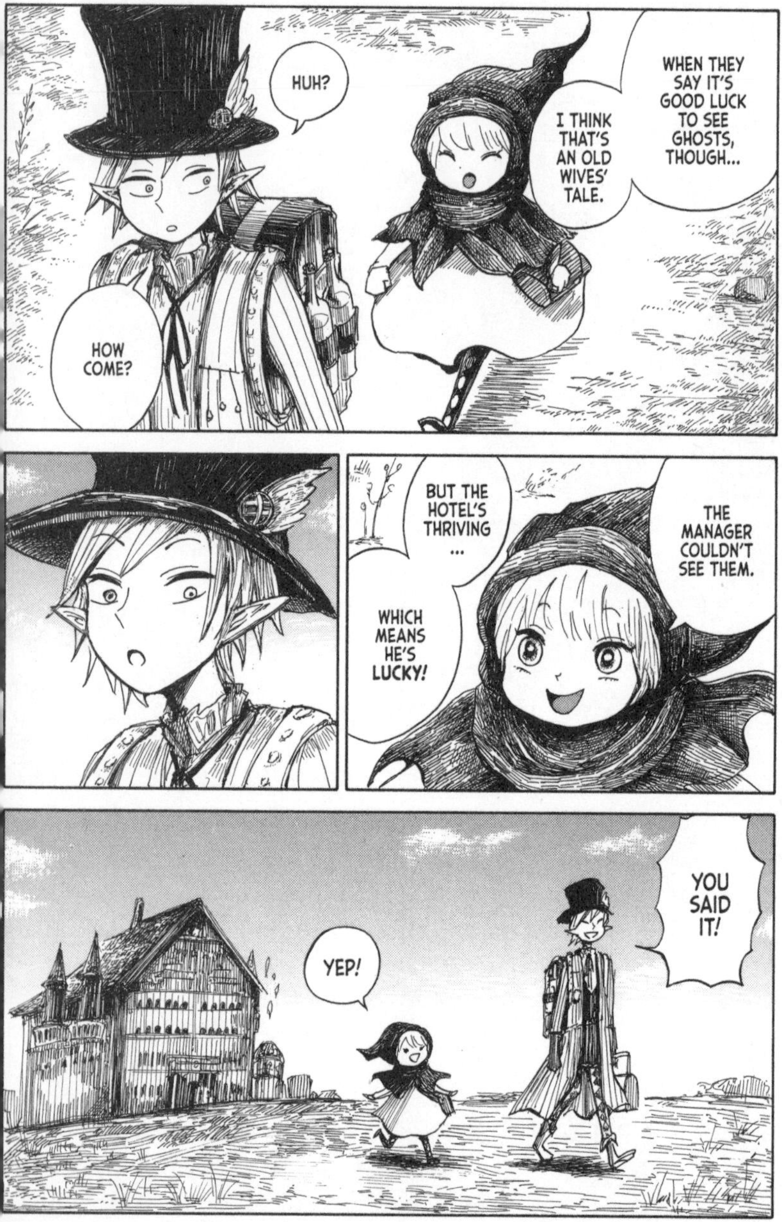
WHEN THEY SAY IT'S GOOD LUCK TO SEE GHOSTS, THOUGH...
I THINK THAT'S AN OLD WIVES' TALE.
HUH?
HOW COME?
THE MANAGER COULDN'T SEE THEM.
BUT THE HOTEL'S THRIVING ...
WHICH MEANS HE'S LUCKY!
YOU SAID IT!
YEP!

Chapter **5** END

After the Visit 5

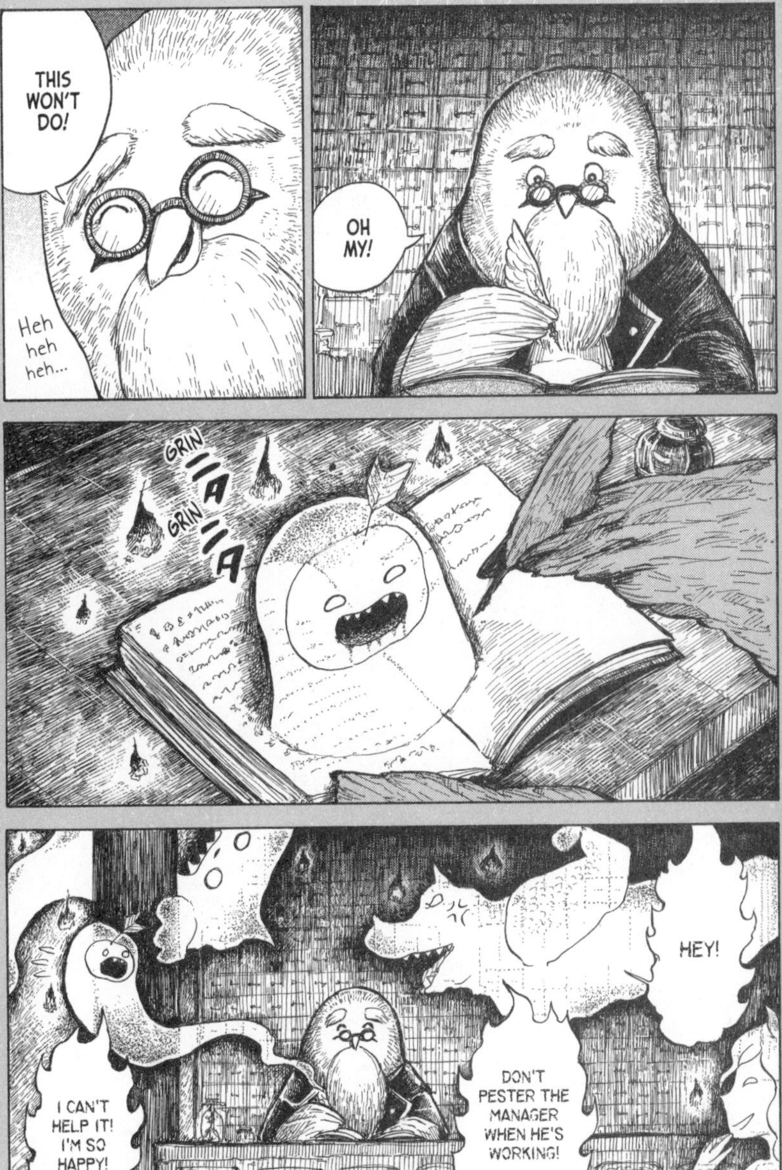
OH MY!
THIS WON'T DO!
Heh heh heh...
GRIN A GRIN A
HEY!
DON'T PESTER THE MANAGER WHEN HE'S WORKING!
I CAN'T HELP IT! I'M SO HAPPY!

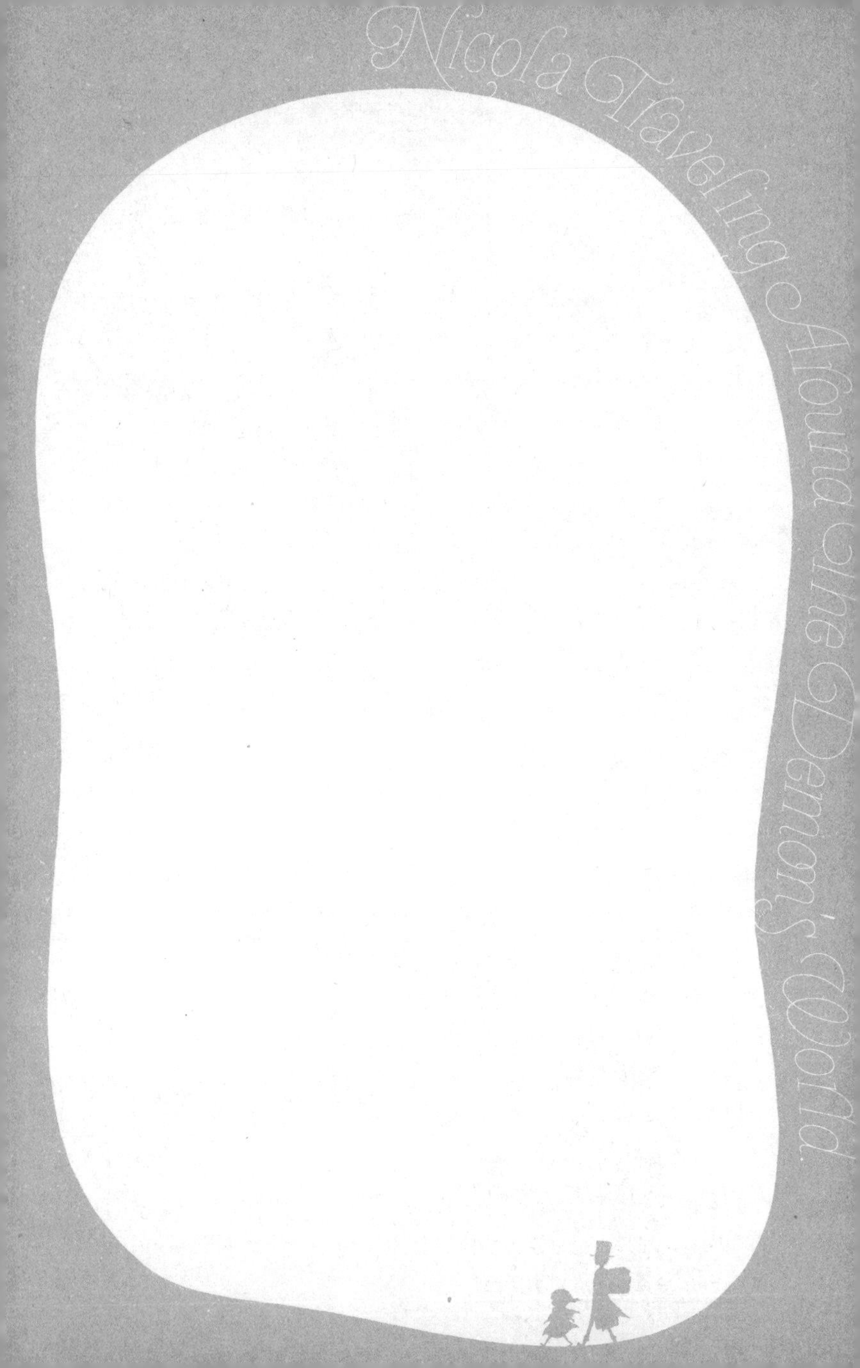
Nicola Traveling Around the Demon's World

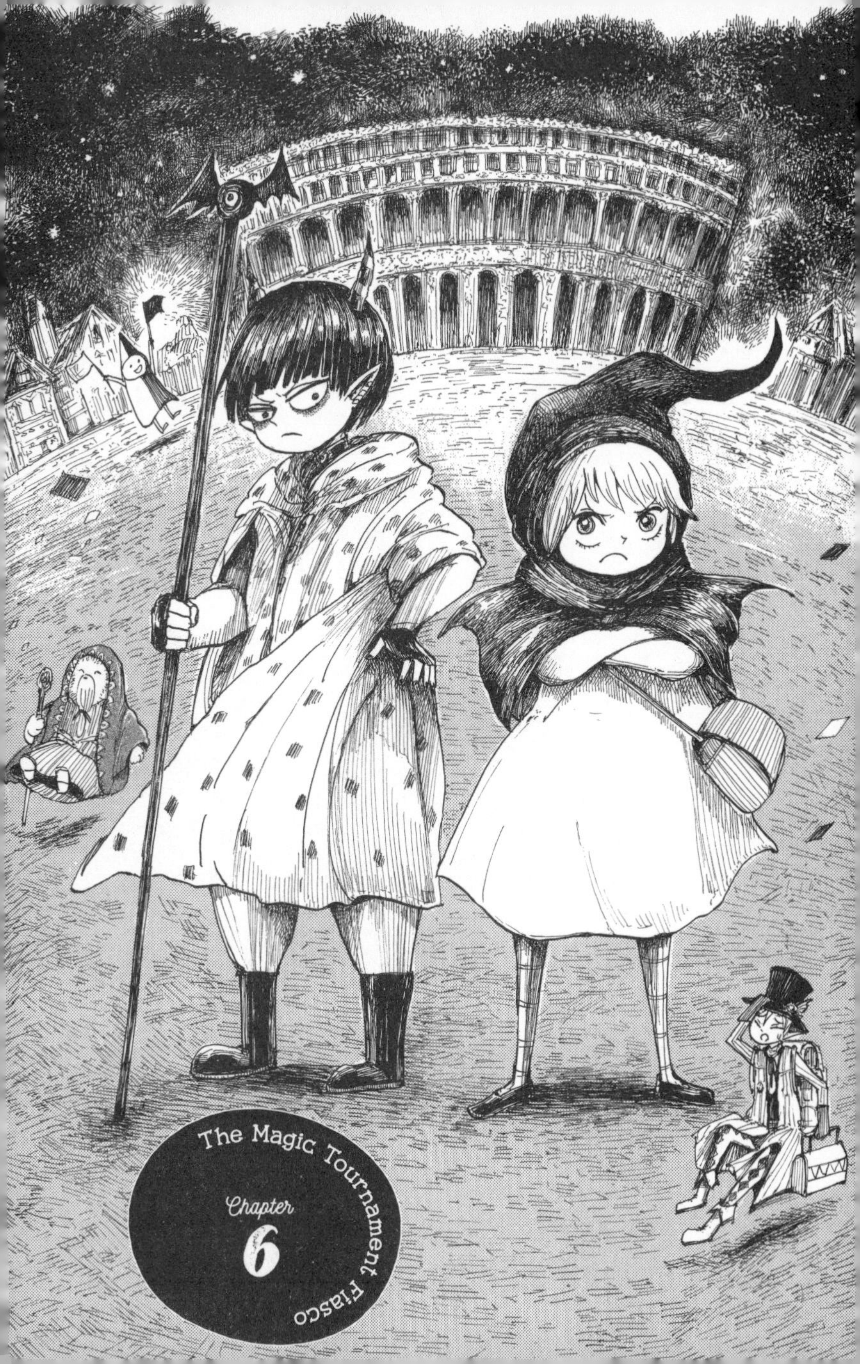
The Magic Tournament Fiasco
Chapter
6

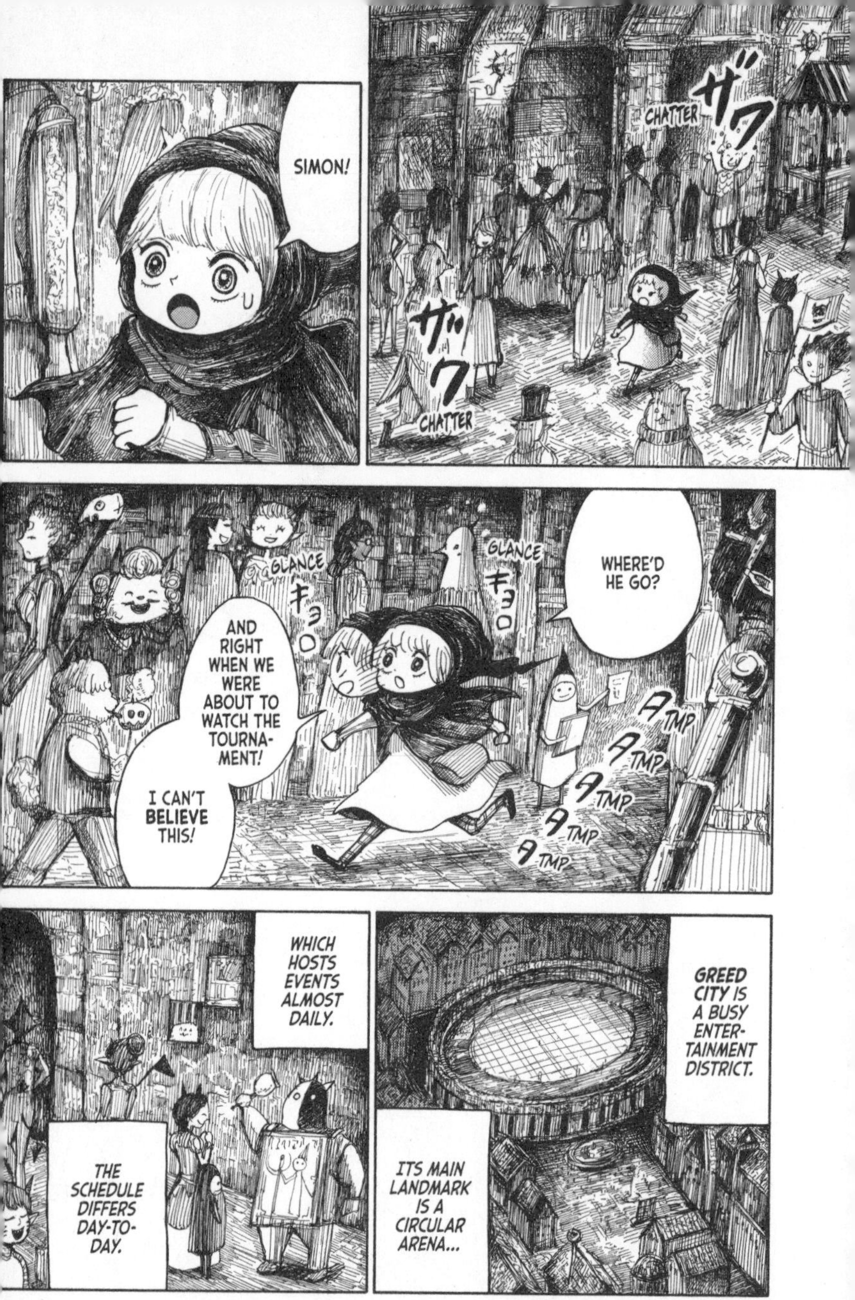
CHATTER ザワ
ザワ CHATTER
SIMON!
WHERE'D HE GO?
GLANCE キョロ
GLANCE キョロ
TMP TMP TMP TMP TMP
AND RIGHT WHEN WE WERE ABOUT TO WATCH THE TOURNA-MENT!
I CAN'T BELIEVE THIS!
GREED CITY IS A BUSY ENTER-TAINMENT DISTRICT.
ITS MAIN LANDMARK IS A CIRCULAR ARENA...
WHICH HOSTS EVENTS ALMOST DAILY.
THE SCHEDULE DIFFERS DAY-TO-DAY.

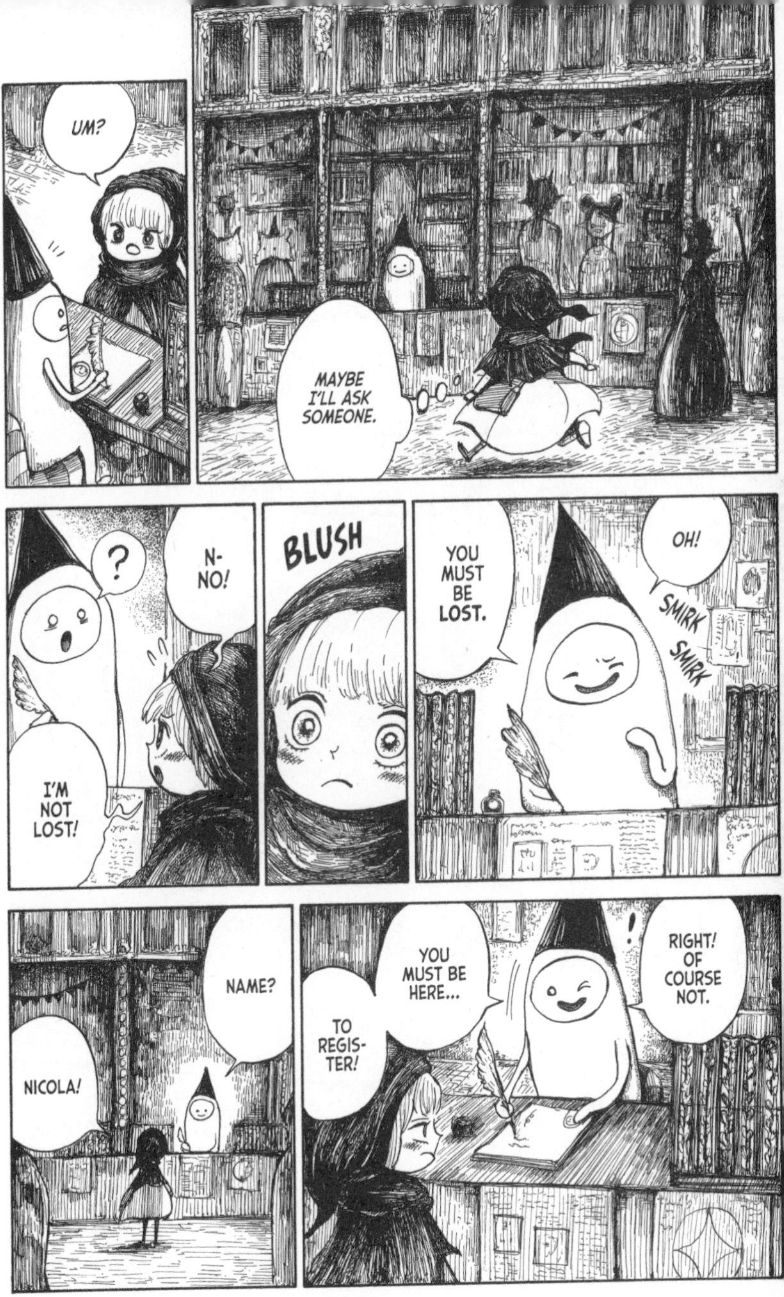

MAYBE I'LL ASK SOMEONE.
UM?
OH!
SMIRK SMIRK
YOU MUST BE LOST.
BLUSH
N-NO!
?
I'M NOT LOST!
!
RIGHT! OF COURSE NOT.
YOU MUST BE HERE...
TO REGISTER!
NAME?
NICOLA!

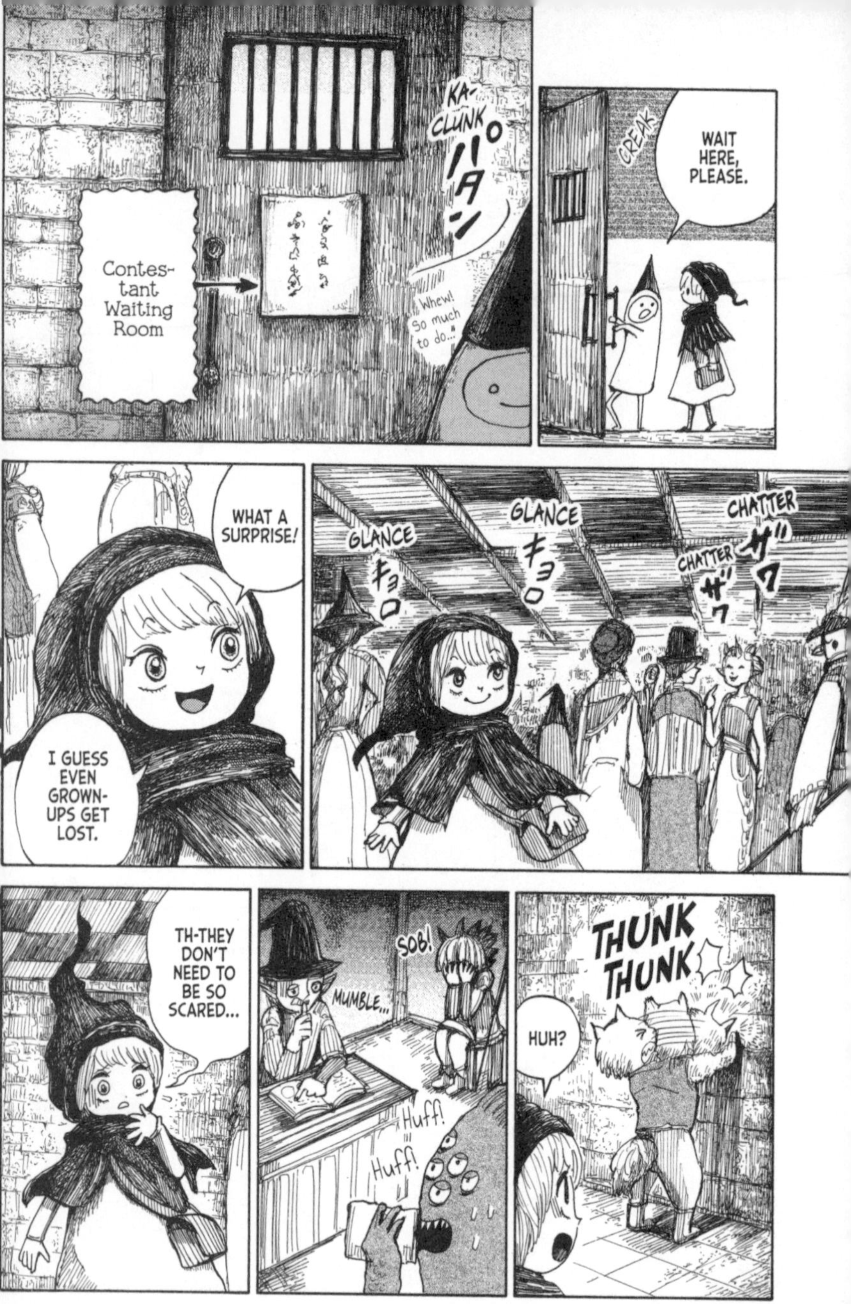
CREAK
WAIT HERE, PLEASE.
KA-CLUNK
バタン
Whew! So much to do..!
Contestant Waiting Room
CHATTER
ザワ
CHATTER
ザワ
GLANCE
キョロ
GLANCE
キョロ
WHAT A SURPRISE!
I GUESS EVEN GROWN-UPS GET LOST.
THUNK THUNK
HUH?
SOB!
MUMBLE...
Huff!
Huff!
TH-THEY DON'T NEED TO BE SO SCARED...

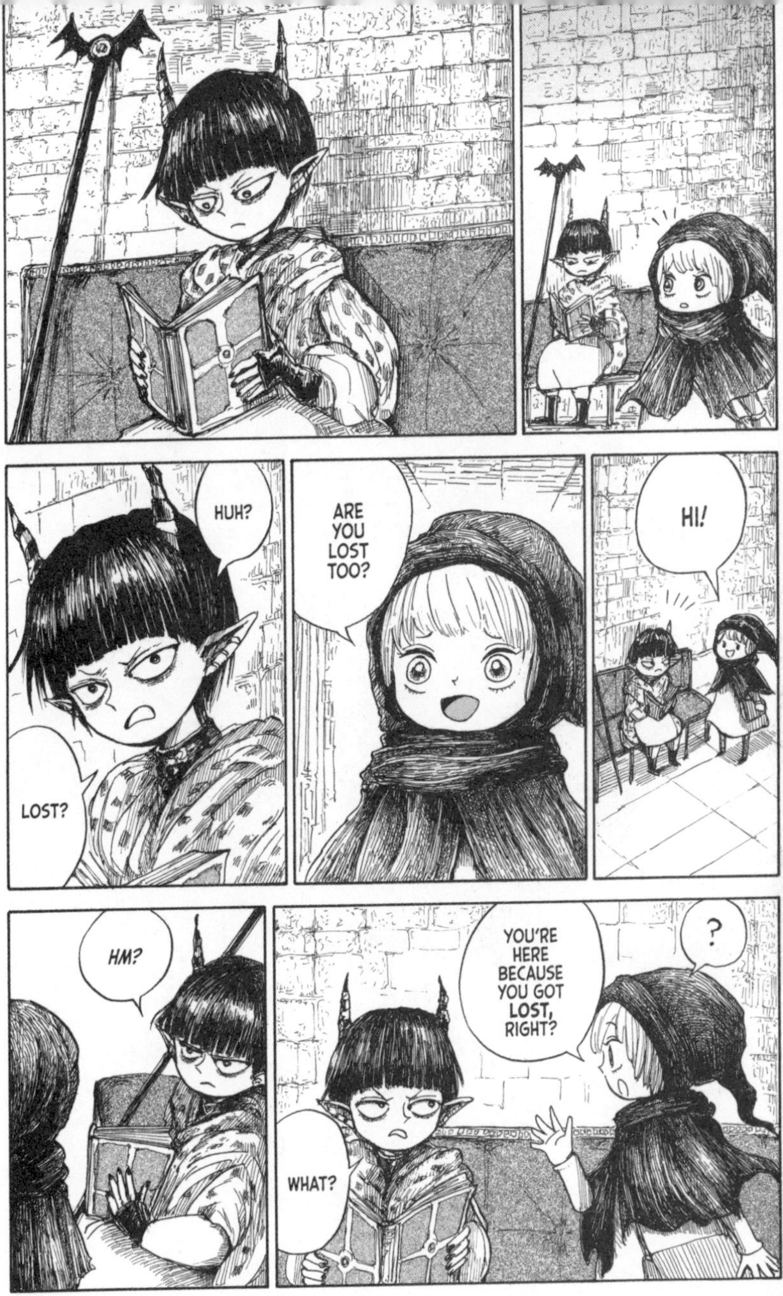
HI!
ARE YOU LOST TOO?
HUH?
LOST?
?
YOU'RE HERE BECAUSE YOU GOT LOST, RIGHT?
WHAT?
HM?

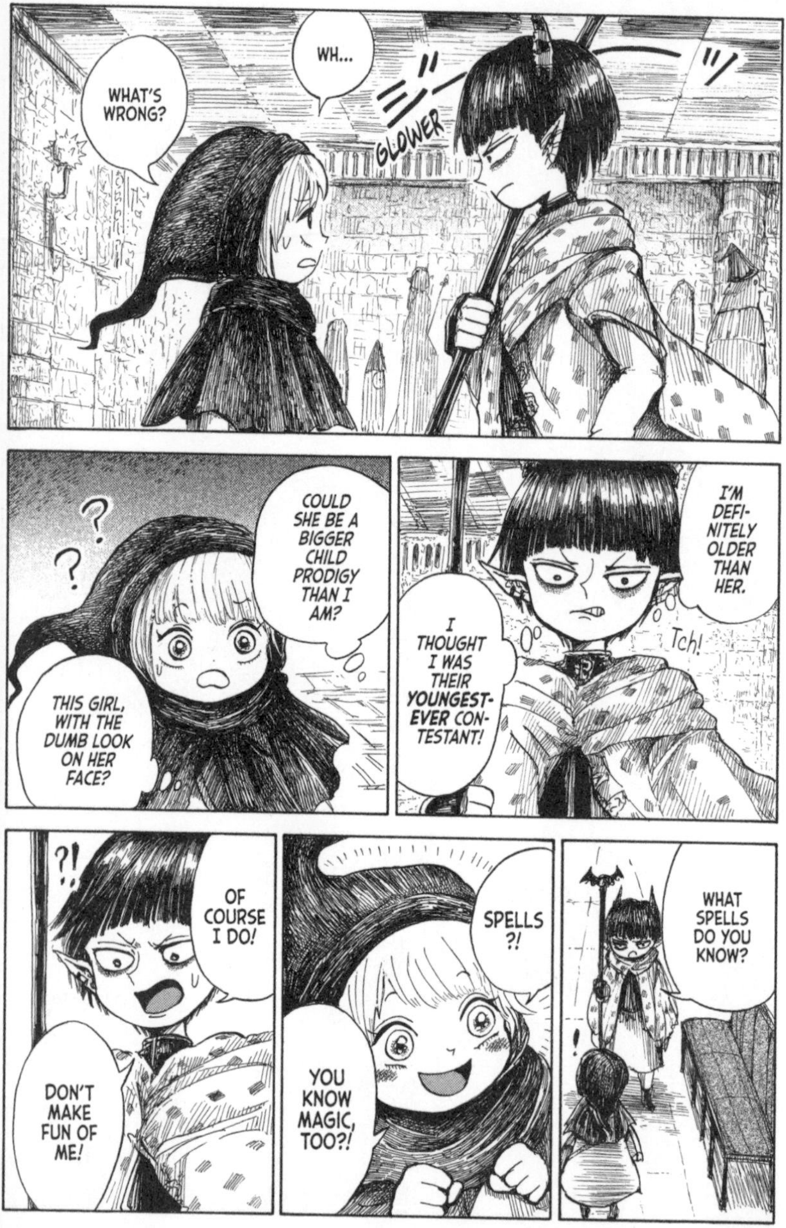
GLOWER
WH...
WHAT'S WRONG?
I'M DEFINITELY OLDER THAN HER.
Tch!
I THOUGHT I WAS THEIR YOUNGEST-EVER CONTESTANT!
COULD SHE BE A BIGGER CHILD PRODIGY THAN I AM?
??
THIS GIRL, WITH THE DUMB LOOK ON HER FACE?
WHAT SPELLS DO YOU KNOW?
!
SPELLS?!
YOU KNOW MAGIC, TOO?!
?!
OF COURSE I DO!
DON'T MAKE FUN OF ME!

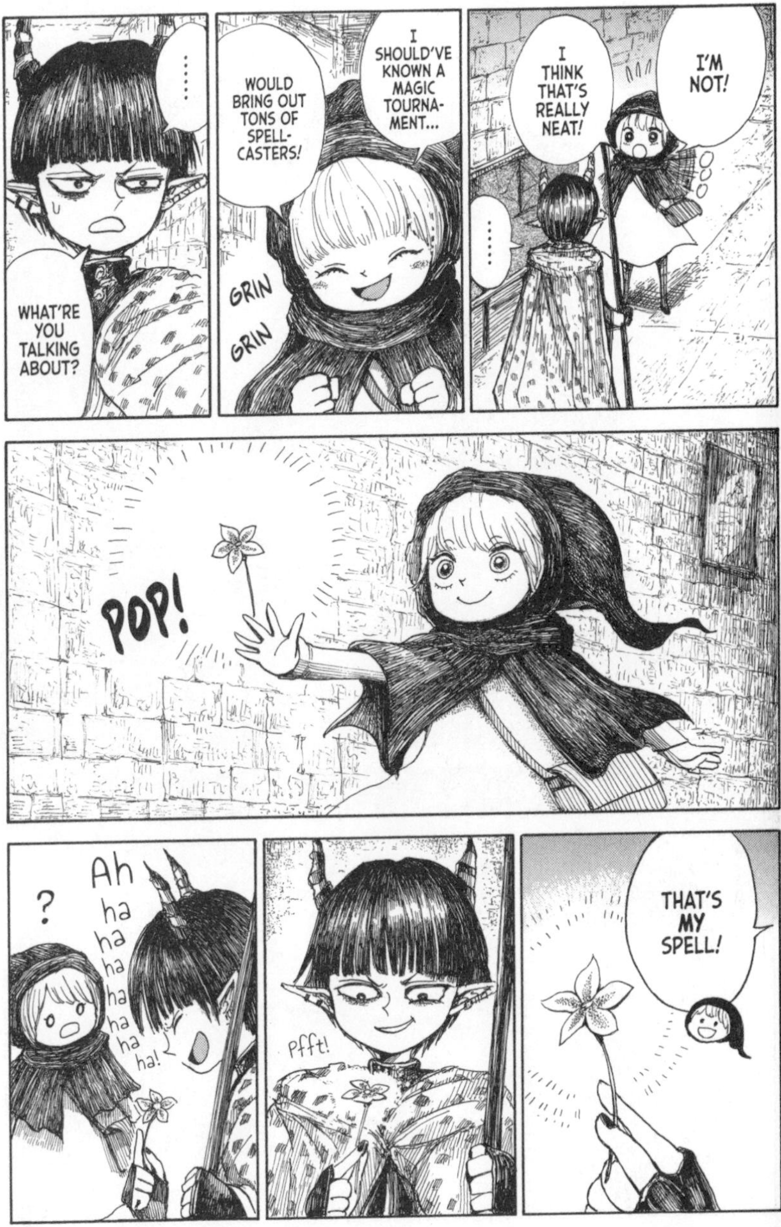
I'M NOT!
I THINK THAT'S REALLY NEAT!
……
I SHOULD'VE KNOWN A MAGIC TOURNAMENT...
WOULD BRING OUT TONS OF SPELL-CASTERS!
GRIN
GRIN
……
WHAT'RE YOU TALKING ABOUT?
POP!
THAT'S MY SPELL!
Pfft!
Ah ha ha ha ha ha ha ha ha!
?

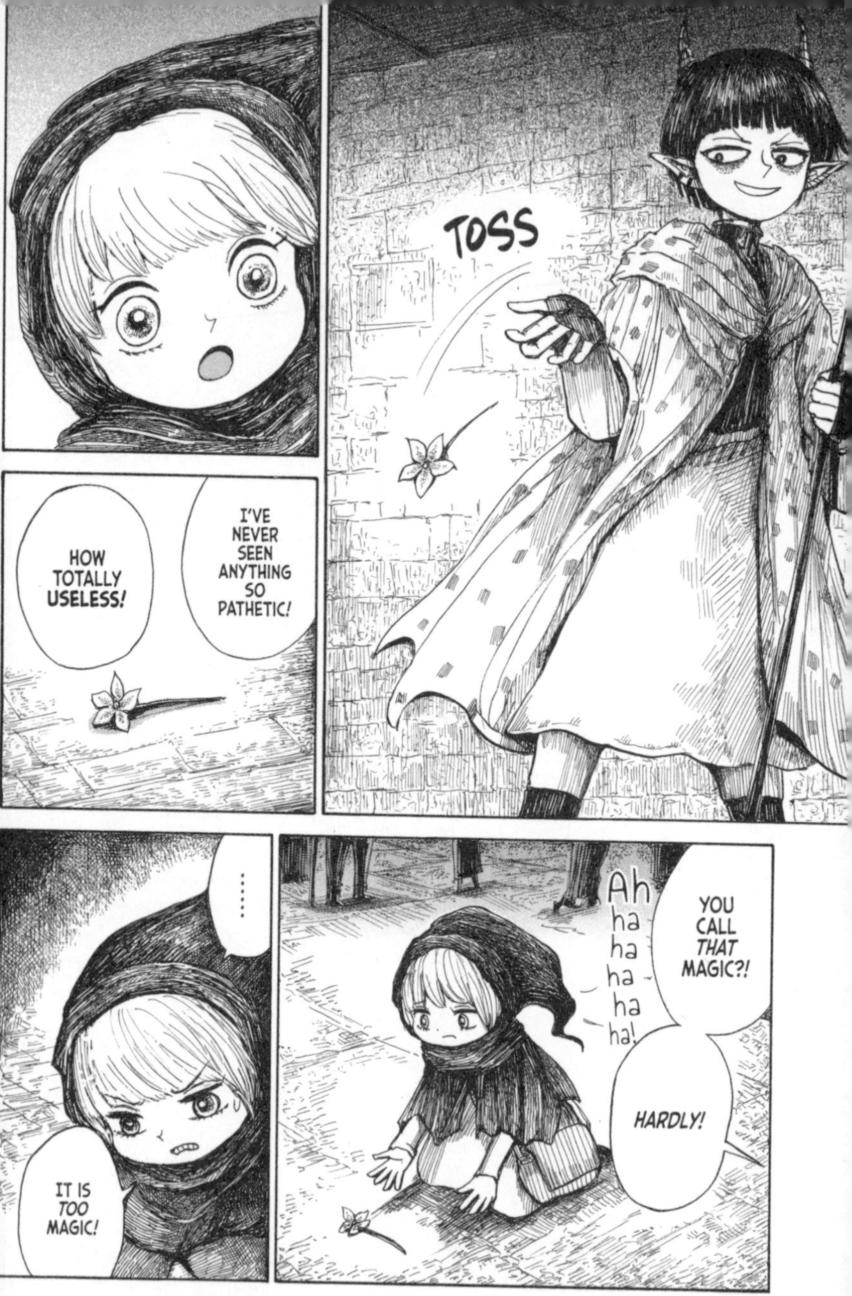

TOSS
I'VE NEVER SEEN ANYTHING SO PATHETIC!
HOW TOTALLY USELESS!
YOU CALL *THAT* MAGIC?!
Ah ha ha ha ha ha!
HARDLY!
……
IT IS *TOO* MAGIC!

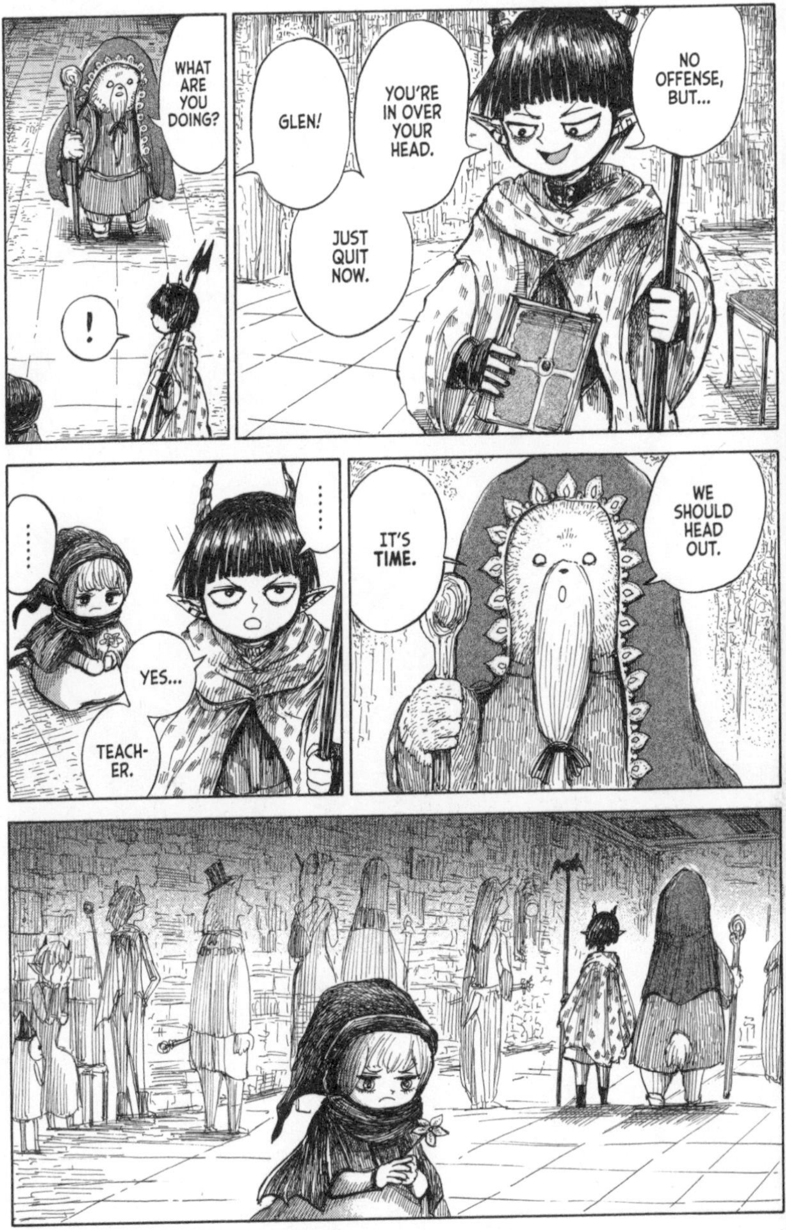
NO OFFENSE, BUT...
YOU'RE IN OVER YOUR HEAD.
JUST QUIT NOW.
GLEN!
WHAT ARE YOU DOING?
!
WE SHOULD HEAD OUT.
IT'S TIME.
......
......
YES...
TEACHER.

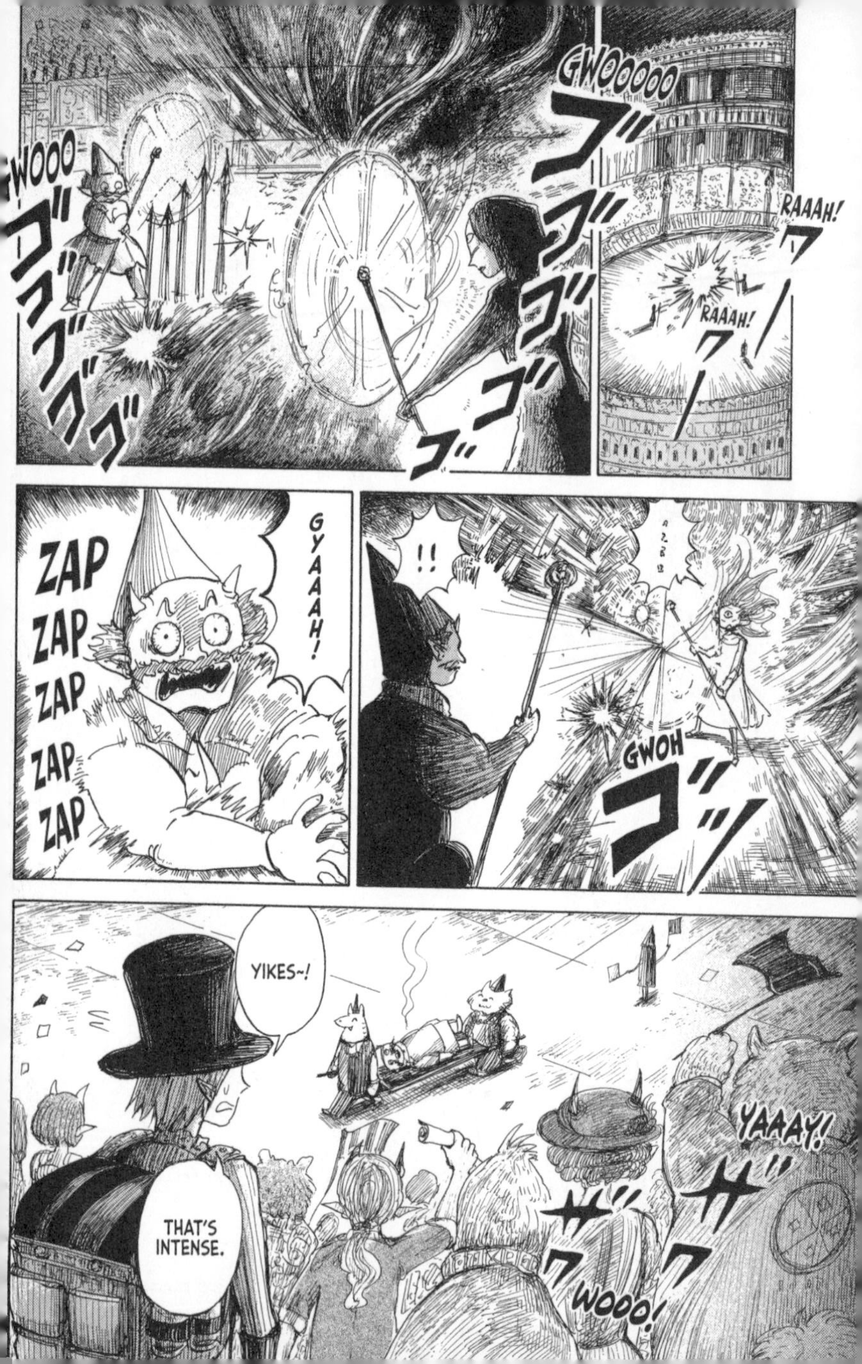
RAAAH!
RAAAH!
GWOOOOO
GWOOO
!!
GWOH
GYAAAAH!
ZAP
ZAP
ZAP
ZAP
ZAP
ZAP
YAAAY!
YIKES~!
WOOO!
THAT'S INTENSE.

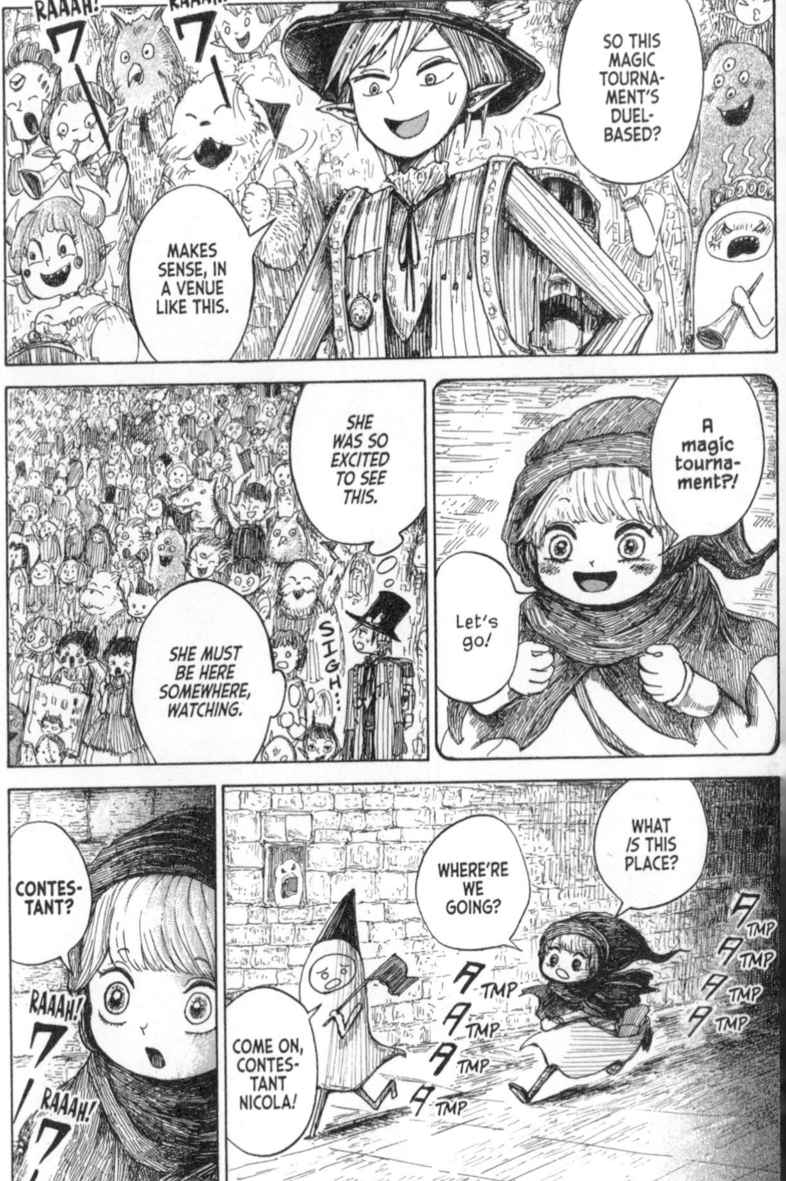
SO THIS MAGIC TOURNAMENT'S DUEL-BASED?
RAAAH!
RAAAH!
MAKES SENSE, IN A VENUE LIKE THIS.
A magic tournament?!
Let's go!
SHE WAS SO EXCITED TO SEE THIS.
SIGH...
SHE MUST BE HERE SOMEWHERE, WATCHING.
WHAT *IS* THIS PLACE?
WHERE'RE WE GOING?
TMP TMP TMP TMP
TMP TMP TMP TMP
COME ON, CONTESTANT NICOLA!
CONTESTANT?
RAAAH!
RAAAH!

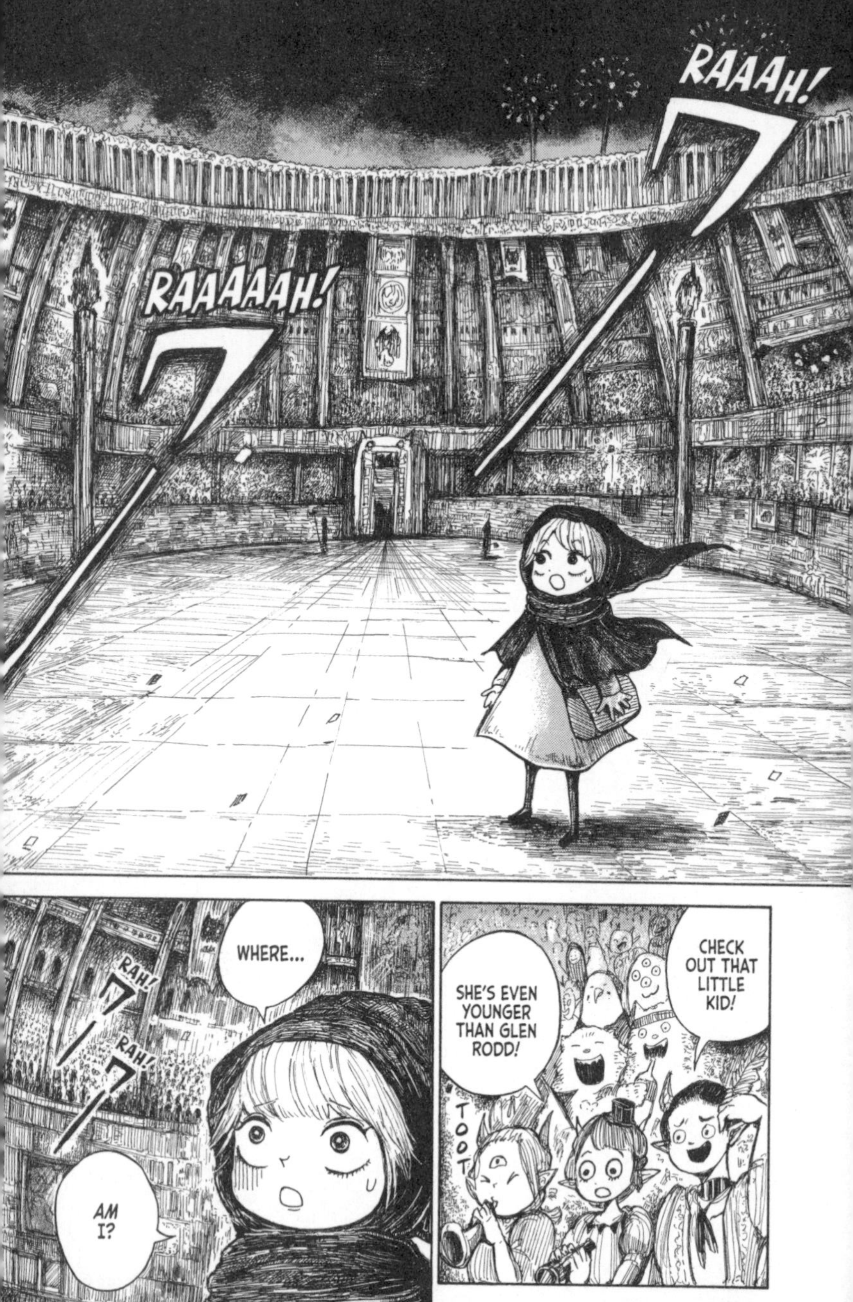
RAAAH!
RAAAAAH!
CHECK OUT THAT LITTLE KID!
SHE'S EVEN YOUNGER THAN GLEN RODD!
TOOT
WHERE...
RAH!
RAH!
AM I?

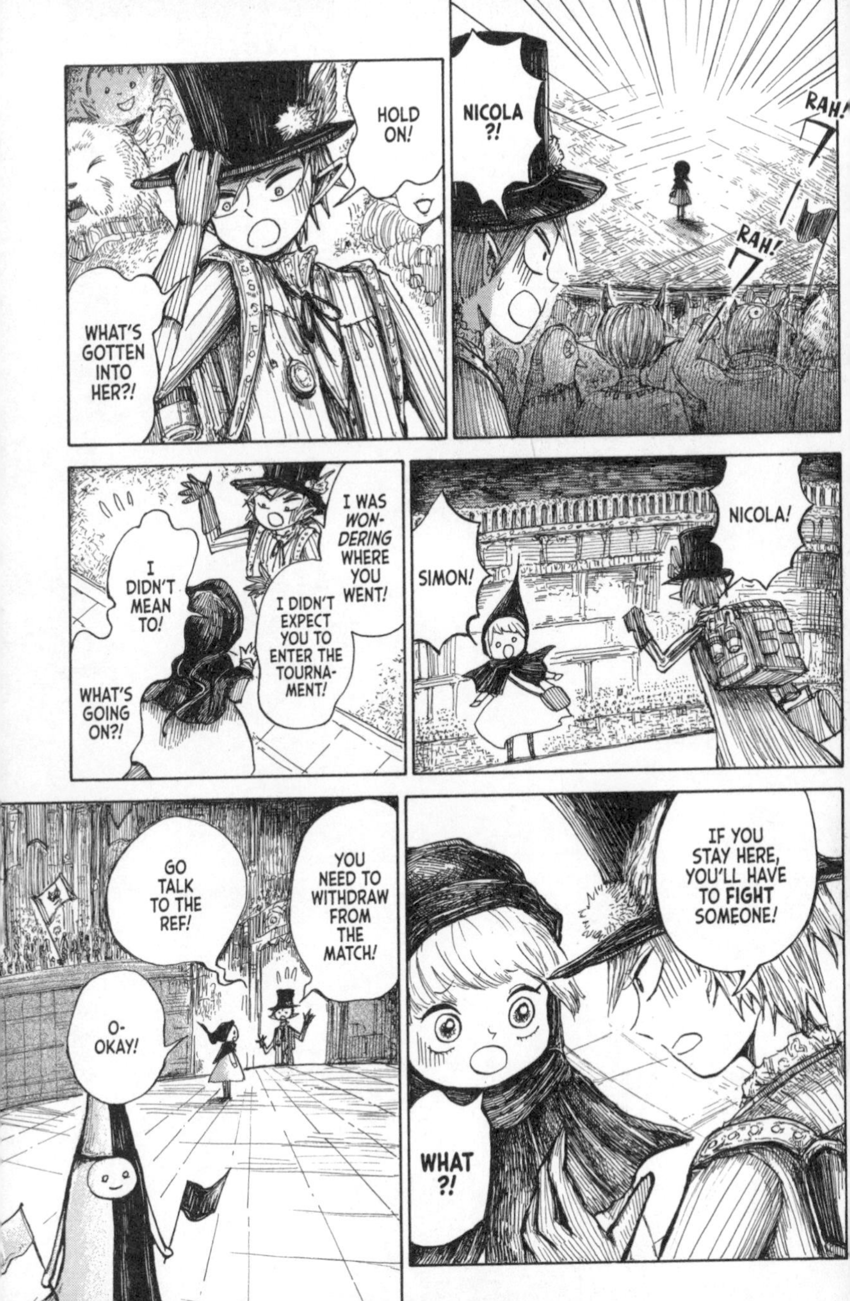
RAH!
RAH!
NICOLA ?!
HOLD ON!
WHAT'S GOTTEN INTO HER?!
NICOLA!
SIMON!
I WAS *WONDERING* WHERE YOU WENT!
I DIDN'T EXPECT YOU TO ENTER THE TOURNAMENT!
I DIDN'T MEAN TO!
WHAT'S GOING ON?!
IF YOU STAY HERE, YOU'LL HAVE TO **FIGHT** SOMEONE!
WHAT ?!
YOU NEED TO WITHDRAW FROM THE MATCH!
GO TALK TO THE REF!
O-OKAY!

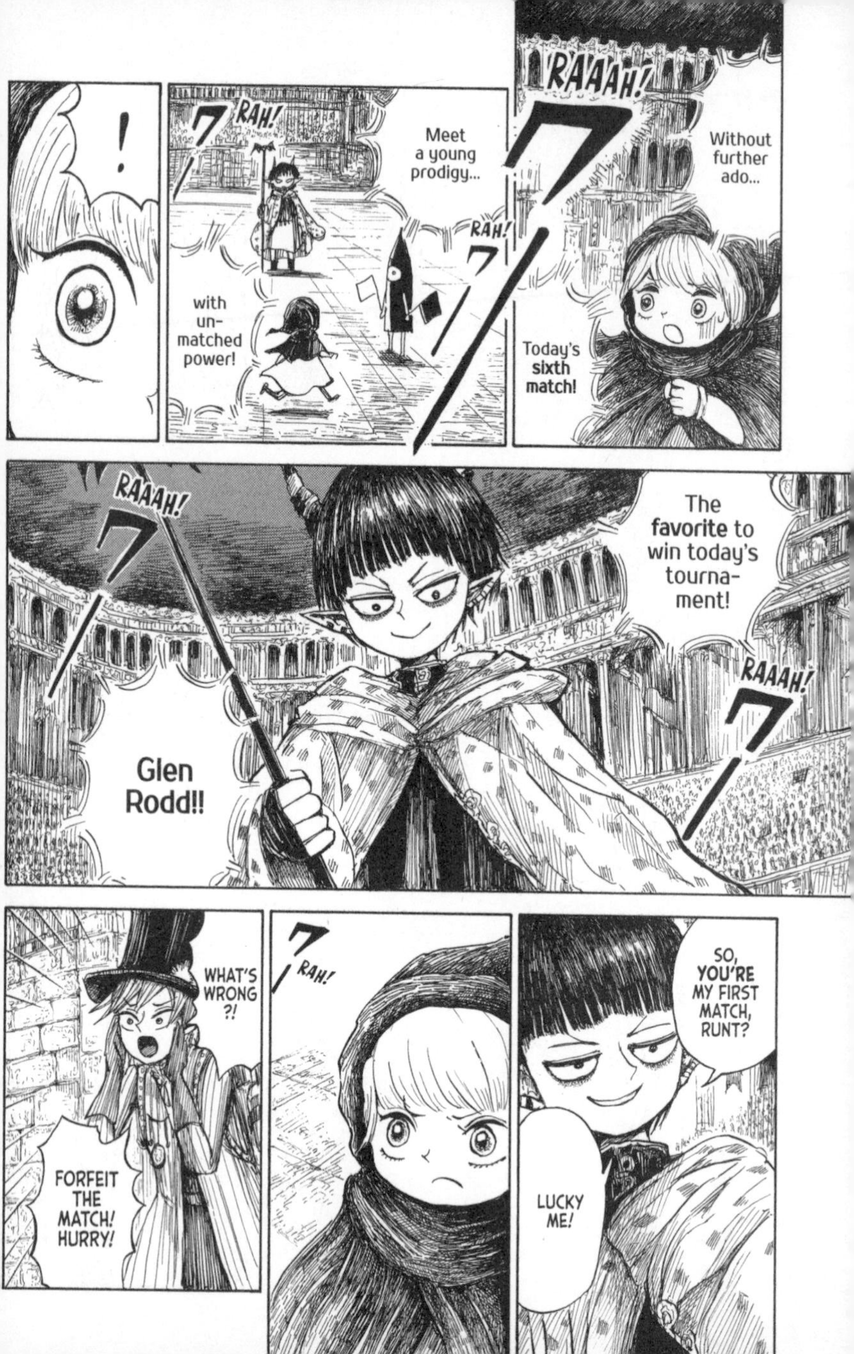
RAAAH!
Without further ado...
Today's **sixth** match!
RAH!
Meet a young prodigy...
RAH!
with un-matched power!
!
The **favorite** to win today's tourna-ment!
RAAAH!
RAAAH!
Glen Rodd!!
SO, **YOU'RE** MY FIRST MATCH, RUNT?
LUCKY ME!
RAH!
WHAT'S WRONG?!
FORFEIT THE MATCH! HURRY!

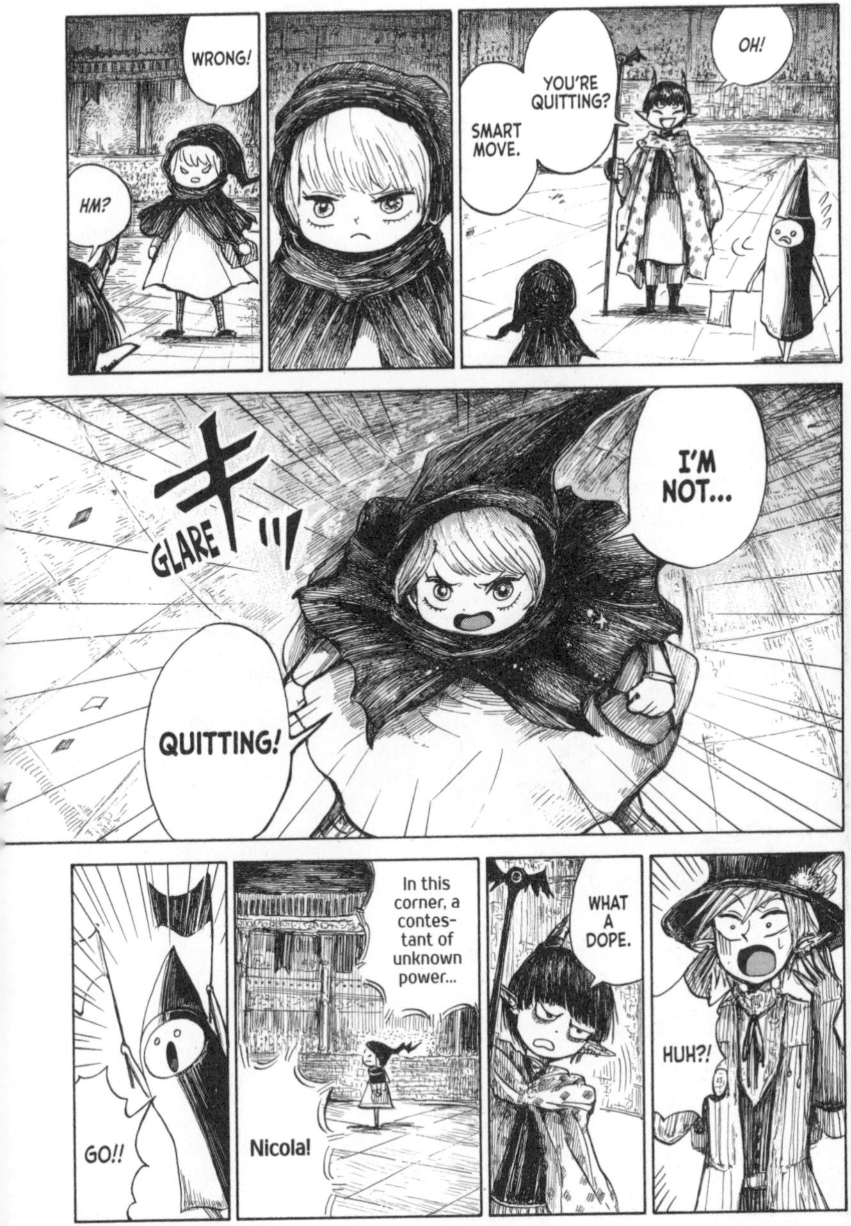
OH!
YOU'RE QUITTING?
SMART MOVE.
WRONG!
HM?
I'M NOT...
GLARE
QUITTING!
HUH?!
WHAT A DOPE.
In this corner, a contestant of unknown power...
Nicola!
GO!!

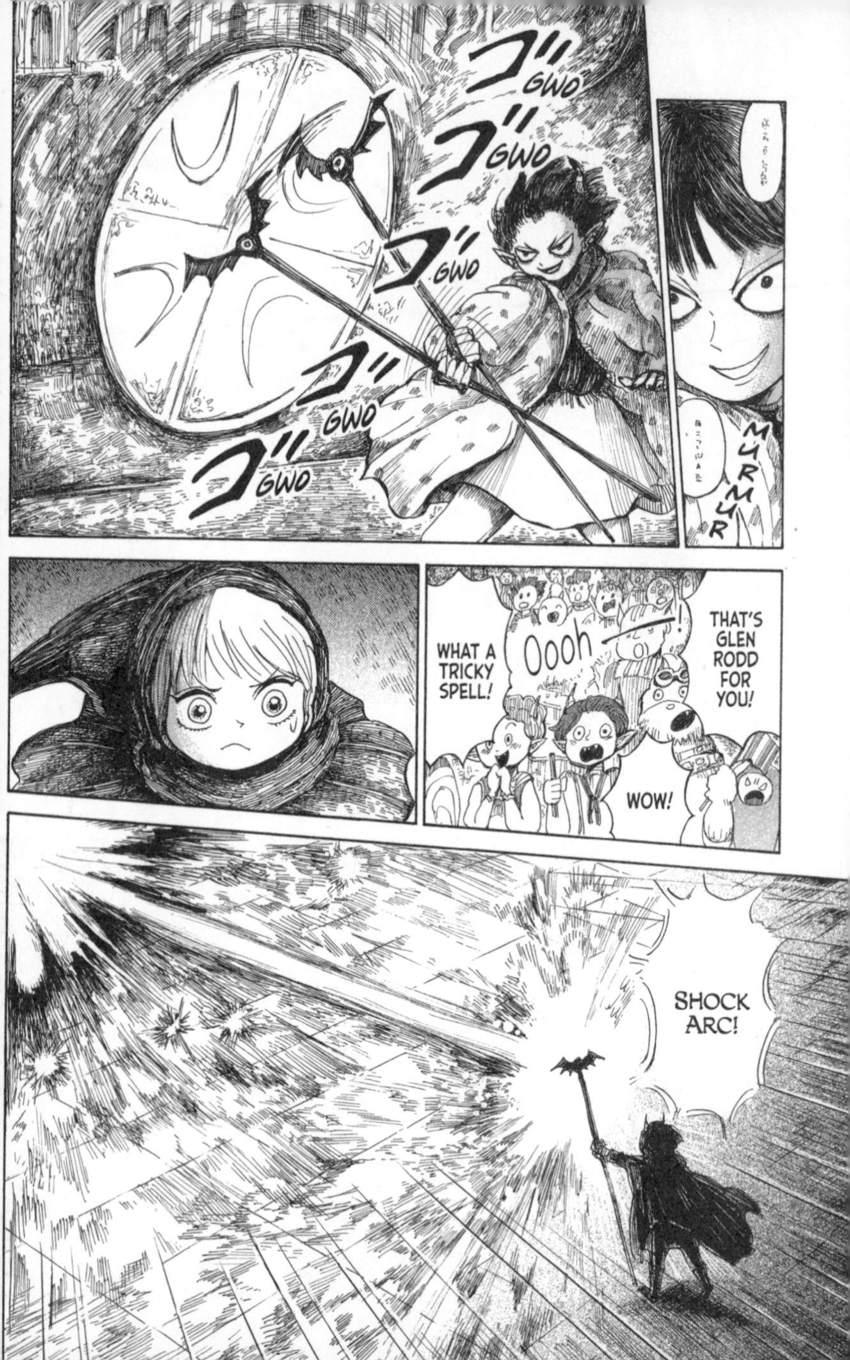
MURMUR
GWO
GWO
GWO
GWO
GWO
THAT'S GLEN RODD FOR YOU!
Oooh
WHAT A TRICKY SPELL!
WOW!
SHOCK ARC!

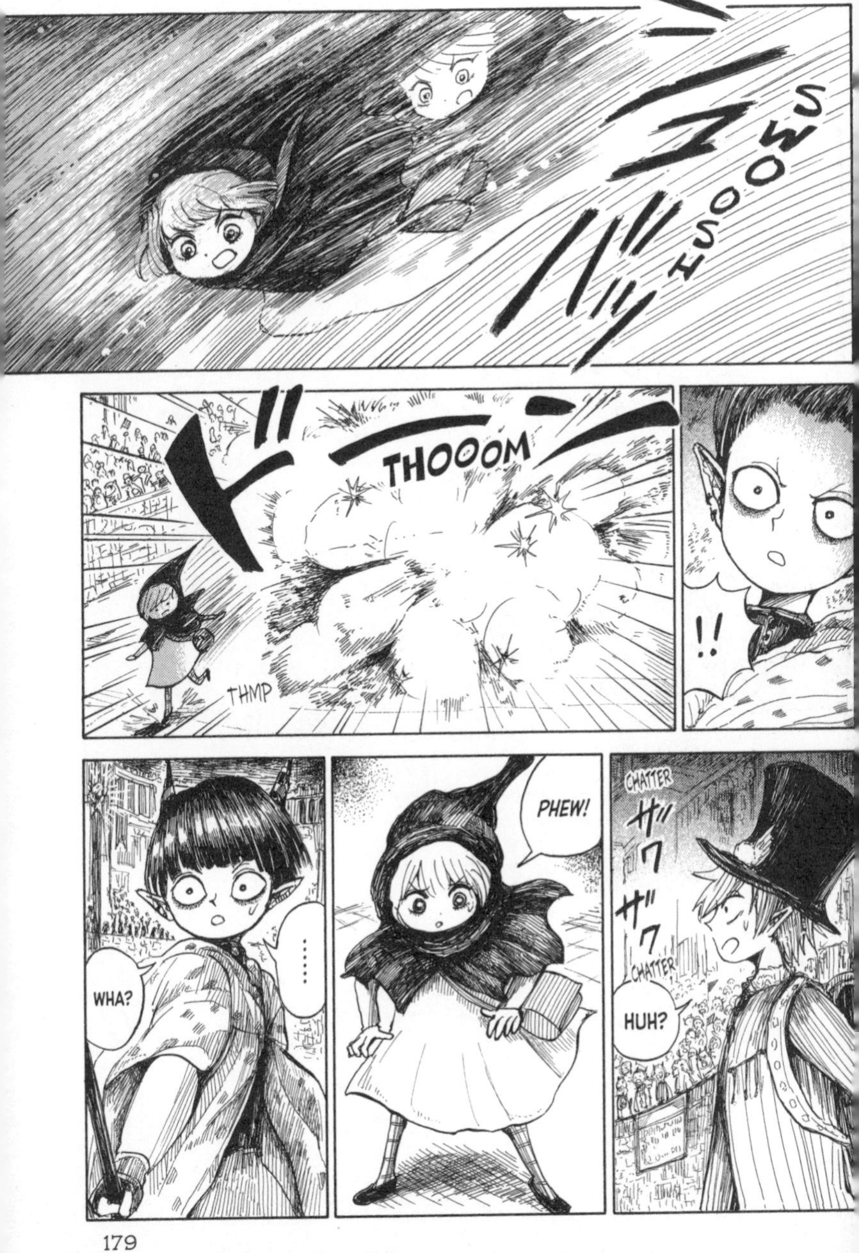
SWOOSH
!!
THOOOM
THMP
CHATTER
ザワ
ザワ
CHATTER
HUH?
PHEW!
......
WHA?

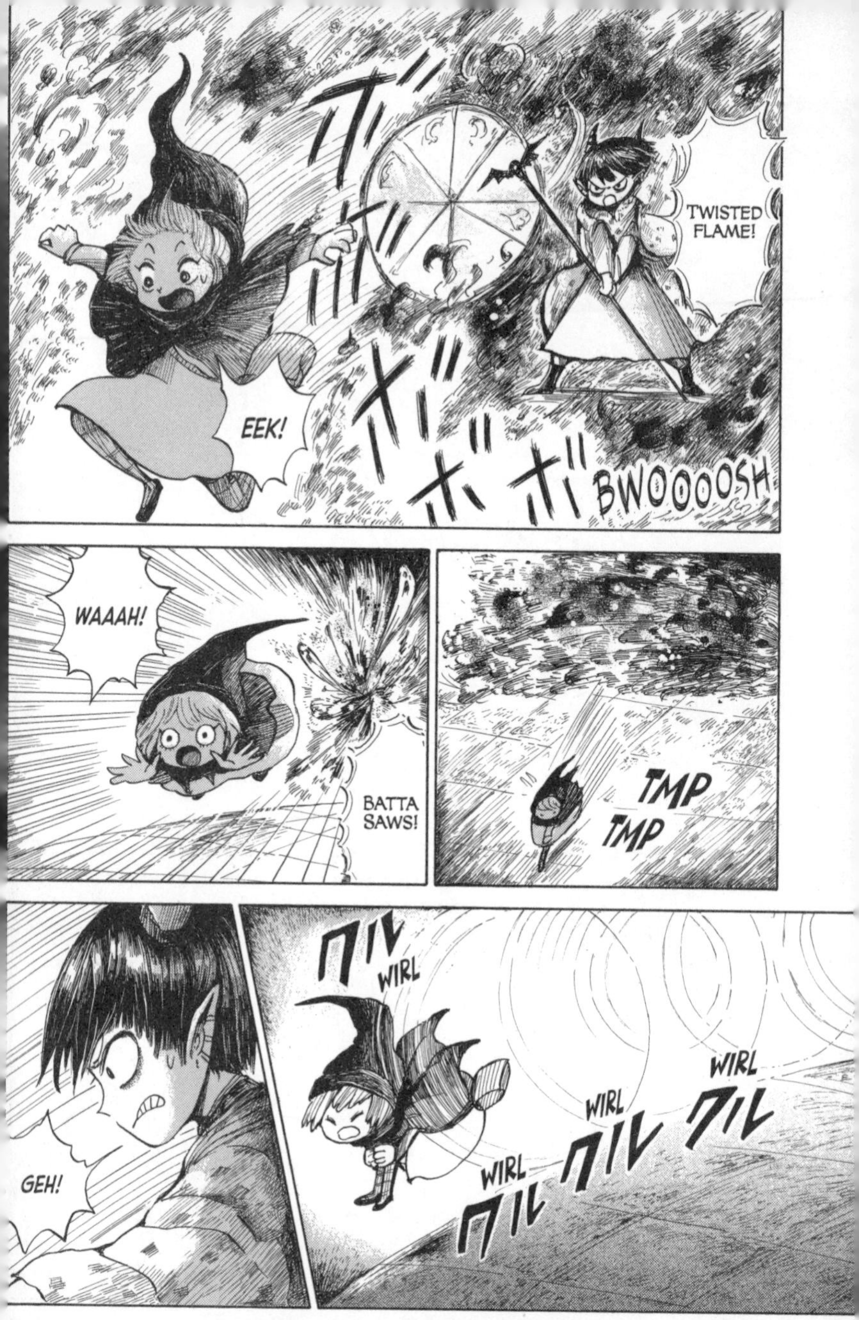
TWISTED FLAME!
EEK!
BWOOOOSH
TMP
TMP
WAAAH!
BATTA SAWS!
WIRL
WIRL
WIRL
WIRL
GEH!

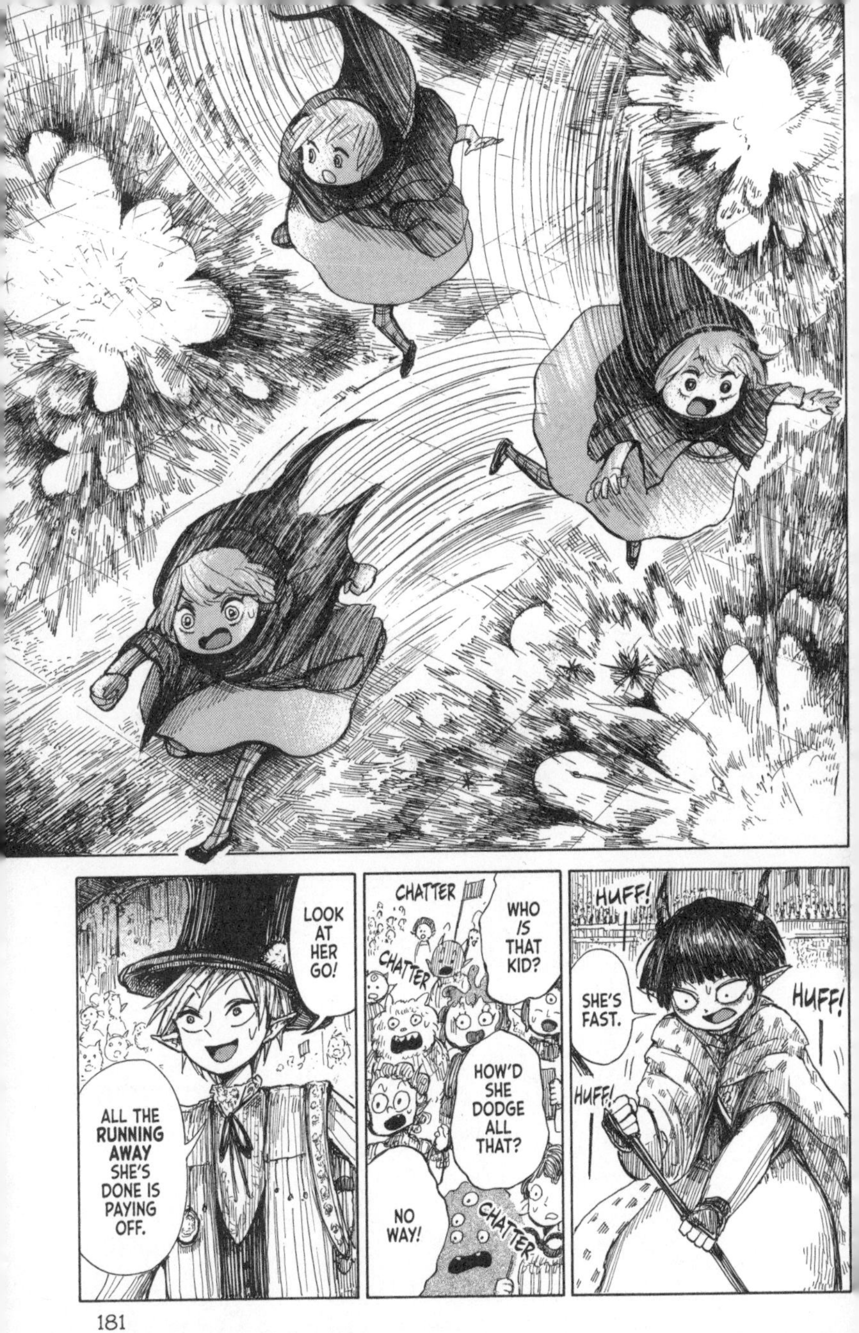
HUFF!
SHE'S FAST.
HUFF!
HUFF!
CHATTER
WHO IS THAT KID?
CHATTER
HOW'D SHE DODGE ALL THAT?
NO WAY!
CHATTER
LOOK AT HER GO!
ALL THE RUNNING AWAY SHE'S DONE IS PAYING OFF.

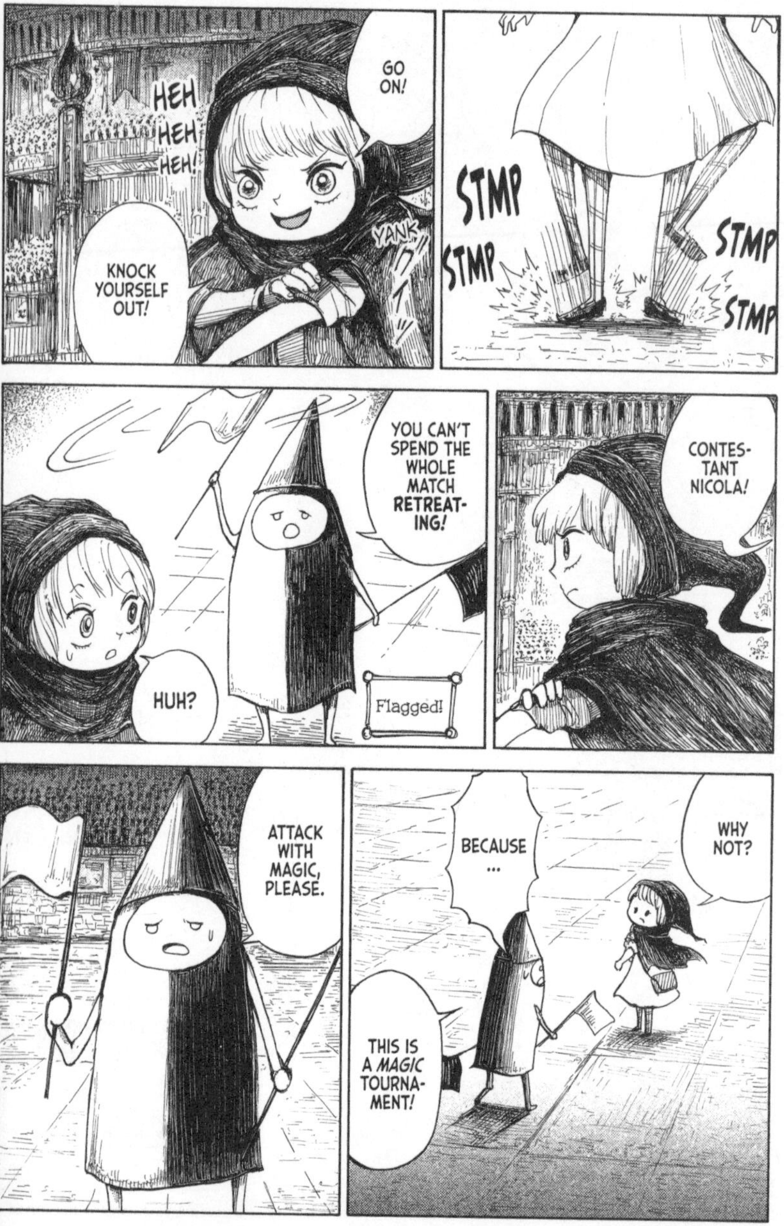
STMP
STMP
STMP
STMP
GO ON!
HEH HEH HEH!
YANK
KNOCK YOURSELF OUT!
CONTESTANT NICOLA!
YOU CAN'T SPEND THE WHOLE MATCH RETREATING!
Flagged!
HUH?
WHY NOT?
BECAUSE...
THIS IS A *MAGIC* TOURNAMENT!
ATTACK WITH MAGIC, PLEASE.

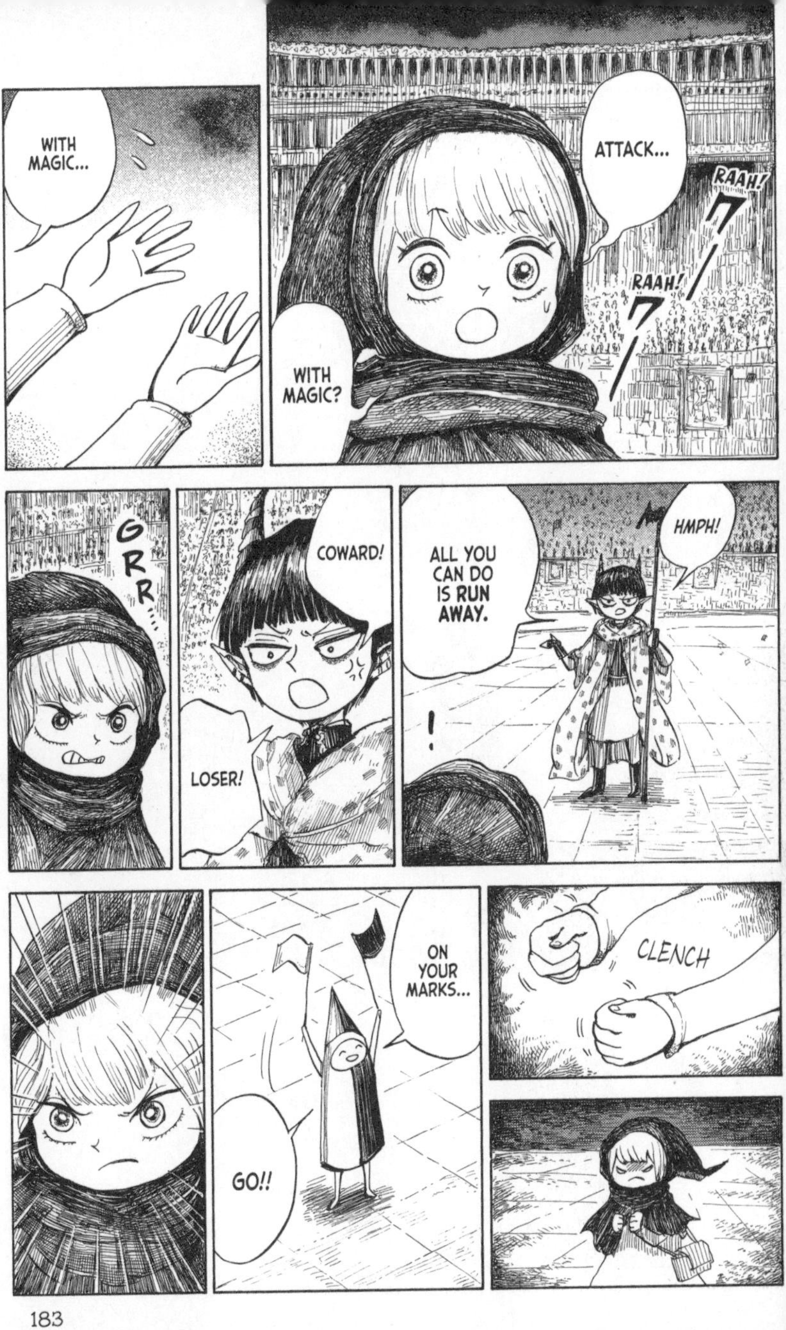
ATTACK...
RAAH!
RAAH!
WITH MAGIC?
WITH MAGIC...
HMPH!
ALL YOU CAN DO IS RUN AWAY.
!
COWARD!
LOSER!
GRR...
CLENCH
ON YOUR MARKS...
GO!!

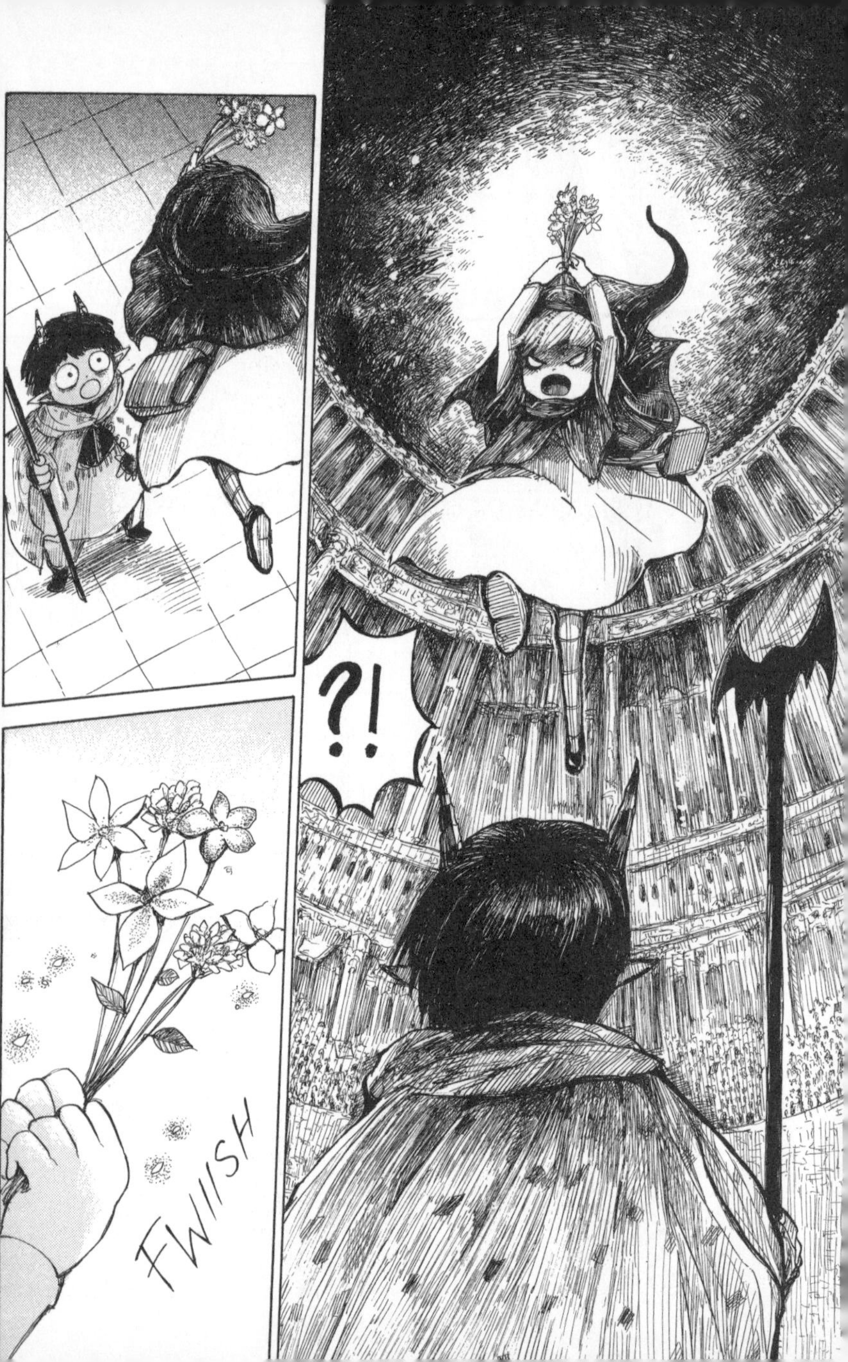
?!
FWIISH

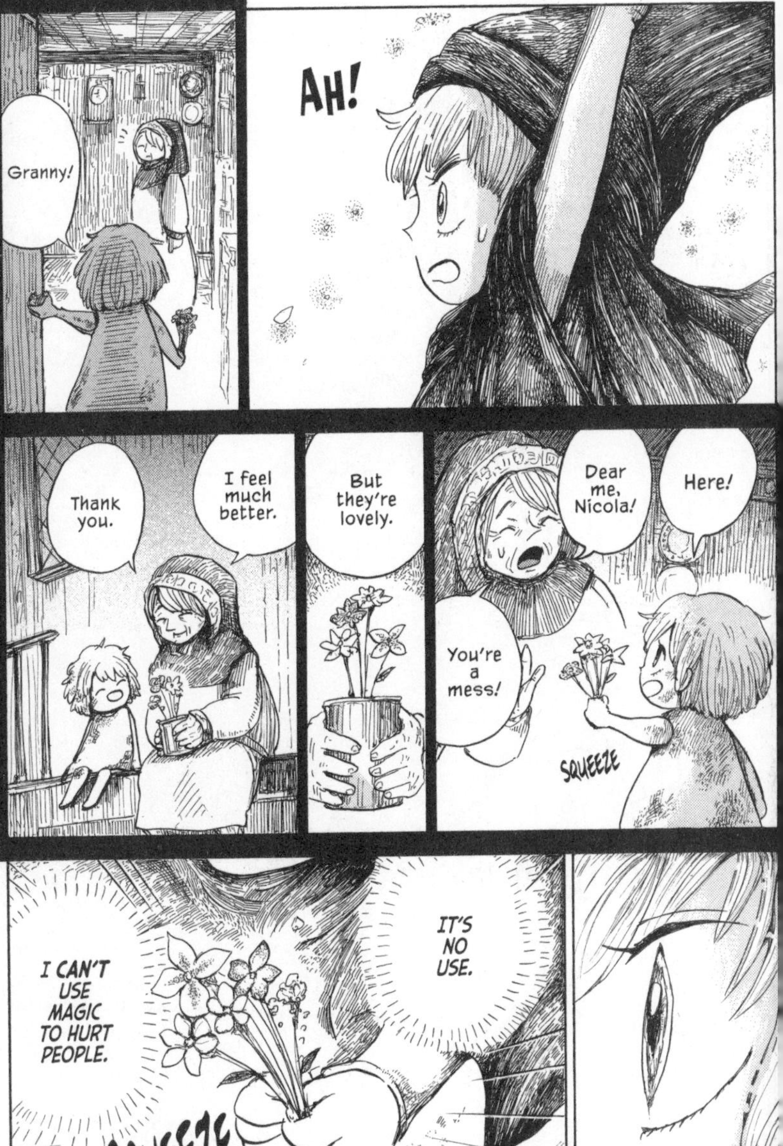
AH!
Granny!
Here!
Dear me, Nicola!
You're a mess!
SQUEEZE
But they're lovely.
I feel much better.
Thank you.
IT'S NO USE.
I CAN'T USE MAGIC TO HURT PEOPLE.
SQUEEZE

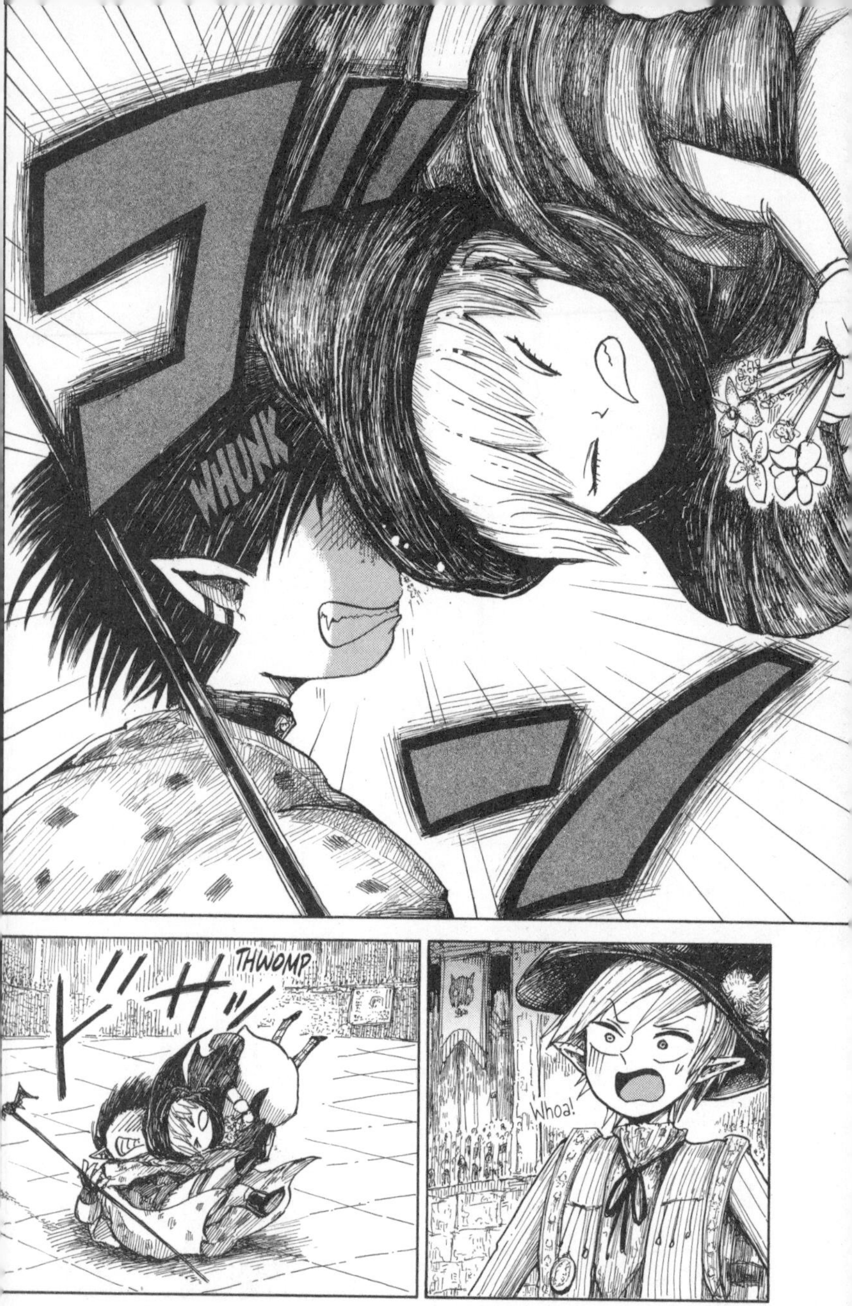
WHUNK
Whoa!
THWOMP

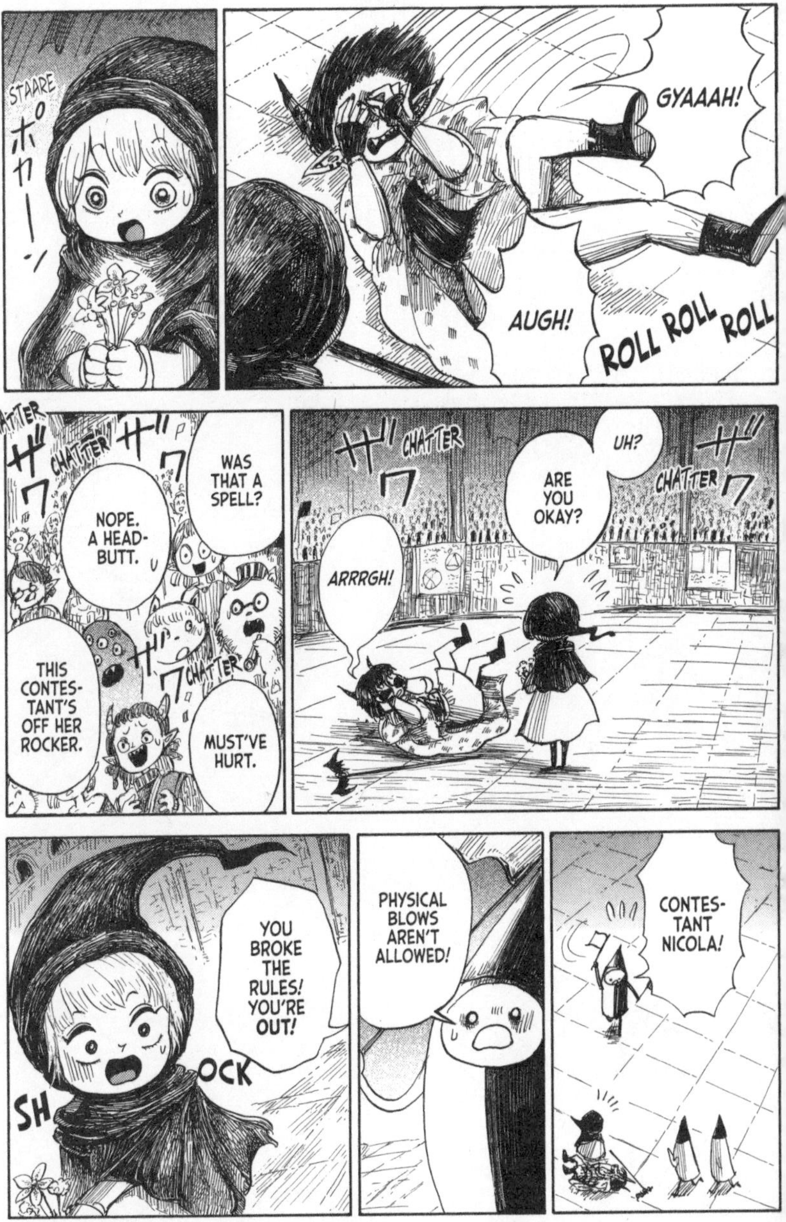
GYAAAH!
ROLL ROLL ROLL
AUGH!
STAARE
ホカー
UH?
ARE YOU OKAY?
CHATTER ザワ
CHATTER ザワ
ARRRGH!
WAS THAT A SPELL?
NOPE. A HEAD-BUTT.
CHATTER ザワ
CHATTER
CHATTER ザワ
MUST'VE HURT.
THIS CONTES-TANT'S OFF HER ROCKER.
CONTES-TANT NICOLA!
PHYSICAL BLOWS AREN'T ALLOWED!
YOU BROKE THE RULES! YOU'RE OUT!
SHOCK

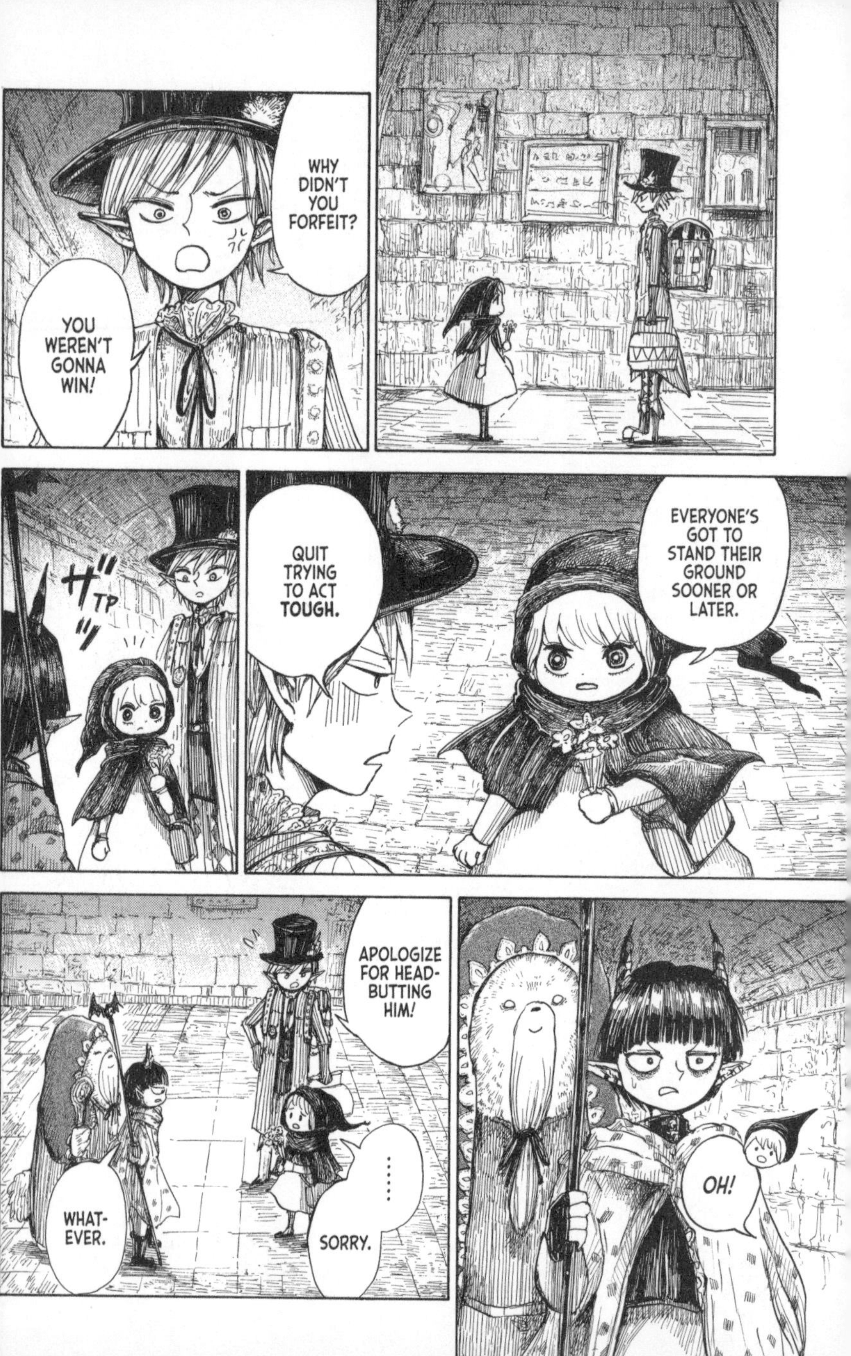
WHY DIDN'T YOU FORFEIT?
YOU WEREN'T GONNA WIN!
EVERYONE'S GOT TO STAND THEIR GROUND SOONER OR LATER.
QUIT TRYING TO ACT TOUGH.
ザッ
TP
OH!
APOLOGIZE FOR HEAD-BUTTING HIM!
......
SORRY.
WHAT-EVER.

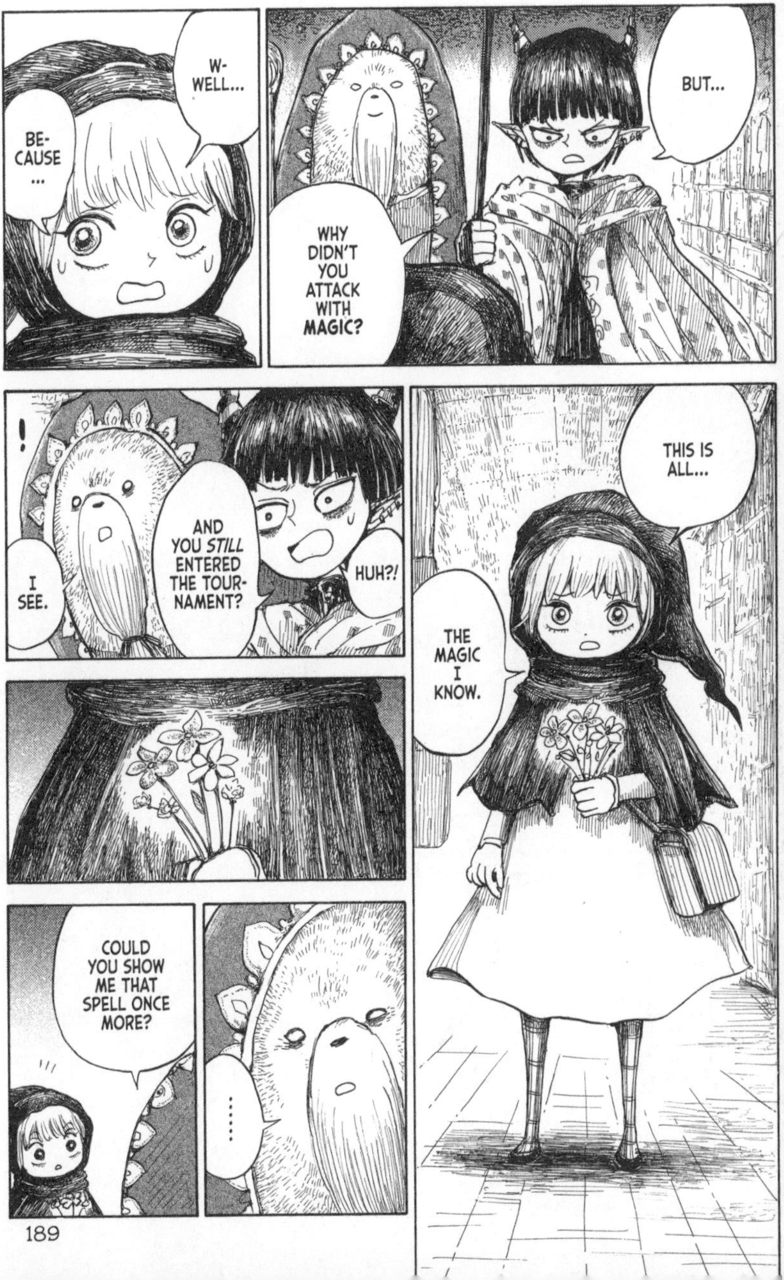
BUT...
WHY DIDN'T YOU ATTACK WITH MAGIC?
W-WELL...
BE-CAUSE...
THIS IS ALL...
THE MAGIC I KNOW.
!
HUH?!
AND YOU *STILL* ENTERED THE TOURNAMENT?
I SEE.
......
COULD YOU SHOW ME THAT SPELL ONCE MORE?

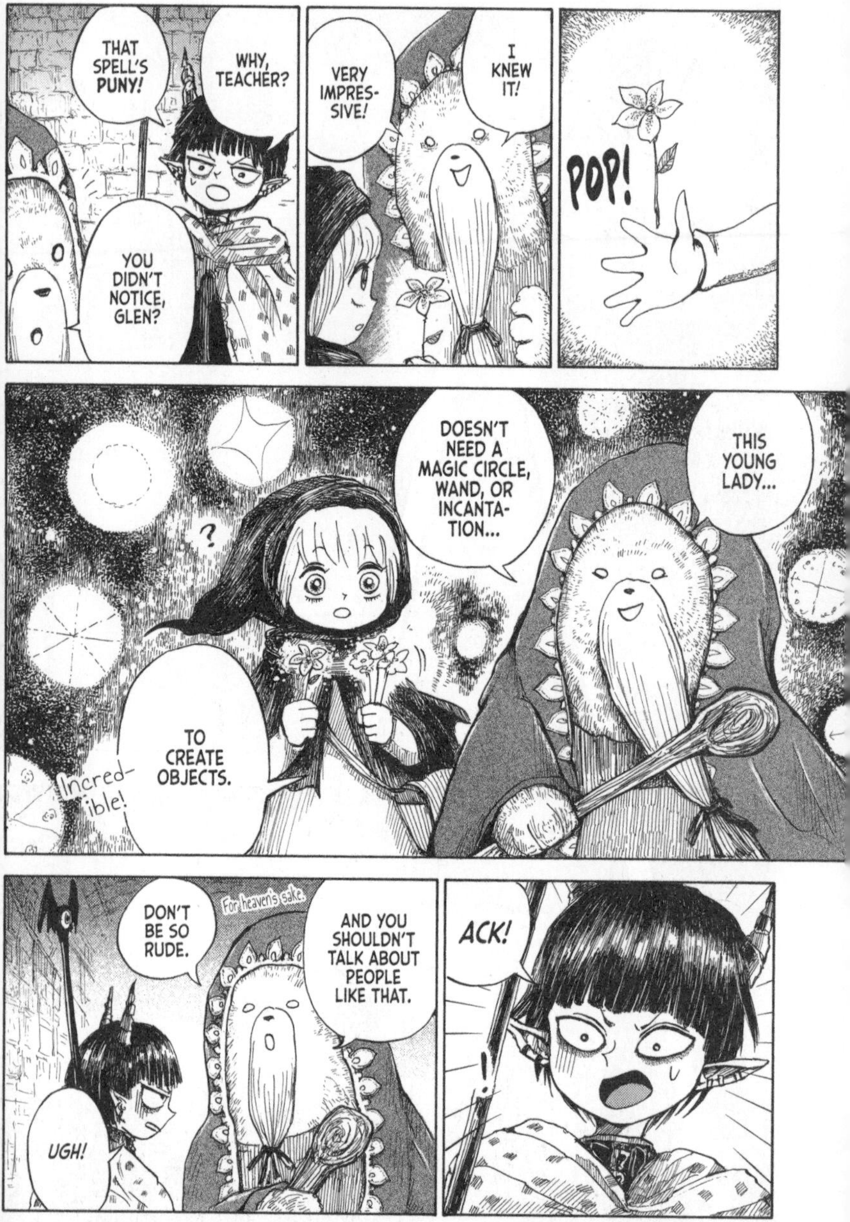
POP!
I KNEW IT!
VERY IMPRESSIVE!
WHY, TEACHER?
THAT SPELL'S PUNY!
YOU DIDN'T NOTICE, GLEN?
THIS YOUNG LADY...
DOESN'T NEED A MAGIC CIRCLE, WAND, OR INCANTATION...
?
TO CREATE OBJECTS.
Incredible!
ACK!
AND YOU SHOULDN'T TALK ABOUT PEOPLE LIKE THAT.
For heaven's sake.
DON'T BE SO RUDE.
UGH!

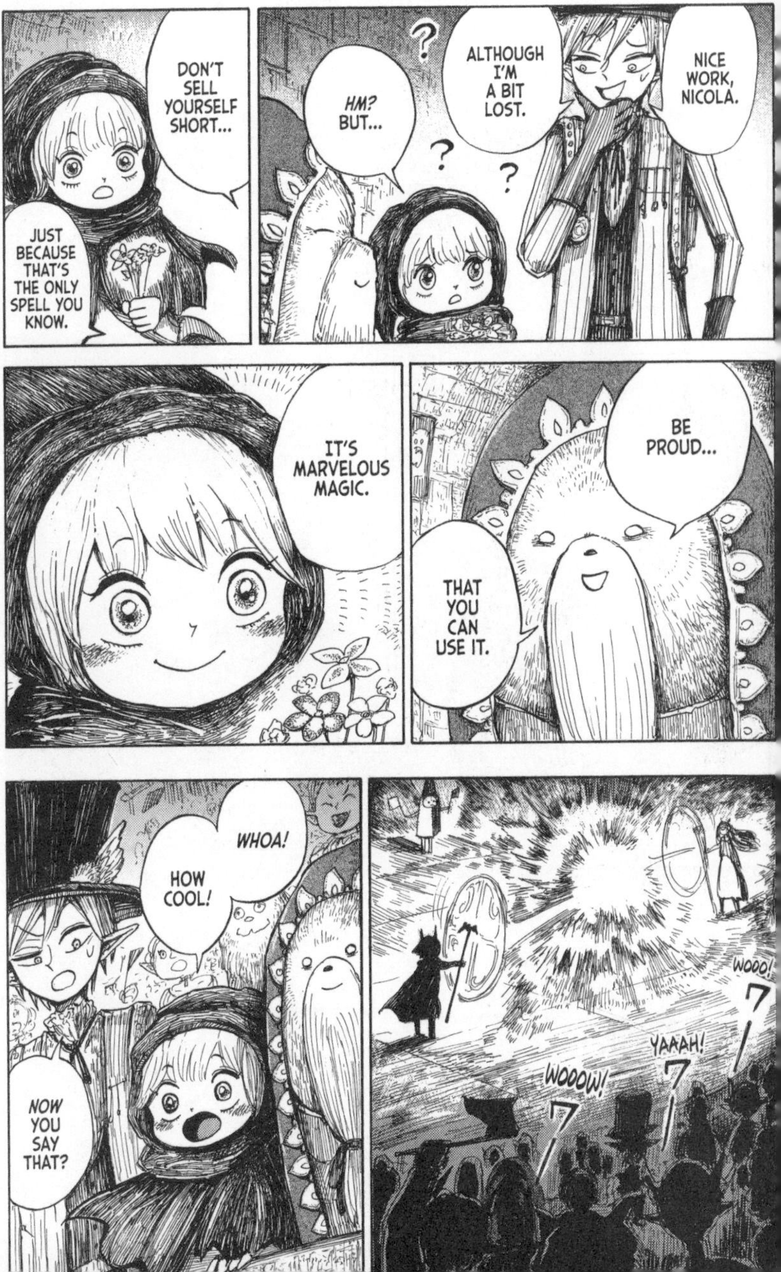
NICE WORK, NICOLA.
ALTHOUGH I'M A BIT LOST.
HM? BUT...
DON'T SELL YOURSELF SHORT...
JUST BECAUSE THAT'S THE ONLY SPELL YOU KNOW.
BE PROUD...
THAT YOU CAN USE IT.
IT'S MARVELOUS MAGIC.
WOOO!
YAAAH!
WOOOW!
WHOA!
HOW COOL!
NOW YOU SAY THAT?

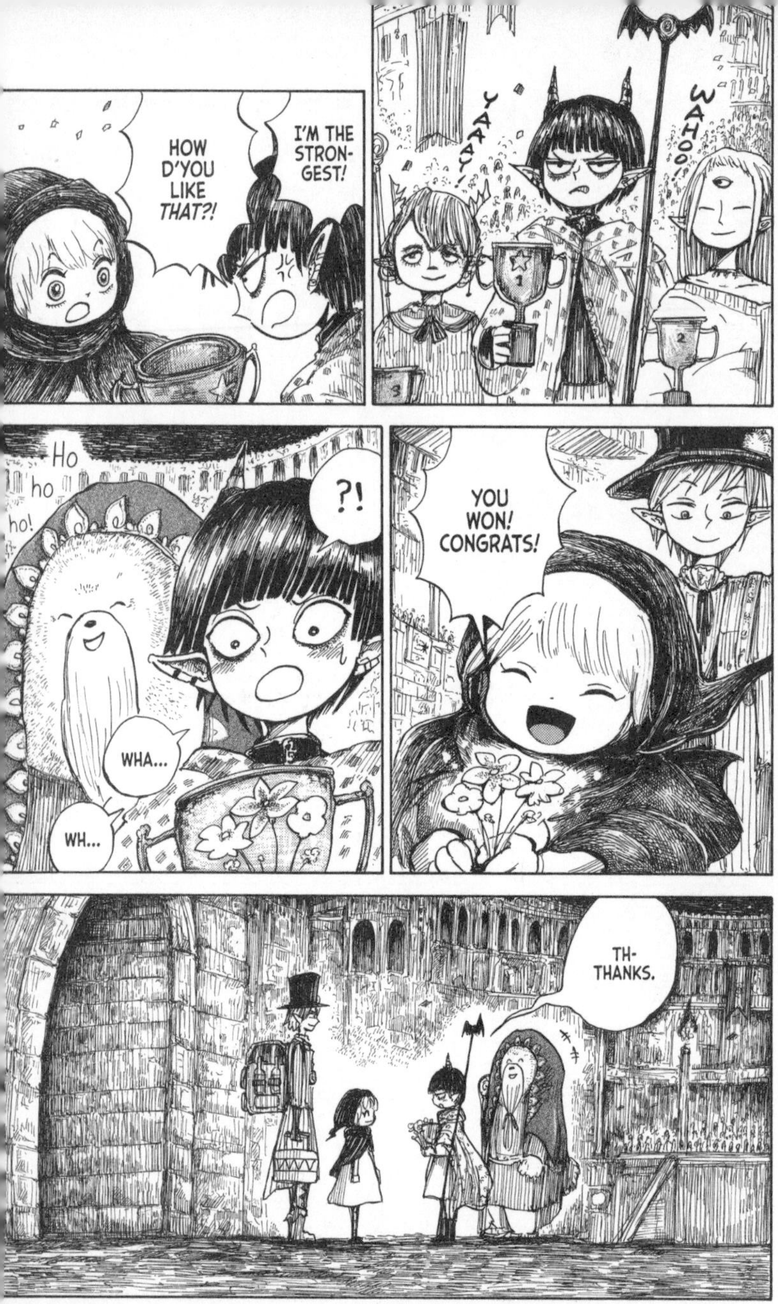
WAHOO!
YAAAY!
I'M THE STRONGEST!
HOW D'YOU LIKE THAT?!
YOU WON! CONGRATS!
?!
Ho ho ho!
WHA...
WH...
TH-THANKS.

Chapter 6 END

After the Visit 6

after that

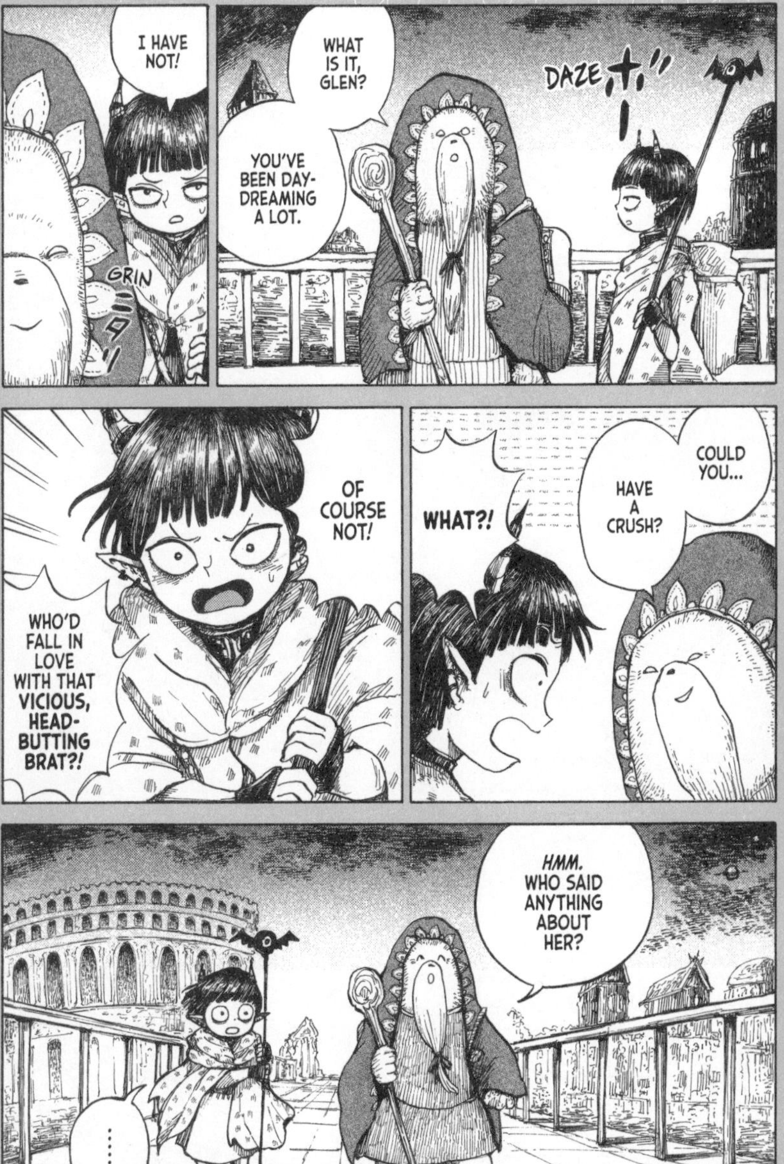

WHAT IS IT, GLEN?
YOU'VE BEEN DAY-DREAMING A LOT.
DAZE
I HAVE NOT!
GRIN
COULD YOU...
HAVE A CRUSH?
WHAT?!
OF COURSE NOT!
WHO'D FALL IN LOVE WITH THAT VICIOUS, HEAD-BUTTING BRAT?!
HMM. WHO SAID ANYTHING ABOUT HER?
......

SEVEN SEAS ENTERTAINMENT PRESENTS

Nicola Traveling Around the Demons' World.

story and art by ASAYA MIYANAGA

VOLUME 1

TRANSLATION
Christine Dashiell

ADAPTATION
Rebecca Schneidereit

LETTERING
Lys Blakeslee

COVER DESIGN
KC Fabellon

PROOFREADER
Stephanie Cohen
Danielle King

EDITOR
Shannon Fay

PRODUCTION MANAGER
Lissa Pattillo

MANAGING EDITOR
Julie Davis

EDITOR-IN-CHIEF
Adam Arnold

PUBLISHER
Jason DeAngelis

NICOLA TRAVELING AROUND THE DEMONS' WORLD VOL. 1
© Asaya Miyanaga 2018
First published in Japan in 2018 by KADOKAWA CORPORATION, Tokyo.
English translation rights reserved by Seven Seas Entertainment
under the license from KADOKAWA CORPORATION, Tokyo.

Seven Seas press and purchase enquiries can be sent to Marketing Manager
Lianne Sentar at press@gomanga.com. Information regarding the distribution
and purchase of digital editions is available from Digital Manager CK Russell
at digital@gomanga.com.

Seven Seas and the Seven Seas logo are trademarks of
Seven Seas Entertainment. All rights reserved.

ISBN: 978-1-64275-337-0

Printed in Canada

First Printing: October 2019

10 9 8 7 6 5 4 3 2 1

FOLLOW US ONLINE: *www.sevenseasentertainment.com*

READING DIRECTIONS

This book reads from *right to left*, Japanese style.
If this is your first time reading manga, you start
reading from the top right panel on each page and
take it from there. If you get lost, just follow the
numbered diagram here. It may seem backwards at
first, but you'll get the hang of it! Have fun!!

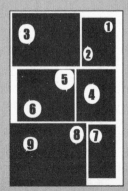